A Social History of Maoist China

When the Chinese communists came into power in 1949, they promised to "turn society upside down." Efforts to build a communist society created hopes and dreams, coupled with fear and disillusionment. The Chinese people made great efforts towards modernization and social change in this period of transition, but they also experienced traumatic setbacks. Covering the period 1949 to 1976 and then tracing the legacy of the Mao era through the 1980s, Felix Wemheuer focuses on questions of class, gender, ethnicity and the urban–rural divide in this new social history of Maoist China. He analyzes the experiences of a range of social groups under Communist rule – workers, peasants, local cadres, intellectuals, "ethnic minorities," the old elites, men and women. To understand this tumultuous period, he argues, we must recognize the many complex challenges facing the People's Republic. But we must not lose sight of the human suffering and political terror that, for many now ageing quietly across China, remain the period's abiding memory.

FELIX WEMHEUER is Chair Professor of Modern China Studies at the University of Cologne. He belongs to a new generation of Western scholars who are rewriting the history of Maoist China. His publications include *Famine Politics in Maoist China and the Soviet Union*, 2014.

New Approaches to Asian History

This dynamic new series publishes books on the milestones in Asian history, those that have come to define particular periods or to mark turning points in the political, cultural and social evolution of the region. The books in this series are intended as introductions for students to be used in the classroom. They are written by scholars whose credentials are well established in their particular fields and who have, in many cases, taught the subject across a number of years.

Books in the series

A SOCIAL HISTORY OF MAOIST CHINA

Conflict and Change, 1949–1976

FELIX WEMHEUER
University of Cologne

CAMBRIDGE
UNIVERSITY PRESS

CAMBRIDGE
UNIVERSITY PRESS

University Printing House, Cambridge CB2 8BS, United Kingdom

One Liberty Plaza, 20th Floor, New York, NY 10006, USA

477 Williamstown Road, Port Melbourne, VIC 3207, Australia

314–321, 3rd Floor, Plot 3, Splendor Forum, Jasola District Centre,
New Delhi – 110025, India

79 Anson Road, #06–04/06, Singapore 079906

Cambridge University Press is part of the University of Cambridge.

It furthers the University's mission by disseminating knowledge in the pursuit of
education, learning, and research at the highest international levels of excellence.

www.cambridge.org
Information on this title: www.cambridge.org/9781107123700
DOI: 10.1017/9781316421826

© Felix Wemheuer 2019

First published 2019
3rd printing 2021

Printed in Great Britain by Ashford Colour Press Ltd.

A catalogue record for this publication is available from the British Library.

Library of Congress Cataloging-in-Publication Data
Names: Wemheuer, Felix, author.
Title: A social history of Maoist China : conflict and change, 1949–1976 / Felix Wemheuer,
University of Cologne.
Description: Cambridge, United Kingdom ; New York, NY : University Printing House, 2017. |
Series: New approaches to Asian history | Includes bibliographical references and index.
Identifiers: LCCN 2018046551 | ISBN 9781107123700
Subjects: LCSH: China – Social conditions – 1949–1976. | China – Politics
and government – 1949–1976. | China – History – 1949–1976.
Classification: LCC HN733.5 .W46 2017 | DDC 306.0951–dc23
LC record available at https://lccn.loc.gov/2018046551

ISBN 978-1-107-12370-0 Hardback
ISBN 978-1-107-56550-0 Paperback

For my mother, Christina Wemheuer

CONTENTS

FIGURES

MAPS AND TABLES

Maps

Tables

DOCUMENTS

ACKNOWLEDGMENTS

I am deeply grateful to the many colleagues and anonymous reviewers whose feedback has enriched this manuscript, and above all for the patient guidance of Lucy Rhymer, my editor at Cambridge University Press. Cameron Henderson-Begg and Lisa Kindervater worked tirelessly to improve the English style and the flow of my arguments. Their diligence has made this a better and more readable book.

Several colleagues provided comments on drafts of individual chapters. For their invaluable suggestions, I am indebted among others to Björn Alpermann (University of Würzburg), Wu Yidi (University of California, Irvine), Wu Yiching (University of Toronto), Neil Diamant (Dickinson College), Cui Jinke (University of Vienna), Brian Demare (Tulane University), Eddy U (University of California, Davis), Puck Engman (University of Freiburg), Susanne Weigelin-Schwiedrzik (University of Vienna), Andrew Walder (Stanford University), Li Minqi (University of Utah), Cormac O'Grada (University College Dublin), Daniel Fuchs (SOAS, University of London), Daniel Leese (University of Freiburg), Kimberely Ens Manning (Concordia University of Montreal), Jessica Pflüger (University of Bochum), Suy Lan Hopmann (Free University of Berlin), Klaus Mühlhahn (University of Berlin), Zhu Meiting (University of Cologne), Jörn Goldberg (University of Frankfurt), Thomas Scharping (University of Cologne) and Xu Mengran (University of Toronto).

I would like to thank Cao Shuji (Jiaotong University, Shanghai) for sharing historical documents for this project. I am also grateful to all the eyewitnesses of the Great Leap Forward and the Cultural Revolution in China who have allowed me to interview them over the years. Their contributions have been immensely valuable. Jing Wenyu (University of Cologne) supported me with helpful editorial work. Vivienne Guo (University of Exeter) completed early translations of several documents into English. I wish to thank Gleb Netchvolodov for drawing graphs and maps.

For access to the extraordinary photographs of Eva Siao, I wish to thank the Museum Ludwig in Cologne. Helmut Opletal (University of Vienna) generously permitted me to use unpublished photographs from his private collection, which provide a glimpse into the views on Chinese society of Western journalists and travelers who visited the country in the 1970s. The Leonhard Gymnasium in Basel provided me with photographs by the Swiss-French teacher Jean Moser and his wife Marie-Louise, who were among the few Westerners living in Beijing in 1966 and 1967.

Last but not least, I extend my thanks to my home institution, the University of Cologne. My appointment in 2014 as Professor of Modern China Studies allowing me to focus on areas that I consider of key importance and interest for understanding twentieth century China and the history of state socialism. It is remarkable what can be achieved when one is freed from worrying about rankings, mainstream academic trends or the financial implications of a particular piece of research. I hope this book represents a productive use of that freedom.

ABBREVIATIONS AND MEASUREMENTS

Abbreviations

CCP   Chinese Communist Party
CPSU   Communist Party of the Soviet Union
GDP   Gross Domestic Product
GDR   German Democratic Republic
GMD   Guomindang (Nationalist Party)
IUD   Intrauterine Device
PLA   People's Liberation Army
PRC   People's Republic of China
ps.   pseudonym
UN   United Nations
USSR   Union of Soviet Socialist Republics

Measurements

1 *liang* = 50 grams
1 *jin* = 500 grams
1 *mu* = 1/15 hectare

INTRODUCTION

On October 1, 1949, standing before the crowds on Tiananmen Square in Beijing, Mao Zedong declared the founding of a state, the People's Republic of China (PRC). As he did so, the armed forces of the Chinese Communist Party (CCP) were pressing home the advantage in the civil war against the Nationalist Guomindang (GMD). As the official version of Chinese history would have it, all the struggles of the Chinese people for liberation from feudalism and imperialism culminated in this moment in a final victory led by the glorious Communist Party.

The Mao era began with the founding of the PRC and ended with death of the chairman in 1976. During these twenty-seven years, society was "turned upside down." Millions of people experienced social upward mobility, while others were marginalized or lost their lives. Efforts to build a communist society created hopes, dreams, fear, enthusiasm, disillusion, painful disappointments and nostalgia. The Chinese people made great strides, but they also experienced traumatic setbacks.

When the CCP came into power, China was in a desperate position. The war with Japan (1937–1945) and the subsequent civil war between the Communists and Nationalists had had a devastating impact on economy and society.[1] The GMD government had been too weak to re-establish effective control over national territory, due to the influence of foreign powers. At its height in the eighteenth century, the Qing Empire (1644–1911) had been a global economic power, but in the aftermath of the Opium War of 1840, it had proved unable to prevent a semi-colonization of the country by Western powers and Japan. With the revolution of 1911 and the overthrow of the Qing Dynasty, China became a republic. However, prior to the founding of the PRC, central governments were able to exercise control only over parts of the Han Chinese heartland, ceding control of peripheral regions such as Tibet and Xinjiang.

---

1 For detail see: Diana Lary, *The Chinese People at War: Human Suffering and Social Transformation, 1937–1945* (Cambridge: Cambridge University Press, 2010) and *China's Civil War: A Social History, 1945–1949* (Cambridge: Cambridge University Press, 2015).

The CCP promised to reunify the nation and to alleviate a deepening social crisis. In 1949, China was one of the poorest countries in the world.[2] The national census of 1953 recorded an average life expectancy of forty years.[3] China was still an agrarian society, with the vast majority of the population both rural and illiterate. The urbanization rate in 1949 was as low as 10.6 percent.[4] The CCP saw industrialization as the key task in the struggle to overcome poverty and backwardness. A strong new China was to be built, one that would be able to survive in a hostile international environment.

In the first half of the 1950s, the communist government launched a transformation of land ownership structures. Landlords and capitalists were expropriated. By 1956, China had established a Soviet-style planned economy based on state industries in the cities and agricultural cooperatives in the country-side. The party promised to "serve the people" and to improve the lives of workers and peasants – the new "masters of the country." In 1958, the CCP launched the Great Leap Forward, promising industrialization in double quick time. Instead, over-ambitious plans resulted in a great famine that killed millions of peasants between 1959 and 1961. By 1963, the country had recovered, but the party was divided as to which road of development should be taken. What followed, the Cultural Revolution of 1966–1976, remains to this day the most controversial period of the Mao era. In autumn 1966, Mao called on the masses to rebel against so-called "capitalist roaders inside the party." Millions of students and workers founded independent rebel organizations to attack the local government bureaucracies accused of acting against the interests of the masses. Cadres were paraded through the streets and criticized at sometimes deadly "struggle meetings." By 1967, fighting between different rebel factions had left several provinces in a state of virtual civil war, and Mao was forced to send in the army to restore stability.

For some in China today, the Cultural Revolution was a justified attempt to discipline bureaucrats and to find new forms of mass democracy. Others see in it little besides the brutal destruction of China's traditional culture and civilization. By the time of Mao's death in 1976, the country had partly industrialized and an impressive railway network had been built. Basic education, public health care, average life expectancy and women's rights had all seen significant improvements. The United States and other Western capitalist countries had recognized

2 Cormac O'Grada, "Great Leap into Famine: A Review Essay," *Population and Development Review*, Vol. 37, No. 1 (2011), pp. 192–193.

3 Andrew Walder, *China under Mao: A Revolution Derailed* (Cambridge, MA: Harvard University Press, 2015), pp. 320–321.

4 Lu Yu, *Xin Zhongguo renkou wushi nian* (Beijing: Zhongguo renkou chubanshe, 2004), Vol. 1, p. 633.

the PRC as a state. But it remains a matter of debate whether the human cost of development in Maoist China, such as the Great Famine, can be said to have outweighed the achievements over which the regime presided.

Between the 1950s and the mid-1970s, as the decolonization of the Global South continued apace, Maoist China emerged as a powerful inspiration for national and social liberation movements. China played an important role in the so-called "Non-Aligned Movement," composed mainly of former colonies such as India, Indonesia and Egypt. The Cultural Revolution also served as an imaginary space for various movements of the New Left in the United States, Western Europe and Japan, both before and after the explosion of social and political activism that rocked cities across the world in 1968. The Cultural Revolution in China was seen as a revolt of the youth against Establishment forces opposed to revolutionary change. For millions of people around the globe, Maoist China represented the promise of a better and truly socialist society, as well as an alternative to the bipolar Cold War order represented by the United States and the Soviet Union.[5] More brutal elements of the Chinese reality – the Great Famine, the mass killings of "class enemies," mostly members of the former elites – were either little heard of or simply ignored.

By the late 1970s, the liberation movements of the postcolonial world had fallen into abeyance. In place of "Arab Socialism" or "African Socialism," the neoliberal economic policies advanced by the World Bank under the aegis of the US and Western Europe became *de rigeur*. Under their influence, governments began programs of privatization in welfare and industry and deregulation in the financial sector. China itself became a global trend-setter in turning away from its revolutionary past. In the early 1980s, a new leadership under Deng Xiaoping condemned the Cultural Revolution and many other policies of the Mao era. The Chinese regime now launched a policy of Reform and Opening (*gaige kaifang*), promoting market reforms including privatization. The state still retained control over sectors of strategic importance such as finance, raw materials, national defense industries and land ownership. But the period of "permanent revolution" and mass mobilization came to an end in the Deng era. China reintegrated itself into the global capitalist economy, becoming "the workshop of the world" in the 1990s. For the Chinese party-state, calls for world revolution gave way to the rules of free trade, global capitalism and the institutions that went with it.

Today, China's economic power is challenging Western dominance. The CCP has not entirely abandoned the Chinese revolution and the Mao era: Chinese

---

5 For case studies see: Alexander C. Cook (ed.), *Mao's Little Red Book: A Global History* (Cambridge: Cambridge University Press, 2014).

Figure 0.1: A demonstration during the Cultural Revolution celebrates the overthrow of Liu Shaoqi, Deng Xiaoping and Tao Zhu, circa 1967.
Source: Collection Jean Moser, Gymnasium Leonhard, Basel.

President Xi Jinping has argued that people should not use the Mao era to discredit the Reform era or vice versa.[6] Dissidents and the Western media often warn that China under Xi could return to Maoism.[7] At the other end of the political spectrum in China, Neo-Maoists hope for a new Cultural Revolution in which the masses will be mobilized to overthrow "corrupt bureaucrats" and "capitalist roaders." China is still far from a consensus on evaluating the Mao era.

This book approaches the Mao period from a new angle, focusing on three key elements: social change, classification and conflict. Before turning to these issues, we will first consider recent developments in the field of PRC history, particularly changes around access to archives in China. I will also reflect briefly on the methodological challenges, different approaches and controversies that face historians of Maoist China.

6 Wei Riping, "Zhidao sixiang shangde 'liangjian': Shibada yilai Xi Jinping guanyu Mao Zedong sixiang zhidao diwei de zhongyao sixiang shulun," http://dangshi.people.com.cn/n/2014/0814/c85037-25467371-2.html, (accessed June 26, 2017).
7 For example see, "The Return of Mao: A New Threat to China's Politics," *Financial Times*, September 29, 2016.

The Mao Era as History

Countless popular and academic books on Mao Zedong have appeared in the last four decades. Within this vast body of material, a number of important new histories of elite politics stand out.[8] The most innovative academic research on Maoist China in recent years, however, has focused not on the "Great Helmsman" himself, but on particular aspects of Chinese society and on individual case studies. The current generation of scholars has benefited from better access to archives and the ability to record oral testimony from living witnesses. Some scholars have begun to make use of so-called "garbage materials" (*laji ziliao*). These documents, bought in old paper or second hand book markets, include a wealth of material for the creation of micro-histories, such as petition letters, personal files, diaries or outsourced archival files, all of which were considered "waste" by archivists or private owners. Meanwhile, Chinese scholars have been able to publish important books from within the PRC or, for more sensitive topics, in Hong Kong. The new sources at their disposal have enabled these authors to ask important new questions.

In the West, too, the Mao era has become something of a hot topic in China studies. In both the United States and Germany, the number of PhD candidates working on this era continues to increase. 2013 saw the foundation of the PRC History Group and a website devoted to the topic (www.prchistory.org), drawing on an international network of scholars. Thus the study of the Mao era, long dominated by political scientists and focused on the central leadership, has opened up more and more to the work of historians. That new research, by both Western and Chinese colleagues, informs much of the discussion in this book.

A New Approach to Social History: Change, Classification and Conflicts

This book presents a social history of Maoist China, focusing on class, gender, ethnicity and the urban–rural divide. I analyze the experiences of a range of social groups under CCP rule – workers, peasants, local cadres, intellectuals, "ethnic minorities," members of the old elites, men and women – across three key areas.

---

8 For example: Roderick MacFarquhar and Michael Schoenhals, *Mao's Last Revolution* (Cambridge, MA: The Belknap Press of Harvard University Press, 2006); Fredrick Teiwes and Warren Sun, *The End of the Maoist Era: Chinese Politics during the Twilight of the Cultural Revolution, 1972–1976* (Armonk, NY: M. E. Sharpe, 2007); Alexander V. Pantsov with Steven I. Levine, *Mao: The Real Story* (New York, NY: Simon and Schuster, 2012).

The first key dimension I identify is **social change**, by which I mean the transformation of economic and ownership structures, urbanization, social mobility, state-directed and self-organized migration, rationing systems, expansion and downsizing of the socialist welfare state and changes in family and gender relations.

A second important dimension in this context is **classification**. How did the party-state structure society by assigning official labels of urban or rural under the household registration (*hukou*) system? What was the impact of other labels – of class status, gender and ethnicity – applied by the state to almost every Chinese citizen? These complex intersecting systems of official classification determined social hierarchies, distribution of jobs and food, access to higher education and party or army membership.

The final dimension on which my analysis rests is **conflict**. Under Mao, conflicts (both within the party and in society at large) emerged partly in response to fundamental social changes, but also in relation to official systems of classification and distribution. Whether at the central or local level, the party-state played a crucial role in assigning labels and served as a "gatekeeper" regulating social mobility. In this context, how the various levels of the CCP understood the state of Chinese society and interpreted its developments and conflicts becomes an essential question.

Mao's own decisions and judgments had an undeniable impact across all three of these areas, and no social history can be complete without some reference to his ideas and writings. Nevertheless, Mao himself, either as a charismatic leader or an innovative Marxist-Leninist theorist, is not the focus of this book. Important sources beyond the Chairman's writings include decisions of central government and party organs, internal reports, statistics, official newspapers and numerous databases and files from county archives. Moving beyond official circles, I also make extensive use of a series of interviews conducted in China between 2001 and 2016 with intellectuals in Beijing, peasants in Henan province and Cultural Revolution-era rebels in Shandong and Shanxi. Published and unpublished memoirs, if used with caution, can further enrich our picture of the experiences of ordinary men, women and children.

The past few decades have seen a shift in approaches to the role of the Chinese people in their own recent history. Against the backdrop of the emerging Cold War in the 1950s, Western scholars tended to see China as a totalitarian society in which the CCP exercised total control over its people. Observers described a Chinese society populated by "blue ants," a homogeneous, Mao-suit–wearing mass blindly following orders from above.[9] Official propaganda promoted a similar picture of natural unity between the ruling party and the laboring masses.

9 George Paloczi-Horvath, *Mao Tse-tung: Emperor of the Blue Ants* (London: Secker and Warburg, 1962).

Figure 0.2: Larger than life: Heroes of the People's Liberation Army around 1966/1967.
Source: Collection Jean Moser, Gymnasium Leonhard, Basel.

Access to more varied sources has brought a different picture to light, unearthing practices of "everyday resistance" such as under-reporting, fraud, theft, black markets and illegal migration.[10] Over-emphasis on these practices, however, can result in a narrative that portrays ordinary people mainly as resistance fighters against the party-state. In fact, in many cases people willingly adopted state policies or the language of class, either to promote their own interests in negotiations with agents of the state or simply to protect their position.[11] Cooperation with the party stemmed from a range of motives, varying from enthusiastic support to opportunism to fear. Ordinary Chinese people in the 1950s and the younger generation involved in the early Cultural Revolution related to the socialist project in widely varying ways, from optimistic hopes and dreams to disillusion and perhaps even apathy. "Everyday resistance" was not the only game in town.

The Limits of Written and Oral Sources

Research on the Mao era still presents considerable challenges, and it is essential to retain an awareness of the limitations we face. Students of the Mao era must

---

10 The most detailed study is: Gao Wangling, *Zhongguo nongmin fan xingwei yanjiu, 1950–1980* (Hong Kong: Zhongwen daxue chubanshe, 2013).
11 Zhang Xiaojun, "Land Reform in Yang Village – Symbolic Capital and the Determination of Class Status," *Modern China*, Vol. 30, No. 1 (2004), pp. 41–42.

keep in mind that we are working on an authoritarian state that has persisted without regime change right through to the present day. In this regard, the conditions under which research is conducted differ from those prevailing in the post-socialist countries of Eastern Europe. In China, official collections of party documents and speeches by central leaders are still carefully selected and edited. Biographies of party leaders have been published based on files from the State Archives Administration (the Central Archive in Beijing), but no academic outside the central government has ever seen the original documents.[12] The Central Archive is not open to Chinese scholars, let alone Western academic researchers. Furthermore, all public archives in China are part of the state bureaucracy. According to the national Archives Law, documents are theoretically open to the public after thirty years, but files can be reclassified at any time if authorities consider a topic sensitive. In general, local archives at the city or county level are much easier to access than those at the provincial level, and one scholar has argued that the archival landscape in China is in fact quite diverse, with county archives sometimes failing to handle files according to strict legal procedure.[13] Nevertheless, access to documents at the local level depends on timing, personal connections and occasionally coincidence. Who is in the office on a given day can often be decisive.

This issue of archival accessibility has a considerable influence over the local case studies that eventually make their way into the academic literature. Western and Chinese research on the history of the PRC, at least that based on written sources, has tended to focus most strongly on the early 1950s and on Shanghai. The preponderance of studies in these areas is a more or less direct result of two phenomena. First, archivists overwhelmingly see the early 1950s as the "golden years" of the PRC, treating them far less sensitively than later periods such as the famine or the Cultural Revolution. Meanwhile, in Shanghai, the local Municipal Archives gained a well-earned reputation for being the most professional and most open institution in China to foreign researchers. This ready access to materials went hand in hand with the development of the so-called "Shanghai school," consisting mainly of scholars from Fudan University and East China Normal University, who focused primarily on local social history.[14] Historians in Beijing, by contrast, have generally been more involved with national and official party history.

---

12 For example: Jin Chongji (ed.), *Mao Zedong zhuan (1949–1976)* (Beijing: Zhongyang wenxian chubanshe, 2003), two volumes.

13 The most detailed study is: Vivian Wagner, *Erinnerungsverwaltung in China: Staatsarchive und Politik in der Volksrepublik* (Cologne: Böhlau Verlag, 2006).

14 See a book series with over two dozen volumes: *Shanghai chengshi shehui shenghuoshi congshu* (Shanghai Cishu chubanshe).

Figure 0.3: Shanghai, 1974.
Source: Photograph by Olli Salmi.

The uneven availability of archival documents has produced a local history of the PRC dominated by Shanghai, which for all its interest is hardly a representative sample. In 1949 Shanghai was China's most important industrial city, with a degree of Western influence on its culture and commerce that was unique across the country. Only limited academic research has been conducted on the history of the Mao era for those living away from the coastal urban centers in provinces such as Gansu, Qinghai, Ningxia, Guizhou, Guangxi or Tibet. The state has published a range of official provincial and county chronicles, but these documents give us only the official narrative of the CCP, and the information they provide on events such as the famine or the Cultural Revolution is unsurprisingly limited. Local academic institutions, meanwhile, generally lack the resources and standing to produce their own research on the more sensitive topics of the Mao era.

My own experience suggests that the years between the mid-1990s and 2012 were somewhat easier for research on the early PRC. Access to local archives was relatively open in this period, while in its early years an abundant supply of supposedly worthless "garbage materials" was available on the open market. In recent years, prices for "garbage materials" or Red Guard magazines have increased markedly as traders have become aware of their growing value. Meanwhile, the ascent of Xi Jinping since 2013 has coincided with increasing restrictions on access to local archives. Many files that were previously open to the public are now no longer available. (In this book, I do not give archival numbers for files in footnotes where it cannot be tracked down which employee of an archive provided the document.) Historians of the Mao era based in the PRC are under renewed political pressure to steer clear of sensitive topics, and only a few PhD candidates in China now dare to work on the period. The unintended result of tighter controls in China is that collections outside the PRC – the Chinese Service Center of the Chinese University of Hong Kong, for instance, or the research libraries of Harvard, Stanford and Berkeley – are becoming more valuable. It is now increasingly common to encounter Chinese scholars who have to travel to these institutions to access material from their homeland.

On the other hand, the past twenty years have seen Western and Chinese scholars of the Mao period gain access to rich new sources of history, including oral history, memoirs and published and unpublished diaries. Until the early 1990s, Western scholars seeking insight into mainland society would travel frequently to Hong Kong to interview refugees and migrants from neighboring Guangdong province.[15] Since the 2000s, however, it has become much easier to conduct interviews in Chinese villages or cities without state supervision. Eyewitnesses have also found new ways to circulate their views on history online, and many who cannot find an official publisher in the PRC will copy and distribute their memoirs as self-printed books or publish them in Hong Kong if they have the money. These written memoirs tend to be the product of retired cadres and intellectuals working in urban settings, but they remain valuable nevertheless.

For the large, mainly rural parts of the Chinese population that were illiterate in the 1950s and 1960s, oral history is often the only means by which people's sense of their own lives can be recovered. Needless to say, memories recounted in interviews decades after the event are subject to influence by later personal experiences and change of narratives or political trends. The impact of the present on the narration of the past always has to be part of the analysis: it is not possible to isolate an event from the history and social identity of the eyewitness, and official narratives also have an impact on people's sense of their personal encounters with historical events. During the campaigns of the Mao era, elderly people were called on to "speak bitterness" (*suku*), recalling the indignities of the past in order to praise the socialist present. Several scholars have noted that the techniques of "speaking bitterness" tend to seep into the ways ordinary people today describe other incidents in their lifetime.[16] The selective

15 For example: Andrew Walder, *Communist Neo-Traditionalism: Work and Authority in Chinese Industry* (Berkeley, CA: University of California Press, 1988).

16 Charlene Makley, "'Speaking Bitterness': Autobiography, History, and Mnemonic Politics on the Sino-Tibetan Frontier," *Comparative Studies in Society and History*, Vol. 47 (2005), pp. 40–78; Guo Yuhua, *Shoukuren de jiangshu: Jicun lishi yu yizhong wenming de luoji* (Hong Kong: Zhongwen daxue chubanshe, 2013).

adoption of party language and official narratives becomes a means to make sense of life in general. It would be naïve of the researcher to trust too implicitly in their ability to tease out any "hidden truth" behind these narratives.[17]

Furthermore, memories of the Cultural Revolution are often fragmentary and structured by the factional struggles of the time.[18] The accounts of ordinary people can provide new perspectives, but we should be wary of expecting some mysterious kind of "real history" to suddenly come to light, unburdened by the official perspectives represented in many of our textual sources. Scholars of rural societies have too often romanticized the local as "authentic" against an "alien" state, a trap that the Chinese case should encourage us to avoid.[19] Even with these limits in mind, however, oral history should not be too readily discarded, first because eyewitnesses who were adults in the Mao era are dying out, and second because, in general, it is easier for Chinese authorities to restrict access to archives than to interviews.

National, Local and Micro: History at Different Scales

Social history can operate at the national, local or micro level, running from the largest social groups to the life experiences of a single individual. The level of analysis at which a scholar chooses to work is related both to their research questions and to ease of access to relevant sources. An appreciation of local variation can be crucial: the extent of famine during the Great Leap Forward and the spread of rebellion during the Cultural Revolution varied widely across different counties and provinces. In the more developed regions on the east coast, industrialization impacted local society in different ways and at different times than in the poor western parts of the country. The effects of Maoist agricultural campaigns differed between the rice-growing economies of the south and wheat-growing zones in the north. Different social groups experienced change differently across time and space.[20] Some scholars have questioned the utility of any attempt to narrate history on the national level. The historian Gail

---

17 Gail Hershatter, *The Gender of Memory: Rural Women and China's Collective Past* (Berkeley, CA: University of California Press, 2011), p. 235.

18 Susanne Weigelin-Schwiedrzik, "In Search of a Master Narrative for 20th-Century Chinese History," *The China Quarterly*, No. 188 (2006), pp. 1084–1085.

19 Tom Brass, "On Which Side of What Barricade? Subaltern Resistance in Latin America and Elsewhere," *The Journal of Peasant Studies*, Vol. 29, No. 3 (2002), p. 339.

20 Jeremy Brown and Paul G. Pickowicz (eds.), *Dilemmas of Victory: The Early Years of the People's Republic of China* (Cambridge, MA: Harvard University Press, 2007), p. 8.

Hershatter, for instance, argues that all socialism in China is fundamentally local in character:

> Even the most prescriptive edicts of a centralized state must be implemented in widely varied environments, by local personnel who interpret, rework, emphasize, and deflect according to particular circumstances. The working out of state policies was everywhere contingent upon geography, prior social arrangements, and local personalities.[21]

Local variation in the implementation of policy is scarcely unique to Maoist China. However, an interest in the specific should not prevent us from analyzing and describing society as a whole. In her study of rural women in Shaanxi, based on over a decade of research across several counties, Hershatter herself goes far beyond the local to theorize the impact of gender and the everyday experiences of women on historical memory more widely. Scholars can usefully seek to explain how the Marriage Law of 1950 changed family and gender structures across China as a whole, or what impact the state rationing system had on the diet of the peasantry, or what social benefits so-called "temporary workers" gained during the Cultural Revolution. This work demands a huge variety of sources, including an array of central documents and sophisticated statistical analysis, but it is not beyond our capabilities.

At the other end of the scale, recent debate has also called the usefulness of micro and grassroots history into question. One area where the techniques of micro-history have been extensively applied is queer history, a topic about which we are still largely in the dark for the Maoist period. The concept of "coming out" into openly gay, lesbian or queer identities seems to have been largely unknown in China at this time. Some accounts speak of outright repression, while others instead emphasize the ignorance of society at large around queer issues. To examine, as one recent study does, a single personal file of a worker accused of having sex with men (alongside other political problems) can provide new insights into how a work unit dealt with the issue of homosexuality.[22] Clearly, however, it would be unwise to generalize from a single case.

The larger methodological question is whether micro-histories of this kind can even attempt to answer "big questions" such as, say, the overall character of state-society relations in Maoist China. The political scientist Elizabeth Perry has criticized historians who work with "garbage materials" for refusing to relate

---

21 Hershatter, *The Gender of Memory*, p. 14.

22 Yang Kuisong, "How a 'Bad Element' was made: The Discovery, Accusation and Punishment of Zang Qiren," in Jeremy Brown and Matthew Johnson (eds.), *Maoism at the Grassroots: Everyday Life in China's Era of High Socialism* (Cambridge, MA: Harvard University Press, 2015), pp. 19–50.

their findings to broader issues of comparative and contemporary relevance. Her critique is cutting indeed: "Intoxicated by the wealth of newly discovered sources that allow for the investigation of everyday life," she writes, micro-historians have accepted "a division of labor in which social scientists explore the 'commanding heights' of the Chinese state and its policies, while historians grub for diversity in the dustbins of grassroots society."[23] Jeremy Brown and Matthew Johnson, by contrast, argue for establishing an entire field of grassroots history, defined as "a complex interplay between provincial, county, commune, and village officials, and among people who had no official titles whatsoever."[24] To those actors one might add some uniquely urban players, such as municipal officials and the individual factories or neighborhoods with which they had dealings.

Good grassroots history goes beyond descriptive summaries of individual files and interesting local anecdotes. I see no necessary contradiction between micro-history based on "garbage materials" and the study of the "commanding heights" of the party-state. My work for this book has involved a systematic study of decisions of the Central Committee regarding the classification of class status, coupled with an examination of personal class files from collections of "garbage material." The differences between these two groups of sources have often been instructive. Without a deeper understanding of central policies, it is often not possible to make sense of the local record.

Moreover, there are many levels of social history that sit between the micro and the central. Documents at the commune level often feature discussion of events both above at the county level and below on the level of the villages. The county level, meanwhile, often leads to documents sent from the provincial administration. This book argues against the opposition of local against national history, instead favoring a multi-level approach built on as wide a variety of sources as possible.

Organization of the Book

Each chapter of the book opens with an individual story, drawn from a memoir or oral history, which serves as a springboard for the discussion that follows.

23 Elizabeth Perry, "The Promise of PRC History," *Journal for Modern Chinese History*, Vol. 10, No. 1 (2016), p. 116. For response see: "Maoism at the Grassroots: An Interview with Jeremy Brown and Matthew Johnson," Age of Revolutions (2016), https://ageofrevolutions .com/2016/10/24/maoism-at-the-grassroots-an-interview-with-jeremy-brown-and-matthew-johnson/ (accessed July 13, 2017).

24 Jeremy Brown and Matthew Johnson, "Introduction," in Jeremy Brown and Matthew Johnson, (eds.), *Maoism at the Grassroots: Everyday Life in China's Era of High Socialism* (Cambridge, MA: Harvard University Press, 2015), p. 4.

At the end of each chapter I present a wider selection of written sources from archives, internal reports, private collections of "garbage material" or databases. In Chapter 1, "Chinese Society under Mao: Classifications, Social Hierarchies and Distribution," I outline the character of Chinese society in general, presenting an overview of the most important official classifications of the Mao era and their impact on social hierarchies and structures of distribution. The following chapters explore these fundamental questions in more detail. Chapter 2, "New Democracy and the Making of New China (1949–1952)," focuses on the remaking of the rural order during Land Reform and the destruction of the old economic and political elites in the PRC's early years. Chapter 3, "The Transformation to State Socialism (1953–1957)," analyses the experiences of workers, peasants, intellectuals and inmates of labor camps during the mid-1950s. Chapter 4, "The Great Leap into Famine (1958–1961)," opens with a discussion of the failure of women's liberation and of attempts to organize care work in public institutions. It then examines how peasants struggled for survival during the Great Leap Famine and outlines the demographic impact of the catastrophe. The social conflicts that developed around the subsequent de-urbanization program and the early 1960s "austerity policies" are the subject of Chapter 5, "The Post-Famine Years: From Readjustment to the Socialist Education Campaign (1962–1965)," which also considers the impact of the Socialist Education Campaign on local cadres and peasants. In Chapter 6, "The Rebellion and Its Limits: The Early Cultural Revolution (1966–1968)," the focus turns to the rebellion of students and workers against the system of class status and rank. I also discuss the contradictory role of cadres, some of whom fell victim to the movement while others sided with the rebels. Chapter 7, "Demobilization and Restoration: The Late Cultural Revolution (1969–1976)," shows the impact of the Cultural Revolution on rural society and discusses the life of the "sent-down youths" exiled from the cities to the countryside. The end of the chapter examines the achievements and failures of the Mao era in terms of living standards, economic growth and social reform. The final chapter, "Legacies and Continuities of the Mao Era in Reform China," examines how the legacy of the Mao regime has continued to influence state classifications and social hierarchies in later years. The overriding question is the extent to which present class structures under "capitalism with Chinese characteristics" can be related to the inequalities of the Mao era.

This book is an attempt at a multifaceted, multi-source approach to the social history of Maoist China. Faced with the complexity of this tumultuous period, I have strived to maintain a reasonable balance, recognizing the PRC's efforts at modernization and social reform without losing sight of the famine and political terror that, for many now aging quietly across China, remain the period's abiding memory.

1 CHINESE SOCIETY UNDER MAO: CLASSIFICATIONS, SOCIAL HIERARCHIES AND DISTRIBUTION

铁饭碗
The iron rice bowl
靠天吃饭
Relying on heaven to eat
上有政策，下有对策
Policy above meets counter-policy below

In 1968, aged eighteen, Ye Weili, an "educated youth" (*zhiqing*) from Beijing, was sent down to a poor village in Shanxi Province. As the child of two mid-level cadres, Ye's schooling had been characterized by a high degree of gender equality, and at home domestic work was done by a maid, whom her parents were entitled to employ because of their work for the CCP. In the villages, Ye experienced very different forms of gender relations:

> I was the only female laborer on my team regularly working in the field. Only occasionally would some unmarried young women join us (...). When we first arrived some villagers privately inquired whether any of us would consider taking a local husband, assuming a city girl would not fetch a big bride price. Once they realized that we were not interested, they left us alone.[1]

The food too was different, both in kind and in quantity, from what she had been accustomed to under the urban rationing system:

> What we ate every day at the *zhiqing* canteens was corn bread, millet porridge and preserved cabbages and carrots. At first food was rationed because there wasn't enough of it (...). Later grain was no longer

[1] Weili Ye with Xiaodong Ma, *Growing Up in the People's Republic: Conversations between Two Daughters of China's Revolution* (New York, NY: Palgrave Macmillan, 2005), p. 118.

a problem, but there were hardly any fresh vegetables, let alone meat. Because of this poor diet, every time we went back to Beijing for a visit we would bring back foodstuffs such as sausages and dried noodles.[2]

As her time in Shanxi wore on, Ye came to worry that she might never be permitted to leave the countryside. However, in 1972, universities across the country were finally able to begin enrolling new students – the first round of admissions since 1966. Ye was selected to become a "worker-peasant-soldier student" at Beijing Normal College, and she returned to the urban world. Social status had played an important role in her selection. Ye's background as the daughter of middle-ranking party cadres had been displaced by a new, more favorable classification as a "peasant." Ye, who graduated in 1976, would go on to leave China for an academic career in the United States.

Ye's story makes clear the importance of hierarchies – gender, age, class, urban versus rural – to understanding life in Maoist China. It is also obvious that these hierarchies and labels intersected with one another: the position of urban women in society differed from that of rural women, for instance. Furthermore, Ye's experience shows that these social categories did not necessarily remain stable over time during the Mao era. In the countryside, Ye was excluded from the urban rationing system and could not be sure of ever returning to Beijing, let alone enrolling at university. We should keep in mind that labels that were important in one context might have no currency in another. Ye's official ethnicity had little significance in Shanxi, where her fellow villagers, like her, came from the Han majority.

In this chapter, I characterize Maoist China as a society in transition. Unlike a capitalist society, social hierarchies were determined less by wealth and private ownership than by a series of official classifications. As suggested above, the four most important classifications (class status, urban/rural registration, gender and ethnicity) were never independent of each other.

By the early 1960s, almost every Chinese citizen was classified by the state according to the four major categories. The official distribution system for food and goods, along with access to information, higher education, employment, party membership and military service were all based on this complex system of classifications. This chapter also discusses informal modes of distribution of material goods that sat outside of official channels, such as theft or under-reporting. Finally, we consider the various waves of internal migration and show how they were linked to the classification system.

2 Ibid., pp. 119–120.

A Society in Transition

The fundamental dynamic driving Maoist China was the transition from a semi-colonial, underdeveloped country to state socialism. The stage was set for this transition by the twin victories of the 1940s. The triumph of the Allies over imperial Japan in 1945 and the Chinese communist revolution of 1949 freed China from its peripheral position in the global capitalist system, allowing the party to pursue one of its central goals: transforming a poor agrarian country into a modern industrial nation within a few decades. In the early 1950s, Cold War tensions and a US economic embargo kept China isolated from the Western world. American policymakers sought to cut off China's supply of high technology and military hardware, compelling the PRC to "lean to one side" and seek closer links with the Soviet Union and the socialist bloc. However, in the late 1960s, Chinese concerns over the Soviet threat encouraged a rapprochement with the United States, setting the PRC on its way to becoming an internationally recognized state. This changing geopolitical background, however, did not result in China's immediate integration into the capitalist world market. Once the attempt to create an alternative "socialist world market" with the Soviet Union and Eastern Europe had stalled in the early 1960s, the PRC adopted a strategy of self-reliance, remaining mainly outside global production chains until 1978.

By 1957 China's urban economy and population were mainly organized along state-socialist lines. State-owned and collective enterprises were embedded in a Soviet-style planned economy. Private accumulation of wealth through property ownership and exploitation of wage labor was prohibited from the socialist transformation in the mid-1950s until the beginning of the Reform era in the early 1980s. Leading cadres managed state-owned enterprises, but they exercised no rights of ownership and had no legal way to transfer profits from the work unit to their personal holdings. In place of the hiring and firing practices of a capitalist system, the permanent workforce in state-owned industries ate from the so-called "iron rice bowl" (*tiefanwan*), meaning that they "owned" their jobs and the associated social welfare benefits for life. Their labor was decommodified, with almost all employment being assigned by the state rather than sold on the open market.[3] Commodified labor did exist in the form of short-term contract work, but this practice remained marginal throughout the Maoist period.

3 Joel Andreas, "Industrial Restructuring and Class Transformation in China," in Beatriz Carrillo and David S. Goodman (eds.), *China's Peasants and Workers: Changing Class Identities* (Cheltenham: Edward Elgar Publishing, 2012), p. 107.

By contrast, rural China under Mao was never more than semi-socialist. Attempts to eliminate private property and natural village boundaries failed spectacularly during the Great Leap Forward, forcing the CCP to allow mixed ownership structures in the People's Communes and to distribute plots of land for private use to peasant families in 1961. Even at the height of the Cultural Revolution, this compromise with the peasantry never came under real attack in more than a few regions. Further socialization of land and the means of production proved impossible, and the peasant family remained an important unit of production and consumption. Nor was it possible to expand the socialist welfare state into the countryside. In general, the reach of the state remained far stronger in urban society than in the villages.[4] This was a critical point of difference between the PRC and the Soviet Union or the GDR (German Democratic Republic), where by the 1970s the whole population was integrated into the welfare state from birth to death. Chinese peasants, almost 80 percent of the population, never tasted the fruits of the "iron rice bowl."

Marxism-Leninism and Equality

Critics of communism are fond of pointing out that in socialist states not everyone was equal. The ideology of communism, the argument goes, was little more than hypocritical cynicism, a rhetoric of convenience used by ruling cadres to dress up their dictatorship. This critique, however, fundamentally misrepresents Marxist theory. Marx and Engels themselves asserted that communism would not be delivered immediately following any revolution; instead, a transitional "dictatorship of the proletariat" would be necessary. The function of this dictatorship would not be to proclaim the equality of all people, but to create the conditions for the elimination of private ownership of the means of production, which would in turn render wage labor obsolete and dissolve class distinctions. It was only after these goals were achieved that the state as an instrument of class struggle would finally be extinguished.[5] Furthermore, Marx explicitly argued that the "bourgeois law" of distribution according to labor performance would continue to apply during the transitional period. Distribution according to individual needs was to be the province of communism, not the socialist state, and the achievement of such a system of distribution would have to await the development of appropriately advanced forces of production. Given the

4 For example see: Vivienne Shue, *The Reach of the State: Sketches of the Chinese Body Politics* (Stanford, CA: Stanford University Press, 1988); Susanne Weigelin-Schwiedrzik, "The Distance between State and Rural Society in the PRC: Reading Document No. 1," *Journal of Environmental Management*, Vol. 87 (2008), pp. 216–225.

5 Karl Marx, "Critique of the Gotha Programme" (1875), www.marxists.org/archive/marx/works/1875/gotha/cho4.htm (accessed September 7, 2017).

diverse needs of individuals, even this would not be an *equal* distribution, merely an equitable one.

Whatever their attitude to equality, communism's founding theorists certainly never envisioned the "dictatorship of the proletariat" as requiring a one-party system. Nor could they have imagined the hierarchical system of ranks that would come to characterize Soviet-style Leninist parties. In contrast, Marx saw the Paris Commune of 1871, a decentralized grassroots democracy, as the best model for proletarian government.[6] The Chinese notion of a vanguard party that would first lead the revolution, then become a party-state after victory, was not a Marxist idea, but an import from the Soviet Union in the 1920s. It was this vanguard role that formed the justification for the special treatment and privileges afforded to CCP cadres after 1949. In another line of reasoning, the party claimed that such privileges were a necessary acknowledgment of the contributions and sacrifices of "old cadres" during the revolution. For the CCP, the vanguard party would be needed as an instrument of class struggle until the transition from socialism to communism had been completed.

The worldview of the CCP in the early 1950s was strongly influenced by Soviet Marxism-Leninism. However, during the Great Leap Forward in 1958 and later during the Cultural Revolution, Marx's early writings such as "Critique of the Gotha Program" and "German Ideology" were widely discussed. Marx imagined a society in which the division between urban and rural, and between manual and intellectual labor, would be abolished. In his vision of communism, every citizen was to have a free choice of occupation according to their needs and skills, so that the same person could be a hunter in the morning, a fisherman at noon and a "critical critic" in the evening.[7] This focus on utopian thinking seems to me to make terms such as "fair wage" or "fair distribution" largely irrelevant in a Marxist context. These notions are more the province of traditional social democracy and Western welfare state. If we are to approach revolutionary regimes on their own terms we may need to abandon these notions, or at least recognize that they were not necessarily native to Marxist debate.

Marx's ideas, especially the prospect of eliminating the city/countryside and intellectual/manual division of labor, had widespread currency in the second decade of CCP rule. Compared to its Soviet counterpart, the Chinese Party proved more interested in the "utopian" elements of Marx's ideas,[8] but ignored his warning that

---

6 Karl Marx, "The Civil War in France" (1871), www.marxists.org/archive/marx/works/1871/civil-war-france/cho5.htm (accesssed September 7, 2017).

7 Karl Marx, "The German Ideology" (1845), www.marxists.org/archive/marx/works/1845/german-ideology/cho1a.htm (accessed March 28, 2018).

8 For detail see: Felix Wemheuer, "Die Konstruktion des neuen Menschen: Diskurse des chinesischen Kommunismus während des Großen Sprungs nach vorne, 1958," in Lena Henningsen and Heiner Roetz (eds.), *Menschenbilder in China* (Wiesbaden: Harrassowitz, 2009), pp. 95–114.

the introduction of communism based on a backward means of production would only "generalize the dejection" that existed in pre-revolutionary society.[9]

By comparison with other notable revolutions such as the French Revolution of 1789 or the Russian "October Revolution" of 1917, the Chinese revolution in 1949 was characterized by a high degree of mass participation.[10] This did not mean, however, that it was an organic, "bottom-up" revolution. Indeed, China in the 1940s experienced few spontaneous uprisings of workers and peasants compared to the Russian Revolution of 1917. Instead, the CCP expanded its power from its base in northern China via a civil war with Chiang Kai-Shek's Nationalists (1946–1949) – in other words, through military conquest. The party built socialism from above, albeit with considerable mass support from below. Workers may have had more power on the shop floor after 1949, but the CCP's dictatorial authority was always exercised *in the name* of the proletariat, never by the proletariat themselves. Workers had no democratic control over production.

Nevertheless, in the 1950s and 1960s the party leadership could count on millions of activists and "true believers" at the grassroots. Some scholars have argued that Mao was little more than a cynic, focusing on maintaining his own power to the exclusion of all else.[11] A desire for power, however, is not in itself incompatible with Leninist ideology, which sees taking and defending the apparatus of the state as key to effecting genuine political and social change. Allowing power to fall into the hands of "class enemies" or "revisionist elements" inside the party would inevitably lead, in this view, to a restoration of the old society. Neither Mao's unceasing defense of the power of his so-called "proletarian headquarters," nor the gruesome determination the CCP showed in eradicating its perceived enemies, necessarily prove that Mao and his followers were not genuine believers in the communist cause. Whatever his ultimate motivations may have been, no available archival evidence gives any sense that Mao did not believe in the communist agenda that he publicly espoused. That agenda, to be sure, was never realized, and people in Maoist China were very far from equal. That does not mean, however, that everything the CCP did under Mao was a cynical power play. The content of CCP policies mattered, and it is therefore necessary to ask questions about how those policies worked in practice and how the party dealt with the results.

---

9 Karl Marx, "Die deutsche Ideologie," *Marx-Engels Ausgewählte Werke* (Berlin: Dietz Verlag, 1972), Vol. I, p. 226.

10 Maurice Meisner, "The Significance of the Chinese Revolution in World History," *Asia Research Working Paper 1*. http://eprints.lse.ac.uk/21309/1/Significance_of_the_Chinese_Revolution_in_world_history.pdf (accessed April 12, 2018).

11 As an example for this kind of narrative see: Jung Chang and Jon Halliday, *Mao: The Unknown Story* (New York, NY: Anchor Books, 2005).

The Intersectionality of Hierarchies in China

Intersectional approaches are well established in sociology. Current intersectional theory traces its roots to the 1970s, when feminists from minority backgrounds forcefully critiqued the mainstream movement for focusing on a binary opposition of "patriarchy" against "sisterhood."[12] In their view, this simplified vision of gender relations failed to account for the race and class discrimination faced by women beyond the wealthy white communities of the Global North, forms of discrimination that were interwoven with gender prejudices in a complex tapestry of injustice. Gender, race and class, in other words, are intersecting qualities, and social hierarchies cannot be understood if each category is studied in isolation from the others. Class is gendered and gender has a class component; ethnic labeling tends to disadvantage the poorest the most. Industrial workers often draw their identities from particular definitions of masculinity: physical strength and a pride in manual skills. Light industry, by contrast, has historically been viewed as nimble, dexterous "women's work." From the 1980s, the textile, garment and electronics industries of developing countries were dominated by women.[13] These female workers were often (and continue to be) seen as easier to control than their male counterparts.

In approaching intersectionality in the Chinese case, I take account not only of systems of production and distribution, but also of reproductive labor, encompassing sexuality, child birth, child care and housework. This unacknowledged, unpaid "invisible labor" continues to be done, in large part, by women, and is existentially important to the functioning of societies across the globe. Much mainstream economic theory, however, either ignores the impact of this unremunerated labor, or else takes it as read that women are natural care givers for whom reproductive work is an automatic instinct. Orthodox Marxist approaches likewise discount care work as "non-productive," in the sense that it fails to produce surplus value. My own research adds to the growing consensus that the invisible labor of reproduction is not only the province of gender studies, but is in fact an essential part of the wider socio-economic picture.

12 For example see: Leslie McCall, "The Complexity of Intersectionality," *Signs*, Vol. 30, No. 3 (2005), pp. 1771–1800; Sabine Hess, Nikola Langreiter and Elisabeth Timm (eds.), *Intersektionalität Revisited. Empirische, Theoretische und Methodische Erkundungen* (Bielefeld: Transcript, 2011); Vera Kallenbacher, Jennifer Meyer and Johanna M. Müller (eds.), *Intersectionality und Kritik. Neue Perspektiven für alte Fragen* (Wiesbaden: Springer, 2013); Björn Alpermann, "Class, Citizenship, Ethnicity: Categories of Social Distinction and Identification in Contemporary China" in Caniela Célleri, Tobias Schwarz and Bea Wittger (eds.), *Interdependencies of Social Categorisations* (Madrid: Vervuert, 2013), pp. 237–261.

13 Teri L. Caraway, *Assembling Women: The Feminization of Global Manufacturing* (Ithaca, NY: Cornell University Press, 2007), p. 22.

In a capitalist society, surplus value is extracted by ownership of the means of production, land and capital and through the control of wage labor. In modern societies, the state plays a significant but generally limited role in distributing the resulting wealth through taxation, subsidies, investment programs, social welfare, provision of education and so on. In Maoist China, the limitations on private accumulation of wealth made the state a far more important distributor of resources than in most contemporary societies. Distribution of goods, along with access to economic and political organizations, programs of affirmative action and the allotment of social capital, was based on a systematic categorization of the population.

The most important division concerned participation in the urban welfare state, with every Chinese citizen labeled as either "inside the system" (*tizhinei*) and "outside the system" (*tizhiwai*). This division ran largely along urban/rural lines: anyone with a rural household registration fell "outside the system" (Figure 1.1). This included peasants in the urban suburbs, who retained their rural registrations but were counted in the urban population statistics in the 1950s. Some urban residents, such as temporary workers and small traders with no assigned work unit, also remained "outside the system." Minimal welfare provision existed for those categorized in this way: outside the cities, even cadres were not paid by the state or entitled to welfare benefits unless they worked above the level of the People's Communes. Inside the cities, meanwhile, a complex system of ranks governed wages and the distribution of goods.

Beyond the urban–rural divide, every Chinese citizen was officially labeled in terms of class, gender and ethnicity. I therefore identify the following major types of classification:

household registration (agricultural versus non-agricultural)
"rank" (a sub-categorization assigned to urban residents)
class status (combining occupational status, family background and political labels)
gender (male versus female)
ethnicity (Han versus ethnic minority).

It is important to note that classification under these categories did not necessarily reflect the self-identity of the person concerned: some of China's fifty-five recognized national ethnic minorities, for instance, were 1950s inventions that bore only a partial relationship to the autonyms used by people on the ground.

By the late 1950s, labeling according to these five categories was complete for almost the entire population, with the exception of some minority areas such as Tibet where the process would continue until the mid-1960s. Household registration, class and ethnicity were all closely linked to family. Ethnicity and family

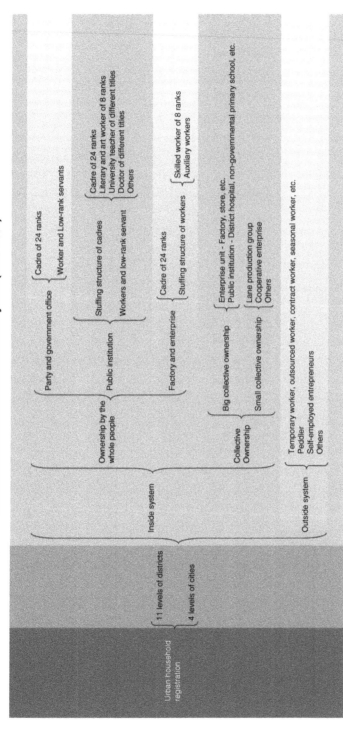

Institutional Status in and outside the System (1958–1982)

Inside system

Urban household registration

Ownership by the whole people
- Party and government office
  - { Cadre of 24 ranks
  - { Worker and Low-rank servants
- Public institution
  - Stuffing structure of cadres
    - { Cadre of 24 ranks
    - { Literary and art worker of 8 ranks
    - { University teacher of different titles
    - { Doctor of different titles
    - { Others
  - Workers and low-rank servant
- Factory and enterprise
  - { Cadre of 24 ranks
  - { Stuffing structure of workers
    - { Skilled worker of 8 ranks
    - { Auxiliary workers

Collective Ownership
- Big collective ownership
  - { Enterprise unit - Factory, store, etc.
  - { Public institution - District hospital, non-governmental primary school, etc.
- Small collective ownership
  - { Lane production group
  - { Cooperative enterprise
  - { Others

Outside system
- { Temporary worker, outsourced worker, contract worker, seasonal worker, etc.
- { Peddler
- { Self-employed entrepreneurs
- { Others

11 levels of districts
4 levels of cities

Rural household registration – Three-level ownership of People's Commune, production brigade and production team

Figure 1.1: Institutional status in and outside the system (1958–1982). Based on Li Xun, *Geming zaofan niandai: Shanghai wenge yundong shigao* (Hong Kong: Oxford University Press, 2015), Vol. 1, p. 4.

background were defined through the paternal line, while household registration was passed down on the mother's side.

The Urban-Rural Divide (Household Registration)

The difference in the treatment of urban and rural areas in the early PRC was so stark that China under Mao is sometimes described as a "dual society."[14] By 1958, almost every citizen in the country's Han Chinese areas was classified with an agricultural or non-agricultural household registration (*hukou*).[15] People with urban status were entitled to buy food and important consumer goods at low prices using ration cards provided by the state. Most of the urban population was organized into work units (*danwei*) and entitled to social welfare and cheap housing.

This state-subsidized urban society was made possible by extracting resources from rural areas. Rural-registered peasants were organized into collectives and compelled to sell any agricultural surplus above a prescribed level to the state, which had a monopoly on sale and purchase and imposed consistently low prices. A rural *hukou* carried no entitlement to a state ration card, wages or social security, which were replaced in the collectives by work points (*gongfen*) that could be exchanged for grain. Almost every peasant was a member of an agricultural cooperative from 1956 and of a larger People's Commune between 1958 and the early 1980s. Within communes, party branches were established on the level of the production brigade, and at the lower levels individual households were grouped together in small production teams from 1961 onwards.

For much of the Mao period only small amounts of currency circulated in the countryside. A production team's income depended heavily on labor performance. The lack of an effective system of redistribution in rural areas meant that weather could have a serious impact on local collectives, and peasants in more developed areas typically ate better than those in poorer ones. In provinces such as Henan, the diet of the rural population would rely on sweet potatoes, widely regarded as "pig food" in the richer south, until the early 1980s. In addition, because minimum rations were not clearly defined, rural distribution was subject to far greater manipulation by local actors than was possible in the state-organized urban supply system. In times of crisis, rations might still be distributed, but the food was of poor quality and had little nutritional value.

14 Xiao Donglian, "Zhongguo eryuan shehui jiegou xingcheng de lishi kaocha," *Dangshiyanjiu*, No. 1 (2005), pp. 8–11.
15 For detail see: Tiejun Cheng, Mark Selden and Timothy Cheek, "The Construction of Spatial Hierarchies: China's *Hukou* and *Danwei* System," in Timothy Cheek and Tony Saich (eds.), *New Perspectives on State Socialism in China* (London: M. E. Sharpe, 1997), pp. 23–50.

Rural welfare did exist in the form of initiatives like the "five guarantee household" program, which provided food, clothing, heating, medical care and burial. These, however, were locally financed and reached only a few percent of the rural population, mainly orphans and disabled or elderly people without family support. Beyond these protected groups, rural society was mainly self-reliant, with peasants receiving relief from central state funds only in the case of severe natural disasters. Some people in the countryside did escape rural registration: workers on state-owned farms and factories could often maintain their urban *hukou*.[16] Genuine upward mobility from rural to urban status, however, was very limited during the Mao era after 1962. It was much more usual for the government to downgrade the status of urban people and send them to the countryside, as in case of the "urban youth" exiled from the cities during the Cultural Revolution.

It is often argued that class was the most important category in Maoist China, but in terms of the distribution of basic goods and services such as food, clothing, housing or health care, class was actually less important than the urban/rural divide. The urban supply system ensured that a "capitalist" in Beijing would eat better than a "poor peasant" in central China, despite the latter's far more favorable class status. Moreover, the "dual society" phenomenon was one of the major push factors for internal migration. The state attempted to control this migration, especially after 1962, by linking access to the supply system to legal residency in the cities. The limited options left open to peasants seeking an urban household registration included serving in the People's Liberation Army (PLA), passing the national university entrance examination or being recruited by an urban work unit as a permanent worker. All were a realistic prospect for only a vanishingly small segment of the rural population. Marrying a worker with an urban household registration was a dream for many women in the countryside, but this form of upward mobility was neutered by the fact that the *hukou* status of children was passed down through the maternal line.

For the vast majority of people, therefore, being a rural citizen meant exclusion from the socialist welfare state in an existence tied to village and land. The model of development during the Mao era was essentially to develop urban heavy industry through exploitation of the peasantry and extraction of rural resources at artificially low prices.[17] The urban–rural divide was the foundational division of Chinese society under Mao, the matrix on which class, gender and ethnicity intersected. To put it in more Maoist terms, the divide was an expression of the contradiction

16 Jeremy Brown, *City versus Countryside in Mao's China: Negotiating the Divide* (Cambridge: Cambridge University Press, 2012), pp. 169–199.

17 Wen Tiejun, *Zhongguo nongcun jiben jingji zhidu yanjiu* (Beijing: Zhongguo jingji chubanshe, 2000), pp. 175–177.

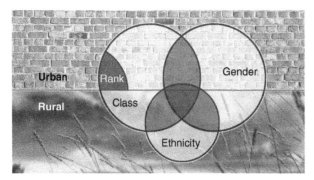

Figure 1.2: Intersectional hierarchies in Maoist China.

between the socialist and semi-socialist elements of Chinese society under the early PRC. (See Figure 1.2.)

This great divide, enduring though it has proved, did not go unchallenged. Despite the difficulties, people could try to change their status from rural to urban. The urban bias of the distribution system and exclusion of the rural population from the welfare state also came under occasional attack as unfair and unjust, particularly in 1956–1957 and during the early Cultural Revolution. In these periods the party leadership struggled to justify why expansion of the "iron rice bowl" was not possible, and some concessions for people "outside the system" were eventually made.

Urban Ranks

Geography played a key role in consumption and distribution during the Mao period. Four levels of administration existed within each of the Chinese provinces, from municipalities under the authority of the central or provincial government down through districts, counties and townships (see Figure 1.1). Below the county level even cadres were in most cases not on the state payroll but drew their salaries from local coffers. For those "inside the system" above this level, a scheme of subranks governed the distribution of resources, and here again spatial stratification was at work. The country was divided into eleven urban areas with varying wage levels to take account of differences in the cost of living, with Shanghai top of the pile.

Figure 1.1 highlights the role of another important division, that between state-owned and collectively owned enterprises. Workers in the state sector were entitled to much better welfare than in the collective sector and enjoyed a far higher degree of job security. The state-owned sector was divided into political

Figure 1.3: Diplomatic compounds in Beijing, Jianguomen, 1974.
Source: Photograph by Olli Salmi.

work units (covering the party and the state apparatus), public work units (covering education and culture), and industrial work units. Within these three kind of units, employees were divided between cadres and workers, with university graduates considered professional cadres.

Among industrial units, heavy industry received more resources than light industry, while state-owned enterprises were prioritized over those under collective ownership. Manual workers in key heavy industries received higher grain rations than those engaged in light or intellectual labor such as cadres or students.[18] These differences were justified mainly through Marxist-Leninist ideas of productivity, under which labor outside of industry and agriculture (such as housework) was regarded as non-productive. Differing rations were also an acknowledgment that manual labor was simply more calorie intensive than other forms of work. In 1955, cadres were divided into thirty ranks, with salaries and access to goods varying accordingly.[19] For instance, the two officials of the first rank (the chairman of the CCP and the prime minister) received a monthly salary of 560 yuan. The lowest rank consisted of service staff, who received 18 yuan per month. A number of scholars have therefore argued that the

18 Felix Wemheuer, *Famine Politics in Maoist China and the Soviet Union* (New Haven, CT: Yale University Press, 2014), pp. 94–96.
19 Yiching Wu, *The Cultural Revolution at the Margins: Chinese Socialism in Crisis* (Cambridge, MA: Harvard University Press, 2014), pp. 26–27.

wage gap between top and bottom in the Chinese public sector was actually larger than in developed capitalist countries in the same period.[20]

As well as formal position, length of service also played a role in the ranking system. Skilled "old workers" who had entered the workforce before 1949 received higher salaries than those who became members of work units later. This applied even to workers at the same level of seniority within an enterprise. To this day, "old workers" continue to receive more generous retirement benefits than their colleagues. For cadres, the year in which they joined the party was the key factor. "Revolutionary cadres" who had joined before the founding of the PRC were understood to have risked far more for the cause than those who entered the party after 1949, and this signal of political reliability meant deficiencies in their family background could be more readily overlooked.

As well as goods and services, rank also determined access to information. News on sensitive topics such as local protests, the underground economy or developments in other socialist countries was shared with only a select few. The so-called "internal reference" documents (*neibu cankao*), internally circulated news reports collected by the state-owned Xinhua News Agency, were received only by high-ranking cadres. Likewise, only people at the higher levels could read speeches and documents in full. For lower-ranking cadres, speeches by Mao and other leaders were often cut, while the ordinary reader would have access only to a newspaper summary.[21] Instructions and documents from the CCP Central Committee, its central decision-making body, were often circulated only at the provincial and county level but not below, with local cadres seldom gaining access to any central documents. In poorer parts of rural China, society remained almost completely paperless and peasants had little access to newspapers or books, leaving rural cadres to circulate instructions and propaganda orally or on blackboards. Many foreign non-fiction books were translated for "internal use" only. "Internal screenings" of Western movies were organized for cadres and party members, who were considered more capable of withstanding "bourgeois influence" than the general public and were trusted to watch for the purpose of information only.

This system of information control was effective but not flawless. Relatives of cadres would sometimes lend "internal books" to their friends, expanding their circulation beyond the government's intended readership. Timely access to information about the twists and turns of central policies could save one's career, and the regulation of information according to rank soon spawned a cottage

---

20 Yang Kuisong, "Guanyu jianguo yilai dangzheng ganbu shouru de wenda," *Nanfang Zhoumo*, 30 August (2007), http://news.qq.com/a/20070830/001836_4.htm (accessed November 28, 2016).

21 For example see: Jean-Luc Domenach, *The Origins of the Great Leap Forward: The Case of One Chinese Province* (Oxford: Westview Press, 1995), p. 71.

industry of rumors and "news from the byways" (*xiaodao xiaoxi*) circulated by word of mouth.

Class Status

As intimated above, a person's class status played only a limited role in the supply system. Class mattered far more, however, in terms of access to institutions such as universities, the army or Communist Party after 1949.[22] The categorization of classes began in rural China as part of the Land Reform campaign (1947–1952), where class labels determined whether an individual would be allotted land and a house or have their property confiscated. In urban areas, the state's assignment of class labels was less systematic.

The system of class status was complex, generating labels based on three dimensions: the pre-1949 economic status of the family, called family origin (*jiating chushen*); the personal status of an individual based on current occupation (*geren chengfen*); and the individual's political performance (*biaoxian*), including their attitude towards the revolution and the ongoing construction of socialism as well as their "social relations" (*shehui guanxi*). For people of bad family origins, it was important to "draw a line" and break with their problematic relatives. Party members were warned against forming friendships with "landlords" and other undesirable elements. Before the Cultural Revolution, members of the CCP or mass organizations like the Communist Youth League were seen as more politically conscious and reliable than the ordinary masses. The CCP in particular considered itself the vanguard of the proletariat and the Chinese nation, with membership restricted to only a small percentage of the population during the Mao era.

It is important to emphasize that the leadership of the CCP never clearly defined how the three elements (family origin, personal status and performance) were weighted when evaluating individuals' class status. Cadres in some parts of the countryside made no distinction between family origin and personal status. In these areas, the son of a "rich peasant" could expect to receive the same label as his parents even if he was born after Land Reform. The class statuses themselves were a mixture of economic and political categories. In the cities, the most favorable categories were "revolutionary cadre," "family of a revolutionary martyr" and "industrial worker." At the other end of the spectrum sat categories such as "capitalist," "rightist" or worse still "counterrevolutionary." This last group was divided into "historical counterrevolutionaries" and "active

---

22 The most comprehensive study on this system remains: Richard Kraus, *Class Conflict in Chinese Socialism* (New York, NY: Columbia University Press, 1981).

counterrevolutionaries." "Historical counterrevolutionary" might mean that a person had opposed the party before 1949 or had served as an official for the Nationalist government or in the Japanese occupied areas. Even somebody without historical problems could be labeled an active counterrevolutionary for recent actions or complaints. A cadre who had confessed to crimes while a prisoner in enemy territory would also be said to have "historical problems." The various political campaigns of the Mao era added many new political labels for their targets, whether cadres, intellectuals or ordinary people.

In the countryside, "poor and lower middle peasants" were regarded by the party as its most reliable allies, while "middle peasants" who had more to lose from the collectivization of agriculture were to be neutralized. "Rich peasants," "landlords," "counterrevolutionaries" and "rotten elements," meaning criminals, were viewed as enemies to be isolated. These foes, collectively known as "the four elements" (*silei fenzi*), were attacked in various campaigns and placed under "the supervision of the masses." Cadres would frequently assign them undesirable or dangerous work such as cleaning out village latrines.

In this context, it was of little importance whether labels imposed by the state matched social and economic realities. Whether a middle peasant was really a middle peasant or rural residents identified with the Marxist-Leninist class system did not change the impact that these classifications had on their day-to-day existence. Class status was the primary factor determining access to or exclusion from the Youth League, the party, the army, public service and higher education. Those with a favorable class status often adopted the Maoist lexicon to bolster their social capital in negotiation with state agents or in struggles over resources.[23] The classification system thus became something of a self-fulfilling prophecy. People in the various classes either adapted to it or else resisted the labels which they were assigned. A constructed "class" consciousness became a reality for many Chinese after 1949.

With no clarity from the party on the issue, the relative importance of the three elements of class status continued to shift over the course of the Mao period. People were born into their family origin, but it was the job assigned to them by the state that often did more to define their individual status in urban society. The impact of family labels on personal behavior was also limited by the fact that such labels were essentially set in stone. It was possible to petition the government for a change in family origin if it had been inappropriately assigned, but such changes were rarely granted. A more common way to improve one's status was to use the opportunity of a new political campaign to display a good political

---

23 Zhang Xiaojun, "Land Reform in Yang Village: Symbolic Capital and the Determination of Class Status," *Modern China*, Vol. 30, No. 1 (2004), pp. 41–42.

performance. As the element of their political status over which people had the most control, performance was crucial to future prospects.[24]

With the exception of the chaotic years of the early Cultural Revolution, it was the party and its organs that acted as the institutional gatekeepers regulating inclusion or exclusion from, say, university or the PLA. At the same time, party organizations were also the "referees" who approved changes in status and evaluated political performance. Hence, every Chinese citizen was dependent on the CCP, making it impossible, given the speed with which the political winds shifted and performance metrics changed, to ever feel entirely secure in one's position. During the early Cultural Revolution, young people from families with an unfavorable class status demanded the right to participate in the movement, with some even questioning the system of class status as a whole (see Chapter 6). The ambiguity of class categories and their potential to produce conflict led the party leadership to produce several decisions during the Mao era clarifying labels and the meaning of the "class line." Nevertheless, the importance of these labels in everyday life meant that they would continue to be a source of social conflict throughout Mao's rule.

Gender

As with many other modern societies, the Chinese state has elected to categorize its citizens as either men or women. Third genders, like those now recognized across the Tibetan border in Nepal, have been ignored in official circles, as have gender, queer and other non-binary identities. Communist regimes have by and large struggled with queer issues just as much as more liberal political systems. By the time the CCP came to power, for instance, homosexuality had been recriminalized in the Soviet Union (where it had briefly been legalized by the Bolsheviks following the 1917 revolution). In the 1920s there was widespread support for gay rights in communist worker movements across the world, but this was largely abandoned following the rise of Stalinism. Maoist China did not specifically outlaw homosexuality, but gay people nevertheless could face severe and potentially crippling persecution.

Very little research has been done on homosexual or queer identities in Maoist China.[25] Our understanding of those beyond the gender binary is particularly scant: our view of the early PRC remains almost exclusively a *cis* one. Certainly

---

24 Li Xun, *Geming zaofan niandai: Shanghai wenge yundong shigao* (Hong Kong: Oxford University Press, 2015), Vol. 1, p. 11.

25 Heather Worth, Jing Jing and Karen McMillan, "Under the Same Quilt: The Paradoxes of Sex between Men in the Cultural Revolution," *Journal of Homosexuality*, Vol. 64, No. 1 (2017), pp. 1–14.

Mao and his comrades seem to have had no conception that any alternative to binary notions of gender – or indeed to heterosexual identity – might be possible.

In the CCP's Marxist-Leninist worldview, gender was subordinate to class. Only socialism had the ability to liberate women, and female peasants and workers were therefore expected to ally with their "class brothers" to fight class enemies. The party did criticize male chauvinism among laborers, but equally "bourgeois" feminism was seen as a plot to divide the working class along gender lines. The party-state declared a goal of "equality between men and women" and spoke of a "women's movement," but the leadership of the CCP never used "feminism" as a term of praise.

Over time, what it meant to be a man or woman under the CCP began to change. After the founding of the PRC, labor began to be re-divided along traditional gender lines. Party leaders such as Zhou Enlai defined child bearing as the "natural duty" of women, and it was taken for granted by the party and most of society at large that every "normal" person should be expected to marry and have children. When female revolutionary activists, some of whom had fought on the front line in the communist guerrilla forces during the Anti-Japanese War, came back from the revolutionary struggle, many felt that they did not know how to be women or how to (re)integrate into traditional family life.[26] Military service, however, was no longer open to them, as women were largely excluded from combat units when the PLA's forces were regularized in the 1940s.[27]

For politically active women there was often pressure to take positions, not as cadres in the regular party organs, but in the All China Women's Federation or the various task forces working on family planning. This form of women's work was considered less political than other kinds of activism, and like other mass organizations the Women's Federation was under the leadership of the CCP and unable to openly contradict party policies. However, women did have some success in using official organizations to champion gender equality, especially when feminist demands could be cloaked in the language of class, making elements of gender contradiction less visible.[28]

26 Kimberley Ens Manning, "The Gendered Politics of Woman-Work: Rethinking Radicalism in the Great Leap Forward," in Felix Wemheuer and Kimberley Ens Manning (eds.), *Eating Bitterness: New Perspectives on China's Great Leap Forward and Famine* (Vancouver: UBC Press, 2011), p. 80.

27 Nicola Spakowski, *"Mit Mut an die Front." Die militärische Beteiligung von Frauen in der kommunistischen Revolution Chinas [1925–1949]* (Cologne: Böhlau Verlag, 2009), p. 371.

28 Wang Zheng, *Finding Women in the State: A Socialist Feminist Revolution in the People's Republic of China, 1949–1964* (Berkeley, CA: University of California Press, 2016), p. 246.

In some aspects of its work the CCP actively promoted the voices of women. Particularly in urban China, the party appreciated that female cadres were more likely than men to gain admission to people's homes, particularly when the visit related to sensitive issues such as the new marriage law or family planning. For local home visits, the party therefore preferred to use female activists. In leadership roles, however, the picture was less rosy. No woman served as a provincial party secretary at any point during the Mao era, nor did any woman ever serve on the Standing Committee of the Politburo, the PRC's most powerful political institution. Indeed the only woman to become a member of the Politburo at any level during this period was Mao's wife Jiang Qing, between 1973 and 1976.

A key political role for women during the Mao era was to be one-half of a model "revolutionary couple." In these couples, usually moving in elite political circles, the husband would generally hold the more senior position, but the wife also contributed to the revolution and the building of socialism. Among the most famous revolutionary couples were Mao and Jiang Qing, President Liu Shaoqi and his wife Wang Guangmei, Premier Zhou Enlai and Deng Yingchao, Minister of Defense Lin Biao and Ye Qun, founder of the Red Army Zhu De and Kang Keqing, and economic planner Li Fuchun and Cai Chang. Kang and Cai both served as chairwoman of the All China Women's Federation, while Ye was a member of the PLA's Cultural Revolution Leading Group. In political couples at the local level, a husband might serve as the party secretary while his wife acted as head of the local branch of the Women's Federation.[29]

After 1949, the CCP's treatment of "invisible" domestic labor oscillated between extremes. A mid-1950s campaign to honor "socialist housewives," for instance, was replaced during the Great Leap Forward by plans to "socialize housework" under the auspices of the collective. Exactly what, then, did Mao's famous maxim that "women may hold up half of the sky" mean in practice? In industry, women do seem to have enjoyed greater opportunities under the CCP. Under the slogan "What men can do, women can do too," women were permitted to take up jobs such as steel worker, mechanic or tractor driver that had traditionally been a male preserve. Heavy manual labor in the fields also became a less exclusively male job, and women were able to join political meetings. The slogan, however, seems to have been a one-way street. There was no parallel effort from the CCP to encourage men to take up housework, spin cloth or take care of children and the elderly. At least after the socialization of housework was abandoned in rural China, the CCP leadership appears to have been more interested in mobilizing women to boost the "productive" sectors of the

29 Manning, "The Gendered Politics of Woman-Work," pp. 91–92.

economy than in encouraging a fair share of domestic work. It is possible to argue, as some scholars have done, that women fulfilled the function of a reserve labor force, to be mobilized as the party required. Millions of women were recruited into industry at the start of the Great Leap Forward in 1958, only to be demobilized in 1961 when the failure of economic development necessitated a downsizing of the workforce. The well-known campaign to mobilize "iron girls" (*tieguniang*) into special production teams for heavy labor in agriculture, promoted by the party during the Cultural Revolution, was partly related to a shortage of male labor in this sector.[30]

As with so much in Maoist China, the gendered division of labor differed across the urban/rural divide. In urban work units, domestic labor was socialized to a much higher degree than in the countryside, with state-owned enterprises providing canteens, nurseries and kindergartens. The principle of "equal pay for equal work" was by and large adhered to. In terms of labor force participation, however, women tended to be most numerous in collective enterprises, where jobs were less attractive and secure.

In the countryside, most care work was done by women within the family unit. In Shaanxi and many other provinces prior to 1949, rural women would contribute to the income of the household by weaving and clothes-making, but their markets disappeared after the state monopoly for the sale and purchase of cotton was established in the 1950s. The CCP saw domestic weaving not as a form of manual labor (*laodong*) but as less valued housework (*jiawu*), and a permanent shortage of cotton meant that it became a challenge for rural women to clothe the family, let alone sell on the open market. In place of weaving, largely done during night hours under poor light,[31] the party mobilized rural women to work by day in the fields. Pay, however, was more unequal than in the cities. Adult women would usually receive seven or eight work points a day compared to the ten given to men, with men's greater physical strength being the most common justification for the difference.

It is important to understand that in the countryside, the family was not only a unit of consumption, but also of production. The semi-socialist order that remained in place after 1962 provided plots for private use for every family. Although their harvest could not be legally sold at market, these plots were important for nourishing the family. The productivity of a family's private plots and its ability to earn work points in the collective were both related to its ratio of strong, working-age people to children and the elderly. Family structure,

---

30 Jin Yihong, "'Tieguniang' zai sikao: Zhongguo wenhua da geming qijian de shehui xingbie yu laodong," *Shehuikexue yanjiu*, No. 1 (2006), pp. 178–179.

31 Gail Hershatter, *The Gender of Memory: Rural Women and China's Collective Past* (Berkeley, CA: University of California Press, 2011), pp. 264–266.

particularly in terms of age and the gender balance, therefore had an important impact on income and levels of reliance on the production team.[32] As a result young and elderly women had different experiences of the social transformations of the early PRC. With the participation of women in manual labor outside the house and in political campaigns, the social control previously exercised by older women over the young weakened. The stereotypical Chinese mother-in-law, lording it over her hapless daughter-in-law, found her power under threat in the Mao era.

Ethnicity

As with gender issues, CCP ideology viewed ethnicity as secondary to class and class struggle. Building on orthodox Marxism-Leninism, Mao emphasized several times that the national question was at its root a class issue. In this reading, the Han chauvinism and local nationalism of the "old society" were both instruments of the ruling class to divide the laboring masses. Suppressed minorities, it followed, could only be liberated in alliance with Han workers and peasants. Socialism was the way to improve their life, and in a future communist society the importance of ethnicity and nation states would ultimately disappear.

The CCP rejected the Republican concept of a single Chinese nation (*zhonghua minzu*) divided into five races (Han, Manchu, Tibetan, Mongol and Hui). Instead, the PRC was founded as a multi-ethnic state. The concepts of ethnicity (also *minzu*) and local autonomy articulated by the CCP borrowed heavily from the Union of Soviet Socialist Republics (USSR), but several points of difference from Soviet practice emerged. Whereas Russians comprised less than 50 percent of the Soviet population, the Han made up over 90 percent of the Chinese. No union of republics or ethnic branches of the Communist Party were established in China. In contrast to the USSR, the Chinese constitution guaranteed local autonomy, but included no right of self-determination to declare independence. This reduced autonomy was perhaps related to the strategic importance of the non-Han areas, which cover more than one-third of the PRC's territory and border India, Burma (now Myanmar), Vietnam, Russia and North Korea.

Today it tends to be taken for granted that China's population consists of the Han Chinese plus fifty-five ethnic minorities. However, the emergence of the minorities is the result of a complex process stretching back several decades. The PRC began to label its citizens according to ethnic categories in the first half of the 1950s. The identity of large groups like the Han, Tibetans and Mongols

---

32 Li Huaiyin, *Village China under Socialism and Reform: A Micro-History, 1948–2008* (Stanford, CA: Stanford University Press, 2009), pp. 345–346.

Map 1.1: Major ethnic groups in China

was taken for granted, but for the multi-ethnic borderlands such as Yunnan and Guangxi in the south, the government decided to send teams of ethnographers and cadres to determine what classification scheme ought to be adopted. This determination was considered a necessary first step towards defining local autonomous territories and admitting the appropriate number of minority representatives into the People's Congress. Most of the PRC's efforts in ethnic classification spanned the years from the early 1950s to 1964. By 1953, the government had recognized thirty-eight groups as "ethnic minorities," and a further fifteen new groups were added by 1964. After this period, only two new groups would be recognized.[33]

Especially in 1954, this classification was hastily carried out. The Soviet criteria for defining a nationality (common language, territory, economic life and

33 Huang Guangxue, *Zhongguo de minzu shibie* (Beijing: Minzu chubanshe, 1995), pp. 147–153.

common psychological make up, with tribal communities excluded) proved too complex to adhere to rigorously. As a result, the Chinese investigation teams relied heavily on linguistic criteria to classify nationalities, particularly in the western part of the country.[34]

In contrast to class status and the urban/rural divide, however, classification according to gender and ethnicity caused only minimal conflict. Some ethnic groups did resent being classified inappropriately: a number of communities of "Tibetans," for instance, considered themselves to be Mongolians, while the largest ethnic minority, the Zhuang, was something of a hodge-podge, encompassing numerous different self-identified groups.[35] Minor adjustments to the classification system continued after 1979, when the state recognized the last official minority, the Jinuo in Yunnan. In the early 1980s, the state launched a series of investigations into minority groupings in the western provinces, aiming to improve the accuracy of its labeling and to better distinguish between smaller ethnic groups such as the Dong and Miao or the Tujia and Man (see Chapter 8 for more detail).[36]

The PRC's classification system is premised on the notion that each person belongs to a single, specific ethnic group. It remains impossible in China to register a child as having a dual ethnicity such as "Han-Tibetan" when the parents are from two different groups. Nor is it possible to simply register as "Chinese" (unlike, say, socialist Yugoslavia, where people could eschew labels such as "Croatian" or "Serb" and register simply as "Yugoslavian"). Since the 1950s, China's ethnic categorization system has been the foundation for affirmative action in higher education and for the training of minority cadres. It is the stated belief of the CCP that the GMD discriminated against minorities and that the Han's "little brothers and sisters" needed support to develop after 1949.

The vast majority of minorities lived in poor, rural areas or in the western provinces as peasants and nomads. Most were therefore excluded from the state-subsidized urban economy. Moreover, the CCP considered minorities as generally more "backward" than the Han Chinese. The official party theory of historical materialism held that the history of mankind was marked by development through several stages, from primitive society through slavery, feudalism, capitalism and finally socialism. The minorities, the party asserted, were by and large still mired in slavery or feudalism, whereas the Han, had progressed to a "semi-feudal" society before 1949.

34 Thomas Mullaney, *Coming to Terms with the Nation: Ethnic Classification in Modern China* (Berkeley, CA: University of California Press, 2011), pp. 89–91.

35 Katherine Palmer Kaup, *Creating the Zhuang: Ethnic Politics in China* (Boulder, CO: Rienner, 2000).

36 Huang Guangxue, *Zhongguo de minzu shibie*, pp. 156–158.

This perceived backwardness meant that minority regions would need more time to enforce the social change the party demanded. In Tibet and Mongolia, the CCP promoted a United Front with "patriotic" local elites in the early 1950s, leaving class labeling for a later period. Minority cultures and religions were always officially supported by the state. However, the relatively tolerant and gradualist approach of the early 1950s gave way to more assimilationist policies during the Great Leap and the Cultural Revolution. The United Front's work with the upper stratum of the minorities was replaced with a new program of class struggle. In language policy, the government from the 1950s onwards supported programs to create a written language in some previously oral minority communities. Existing scripts and terms were reformed to create languages that better fitted the necessities of modernization and the ideology of the CCP – Tibetan is a particularly well documented case. The top-down nature of these reforms is emphasized by the fact that most cadres in the minority areas were Han Chinese from other regions. By and large, these representatives of the state could not speak or understand local languages before arriving, and some made no effort to learn.

Although the fifty-six recognized ethnic groups had nominally equal standing, in practice a hierarchical binary existed, with minorities on one side and the Han on the other.[37] For the minorities, ethnic labels played a central role in everyday relations with the state, while for the Han ethnic status was important mainly as a mark of distinction against a minority "other." The Han had no special representatives in the People's Congress, and it was taken for granted that the leaders of the party-state, almost all Han, were well equipped to represent the interests of the Chinese nation as a whole and even to lead "autonomous" minority areas. No Tibetan ever served as the first party secretary of the Tibetan Autonomous Region, while one Uygur, Seypidin Azizi, served in the same position in the Xinjiang Uygur Autonomous Region. The CCP promoted the education of minority cadres, but only a few, such as the ethnic Mongol Wulanfu (Ulanhu in Mongolian), a party member since 1925, were considered reliable enough to serve in leading positions (in Wulanfu's case as a vice-premier and alternate member of the Politburo).

Little research has been done on the question of how ethnicity and class status interacted with gender during the Mao era. There was clearly considerable crossover. In Tibet, for instance, the CCP used "Liberation of Women" as a slogan to promote class struggle. Poor rural women, whose status in their own communities was low, were recruited to work on state farms in the 1950s,

---

37 For more detail see Dru C. Gladney, "Representing Nationality in China: Refiguring Majority/Minority Identities," *The Journal for Asian Studies*, Vol. 53, No. 1 (1994), pp. 98–103.

becoming part of the state project to build a new Tibet.[38] In state media and films, meanwhile, exotic images of minority women in colorful ethnic costumes were already a staple. It seems to me that both the state and the Han majority viewed minorities in primarily ethnic terms, but issues of gender and class clearly cannot be overlooked.

Classification, Files and Registration

Classifying the population was a great bureaucratic challenge for the state. In the early PRC, every family had a household registration document, but identity cards (*shenfenzheng*) were issued only in the Reform era after 1984. The other most common identity document, the passport, was available only to the very few who were allowed to travel abroad as diplomats or students or to attend conferences. Every such trip had to be approved by the work unit or even by higher levels of government.

"Inside the system," members of work units had a personal file (*dang'an*). To enter a work unit, the party or mass organizations, people had to complete forms covering family origin, individual status, gender, ethnicity and so on, and the unit could check these against the official record. Providing false or misleading information could lead to serious consequences if, for example, a "landlord who had escaped the net" was uncovered. *Dang'an* files included evaluations of political performance by superiors or party secretaries, as well as documents related to any "historical problems," and a separate system of individual files, containing similar information, existed for CCP cadres.

During political campaigns, files were often rechecked to uncover hidden enemies. Individuals, however, had no right to access their own files, and therefore no way of knowing for certain how their superiors had evaluated them. In the early Cultural Revolution, control over personal files became a major source of conflict. Red Guards occupied archives to get access to the files of cadres, seeking to edit "black material" and attack them. Some Red Guards who had faced repression themselves demanded the deletion of negative information.

Prior to 1963, ordinary peasants had no personal files. During the Socialist Education Campaign, however, the Central Committee began creating class files for rural families.[39] Some forms included the class status of the head of the

---

38 Emily T. Yeh, *Taming Tibet: Landscape Transformation and the Gift of Chinese Development* (Ithaca, NY: Cornell University Press, 2013), pp. 60–91.

39 For detail see: Jeremy Brown, "Moving Targets: Changing Class Labels in Rural Hebei and Henan 1960–1979," in Jeremy Brown and Matthew Johnson (eds.), *Maoism at the Grassroots: Everyday Life in China's Era of High Socialism* (Cambridge, MA: Harvard University Press, 2015), pp. 51–76.

household, but in general the family, not the individual, was the main unit of analysis. The creation of these rural files was designed to allow the reinvestigation of class status and also the addition of new information about the "performance" of people during campaigns, along with any rewards or punishments received. Document 1.1, a family registration form from 1966, provides a good example. It draws a clear line between personal status and family origin. The lead householder and his wife were of "middle peasant" and "poor peasant" background, but both were assigned the personal status of "urban poor." Their personal history is also recorded, although the form provides a cautionary tale of how an apparently incorrect class status might be given even with an abundance of information available. The form notes that the husband, Wang Yinquan, sold vinegar in several cities until 1963, while his wife and children stayed in their home village to farm their land. By the time the document was written in 1966, however, the husband had returned to the rural commune and retired. The label of "urban poor" reflected his personal history, not his current situation.

Wang's past as a petty trader might have exposed him to suspicion. However, his political performance was evaluated favorably. His son, Wang Shuangbao, was a member of Communist Youth League, had served in the PLA and was educated to junior high school level. The younger Wang's status, too, seems to have been rather haphazardly determined. He was listed as a student despite a "current occupation" as a soldier. His family origin of "middle peasant," meanwhile, was apparently taken from his grandfather, in defiance of official regulations requiring that family origin was to be inherited from the father (whose rank, as we have seen, was "urban poor"). Local actors, the form suggests, often did not classify according to central standards. The creation of rural class files was also not universally enforced, with many ordinary rural people remaining essentially undocumented, at least in terms of class. However, in many villages, close family ties and a lack of social mobility or out-migration after 1962 meant that any bad class labels assigned during Land Reform were likely to be common knowledge.

Informal Channels of Distribution

Clearly official labels, and the distribution system for goods and services that they supported, were an important part of the Maoist economic system. However, this system faced a serious, unresolved problem: it could not satisfy the needs of people. During the famine of 1959–1961, not even survival was guaranteed in the countryside. Much of the population, but peasants especially, learned the hard way that they could not rely on the state.

In urban areas, the basic needs of the population were met in all except the famine years. If, however, an individual needed more than basic goods, he or she had to find alternative ways of acquiring them. In the GDR, this working around the system was referred to ironically as the "socialist way." While personal relations play a certain role in distributing goods or jobs in all societies, people in socialist states were particularly skillful at navigating the informal distribution of public goods. Because self-interest and critiques of the system could not be openly expressed, much of this informal distribution happened below the surface. As the Chinese expression puts it: "Policy above meets counter-policy below."

In the countryside, theft of grain and "concealing production to distribute privately" (*manchan sifen*) became widespread almost as soon as the collectivization of agriculture began in the mid-1950s. During the famine, many peasants "ate green" (*chiqing*), surviving on unripe crops taken from the field before the harvest. This and other practices for under-reporting production or land usually had to be covered up by cadres in the production team. These cadres, however, were not on the state payroll and often had relatives in the villages, making them potentially receptive allies. The Chinese scholar Gao Wangling calls these strategies "counter-actions" that were not meant to be resistance against the state, but survival strategies.[40] This is true from a peasant perspective, but theft and under-reporting did affect the state's policymaking, reducing the amount that could be taken to feed the cities or for exports.

Peasants could try to get access to the urban rationing system through "blind migration" into the cities. This was relatively easy before 1961 but became challenging during the rest of the Mao era, when the household registration system was strictly enforced. In the cities, workers had fewer reasons to steal food or try to move away, and strike action over wages occurred on a large scale only before 1958 and during the early Cultural Revolution. Many workers and peasants did, however, try to reduce the workload that the cadres demanded. In socialist countries in Eastern Europe, people would say of the government that "they are pretending to pay us and we are pretending to work." The Chinese equivalent was *moyanggong*, "feigning work." One particular popular method was to shop for groceries – often requiring hours of queuing – during the working day.

Another widespread practice during the Mao era was "entering through the backdoor" (*zouhoumen*). This was a form of cronyism whereby a person would gain access to goods or a job thanks to personal connections to officials. During

---

40 On forms of peasant resistance see: Ralph Thaxton, *Catastrophe and Contention in Rural China: Mao's Great Leap Forward Famine and the Origins of Righteous Resistance in Da Fo Village* (Cambridge: Cambridge University Press, 2008); Gao Wangling, *Zhongguo nongmin fan xingwei yanjiu, 1950–1980* (Hong Kong: Zhongwen daxue chubanshe, 2013).

the supply shortages of the Great Leap in 1959, individuals would use this strategy to get much-needed food. Organizations could also "enter through the back door," with work units tapping official connections to secure materials needed to fulfill their production quotas.[41] During the Cultural Revolution, "sent-down youths" seeking a way out of the countryside sometimes used the same tactic to enlist in the PLA or enroll as students (for more detail see Chapter 7). The CCP leadership criticized this informal practice many times, fearful of undermining the image of social justice and fair distribution. However, scarcity of resources, combined with the personal power of cadres to ignore formal rules, ensured "entering through the backdoor" never disappeared.

What exactly was the relationship of these practices to official power? There is no justification for glorifying all forms of informal distribution, as some have done, as "weapons of the weak."[42] It was not only the weak who gained access to goods they were not entitled to, but also the powerful. Moreover it was CCP cadres, not ordinary peasants, who were in the best position to defraud the state. These cadres, as we have seen, were predominantly male and predominantly Han. The more powerful and senior of these cadres also tended to be older, drawn from the "revolutionary cadres" of the pre-1949 days. Unlike today, cadres could not transfer millions of US dollars to foreign bank accounts, but the archives of the anti-corruption campaigns of the Mao era include impressive accounts of fraudulent and illegitimate activities for capturing food and finances. During the famine, many rural cadres took advantage of special canteens to ensure that they remained well fed while others starved. For those outside the CCP's protective umbrella, having a relative working as a cook in a public dining hall might be the difference between life and death.

Based on a case study in Anhui province, one scholar argues that survival in the villages during the famine was often decided by the strength of kin relationships.[43] Some observers suggest that personal relationships (*guanxi*) and the exchange of gifts and favors (*renqing*) helped ordinary people, both men and women, to receive goods through informal means. Other scholars, by contrast, claim that these systems were most profitable to powerful men.[44] More research is required before any definitive answer can be reached.

---

41 For details see: Lü Xiaobo, *Cadres and Corruption: The Organizational Involution of the Chinese Communist Party* (Stanford, CA: Stanford University Press, 2000), pp. 130–134.

42 For this term see: James C. Scott, *Weapons of the Weak: Everyday Forms of Peasant Resistance* (New Haven, CT: Yale University Press, 1985).

43 Chen Yixin, "When Food became Scarce: Life and Death in Chinese Villages during the Great Leap Forward," *Journal of the Historical Society*, No. 2 (2010), pp. 162–164.

44 For example see: Mayfair M. Yang, *Gifts, Favors, and Banquets: The Art of Social Relationships in China* (Ithaca, NY: Cornell University Press, 1994); Yan Yunxiang, *The Flow of Gifts: Reciprocity and Social Networks in a Chinese Village* (Stanford, CA: Stanford University Press, 1996).

The Role of Internal Migration

Internal migration played a crucial role in both upward and downward social mobility and the remaking of territorial space in the Mao-era PRC. As we will see, state-organized and self-directed migration were often connected to the major state classifications (household registration, class status, gender and ethnicity). One of the most pressing questions of the Mao era was who was to be allowed to stay in the cities and enjoy the entitlements of the "iron rice bowl." Following the large-scale demobilization of soldiers in the early 1950s, for instance, many veterans sought permanent employment in the cities. The central government's insistence that they return to their home villages caused considerable frustration, with many questioning why their sacrifices for the nation did not entitle them to better treatment. Some veterans simply moved to an urban center without authorization ("blind migration"), while others protested openly.[45]

The main destination for internal migration was the northern provinces of Inner Mongolia, Xinjiang, Ningxia, Qinghai and Heilongjiang. Between 1952 and 1982, the population of some of these regions doubled, far outstripping the nationwide increase of 50 percent in the same period. Much of this migration consisted of Han Chinese moving into the ethnic minority Autonomous Regions.[46] The government supported this development to "open up" underdeveloped borderlands and establish firmer control over the periphery: in Xinjiang and Tibet, two particular trouble spots, migration was encouraged by establishing a network of military farms.

Some Han Chinese migrated to the border regions voluntarily, either out of patriotism or poverty. Soldiers and cadres, meanwhile, could be ordered to go. These overwhelmingly male settlers and military personnel were supported by a government-organized "supply" of Han Chinese women from Inner China. Criminals and enemies of the regime were also sent to the western periphery: according to the official numbers, over 123,200 "criminals" from all over the country were sent to the labor camps and farms in Xinjiang in the 1950s.[47]

In contrast to Stalin's Soviet Union in the 1930s and 1940s, the Chinese government did not enforce policies to compel "unreliable" ethnic groups from the border regions to resettle in the hinterland. Nor did China experience the

---

45 Neil Diamant, *Embattled Glory: Veterans, Military Families, and the Politics of Patriotism in China, 1949–2007* (Lanham, MD: Rowman and Littlefield Publisher, 2008), pp. 89–90.

46 Thomas Heberer, *China and its National Minorities: Autonomy or Assimilation?* (Armonk, NY: M. E. Sharpe, 1989), p. 94.

47 Shi Jijin, *Zhongguo dangdai shehuishi (1949–1956)* (Changsha: Hunan renmin chubanshe, 2011), Vol. 1, p. 186.

ethnic cleansing seen in other parts of the world. In some regions such as Xinjiang, however, government policy seems to have been designed to ensure Han Chinese would outnumber local ethnic groups (see Chapter 2). The ratio of Han Chinese to Mongolians in Inner Mongolia, for example, increased from 6:1 to 12:1 between 1958 and 1968.[48]

The first major movement of population under Mao was a rapid wave of rural-urban migration. Spanning the years 1949 to 1960, this process saw large numbers of rural Chinese attempt to break into booming new industries in the cities. The earliest state-organized migration, meanwhile, was the sending of cadres from the "old liberated areas" of the north to "go down south" with the advancing PLA in 1949. The goal was to establish control in the "newly liberated areas," where activists and party members were few. Incomplete statistics suggest that over 130,000 cadres were sent out, while 400,000 family members also went south with the army.[49] These people often struggled to communicate with local rural communities due to language differences. Between 1952 and 1958, more than 379,000 migrants, mainly from Shandong, went to Heilongjiang in the far north to open up uncultivated land or to work in industry. Major infrastructure projects such as the construction of reservoirs and hydroelectric power plants led to the displacement of about 5.68 million people in the first three decades of the PRC.[50]

The Great Leap Forward also led to a massive wave of rural-urban migration in 1958. This was partly uncontrolled and unwanted by central authorities, partly a result of labor recruitment by work units to meet their ambitious new targets. During the famine, millions tried to escape to less badly affected regions, some to nearby provinces and counties, and others to Xinjiang or the north-east. In order to stabilize the economy and the distribution system in aftermath of the famine, the government sent over 26 million people from cities and towns to the countryside between late 1960 and 1963.[51] Between 1963 and the early 1970s, millions of workers, along with equipment, resources and factories, were transferred from the east coast to western China in order to build the so-called "Third Front," designed to minimize industrial losses in the event of an attack on the coastal cities. In 1966, during the early Cultural Revolution, hundreds of thousands of people with a bad class status were deported from the cities and forced to settle in the countryside. Red Guards organized these deportations with the support of Public Security Departments in order to "cleanse" the cities of "non-proletarian elements." According to official statistics, between July and October

48 Heberer, *China and its National Minorities*, p. 93.
49 Shi Jijin, *Zhongguo dangdai shehuishi*, Vol. 1, p. 183.   50 Ibid., p. 182.
51 Lu Yu, *Xin Zhongguo renkou wushi nian* (Beijing: Zhongguo renkou chubanshe, 2004), Vol. 1, p. 594.

of 1966, 397,400 "ox ghosts and snake demons," as these people were called, were deported from cities across the country.[52] Starting from late 1968, the government intensified its program of sending "urban youths" down to the countryside. Over the course of the Cultural Revolution, in excess of 16 million people were "sent down" in this way.[53]

These numbers suggest it would be wrong to imagine Maoist China as a society with a static population. The factors underlying internal migration in the PRC, however, owed less to economics than to state policies. The state's motives in instigating these migrations, and the popular responses to them, form a crucial part of the narrative of Maoist China. These and other social changes, and the classifications and conflicts that went with them, will be discussed in more detail in the following chapters.

52 Ma Yuping and Huang Yuchong, *Zhongguo zuotian yu jintian: 1840–1987 guoqing shouce* (Beijing: Jiefangjun chubanshe, 1989), p. 754.
53 Lu Yu, *Xin Zhongguo renkou wushi nian*, Vol. 1, p. 601.

DOCUMENT 1.1 Class status registration form (1966).
First production team, Dingxing zhuang production brigade, Dong Village commune, Xin County, Shaanxi Province

Name of householder	Gender	Male	Family Origin	Middle peasant	Family size	Population at home	3
	Age	63					
Wang Yinquan	Nationality	Han	Personal status	Urban poor		Population outside home	1
Family economic conditions	During Land Reform		Before Land Reform, the household made vinegar in the towns. They could hardly make a living and went back home after Land Reform (in 1948 and 1949). They made a living afterwards with three rooms and eight mu of land that their elderly parents gave to them.				
	During the advanced cooperative		During the advanced cooperative, the household possessed eight mu of land and three rooms. Nothing else.				
	At present		The household currently possesses three rooms and eight fen of plots for private use. Nothing else.				
Major family social relations and their political appearance			Wang Nongquan: Third younger brother, commune member of the first production team. Wang Runquan: Second younger brother, commune member of the second production team. Wang Gaozhuan: Sister, Dong Village				
Description of family history			[Wang's] grandfather was a farmer his whole life (both for himself and others). After his father died around 1913, he began to participate in agricultural labor at the age of 10. He went to Feng Town in Inner Mongolia to make vinegar in 1921 (at age 18). Due to economic depression in his business after 1943, he survived by selling his property (the equipment to make vinegar). When he could no longer earn a living, he returned home in 1948. Before 1943, he was running a self-sufficient vinegar business in Feng Town. From 1951–1963, he successively engaged in the vinegar business in Taiyuan, Sanmenxia and Kaifeng in Henan, until he retired and went back home. During this period, his wife and children stayed in his home village. The household has lived in the commune since 1963.				
Remarks							

Signed: Chen written in May 1966

DOCUMENT 1.1 (cont.)

Profile of family members

Name	Wang Yinquan	Sun Hua	Wang Shuangbao
Relation to head of household	Head of household	Wife	Son
Sex	Male	Female	Male
Age	63	52	22
Nationality	Han	Han	Han
Family origin	Middle peasant	Poor peasant	Middle peasant
Personal status	Urban poor	Urban poor	Student
Education	Primary school	Illiterate	Junior high school
Religion	No	No	No
Commune member	Yes	Yes	No
Current occupation and duty	Commune member	Commune member	Soldier
Member of revolutionary organizations	None	None	Communist Youth League
Member of reactionary organizations	None	None	None
Rewards and punishments	Rewarded for making vinegar after liberation	None	Five-good soldier
Main experiences and political performance	At the age of 18, he went out and made vinegar till the age of 45. He made vinegar again from age 47 to 60. His political performance is very progressive.	Married in 1933 and made vinegar with her husband. She returned home for farming in 1949. Her political performance is progressive.	

Source: Collection of the author, "garbage material."

2 NEW DEMOCRACY AND THE MAKING OF NEW CHINA (1949–1952)

中国人民站起来了
The Chinese people have stood up
打土豪分田地
Attack local tyrants, divide up the farmland
抗美援朝, 保家卫国
Resist the US, support Korea; defend your family, protect the country

In 1947, Liu Lian, a 22-year-old student, participated in the Land Reform movement in the communist controlled areas in Hebei province. There she met
professor He Ganzhi (1906–1969), the faculty dean at the United University of
North China. Already the author of several well-regarded books on the history of
the Chinese revolution since 1911, He was considered one of the most important
historians of the CCP. He and Liu grew increasingly close, and, following her
acceptance into the CCP in 1949, the party permitted the couple to marry in
1950. This union, and the political problems it brought, would dictate much of
Liu's life over the following decades.

   Liu's 1998 memoir describes her experiences during Land Reform. When the
work team of cadres and activists entered one particular village, they found it
almost empty. The GMD had spread rumors that communists would encourage
immoral gender relations and forcibly recruit women for their army, and the
Land Reform team had to convince peasants to return. According to Liu, the
team found that 90 percent of the local population was comprised of two
categories, "poor and lower middle peasants" and "rural laborers," but that
these groups owned on average less than 1 *mu* of land per household.
"Landlords" owned about 17 *mu* and "rich peasants" about 5 *mu*; 2 *mu* of
land were needed for a family to produce enough grain to live on with a small
surplus.

   As Land Reform got underway, the activists encouraged peasants to "speak
bitterness" at struggle meetings. One "local tyrant," Ren Laochao, who had

already relinquished his land, was accused of rape by a mother whose daughter had committed suicide soon after the alleged crime. Emotions ran high, and anger spilled over when the mother brought out her dead daughter's hair and showed it to the crowd. Cries of, "Down with Ren Laochao! Execute Ren Laochao!" went up, and one peasant, brandishing a wooden stick with nails attached, attempted to beat the "local tyrant" to death, only to be held back by the People's Militia. Finally a compromise was reached: instead of allowing him to be beaten, the People's Court sentenced the man to death and he was shot. Liu described her feelings: "This was the first time in my life that I had seen an execution by shooting. My heart was beating fast. Even though I was a little afraid, I felt more excitement (...). The Communist Party was eliminating evil for the people to the satisfaction of everyone."[1]

According to Liu, her husband grew to oppose some of the excesses of Land Reform – "leftist mistakes" in official terminology. When work team cadres beat the sixteen-year-old daughter of a "landlord," who had herself committed no crime, He intervened. He also criticized the unfair labeling of many "middle peasants" as "rich peasants" in a report to the party leadership.

His actions would come back to haunt him. Twenty years later, during the Cultural Revolution in 1967, Red Guards accused him of promoting "the rich peasant line." By that time, He and Liu were both teachers at the prestigious People's University in Beijing. Liu expressed her anger that old party members like He and herself were struggled against in meetings during the Cultural Revolution, just as "landlords" had been during Land Reform. She herself was beaten with a belt by students and imprisoned in a classroom for several months. He would spend two years living under "mass dictatorship" – surveillance by neighbors and colleagues – before he died of a heart attack in 1969, leaving Liu as a widow with five young children. It was not until 1979 that Liu was fully rehabilitated by her university. His manuscripts and personal items were returned to her, along with a personal letter written to him by Chairman Mao in 1939.

The final years of Liu's career were spent teaching and editing her husband's collected works. In two interviews in 2002, she presented herself as a loyal party member who had always defended the CCP's ideals in spite of the leadership's "leftist mistakes," such as the Great Leap Forward or the Cultural Revolution.[2] Her marriage to He Ganzhi provides a good example of a revolutionary couple. As a prominent party historian, his was the more prestigious role, but there is no doubt that Liu was a strong-minded party activist in her own right.

---

1 Liu Lian, *Fengyu banjunxing: Wo yu He Ganzhi de ershi nian* (Nanning: Guangxi jiaoyu chubanshe, 1998), p. 19.
2 Interview with author, Beijing, May 2002.

The early years of the PRC are crucial to any understanding of China's subsequent history. The post-revolutionary state was founded as a "New Democracy" or "People's Democracy" based on a broad class alliance. The official goals of the New Democratic Revolution were to do away with the "semi-feudal" structure of Chinese society and to put an end to semi-colonial oppression by foreign imperial powers. In this context, Land Reform was the early PRC's most radical political project. The reform process destroyed traditional rural elites, labeled as "semi-feudal landlords," once and for all. Indeed, the CCP continues to use the liberation of peasants from exploitation and misery to justify the length and violence of the revolution. Land Reform, coupled with the new regime's success in bringing inflation under control and nurturing economic recovery, meant that many Chinese welcomed the new order.

Scholars, both Western and Chinese, have long described the years between 1949 and 1956 as a "honeymoon period" between party and people.[3] However, these years saw one of the deadliest purges in the history of the PRC, the Campaign to Suppress Counterrevolutionaries (1951–1953). The party leadership also launched the Three-Anti Campaign to reduce corruption among its cadres, and businesses too came under attack. As well as exploring these campaigns, this chapter will examine another important milestone of the early Mao era: the CCP's new Marriage Law, the official goal of which was to end "feudal" oppression of women. The government's strategies for reintegrating Xinjiang and Tibet – Han migration and a United Front with indigenous elites – will also be discussed. The CCP saw the reunification of China as the national task of the New Democratic Revolution.

We should not forget that China in the early 1950s was not a country at peace. The Nationalists had been defeated on the mainland, but the GMD government-in-exile in Taiwan regularly spoke of reconquering the mainland and expelling the communists. In the southwest, the PLA was forced to spend several years dealing with groups of armed anti-communist "bandits." From October 1950 until 1953 China was involved in the Korean War, and throughout this period the Cold War between the United States and the Soviet Union frequently threatened to turn hot.

The Concept of New Democracy

Maoist New Democracy bore little resemblance to the liberal democratic order familiar to Western readers, with its focus on rule of law and electoral systems based on one person, one vote. A major difference was the lack of formal,

---

3 For new approaches to the early 1950s see: Jeremy Brown and Paul G. Pickowicz (eds.), *Dilemmas of Victory: The Early Years of the People's Republic of China* (Cambridge, MA: Harvard University Press, 2007).

independent state institutions, the building of which was low on the government's list of priorities in the period after 1949. In the five years before the ratification of the first PRC constitution in 1954, the only formal rules governing the CCP's exercise of power came from the 1949 "Common Program of the Consultative Conference of the People's Government of China," while for the first two years after the revolution the country was ruled by regional Military Control Commissions. No replacement for the abandoned Republican criminal code was adopted until 1979.

During the Mao era, party and state were not clearly divided. Written law did exist, but it was largely subordinate to decisions and regulations promulgated by the CCP Central Committee, the State Council, and the central government. The People's Congress, established under the 1954 constitution, served as a national parliament, but it was never elected by direct popular vote. All state bodies fell under party control. Until 1959 Mao was both Chairman of the CCP and President of the State, while Liu Shaoqi and Zhou Enlai, his two most senior deputies within the party, were respectively Chairman of the Standing Committee of the National People's Congress and Premier of the State Council.

For the CCP, the term "democracy" meant forming a broad class alliance under CCP leadership to remove power from the old elites, thereby effecting a "democratic revolution" that would place the country in the people's hands. Already in the 1930s, Mao and the Communist International (Comintern) had argued that foreign imperialism had stunted the growth of Chinese capitalism, leaving China's bourgeoisie too weak to lead the kind of democratic change seen in Western Europe in the previous century. This left the working class, led by the CCP, as the only force able to liberate the country from the oppressive forces of feudalism, imperialism and bureaucratic capitalism. This last term was originally used to describe capitalists with close connections to the pre-1911 imperial Qing state, but following the collapse of the United Front between the Communists and the GMD in 1927 the CCP began to use the label for capitalist interests linked to the Nationalist bureaucracy.

New Democracy was premised on the creation of an alliance between the working class, the peasantry, the petty bourgeoisie and the national bourgeoisie. This idea was captured in the PRC's national flag, in which a single large star represented the CCP and four smaller stars stood for the allied classes. For Mao, the New Democratic Revolution was distinct from previous revolutions (the French Revolution of 1789, for instance), because it was to be part of – and sustained by – a broader communist world revolution.[4]

---

4 Mao Zedong, "Zhongguo geming he Zhongguo gongchandang," in *Mao Zedong Xuanji* (Beijing: Renmin chubanshe, 1967), Vol. 2, p. 610.

New Democracy was propelled by the establishment of a so-called United Front with "patriotic" political forces outside the communist movement, such as the national bourgeoisie, old intellectuals and ethnic minority elites. Religious leaders were also included, provided they made clear statements against imperialism and welcomed the new political order. Under the banner of the United Front, the CCP permitted several minor political parties to send delegates to the National People's Congress. From the beginning, however, it was clear that this was no alliance of equals and that the CCP, as the "leading party," retained absolute authority.

In some ways the concept of New or People's Democracy was a fairly inclusive one. Certainly it was more inclusive than the "dictatorship of the proletariat" that replaced it in the latter part of the 1950s, as the CCP sought to eliminate private ownership of land and means of production through "socialist transformation." However, "the people" was not a universal category, and "enemies of the people" were in a potentially precarious position. In his June 1949 article on "The People's Democratic Dictatorship," Mao identified "the people" with the four allied classes, set against three groups of class enemies – landlords, bureaucratic capitalists and counterrevolutionaries – who would need to be suppressed for the revolution to succeed. Mao argued that the suppression of these enemies should be accomplished through the state apparatus, with democratic freedoms and citizens' rights being afforded only to the working class and its allies.[5] In the early years, the party took a slightly more nuanced approach, seeking the cooperation of some capitalists to help operate enterprises and manage urban administration or foreign trade relations. The CCP's distinction between members of the sympathetic "national bourgeoisie" on the one hand and the despised "bureaucratic capitalists" on the other allowed the party to identify a selection of "good" capitalists whose skills could be put to use. The lenient treatment experienced by the national bourgeoisie led some capitalists to heed the government's call to stay in or return to China, even as others fled abroad after the communist takeover.[6] The party's initial reliance on bourgeois elements, however, did not mean that the bourgeoisie as a class was ever equipped to challenge the new regime in any serious way. The oft-mooted "third way," a progressive alliance bypassing the CCP and GMD, was never a realistic option given the power relations on the ground.

The notion of New Democracy was not unique to China. Since 1935, the Comintern and the Soviet leadership had promoted a United Front strategy

---

5 Mao Zedong, "Lun renmin minzhu zhuanzheng," in *Mao Zedong Xuanji*, Vol. 4, pp. 1412–1413.
6 For more detail see: Sherman Cochran (ed.), *The Capitalist Dilemma in China's Communist Revolution* (Ithaca, NY: Cornell East Asia Program, 2014).

Figure 2.1: A market in Beijing.
Source: Photograph by Eva Siao, Museum Ludwig.

calling for a broad class alliance of democratic and patriotic forces against fascism. Following the defeat of Nazi Germany in 1945, the new states of post-war Eastern Europe were founded as People's Democracies. In contrast to the Soviet Union, these states were established, not as one-party dictatorships, but as parliamentary systems with several parties working under the leadership of the communists, who often renamed themselves as "workers' parties." Between 1945 and the early 1950s, each of these European People's Democracies conducted land reforms as the communist parties sought to win over the peasantry to the new order. Such reforms were presented not as socialist, but instead as "anti-feudal." In East Germany, for instance, the Communist Party argued in 1946 that the division of lands held by the old nobility represented not a socialist upheaval but simply the fulfillment of goals articulated in the bourgeois revolution of 1848. At the same time, it was also widely accepted within the communist movement that land reform was not an end in itself, and that the long-term objective should remain the collectivization of agriculture and the establishment of socialist relations of production in the countryside. Land reforms created an ocean of new landholders, but in order to eliminate class divisions and the distinction between industry and agriculture it would be necessary to convert smallholdings into large collectives and the peasants working them into agricultural laborers.

These plans were not kept secret in China, but were downplayed in the early years of the PRC. The "Common Program" of 1949 promised that after Land Reform private ownership of land by the peasants would be protected. Agricultural and consumer cooperatives would be promoted, but only on a voluntary basis, and the private and state capitalist sectors of the economy would be allowed to develop (albeit under the leadership of the state-owned economy). State capitalist enterprises were not privately owned, but were run on a for-profit basis along market lines. The "Common Program" stipulated the transition to a socialist economy as the eventual goal of the new state, but private enterprises and free markets were to be allowed to co-exist with state firms, at least in the immediate term.[7]

The "Common Program" also laid down a number of other goals for the new state. Equality between men and women was to be pursued in economic, cultural, educational and social life, and all ethnic groups, large or small, were to be equal. The state was to help ethnic minorities develop their written languages and to establish a system of regional autonomy. It is important to emphasize that the CCP promoted equality in gender relations and among ethnic groups, but never between classes. In order to establish a classless society, the CCP and the working class would have to take the lead and suppress class enemies.

Many Chinese and Western scholars have questioned whether the CCP's promotion of New Democracy was genuine or simply a political stratagem to garner the support of potentially hostile groups, allowing the CCP to eliminate them gradually at the time of its choosing. Did the party leadership actually see New Democracy as a meaningful economic program? CCP leaders, including Mao, said consistently in the early days of the PRC that the New Democratic settlement should remain unaltered for fifteen years.[8] However, by 1953 the party was already pushing away from New Democracy towards full-blooded socialism with the First Five Year Plan and the beginnings of collectivization in agriculture. There is some evidence that these moves were a source of tension within the leadership: it was provincial actors such as Gao Gang (1905–1954), the party chief in the northeast, and the leaders of Shanxi Province who, along with Mao, pushed most strongly for socialist transformation.[9] Official Chinese scholarship post-1978 has generally presented Liu Shaoqi as the leader most in favor of New Democracy as a long-term economic and political strategy.

---

7 "Zhongguo renmin zhengzhi xieshang huiyi gongtong gangling," in Zhongyang wenxian chubanshe (ed.), *Jianguo yilai zhongyao wenxian xuanbian* (Beijing: Zhongyang wenxian chubanshe, 1992) [hereinafter "*JGYL*"], Vol. 1, p. 7.

8 Bo Yibo, *Ruogan zhongda juece yu shijian de huigu* (Beijing: Zhongyang dangxiao chubanshe, 1991), Vol. 1, p. 47.

9 For detail see: Hou Xiaojia, *Negotiating Socialism in Rural China: Mao, Peasants, and Local Cadres in Shanxi 1949–1953* (Ithaca, NY: Cornell University Press, 2016).

Another area of controversy is whether New Democracy as a concept origi-
nated with Mao or simply reflected wider trends in the Eastern European socialist
camp.[10] By the time the PRC was established, Stalin was encouraging the Eastern
European and Chinese parties to favor a gradualist approach, avoiding the
radical strategies of violent collectivization with which the USSR had experimented in 1929.[11] Moreover, developments in China seem to have tracked the
Eastern European states with uncanny precision. By the early 1950s the
European People's Democracies had moved away from the democratic stage of
revolution and were pushing towards socialist transformation of industry and
agriculture. The pressure on China not to fall behind was intense.

Land Reform: Turning the Rural Order Upside Down (1947–1952)

For decades, many Chinese and Western observers praised Land Reform as
among the most important achievements of the Chinese revolution, heralding
the destruction of a stagnant feudal order and a move towards greater social
justice. The CCP had begun distributing land to peasants in the late 1920s in its
revolutionary base areas and had repeated the process on a larger scale in the "old
liberated areas" of the northeast between 1946 and 1948. Official statistics
suggest that the national Land Reform program saw 43 percent of all China's
agricultural land distributed to 60 percent of its rural population.[12] Officials who
had served in the US government after World War Two believed that rural
support for the communists in China and Vietnam grew largely out of these
redistributive policies, ascribing the "loss of China" in 1949 in large part to the
GMD's inability to carry through land reform. It was this belief that led
American advisers to promote similar reforms during the US occupation of
Japan and South Korea, as well as under the GMD government on Taiwan.

Debates on Land Reform

Today, views on Land Reform tend to be less clear cut. A number of scholars in
China and the West now argue that the reforms pursued by the CCP were
unnecessary in economic terms, suggesting that pre-revolutionary rural China

10 Arlen Meliksetov and Alexander Pantsov, "The Stalinization of the People's Republic of China,"
    in William C. Kirby (ed.), *Realms of Freedom in Modern China* (Stanford, CA: Stanford
    University Press, 2003), pp. 200–201.
11 Gail Kligman and Katherine Verdery, *Peasants under Siege: The Collectivization of Romanian
    Agriculture, 1949–1962* (Princeton, NJ: Princeton University Press, 2011), p. 68.
12 Jürgen Osterhammel, *Shanghai 30. Mai 1925: Die chinesische Revolution* (Munich: Deutscher
    Taschenbuchverlag, 1997), p. 232.

was a relatively homogeneous society without a real landlord class. Many have pointed to 1930s survey work by American experts such as John L. Buck, who found, contrary to Communist Party claims, that exploitation through high rents was not a central reason for rural China's backwardness, and moreover that land distribution on the whole was not strikingly unequal.[13] In this reading, Land Reform was first and foremost a pretext to destroy the traditional rural elites and to divide communities, allowing the state to enforce more effective control in the villages. If any redistribution of land was necessary, a more appropriate course would have been a peaceful reform like that conducted on Taiwan. There the GMD not only did not mobilize peasants in class struggle but even compensated expropriated landlords for their losses.

Other scholars have drawn attention to important nuances in the party's approach to Land Reform. They point to the CCP's decision to allow even "class enemies" to keep some land to supply their needs, and to the fact that the party allowed a "rich peasant economy" to continue to thrive, even if temporarily, for taxation purposes. These concessions meant that, in many villages, there was little extra land actually available to be redistributed. Two Chinese scholars have claimed that the most important aspect of Land Reform was not the expropriation of land but the reduction of rents. As long as tenants were forced to make regular, expensive payments to land owners, the state could not bring inflation under control or tax the rural population efficiently. The abolition of rents was a prerequisite for the state to begin extracting resources from the countryside.[14] It is notable that the destruction of the class of surplus-producing "rich peasants" effectively removed the last barrier between ordinary peasants and the extractive machinery of the state, forcing the burden of the grain tax down a rung on the ladder. The state's desire to control the rural economy more effectively is illustrated by the fact that, during the entire Mao era, only very limited circulation of currency was permitted in rural areas.

I would argue that inequality of land ownership before 1949 is almost impossible to quantify, in the light of the lack of any survey data on the national level. However, a critical reassessment of Republican era land surveys and statistics suggests that to view pre-revolutionary China as a nation of smallholders would be wishful thinking at best. In the 1930s, landlords did indeed own a great deal of land.[15] Buck and his American colleagues were mainly interested in technical

13 Frank Dikötter, *The Tragedy of Liberation: A History of the Chinese Revolution 1945–1957* (London: Bloomsbury, 2013), pp. 70–71.
14 Cao Shuji and Liu Shigu, *Chuantong Zhongguo diquan jiegou jiqi yanbian* (Shanghai: Shanghai jiaotong daxue chubanshe, 2015), p. 243.
15 Joseph Esherick, "Number Games: A Note on Land Distribution in Prerevolutionary China," *Modern China* (1981) Vol. 7, No. 4, p. 407.

solutions to rural China's problems – improving farm management, for instance, alongside new credit systems and infrastructure – and this preoccupation seems to have obscured issues of class.[16] While China had no parallel to the situation seen in South America or eastern Germany, where land ownership was dominated by a small number of vast rural estates, exploitation was still rife, primarily through high rents. National estimates in the 1930s suggested that 42 percent of farmland was rented, with rents generally ranging from 50 to 70 percent of the main harvest.[17]

The villages of pre-revolutionary China were not harmonious communities founded on kinship and Confucian values. If this kind of ideal society ever existed in China, it had vanished by the end of the Anti-Japanese War in 1945. By that time, eight years of conflict had decimated rural families and forced elites in many areas to choose between fleeing and losing their wealth or staying and collaborating with the invader, with all the moral quandaries that entailed.[18] Many villages had experienced an extraordinary spiral of violence, with territory changing hands repeatedly and each new occupying force dividing communities afresh.

Often these depredations made some redistribution of agricultural land unavoidable. The CCP's Land Reform campaign in Manchuria, which began in 1946, was a case in point. There Chinese peasants' land had been expropriated for Japanese settlers before 1945, and 10 to 15 percent of the cultivated land had eventually come into the hands of private individuals, land companies or the puppet government of Manchukuo.[19] The Japanese withdrawal and the repatriation of colonial settlers meant that new owners had to be found for the land they had abandoned.

Advocates for a Taiwan-style land reform in the PRC have failed to make the case that the GMD's methods would have been effective on the much larger mainland. Taiwan's population stood at 7.7 million in 1950, while on the mainland the number of peasants was around 450 million. It is not by any means clear that consensus-based reforms would have been feasible on this scale in the fraught setting of the late 1940s. Moreover, quite apart from the CCP's ideological opposition to paying compensation for land, to do so would have made the

---

16 For a critical review of Buck's work see: Randall E. Stross, *The Stubborn Earth: American Agriculturalists on Chinese Soil, 1898–1937* (Berkeley, CA: University of California Press, 1986), pp. 161–188.

17 Peter Zarrow, *China in War and Revolution, 1895–1949* (London: Routledge, 2005), p. 99.

18 Diana Lary, *The Chinese People at War: Human Suffering and Social Transformation, 1937–1945* (Cambridge: Cambridge University Press, 2010), pp. 6–7.

19 Steven I. Levine, *Anvil of Victory: The Communist Revolution in Manchuria, 1945–1948* (New York: Columbia University Press, 1987), p. 203.

twin goals of ending inflation and controlling the flow of currency in the country-side almost impossible to achieve.

The debate around Land Reform is inevitably highly politicized, since policies of rural redistribution were fundamental to the legitimacy of the 1949 revolution. Land Reform was almost the *raison d'être* of the early PRC state. Furthermore, the CCP continues to narrate the history of this period as a struggle between evil landlords and good poor peasants. That view should not go unchallenged, but the picture painted by some commentators of a contest between a humble Confucian gentry and a "lumpenproletariat" agitated by communist radicals is perhaps just as flawed.

Mobilization and Violence

In terms of violence against "class enemies," Land Reform went through several cycles of radicalization and de-radicalization. The encouragement of violence was central to land reform movements from the mid-1920s on. The most influential text on the practice of "revolutionary terror" was Mao's 1927 "Report on the Peasant Movement in Hunan." Reprinted in many different editions, in May 1947 it became required reading for party cadres involved in the Land Reform program then in progress in the "old liberated areas" of northeast China.[20] Mao's argument on violence was plain: a period of terror, repeated in every village under CCP control, was the only way for peasant associations to overthrow the rule of landlords and the "evil gentry."[21] Mao summarized the tactics of the peasants, from producing lists of all class enemies and forcing them to parade with paper hats in the streets, through to executions, the destruction of temples, forced labor for vagrants and so on. In this eruption of class enmity, suppressed for centuries under the old system, "excesses" would be unavoidable. Nevertheless, Mao contended that it was peasants, as victims of oppression themselves, who were best placed to determine just punishments for the dethroned old elite. If their judgment was that death was the only satisfactory penalty, then that judgment must, within reason, be accepted.

This justification for the execution of landlords, "evil gentry" and counter-revolutionaries is repeated in numerous documents produced by the central party leadership. "Excesses" were simply the cost of doing business, and one should not "pour cold water" on activists or the masses for fear of lessening their enthusiasm. The free rein given to the peasants also affected how people were

20 Yang Kuisong, *Zhonghua renmin gongheguo jianguoshi yanjiu* (Nanchang: Jiangxi renmin chubanshe, 2009), Vol. 1, p. 48.
21 Mao Zedong, "Hunan nongmin yundong kaocha baogao," in *Mao Zedong Xuanji*, Vol. 1, p. 17.

killed. In February 1948, Liu Shaoqi insisted that executions should be by shooting and should take place only after authorization from a party committee above the county level; simply tying prisoners up and beating them to death, he declared, was a "feudal method."[22] Liu's warning was a pertinent one. During Land Reform in the old liberated areas, mass killings, beatings and torture rose to a fever pitch between 1946 and late 1947, when even supposedly "rightist" cadres might be beaten to death. Land Reform itself was accompanied in the northeast by "cleansing" campaigns and in Shandong by a hunt for spies, both of which led to intense violence even after the actual distribution of land had been completed. In one county in Heilongjiang, 35 percent of all "middle peasants" became subjects of struggle at some point during this period.[23]

Although the CCP leadership initially encouraged extrajudicial violence, there was also a recognition that problems might occur. Terms such as "chaotic killing" and "killing at random" are scattered through official documents,[24] indicating either that more people had been killed in a particular area than was considered necessary by the leadership or that local people had taken to targeting groups such as children, poor or middle peasants and innocent party cadres. Such actions were labeled "leftist error." The leadership was aware that "chaotic killings" could have negative consequences for the CCP. By the end of 1947, Mao had begun to argue that "excesses" in the prosecution of Land Reform could alienate "middle peasants" from the party and damage the fragile United Front with the petty bourgeoisie. Moreover, many PLA soldiers were from "middle peasant" backgrounds, and harsh treatment of this group risked impacting on the morale of the armed forces.

In the following months, Mao wrote several instructions and articles calling for "leftist tendencies" to be brought under control. This did not mean an end to the killings, but it did mean that executions should be fewer in number and better targeted. Mao and other CCP leaders also pointed out several times that China's roughly 36 million "rich peasants" constituted a huge labor force, one which could be put to use in the economic construction of the new country – but only if left alive.[25]

---

22 Yang Kuisong, *Zhonghua renmin gongheguo jianguoshi yanjiu*, Vol. 1, p. 92.

23 For Dongbei see: Luo Pinghan, *Tudi gaige yundongshi* (Fuzhou: Fujian renmin chubanshe, 2005), pp. 188–193. For Shandong see Wang Youming, *Geming yu xiangcun: Jiefang qu tudi gaige yanjiu: 1941–1948: yi Shandong Junan xian wei ge'an* (Shanghai: Shanghai shehui ke-xueyuan chubanshe, 2006), pp. 126–139.

24 For example see, Liu Hao, "Lun Guangdong tudi geming zaoqi de hongse kongbu xianxiang," *Xue Lilun*, No. 2 (2009), p. 17; Huang Daoxuan, *Zhangli yu xianjie: Zhongyang suqu de geming (1933–1934)* (Beijing: Shehui kexue wenxian chubanshe, 2011), p. 308.

25 Yang Kuisong, *Zhonghua renmin gongheguo jianguoshi yanjiu*, Vol. 1, pp. 76–77, 85.

One way to limit spontaneous violence against the wrong targets was through more effective labeling. Class labels were an important part of the process of land distribution, but the criteria by which such labels were to be assigned were not always clear to actors on the ground. In extreme cases, cadres turned to proscribed methods of labeling such as "investigating three generations," which could result in people being categorized as landlord based on the economic situation of their grandparents, with no regard to current circumstances.[26] In February of 1948, Mao attempted to address this difficulty by declaring that "landlords" and "rich peasants" accounted for only 8 percent of the rural population, while "middle peasants," "poor peasants" and "rural labors" covered over 90 percent. In addition to limiting the total number of legitimate targets to 8 to 10 percent of the rural population (approximately the percentage of class enemies, with some additional leeway) he declared that the prerogative to order executions was to be restricted to higher levels of the party apparatus:

> Reactionaries must be suppressed, but killing without discrimination is strictly forbidden; the fewer killings, the better. Death sentences should be reviewed and approved by a committee formed at the county level. The power to try and to deal with the cases of political suspects is vested in committees at the district committee level of the CCP.[27]

A number of scholars have argued that violence was a direct result of the ideology of class struggle. Here, however, we see Mao and the party leadership using the same ideology to *limit* targets of violence by setting an upper bound on the number of people who could be designated class enemies.

Nevertheless, even with these stricter targeting criteria, 8 to 10 percent of the rural population still covered many millions of people. The number killed during Land Reform between 1946 and 1952 may never be known. Liu Shaoqi estimated in a report to Moscow in 1950 that 250,000 "landlords" and "rich peasants" had been killed in 1947 alone. For the "old liberated areas," numbers may have been lower after Mao's declaration in 1948, when the most extreme forms of killing largely ceased. A government resolution in August 1950 applied the 1948 declaration to the "newly liberated areas" as well, and methods such as "investigation of three generations" were once again criticized. The resulting drawdown in violence, however, was short-lived. The Campaign to Suppress Counterrevolutionaries and China's entry into the Korean War put an end to "peaceful land reform" in the south and northwest. This new wave of destruction

---

26 Luo Pinghan, *Tudi gaige yundongshi*, p. 177.
27 Mao Zedong, "Xin jiefangqu tudi gaige yaodian," in *Mao Zedong Xuanji*, Vol. 4, pp. 1226, 1227 (for English language version see: www.marxists.org/reference/archive/mao/selected-works/volume-4/mswv4_30.htm (accessed March 3, 2017)).

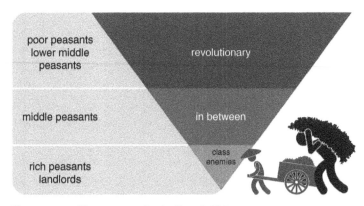

Figure 2.2: Class categories in Rural China.

was perhaps less severe and better controlled than in 1947 and 1948,[28] but even without access to nationwide statistics the scale of the killing remains remarkable. In Guangdong alone, archival documents suggest 170,000 people committed suicide during the campaigns of the early 1950s, to say nothing of the numbers executed.

The Classification of the Rural Population

After passing a Land Reform law soon after the founding of the PRC, the government saw the need not merely to restrict the total number of people who could be targeted but also to provide clear definitions to allow targets to be effectively identified. (See Figure 2.2.) In August 1950, the State Council therefore passed the "Decision Regarding the Classification of Rural Classes."[29] For the next two decades, this document was the government's standard reference when uncertainties arose regarding the classification of individuals in the countryside (see Chapter 5). The definitions were based on regulations passed in 1933 by the Chinese Soviet Republic (1931–1937), the governing authority in the areas of China then under CCP control. However, the 1950 decision was far more detailed than its predecessors. Among the most important points to note is that, in contrast to the criteria employed during land reforms in the GDR or

28 For all numbers of this paragraph see: Yang Kuisong, *Zhonghua renmin gongheguo jianguoshi yanjiu*, Vol. 1, pp. 99, 152–153.
29 "Zhengwuyuan guanyu huafen nongcun jieji chengfen de jueding," in *JGYL*, Vol. 1, pp. 382–407.

Poland around the same time, a "landlord" under the CCP system was not simply anyone whose land holdings exceeded the threshold for seizure. Instead, the party's definition was mainly based on the proportion of income an individual derived from "exploitation" of the labor of others. This statistical element complicated the work of local cadres, who were required to do more than simply measure the amount of land a person possessed.

The decision defined a landlord as a person who did not participate in manual labor and whose income was based on the exploitation of wage labor and tenants through high rents. Next on the ladder came the "rich peasant," who rented out some land but also did some farming of his or her own. The rich peasant's income was still based mainly on exploitation, but in contrast to the idle landlord he or she also participated in manual labor. A "middle peasant" owned some land but usually did not exploit other wage laborers or receive rents. A "poor peasant" owned little or no land and instead made a living by selling his or her labor power, whether directly or through rents. Two further labels, "self-employees" and "professions," covered doctors, teachers, lawyers, artists and others who did not derive their earnings from exploitation. A final label, "intellectual" (*zhishifenzi*), was not a class status or family background. These "brain workers" were generally protected by the new government, and their family status was defined according to the class labels already described, such as "landlord" or "middle peasant."[30]

The decision also outlined a series of relationships between individuals' economic and political status. "Warlords," "local tyrants," "members of the gentry" and "bureaucrats" who had served the old regime were seen as the political representatives of the (economically defined) "landlord class." These were negative political labels, even if the person so designated came from a favorable class background. By contrast, Red Army soldiers could expect to have land distributed to them and their family members even if their family were landlords or rich peasants. Contributions to the revolution outweighed class label. The category "family of a Red Army soldier" to which this protective umbrella extended encompassed a person's parents, spouse, children and siblings below the age of sixteen. Other relatives with bad family backgrounds had no right to receive land.

The decision also defined how to deal with class status in marriage. For example, if a female poor peasant married a landlord, she could keep her own class status as long as she continued to participate in manual labor. If not, she would be labeled as a landlord along with her husband. This dynamic element of class labeling was seen also in the promise that bad labels could eventually be excised. The 1950 decision included an undertaking that any landlord who

---

30 Ibid., pp. 397–398.

worked hard and was not implicated in counterrevolutionary activity could apply to the local government to change their status to "laborer" after a period of five years. In case of a "rich peasant," only a three-year wait was required.[31] In practice, however, such a change of status proved nearly impossible to obtain, and most people with unfavorable class labels had to wait until 1980 to have them expunged.

How criteria for classification were actually implemented in the villages remains an understudied question. The CCP's system was designed for areas where agriculture was the only, or at least the predominant, income source for most rural households. In more developed regions such as Jiangnan, south of the lower reaches of the Yangzi River, many villagers received a large portion of their income from activities other than farming, making the party's model of classification difficult to apply.[32] In fact, the whole project of the rural revolution had a strong northern bias. Cadres "sent down south" after the revolution tended to know little about local social and economic conditions.

The classification of the people in terms of class status gave rise to a new language of good and evil. Abstract class categories took on vivid and concrete form in personal stories delivered through propaganda, literature and films. Exploitation before 1949 was often modeled through tales of sexual violence. One particularly famous story, *The White Haired Girl*, follows Xi'er, a poor peasant forced to serve as a landlord's concubine. Her long suffering at her master's hands ends when she flees to the mountains, where her hair turns white and she takes on a ghostly, almost supernatural appearance. Later, she returns with the Red Army to her village, where, during the Land Reform campaign, she "speaks bitterness" against her former oppressor, leading to his eventual punishment by the local people. Xi'er is then free to reunite with her former fiancé, an honest and hardworking peasant. Where the "old society" had turned humans into ghosts, the "new society," the narrative suggests, makes them fully human again. The details of *The White Haired Girl* vary across different media – the story was performed as, among other things, a Peking opera, an amateur play for rural theatre groups, a 1950 film and a 1965 ballet (later named as one of the eight "revolutionary model operas" during the Cultural Revolution).[33] It is notable that, in some versions of the tale, the

31 Ibid., pp. 400–401, 406–407.

32 Julia Strauss, "Rethinking Land Reform and Regime Consolidation in the People's Republic of China: The Case of Jiangnan 1950–1952," in Mechthild Leutner (ed.), *Rethinking China in the 1950s* (Berlin: Lit-Verlag, 2007), Vol. 31, pp. 28–31.

33 For the large variety of cultural production to promote Land Reform see: Brian James Demare, *Mao's Cultural Army: Drama Troupes in China's Rural Revolution* (Cambridge: Cambridge University Press, 2015).

Figure 2.3: A painting illustrating Land Reform: a struggle meeting against "landlords" through CCP eyes.
Source: Helmut Opletal (ed.), *Die Kultur der Kulturrevolution: Personenkult und politisches Design im China von Mao Zedong* (Wien: Museum für Völkerkunde, 2011), p. 73.

landlord's final act of exploitation is to rape Xi'er, who subsequently falls pregnant only to lose her child during her period in the mountains. Similar narratives prevailed in early PRC schools, where students learned that "landlords" and "rich peasants" had been rapists and blood suckers, while "poor" and "lower middle peasants" had lived a life of misery before being liberated by the Communist Party. The 1950 "Decision on Classification" suggests that, in the real world, the issue of class status was more complex than these narratives implied. The decision, as we have seen, was in some ways surprisingly nuanced, including specific regulations on how to deal with spouses, close and distant family members, inter-class marriage and family background. The focus on "political performance" and the promise of changes in class status after three or five years of good behavior introduced a further complication, offering hope to those with bad backgrounds that their labels might not be set in stone.

The Campaign to Suppress Counterrevolutionaries

Where Land Reform had destroyed the rural elites and broken the power of sects (*huidaomen*) and secret brotherhoods in the countryside, the Campaign to Suppress Counterrevolutionaries was directed against urban targets. In rural China, the CCP mobilized the masses against landlords through a largely bottom-up approach. In attacking GMD supporters and opponents of the new order in the cities, the party preferred a top-down strategy led by its own officials and the public security apparatus. Whereas in the countryside peasants had been allowed to take the lead, in the cities struggle meetings and public trials were stage-managed entirely by party cadres. Mass executions of "enemies of the people" were viewed by live audiences of thousands, reported in the press and sometimes broadcast on national radio.

Because no formal criminal code was ever passed during the Mao period, the government turned to other forms of statutory instrument to determine what counted as counterrevolutionary crimes and how they should be punished. Among the most important was the "Statute on the Punishment of Counterrevolutionary Activity," approved in February 1951, which was less a formal piece of legislation than a political declaration by the central government. The statute criminalized the organization of armed insurrections and espionage, but also less serious transgressions such as "instigating the masses to show resistance to government action in the purchase of foodstuffs and the levying of taxes." Some classes of "counterrevolutionary activity" were very broadly drawn: among the activities outlawed by the statute were "sowing dissension and hostility among the nationalities, democratic classes, parties and people's organizations," "undermining the unity of the people and the government" or "engaging in counterrevolutionary agitation, fabricating and spreading false rumors." All were punishable with a three-year prison term or, in extreme cases, with the death penalty.[34] The inclusion of "spreading rumors" as a counterrevolutionary crime illustrates the new regime's desire to secure a monopoly on information, something it defended by establishing state control over the media, news and publishing. The concern over rumors was a valid one. In the 1950s, instances of mass unrest might be sparked by stories of mysterious local emperors or child-eating demons that roamed across county and even provincial borders.[35] During the Korean War, rumors about the outbreak of a third World War or a US invasion of the Chinese mainland enjoyed a wide circulation.

Killing to Meet Quotas

Like all other purges – and in common with the Land Reform campaign – the Campaign to Suppress Counterrevolutionaries went through several cycles of radicalization and de-radicalization. In July of 1950, the government made clear that "chaotic beatings, chaotic killings" and corporal punishment were not permitted, an order that was subsequently repeated on several occasions. Nevertheless, the same instruction specified that "counterrevolutionaries" were to be executed if they had taken up arms against the People's Government, killed government officials or members of the masses, committed serious acts of sabotage, destroyed public goods or stolen secret information.[36] The CCP Central Committee decreed that the death penalty in such cases should be approved by party committees at the provincial, city and district levels. The only exception was for foreigners or people in the public eye, who were to be executed only with the approval of the State Council.[37] The government designated several groups of enemies, singling out "local tyrants," bandits, backward elements, spies and members of sects. In contrast to rural China, where class labels based on economic categories were key, in urban society the enemy was defined primarily by political labels.

---

34 See Gong'an zhengce falü yanjiushi (ed.), "Zhonghuarenmin gongheguo chengzhi fangeming tiaoli," in *Gong'anbu fagui huibian* (Beijing: Qunzhong chubanshe, 1980), pp. 96–99.

35 Li Ruojian, *Xushi zhijian: 20 shiji 50 niandai Zhongguo dalu yaoyan yanjiu* (Beijing: Shehui kexue wenxian chubanshe, 2011), pp. 27–33.

36 "Zhengwuyuan, zuigaorenminfayuan guanyu zhenya fangeming huodong de zhishi," in *JGYL*, Vol. 1, p. 359.

37 "Zhonggong zhongyang guanyu zhenya fangeming huodong de zhishi," in *JGYL*, Vol. 1, p. 422.

By the end of 1950, the central government in general and Mao in particular had started to complain that cadres were failing to take the campaign seriously enough, resulting in an insufficient number of people being targeted.[38] Cadres were evidently struggling to find the dividing line between too few executions and the equally undesirable "chaotic killings" that had characterized parts of the Land Reform campaign. To encourage more enthusiastic prosecution of the purge, Mao therefore set what amounted to quotas for executions for different areas. In most cities, he declared, 0.5 people per thousand should be executed. In areas where the enemy was particularly active, the number should rise to one person per thousand, and areas with extraordinary problems might reach an upper bound of 1.5 per thousand.[39] It was clear from the outset that these quotas were intended not to tame violence but to press for more executions. The need for more killings was again justified in populist terms, and leading CCP figures took the view that "if we do not kill, [the punishment] is not sufficient to calm the anger of the people." Having set the engine of mass repression in motion, in February 1951 Mao justified the killings in a letter to Huang Yanpei, the Vice-Premier of the State Council:

> If we do not kill bandit leaders and professional bandits, we will never be able exterminate banditry; instead, the harder we try to destroy ordinary bandits the more of them there will be. If we do not kill local tyrants, we will not be able to organize the peasant associations and consequently we will not be able to distribute land to the peasants. If we do not kill key [Nationalist] secret agents, acts of sabotage and assassinations will continue.[40]

In the summer of 1951, the Central Committee attempted to lower the temperature with a call for "killing less." Even with this milder approach, by the end of the campaign Mao's quotas had been overfilled. According to one Chinese scholar, in south-central China 1.5 people in every thousand were killed in the mid-south region.[41] Official statistics report that of 2.62 million people arrested as part of the campaign between 1950 and 1953, 712,000 were executed and a further 1.29 million imprisoned, out of a total population of approximately 574 million.[42] The rate of executions was far lower than during Stalin's infamous

---

38 "Zhonggong zhongyang pizhuan zhongyang gong'anbu 'guanyu quanguo gong'an huiyi de baogao'," in *JGYL*, Vol. 1, pp. 442–443.
39 Yang Kuisong, *Zhonghua renmin gongheguo jianguoshi yanjiu*, Vol. 1, pp. 189, 191.
40 Mao Zedong, "Gei Huang Yanpei de xin," in Zhonggong zhongyang wenxian yanjiushi (ed.), *Jianguo yilai Mao Zedong wengao* (Beijing: Zhongyang wenxian chubanshe, 1993), Vol. 2, p. 124.
41 Yang Kuisong, *Zhonghua renmin gongheguo jianguoshi yanjiu*, Vol. 1, p. 209.
42 Ibid., p. 217.

Great Purge of 1937–1938, in which at least 681,692 people were executed and 2.5 million arrested out of a population of around 168 million.[43] Nevertheless, in terms of raw numbers the Chinese campaign was actually wider in scope.

The purges of the 1950s also had a long-lasting impact on state classification. Hundreds of thousands had the label "counterrevolutionary" written into their personal files, and the consequences of this labeling reached beyond the individual to family members and relatives. Until the early 1980s, application forms for party membership, university entrance and travel abroad almost always asked whether any of the applicant's relatives had been "suppressed, arrested or killed in campaigns in the early years of the foundation of the state." Those who answered "yes" could expect to be met with suspicion and distrust. In 1954, the organization department of the CCP went a step further, determining that people with problematic family backgrounds whose relatives had been arrested, killed or had "committed suicide to escape punishment" should not be allowed to apply for party membership. The mere suggestion of personal contact with such people would see the applicant subjected to serious investigation prior to admission, even if they were clearly well disposed towards the new regime and had a good class background.[44]

Hunting Flies and Tigers

Even in the revolutionary base areas in the 1940s, nepotism, corruption, fraud, "decadent lifestyles" and misuse of public funds by cadres had already begun to pose problems for CCP rule.[45] After the establishment of the PRC, these issues only became more pressing. Many rural cadres entering the cities for the first time after the revolution had little or no experience of urban administration or consumer culture. Concerned that its revolutionaries would be led astray by the "sugar-coated cannonballs" of urban life, the party leadership not only suppressed counterrevolutionary forces, but also attempted to discipline corrupt officials in the state and party apparatus.

43 Wendy Z. Goldman, *Terror and Democracy in the Age of Stalin: The Social Dynamics of Repression* (Cambridge: Cambridge University Press, 2007), p. 5.

44 "Zhongyang zuzhibu tongyi Xi'nanju zuzhibu guanyu zhixi qinshu xi bei zhenya, guanzhi huo weizui zisha de dizhu, eba, fangemingfenzi de gongzuo renyuan rudang wenti de chuli yijian," January 16 (1954), in Song Yongyi (ed.), *Database of the Chinese Political Campaigns in the 1950s: From Land Reform to the State–Private Partnership, 1949–1956*, CD-ROM (Hong Kong: Universities Service Centre for China Studies, The Chinese University of Hong Kong, 2014).

45 Lü Xiaobo, *Cadres and Corruption: The Organizational Involution of the Chinese Communist Party* (Stanford, CA: Stanford University Press, 2000), pp. 37–44.

The result, the so-called Three-Anti Campaign, targeted corruption, waste and "bureaucratism" (denoting an excessive fondness for bureaucratic rules and procedures). The dynamic of this campaign was similar to that seen in the Campaign to Suppress Counterrevolutionaries, with which it was almost exactly contemporaneous. Mao called for mobilizing the masses to hunt not only "flies," cadres guilty of petty corruption, but also "tigers" who had defrauded the state of large sums. The party apparatus initially showed little enthusiasm for the campaign, and as before the central leadership responded by setting quotas for the number of targets to be identified. On February 8, 1951, Mao wrote in a telegram: "Perhaps we have to shoot ten thousand or several tens of thousands of corrupt criminals across the whole country in order to solve the problem."[46] One of the most spectacular cases was the public execution on February 10, 1951 of Liu Qingshan, who had served as the party secretary of the district committee of Tianjin. He was accused of misappropriating millions of yuan from the grain tax, as well as from funds for famine relief and flood control. Corruption was indeed serious, but the radical fervor with which the CCP prosecuted the campaign resulted in significant exaggerations. Methodical combing of accounts in search of fraud was replaced by confessions forced from cadres at often brutal struggle meetings. By mid-1952, over 1.5 million supposedly corrupt officials had been uncovered.[47] As the central government itself acknowledged in internal reports, many of these accusations were false and the confessions supporting them either invented or extracted under duress. These shortcomings led to the implementation of stricter controls and the eventual end of the Three-Anti Campaign.

Document 2.1 shows the wide variety of torture that could take place at the local level in the early PRC, including as many as sixty methods of extracting confessions. Many of these were apparently carried over from the techniques used in GMD prisons before 1949. Even after the Three-Anti Campaign had passed its peak, some local cadres were driven to suicide by Mao's attempt to "rectify the party." Nor were cadres with a good class background and without political problems immune. Document 2.2 recounts the case of one party member who committed suicide out of shame after being accused of "illicit sexual relations." By the time these reports were written, the party leadership was actively trying to avoid violence against cadres.

46 Mao Zedong, "Zhongyang guanyu sanfan douzheng bixu dazhang qigu jinxing de dianbao," in Zhonggong zhongyang wenxian yanjiushi (ed.), *Jianguo yilai Mao Zedong wengao* (Beijing: Zhongyang wenxian chubanshe, 1993), Vol. 2, p. 549.

47 Yang Kuisong, *Zhonghua renmin gongheguo jianguoshi yanjiu*, Vol. 1, pp. 297, 305.

The Three-Anti Campaign shows that local cadres could themselves become the target of repression and violence as "class enemies" if they fell out of favor with the higher levels of government. The prospect of losing office and party membership, with the concomitant fall in social status, was enough to keep many in line. One scholar argues that local cadres were subjected to the discipline of the regime to a greater extent than any social group outside the military.[48]

During the first half of 1952, the Three-Anti Campaign was transformed into a wider Five-Anti Campaign against bribery, tax evasion, fraud and theft of government property and economic secrets. The party leadership argued that some officials had been corrupted by "unlawful merchants" and had turned a blind eye to "illegal economic activities." The new campaign therefore shifted the target from cadres to private businessmen. The central government was not yet openly questioning the United Front with the national bourgeoisie or calling for the elimination of capitalists as a class, but it attacked "speculating unscrupulous businessmen" as fair game. These individuals were accused of violating price regulations by illegally selling subsidized raw materials on the black market. Many companies, the state charged, were keeping two sets of books to falsify profits and tax reports, and businessmen had tried to convert earnings to gold or foreign currencies without proper authorization.[49]

Several scholars have identified the Five-Anti Campaign as an important step on the road to the socialist transformation that began the following year. The CCP attempted to mobilize "lawful merchants" to uncover "unlawful" colleagues under the leadership of urban workers. The government called on children to convince their parents to make confessions or to report them to the authorities. Even the All China Women's Federation tried to mobilize and educate "bourgeois housewives" to contribute to the Five-Anti struggle.[50] The degree of violence at struggle meetings was relatively low compared with that of the Land Reform or the Campaign to Suppress Counterrevolutionaries. However, some targets were unable to endure the humiliation of being struggled against, and once more a significant number committed suicide. The Five-Anti Campaign also disrupted industrial production and resulted in a decline in labor

---

48 Andrew Walder, *China under Mao: A Revolution Derailed* (Cambridge, MA: Harvard University Press, 2015), p. 120.

49 For example see Karl Gerth, "Wu Yunchu and the Fate of the Bourgeoisie and Bourgeois Lifestyles under Communism," in Sherman Cochran (ed.), *The Capitalist Dilemma in China's Communist Revolution* (Ithaca, NY: Cornell East Asia Program, 2014), p. 192.

50 Feng Xiaocai, "Between Class Struggle and Family Loyalty: The Mobilization of Businessmen's Wives and Children during the Five Antis Movement," *European Journal of East Asian Studies*, No. 13 (2014), pp. 288–289.

discipline and the closure of numerous companies. Workers felt empowered to denounce their bosses, and the space for profit-making private businesses contracted. The CCP had promised the liberation of workers from exploitation but promoted cooperation between labor and capital at the same time. This contradiction at the heart of the New Democratic order was now exposed, and the socialist transformation initiated in 1953 would see it decisively resolved.

The Marriage Law: Monogamy and the New Democratic Family

One important component of the early PRC's political landscape was the reform of the family to establish a New Democratic form of marriage. The Marriage Law of April 1950 marked a radical break with "feudal" tradition. In the old China, marriage was not the union of a self-selecting couple but an exchange between two families of patriarchal control over the new bride. Women were subjected to the control of first their fathers, then their husbands and mothers-in-law, and finally their adult sons. Marriage marked the woman's departure from her own family and absorption into her husband's. Men too were not free individuals, but were subject to the orders of their father – the family's emperor – and any elder brothers.

The traditional Confucian or "feudal" family model had been under attack since the May Fourth Movement of 1919, and notions of romantic love, youth rebellion, gender equality and free choice in marriage spread widely in urban China. Decades of war and civil war further undermined and deformed the economic and moral foundations of the traditional family structure.[51] Well before the founding of the PRC, the GMD regime had introduced its own marriage law, including among other things the right to divorce. However, the Republican state lacked the capacity to enforce the law across the full spectrum of Chinese society, and formally sanctioned divorces remained rare before 1949. Moreover, the Republican Civil Code still permitted men to keep concubines, and the marriage law did little to prevent the widespread sale of women. A husband remained able to legally sell his wife to a third party as long as her "consent" had been secured.[52]

The new Marriage Law of 1950 defined marriage as between one man and one woman, enshrining in law the principles of gender equality and freedom of marriage and divorce. Bigamy, concubinage, forced marriage and the adoption

51 Lary, *The Chinese People at War*, pp. 3–4.
52 Phillip C. C. Huang, "Women's Choices under the Law: Marriage, Divorce, and Illicit Sex in the Qing and the Republic," *Modern China*, Vol. 27, No. 1 (2001), pp. 34–38.

of girls as future daughters-in-law were all outlawed. Equality, however, only went so far: the minimum marriage age was set at twenty for men but eighteen for women, suggesting an assumption by the state that a husband should be older than his wife. People suffering from mental disabilities, leprosy or sexually transmitted diseases were not allowed to marry at all. The law also regulated the parent-child relationship, placing a legal obligation on parents to raise and educate their children and a parallel duty on children to support their parents in their old age. The parental obligation applied whether children were born inside of marriage or not, and where parents were unmarried the father was required to provide for his children's living costs and education until the age of eighteen.

Outside the party, the new legislation was popularly known as the "divorce law." The freedom to divorce was guaranteed, but men were not allowed to divorce pregnant women, and military personnel enjoyed special protections meaning they could not be unilaterally divorced.[53] Officials argued that the goal of the new law was not to destroy the family or encourage "chaotic relations" between men and women, but that freedom of marriage and relationships built on mutual feelings provided the best conditions for harmonious and stable families.[54] Marriage and divorce had to be registered and approved under the new law, giving local governments a role in overseeing family relations.

The Marriage Law met with fierce resistance in many parts of China. Across the country, thousands of women were reportedly killed for seeking divorce; official accounts lay the blame for this violence on "backward," "feudal" forces. In addition, a number of cadres charged with disseminating the new Marriage Law were murdered by villagers. Several factors were at work here. Some poor peasants worried that they would be unable to keep their wives once divorce became more widely available. Others who had paid heavy bride prices or dowries to secure a marriage simply felt cheated by the new system. Faced with an uncertain and precarious future, some former concubines committed suicide.

How much impact the Marriage Law actually had on women's lives remains an open question. Feminist scholars have argued that the strength of rural patriarchy precluded many women from exercising their new rights, as local cadres stood in the way of what were now entirely legal requests for divorce.[55]

---

53 "Zhonghua renmin gongheguo hunyinfa," in *JGYL*, Vol. 1, pp. 172–177.

54 Shanghai Jiefang ribao shelun, "Jianjue guanche zhixing hunyinfa," August 5 (1951), in Song Yongyi (ed.), *Database of the Chinese Political Campaigns in the 1950s: From Land Reform to the State-Private Partnership, 1949–1956*, CD-ROM (Hong Kong: Universities Service Centre for China Studies, The Chinese University of Hong Kong, 2014).

55 Kay Ann Johnson, *Women, the Family and Peasant Revolution in China* (Chicago, IL: The University Press of Chicago, 1983), pp. 221–222.

However, Neil Diamant has pointed out numerous cases of rural women bypassing local cadres to seek divorces directly from local courts, often escaping the husband's household back to their natal families. In fact, as Diamant shows, it was more often the "respectable" housewives of the educated urban elite who hesitated to go to court. In the cities, the working class districts had consistently higher divorce rates than wealthier ones. Urban areas actually experienced a downward shift in divorce rates after 1953, whereas in the countryside the rate rose markedly in the early 1960s.[56]

Starting from 1954, the central government seems to have ceased to view enforcement of the Marriage Law as a priority. Divorce was all very well when it was "feudal" marriages being broken up, but the CCP proved more reticent about ending post-1950 "New Democratic" unions, which, after all, it had argued would be more durable than those concluded under the old system. In the 1960s, the state began to impose barriers to divorce, for instance by calling for couples to go through mediation before a separation was granted. The party leadership today continues to believe that every "healthy" Chinese person should marry and have at least one child. In contrast to many other socialist states, the PRC never encouraged single parenthood, instead linking the stability of marriage to the stability of the new society.

Family Reform in Comparative Perspective

Compared to the reforms implemented in the Soviet Union in the 1920s, the family policies of the CCP were relatively moderate. Women Bolshevik leaders such as Alexandra Kollontai had called for the abolition of the family on the grounds that it was institutionally tied to private property and the enslavement of women. They argued for the socialization of housework and education through public institutions such as kindergartens, dining halls, washing facilities and nursing homes. Some Soviet architects planned buildings and even whole cities not for nuclear families but for new forms of collective living. The Bolshevik government introduced civil marriage, along with what was, at the time, the most liberal divorce law anywhere in the world. Compared to the rest of Europe, gender equality (at least under the law) was one of the early Soviet Union's outstanding features. Homosexuality and abortion were decriminalized, and "free love" became a rallying call among the urban youth. At the same time, a lack of men following the destruction of World War One and the

---

56 Neil Diamant, *Revolutionizing the Family: Politics, Love, and Divorce in Urban and Rural China, 1949–1968* (Berkeley, CA: University of California Press, 2000), pp. 320–324.

Russian Civil War (1918–1921) imposed a practical barrier to marriage for millions of women.

Under Stalin in the mid-1930s, the Soviet Communist Party's family policy took a conservative turn, and divorce became markedly more difficult. This change garnered some support among women, many of whom had seen men abuse the concept of "free love" to avoid paying alimony and taking responsibility for their children.[57] In 1935, the Soviet government went a step further, outlawing abortion and recriminalizing homosexuality. Particularly after World War Two, in which the USSR lost over 20 million people, the government's rhetoric became strikingly natalist, with higher birth rates encouraged and "hero mothers" honored in state propaganda. In the early years of the PRC, the Chinese government followed the Soviet model in this regard.

The Marriage Law of 1950 was in many ways a microcosm of New Democracy as a whole. It contained no socialist provisions for replacing the nuclear family and its gendered division of labor with public institutions. The New Democratic family was far closer to the modern bourgeois ideal of nuclear family and monogamous marriage than to the "free love" of the early USSR. In many industrialized countries such as West Germany, France, the Netherlands, and Switzerland family laws continued to stipulate husband or father superiority until the 1970s.[58] It took even longer for most European states to introduce the principle of no-fault divorce, without which women who had neglected their marital duties or taken lovers risked losing any entitlement to alimony if the court decided that the failure of the marriage was their fault. In these respects, the Chinese law of 1950 was well ahead of many Western countries.

The Legacy of the Qing and the New Multi-Ethnic State

The reunification and liberation of the country from foreign domination was central to the CCP's agenda for the New Democratic Revolution. While in the urban centers the party took a hard line against its enemies, on China's periphery it adopted a more flexible and gradualist approach. In doing so it attempted to answer a question that had dogged the Chinese revolution since the fall of the last imperial dynasty in 1911: how was the vast, unwieldy empire the Qing had built to be held together in the modern age? The Guomindang and the CCP were both nationalist parties opposed to all manifestations of Western imperialism in

57 Wendy Z. Goldman, *Women, the State and Revolution: Soviet Family Policy and Social Life 1917–1936* (Cambridge: Cambridge University Press, 1993), pp. 341–342.
58 Göran Therborn, *Between Sex and Power: Family in the World, 1900–2000* (London: Routledge, 2004), p. 100.

China. However, both were also entirely at ease with China's own imperial legacy, including the huge geographical expansion that had pushed the Qing state into non-Han areas on the western periphery. Perhaps unsurprisingly, neither the CCP nor the GMD considered the Qing's westward expansion an imperial project.

The Qing was a multi-ethnic state ruled by the Manchu court. By contrast, the Republican claim to sovereignty after 1911 was modeled on Western ideas of the modern nation state, being premised on defined borders, residents as citizens and the existence of a national "Chinese" identity. Both the revolutionaries of 1911 and, in later years, the GMD realized that this national identity would have to go beyond homogeneous Han culture if they were to have any chance of holding the territories of the Qing Empire together.[59] The weakness of successive Republican governments illustrated the point clearly. Freed from central control, parts of the periphery soon fell away from the Han Chinese heartlands, coming into the hands of warlords (Xinjiang), local theocratic elites (Tibet) and Japanese colonists (Manchuria). Outer Mongolia, meanwhile, became an independent socialist state in 1924 and pursued a close alliance with the neighboring USSR. Even after the defeat of Japan in 1945, the GMD government was unable to establish effective control over these four important parts of the former Qing Empire.

The USSR was a heavy influence on the CCP's approach to the ethnic minorities. In the 1920s and early 1930s, the party modeled its concept of state-building on the Soviet Constitution of 1918 and promoted the idea of a Chinese federal union that would include autonomous republics in Mongolia, Tibet and Xinjiang. These semi-independent polities would protect minority rights to self-determination and regional self-government. However, following the Japanese invasion of Inner China in 1937 the party leadership began to downplay the federalist approach, which was replaced with an emphasis on a multi-nationality United Front.[60] The party's commitment to self-determination morphed into an emphasis on limited autonomy for the national minorities within an unbreakable Greater China. The CCP increasingly pressed anti-imperialist arguments into service in support of its territorial vision. Foreign powers, notably the British in Tibet and the Japanese in Mongolia and Manchuria, had attacked the "unity of the motherland" and the integrity of its borders, which all patriotic citizens were therefore duty-bound to defend.[61]

---

59 James Leibold, *Reconfiguring Chinese Nationalism: How the Qing Frontier and its Indigenes became Chinese* (London: Palgrave, 2007), p. 39.

60 Zhou Minglang, "The Fate of the Soviet Model of Multinational National State-Building in the People's Republic of China," in Thomas Bernstein and Li Hua-yu (eds.), *China Learns from the Soviet Union, 1949–Present* (Lanham, MD: Lexington Books, 2010), p. 480.

61 Zhou Enlai, "Guanyu woguo minzu zhengce de jige wenti," in *JGYL*, Vol. 10, pp. 507–508.

The CCP did, however, accept Stalin's insistence on the independence of Outer Mongolia as the price of cooperation with the Soviet Union.

Given their success in reintegrating Tibet and Xinjiang into the Chinese state, it was arguably the CCP, not the GMD, that was the real successor to the Qing imperial project. It was the CCP, after all, that moved the government back to Beijing, the Ming and Qing capital. Mao's proclamation of the new state was made from the Gate of Heavenly Peace, the entrance to the former royal palaces of the Forbidden City. An image of the gate became part of the national coat of arms, an imperial symbol repurposed for a new age. While the CCP never conducted government business in the Forbidden City, once the threat of GMD air attacks declined the party leadership was headquartered at Zhongnanhai, a former imperial park near the palace complex, where it has remained ever since. The Great Hall of People, seat of the new National People's Congress, was built on Tiananmen Square outside the Gate of Heavenly Peace, integrating national power into the imperial spatial order. In the late 1950s, Tiananmen Square would become the most important symbolic space in the new China, a site of mass rallies and large military parades. The leaders of the CCP did not regard themselves as new emperors, but they made obvious use of the empire's rhetorical and figurative legacy. The party also adopted traditional imperial strategies to strengthen central control over the periphery. Han migration to Xinjiang increased markedly after 1949, and the CCP's initial policies towards Tibet echoed the imperial efforts to integrate the region through alliances with local elites.

The United Front in Tibet

Between 1951 and 1959, Tibetans enjoyed special status within the new People's Republic. This was largely a result of the unique circumstances under which Tibet had been brought back into the Chinese state. In 1913, the region had officially declared its independence. Although this declaration was never recognized internationally, between 1911 and 1950 Tibet arguably was an independent state for all practical purposes, as internal chaos and Japanese occupation left successive Chinese governments too weak to re-establish control.[62] Insulated from Inner China and the Anti-Japanese War by the protective barrier of the Himalayas, Tibet existed as a theocratic state under the Dalai Lama, with most of its land held by monasteries and the local aristocracy. The thirteenth Dalai Lama (1876–1933) initiated reforms intended to construct a modern nation state and education system, but these were thwarted by resistance from the clergy. His

---

62 Melvyn C. Goldstein, *The Snow Lion and the Dragon: China, Tibet, and the Dalai Lama* (Berkeley, CA: University of California Press, 1997), pp. 33–34.

Figure 2.4: Workers enlarging Tiananmen Square.
Source: Photograph by Eva Siao, Museum Ludwig.

successor, the fourteenth Dalai Lama (b. 1935), who was only fourteen years old when the PRC was founded, would himself describe the old system of land ownership in Tibet as "feudal."[63] Local agricultural surpluses were used to

63 Dalai Lama, *My Land and My People* (New York, NY: McGraw-Hill, 1962), p. 67.

support a huge population of Buddhist monks and nuns, few of whom participated in manual labor.

Tibet's de facto independence came to an end with the so-called "peaceful
liberation" of May 1950, sealed by a "17 Point Agreement" between the local
government in Lhasa and the central government in Beijing. To this day, it is
a point of contention whether the Tibetan delegation signed this agreement
voluntarily or was forced to do so under political and military pressure from
the PRC. Under the agreement, the Dalai Lama acknowledged Tibet's "unifica-
tion with the motherland." In return, the Chinese government permitted the
traditional theocracy to remain in power and allowed Tibet the leeway to under-
take economic reforms and political campaigns at its own pace. The agreement
also promised that freedom of religion, local customs and Buddhist monasteries
would be protected. The Tibetan army was to be integrated into the PLA, and
PLA troops would enter Tibet, where the authorities would support them with
a supply of local goods. The Chinese government guaranteed to cover all costs.

Following the agreement, 30,000 PLA troops made the dangerous journey
over the Himalayas to Lhasa by foot or on horseback. Supplying them was
a difficult task. Throughout the early 1950s, it was easier to ship grain from
Guangzhou to India, bring it by train to the foothills of the Himalayas and then
transport it by pack horse over the mountains to Lhasa than to use the shorter
overland route from Sichuan. As Mao argued, this left the Chinese military
presence in Tibet vulnerable to Indian pressure, and building a road over the
Himalayas from Inner China was therefore a top priority.[64] To achieve self-
sufficiency for the Tibetan garrison over the long term, the army also established
a network of state farms. The lack of many Tibetan communist activists and Han
settlers to support the Chinese effort meant that the PLA was forced to take the
lead, and its farms were the first flickering of a state-planned economy in Tibet.
It is interesting to note that many PLA recruits for this and other infrastructure
projects were poor Tibetan women. Their low social status and the refusal of
many Tibetan men to work for the Han made them an ideal resource as the state
sought to integrate the ordinary Tibetan population into the new China.[65]
In 1954, the Dalai Lama and the Panchen Lama (the second most senior figure
in Tibetan Buddhism) were made Vice-Chairmen of the Standing Committee of
the National People's Congress. No other minority leaders were so assiduously
courted by the Chinese government. This period of Sino-Tibetan relations was

---

64 Mao Zedong, "Guanyu Xizang gongzuo de fangzhen," in Zhonggong zhongyang wenxian
yanjiushi (ed.), *Mao Zedong Xizang gongzuo wenxuan* (Beijing: Zhongyang wenxian chubanshe, 2008), p. 62.
65 Emily Yeh, *Taming Tibet: Landscape Transformation and the Gift of Chinese Development*
(Ithaca, NY: Cornell University Press, 2013), p. 91.

Figure 2.5: A young 14th Dalai Lama.
Source: Photograph by Eva Siao, Museum Ludwig.

comparable to the situation under the Qing, when the center had used local elites to rule the periphery and left space for indigenous laws and customs. For several years following the 17 Point Agreement, the CCP did not promote social revolution in Tibet nor attempt to change local landlords' and monasteries' treatment of the peasantry. Instead, the government acknowledged that the transformation to socialism would require more time in minority regions, expressing the hope that Tibet could be incorporated peacefully and Tibetans won over to become loyal citizens of a multi-ethnic new China. In line with Beijing's undertakings under the Agreement, the feudal and religious elites were permitted to remain in power as long as they were not implicated in rebellion against the state.

The Tibetan elite was sharply divided on whether to cooperate with the Chinese government and carry out its proposed reforms. The CCP hoped that the young Dalai Lama would side with them against conservative forces. In 1952, Mao provided a glimpse of the party's rationale for the go-slow in Tibet, arguing that Land Reform and rent reduction should not be sought in the region within the next three years because, in contrast to the situation in Xinjiang, no Han Chinese settlers were available in the region to support the center.[66] Before 1959 the Chinese government seems to have had no intention to change its gradualist strategy or abandon the United Front with the Tibetan elites around the Dalai Lama. We should recall that this was a geographical rather than a strictly ethnic approach. The special arrangements for Tibet did not encompass Tibetan-populated areas in the provinces of Qinghai, Sichuan, Gansu and Yunnan, where Land Reform and collectivization were implemented almost in lockstep with Han parts of the country.

Xinjiang: Control and Development through Han Settlement

CCP policies towards Xinjiang were strikingly different from those adopted in Tibet. Uyghur nationalism had developed in some parts of the region, and between 1944 and 1949 a short-lived, Soviet-backed East Turkestan Republic existed in three districts around Ili in the north of the region. The CCP's victory in the Chinese Civil War saw Stalin abandon his support for the Uyghur national-ists, and Xinjiang was "peacefully liberated," with the PLA meeting little resis-tance as its troops marched westwards.

Xinjiang lies 3,500 kilometers from Beijing and is separated from the Chinese heartland by a vast expanse of desert. Covering around 1.6 million square kilo-meters, the region is the largest political unit of the PRC by area and is home to a multi-ethnic population consisting of thirteen officially recognized groups. In the early 1950s, the Han Chinese accounted for only 6 to 7 percent of the 5 million inhabitants of the region, while Muslim groups (mainly Uyghurs) composed around 75 percent of the total.[67] In 1949 the CCP had only 3,000

---

66 Mao Zedong, "Guanyu Xizang gongzuo de fangzhen," p. 62.
67 Donald H. McMillen, "Xinjiang and the Production and Construction Corps: A Han Organisation in a Non-Han Region," *The Australian Journal of Chinese Affairs*, No.6 (1981), p. 66.

registered members in the whole province.[68] Under these circumstances, establishing control over this large and geographically challenging region, particularly its 3,000-kilometer border with the Soviet Union, presented a serious problem for the party. Especially in times of crisis, this frontier was almost entirely porous, with Kazakh nomads and others moving freely between Chinese and Soviet territory.

As elsewhere, the party initially proposed a form of control based on a United Front with local elites. Compared to Tibet, however, representatives of the Uyghurs enjoyed little influence in government. With no special agreement to delay the CCP's socio-economic revolution, Land Reform was enforced in the early 1950s. As it did in Tibet, the PLA played a central role in the new order, but in Xinjiang its work consisted mainly of supporting large-scale Han Chinese in-migration. In 1952, Mao made patriotic appeals to demobilized soldiers to volunteer to stay in "backward" areas to help build the new China. Initially over 100,000 soldiers were demobilized as part of a program to reclaim agricultural land and build new homes, infrastructure and industries. In 1954 the project was given formal shape in the guise of the newly established Xinjiang Production and Construction Corps (XPCC). This body, known informally as "the corps" (*bingtuan*), also had a role in public security, riot suppression and border control. The party's use of the XPCC echoed strategies of periphery control with considerable historical pedigree. The late Qing government in particular had used hybrid agricultural and military settlements (*tuntian*) to expand its control beyond the Gansu corridor into Xinjiang. The CCP also had its own tradition of producer armies, carried over from the pre-1949 revolutionary base areas.

The size of the corps increased from 175,451 in 1954 to 311,470 in 1957.[69] The overwhelming majority of this substantial labor force was Han. Many were former GMD soldiers hoping to secure better treatment by joining up, but some Han from Inner China also volunteered for patriotic reasons. In the early 1950s, conditions for those living and working in the desert or other remote areas were often exceptionally hard, and new arrivals had to build houses and reclaim land for themselves. As was the case with the PLA soldiers who had crossed the Himalayas into Tibet, the corps' fight against the desert was transformed by CCP propaganda into a heroic narrative of self-sacrifice for the motherland. Han soldiers and settlers were depicted as friendly helpers of the local population.

68 Hauke Neddermann, *Sozialismus in Xinjiang: Das Produktions- und Aufbaukorps in den 1950er Jahren* (Berlin: Lit Verlag, 2010), p. 35.
69 Ibid., p. 115.

A particular challenge to the smooth running of the corps was the question of gender imbalance. In 1953, the Central Military Commission devised a five-year plan to recruit 99,300 women from Inner China to migrate to the new PLA farms.[70] Relatives of landlords and rich peasants who had been suppressed as counterrevolutionaries could volunteer to become workers and wives in Xinjiang, offering a rare opportunity for these women to escape their family backgrounds.

The establishment of the corps turned out to be a highly successful strategy, allowing the new state to fashion a network of developments projecting para-military control out to the remote border regions. Whole new cities such as Shihezi sprung up in previously lawless areas. The policies of the CCP in Xinjiang were obviously in line with the imperial tradition of combined agricultural and military settlements. However, they also bore similarities to the Soviet Union's policies, themselves built in certain ways on the imperial legacy of the tsars. Stalin supported Russian resettlement in the Far East as a strategy to promote industrial development and establish control. In 1949 he advised Chinese leaders to raise the Han population in Xinjiang from 5 to 30 percent through massive, ethnically targeted migration,[71] and sure enough by 1964 the region's Han population had risen to 31 percent.[72] In contrast to European colonial activity in North America and Australia, Han settlers did not drive the native population from their land, nor were Uyghurs and Kazakhs killed by the incoming Han. Instead the network of new oases was established parallel to the Uyghur and Kazakh economy. The local population benefited from new schools, roads, and hospitals but played only a minor role in the workforce of the state economy. It is abundantly clear that, from the first, the central government trusted Han Chinese, even former GMD soldiers, much more than the non-Han local population. The foundations for state control through Han settlement and marginalization of the minority population were laid in the early 1950s.

In a few short years following the foundation of the new China, the CCP had achieved what all nationalist leaders, including Sun Yat-sen and Chiang Kai-shek, had sought since 1911: the reunification of the state almost to the borders of the old Qing Empire, including the non-Han periphery in Tibet and Xinjiang. On its own terms, the new revolutionary government was extremely successful during its early years.

---

70 James Z. Gao, "The Call of the Oases: The 'Peaceful Liberation' of Xinjiang, 1949–53," in Jeremy Brown and Paul G. Pickowicz (eds.), *Dilemmas of Victory: The Early Years of the People's Republic of China* (Cambridge, MA: Harvard University Press, 2007), p. 202.
71 Ibid., p. 190. 72 Neddermann, *Sozialismus in Xinjiang*, p. 44.

DOCUMENT 2.1 The District Party Committee of Wan County, Sichuan.

Behaviors that seriously violate the law and discipline have been covered up

[Xinhua News Agency Southwest Branch]: Last year during the Three Anti and Five Anti Campaigns in Wan City and County, Sichuan province, shocking behaviors of compelling orders by force that seriously violated the law and [party] discipline were covered up for nearly a year.

First, the evident violations of law and discipline. Brutal torture was applied to extract confessions and more than 60 methods of torture were utilized, including hanging up of prisoners, [forced] kneeling, heating, freezing, starving, kicking, lashing, beating with a stick or a rope, use of handcuffs, locking prisoners in a dungeon, standing them in toilets, electric shocks, burning of the beard, confinement in one place, clutching of the hair, hanging by the hair, the "three-point line," pricking the face with a needle, branding with a burning fire-tong, jamming of the fingers, burning with joss sticks, "knocking screw bones," "eating meat in a pod," "sitting in the tiger chair," "locking in the tiger cage," use of the airplane method, "monkeys moving wood piles," hanging firewood on the nipples, and forced inhalation of pepper juice or soapy water through the nose or mouth. Many of these torture methods had been used by the Guomindang special agents.

Source: *Neibu Cankao*, March 21, 1953.

DOCUMENT 2.2 Suicide and escape of party members during the rectification campaigns in Dongbei.

[Xinhua News Agency Northeast Branch]: In a few counties and districts in Dongbei, the basic principles of rectification have not yet been adopted, and some mistakes were made during the first round of training. In some districts, there was a lack of positive education for party members in training, and instead attacks and criticisms were often directed at them. Great effort was made to investigate matters such as the personal histories and personal relationships of party members and to use these to apply pressure to them. A few rectification cadres even held the attitude of "fighting the tiger" and adopted a strategy of "chasing, forcing, and besieging," which resulted in panic among some party members, a number of whom committed suicide and escaped.

According to telephone reports to the Party Rectification Committee for Rural Northeast China (the Northeast Bureau), six party members have committed suicide (two from Heilongjiang and one each from Songjiang, Liaodong, Liaoxi and Rehe); four party members attempted suicide but did not succeed (two each from Jilin and Rehe); and one escaped (Rehe). For example, You Chunfang, the party secretary of Dasizhong Village, Chaoyang County, Rehe had been a poor peasant without any problems in his political background. Simply because he was not very enthusiastic about his job and not show solidarity at the party branch, You offended party member Jiao Yongan. Jiao retaliated against You by claiming that "You Chunfang used to be a bandit in Japanese occupied Manchuria, and he also had illicit sexual relations with three women." You immediately replied with tears in his eyes, "Anyone's luck can turn! What else do you want to accuse me of? Bring it on!" In order to end this confrontation, the cadre in charge of the training had to say: "This is nothing,

DOCUMENT 2.2 (cont.)

it does not matter." After the training, You returned home and hanged himself from a tree outside his village. When training was carried out in Fuyu County, Heilongjiang, party members were asked to confess before they were re-educated. Having confessed that he engaged in corruption and illicit sexual relations, party member Li Guisheng was made an example for the training class. Li then committed suicide out of shame. In other counties and districts, labels were given to persecuted party members, whose [self-]justifications were all rejected. In Chengquercun Village, Longhua County, Rehe, some party members, when forced too hard [to confess], attempted to commit suicide by eating green onions with honey (poisonous when eaten together). Having been stopped in time, they eventually escaped.

In order to avoid the same problems, the CCP Central Committee of the Northeast Bureau has informed the local branches to correct these mistakes.

Source: *Neibu Cankao*, January 31, 1953.

3 THE TRANSFORMATION TO STATE SOCIALISM (1953-1957)

苏联的今天是我们的明天
The Soviet today is our tomorrow

百花齐放、百家争鸣
Let a hundred flowers bloom; let a hundred schools of thought contend

把心交给党
Give your heart to the party

Zhang Chengjue was a student at Jiaotong University in Shanghai when the Anti-Rightist Campaign began in 1957. A matter of weeks earlier, he, like many others, had answered a call from the CCP leadership to help the party identify shortcomings in China's social and political system. As a supporter of the socialist cause, Zhang responded in good faith, suggesting that the country would benefit from a relaxation of party committees' dominance over academic and political life. He was as surprised as anyone to find himself labeled a "rightist" in January 1958, and to be attacked on big-character posters (*dazibao*) and in meetings. Under pressure, Zhang attempted to protect himself by denouncing other students for secretly listening to broadcasts from the US-government–financed Radio Free Asia.

Zhang had a complicated family background. He had been born in Hong Kong in 1939, but his father hailed originally from the city of Dongguan in Guangdong province. Zhang senior, a practicing lawyer and businessman, had worked for the local GMD government in Guangzhou (Canton), but after the founding of the PRC two of Zhang's brothers served as cadres in the new government and the armed forces. In light of the family's contribution to the revolutionary state, Zhang's father assumed it would be safe to return to Dongguan, only to find himself classified as a landlord during the Land Reform campaign. Zhang senior was eventually executed for resisting delivering surplus grain to the government.

Taking this checkered background into account, it is remarkable that Zhang ever managed to gain admission to Jiaotong University, a prestigious institution with a focus on science and engineering. However, his good fortune ended with the Anti-Rightist Campaign. Although his student status was not formally revoked, he was sent to perform manual labor under surveillance in the suburbs of Shanghai, and the resultant bout of depression led him to drop out.

To improve his political situation, Zhang signed up with other Shanghai "rightists" to go to Xinjiang with the Construction Corps (see Chapter 2). There he was assigned to a machinery factory near Urumqi, the provincial capital, until in 1961 the party decided that his rightist label could be provisionally removed, a process referred to colloquially as "taking off the hat." Believing that he was no longer considered an enemy of the people, Zhang contacted his brother in Shanghai to find out if he could return to university. His request was denied, however, and it was a year before a bout of dropsy brought on by malnutrition led to his being sent home to Guangdong for rest and medical treatment. In 1966, the Guangdong authorities decided to send him back to Xinjiang, where he served for almost a decade as a worker before being taken on as a teacher in 1975. It was during this period that Zhang finally married. His wife, who came from a peasant background, agreed to marry him without knowing of his status as a "rightist who had taken off the hat."

As in other similar cases, it was left to the institution that had labeled Zhang to decide whether to fully rehabilitate him. In 1979, the party committee at Jiaotong University revised its original verdict, enabling Zhang to leave Xinjiang for Guangzhou in 1982. In 1988 he moved to Hong Kong, where, until recently, he wrote and published material criticizing the Anti-Rightist Campaign. Discussing his fate after 1957, Zhang references one of the classics of Mao-era literature: "In the opera *The White Haired Girl*, it is said: 'The old society turned humans into ghosts, but the new society turns ghosts into humans' . . . It should say it turns humans into worms."[1] The CCP may have rehabilitated Zhang, but its treatment of him during the Anti-Rightist Campaign and the two subsequent decades meant that it never managed to recapture his loyalty.

The period between 1953 and 1957 saw the most fundamental social revolution of the entire Mao era. In these four years, the party initiated a "socialist transformation," moving the country away from private ownership of the means of production towards a Soviet-style planned economy. By the end of 1956, industry and trade had been integrated into the state economy and peasants were organized into agricultural collectives. Unsurprisingly, the scale of the change led to widespread opposition. In the cities, conflict emerged between workers and the party over the question of representation and the role of labor

---

1 Zhang Chengjue, *Liushi yunian jiaguo: Wode youpai xinlu licheng* (Hong Kong: Kehua tushu chuban gongsi, 2006), p. 313; Interview with the author, Vienna (Austria), March 2013.

unions. In the countryside, the establishment of a state monopoly over the grain market met with massive peasant resistance.

After the elimination of capitalists and landlords as economic classes, the party began to debate abolishing the system of class status itself. This apparent success, however, did not prevent the government establishing a nationwide network of labor camps, operational by the mid-1950s, to re-educate "enemies of the people" through manual labor. In the late 1950s, attempts to solicit comments on party rule from intellectuals and to "reform" undesirable patterns of thinking led to a particularly fearsome crackdown on dissent in the Anti-Rightist Campaign. This movement, which saw huge numbers of intellectuals condemned for allegedly anti-socialist views, marked the end of the de facto United Front between the party and the intelligentsia.

Industrial Workers: Under the Party's Wing?

Workers in Maoist China enjoyed a higher level of prestige than any other officially recognized class. In the language of the CCP, "workers" (*gongren*) was a relatively exclusive term, referring only to the permanent workforce of industrial work units, who the party celebrated as "masters of the country." In the early days of the PRC this was a highly select group: in 1951, Zhou Enlai estimated that there were 3 to 4 million industrial workers across the whole of China, accounting for less than 1 percent of the population.[2] Most modern industry was located in Shanghai and Manchuria.

Labor had had a difficult relationship with successive Chinese governments. In the first half of the 1920s, labor movements had begun to develop in the cities and large strikes had broken out. Antagonism between workers and the state reached a peak in 1927, when a GMD massacre of communists and labor activists dealt organized labor a blow from which it never fully recovered. Urban labor movements would play only a minor role in the Chinese Civil War and the 1949 revolution. As the PLA liberated China's cities, the CCP's outreach to workers was limited to calls to maintain production and ensure they deferred to the party's representatives. Once the new PRC government was established, the CCP restricted representation of workers to the party-backed All China Federation of Trade Unions. In the first years of the new China, urban unemployment remained high. Social security and welfare entitlements were introduced, but only for the permanent workforce of the state-owned enterprises.

---

2 Zhou Enlai, "Guanyu zhishifenzi de gaizao wenti," in Zhongyang wenxian chubanshe (ed.), *Jianguo yilai zhongyao wenxian xuanbian* (Beijing: Zhongyang wenxian chubanshe, 1992) (hereinafter "*JGYL*"), Vol. 2, p. 446.

Figure 3.1: Workers' poster, 1975, Guangzhou. The text proclaims: "We are the masters of the country."
Source: Photograph by Helmut Opletal.

A number of scholars have pointed to continuities between the CCP's approach to managing the urban workforce and that adopted by the GMD before 1949. The establishment of official labor unions and workers' militias under party leadership were both Nationalist innovations, as was the system of work units, which the GMD had set up during the Anti-Japanese War.[3] The party's initial emphasis on increasing production, work discipline, and mutual benefits for labor and capital in a mixed economy had much in common with corporatist regimes across the globe. Evidence from case studies adds to the impression of continuity with the old regime. Archival research on the silk industry in the city of Wuxi has shown that male overseers from the pre-1949 period, some of whom were known to have viciously beaten female workers, were left in charge of shop floors for several years after the communist victory.[4] Workers who had taken the promise of "liberation" seriously were

---

3 For details see: Elizabeth Perry, "Masters of the Country? Shanghai Workers in the Early People's Republic," in Jeremy Brown and Paul G. Pickowicz (eds.), *Dilemmas of Victory: The Early Years of the People's Republic of China* (Cambridge, MA: Harvard University Press, 2007), p. 78; Mark W. Frazier, *The Making of the Chinese Industrial Workplace: State, Revolution and Labor Management* (Cambridge: Cambridge University Press, 2002).

4 Robert Cliver, *Red Silk: Class, Gender, and Revolution in China's Yangzi Delta Silk Industry* (unpublished manuscript, Cambridge, MA: Harvard University Asia Center, forthcoming 2019).

often disappointed that so little had changed, and many believed that the revolution had failed to live up to all its early promise. In Shanghai, labor unrest and strikes in the early years of the PRC put the government under sustained and unwelcome pressure. Against this background, how are we to understand the CCP's lofty assertion that workers were now "masters of the country?" The claim makes sense only in the context of the party's Marxist-Leninist ideology. Marx had argued that, prior to the proletarian revolution that would begin the transition to socialism, the bourgeoisie would seize power from the feudal classes and replace the system of feudal exploitation with one of capitalist exploitation, of which the bourgeoisie itself would be the primary beneficiary.[5] The working class would then lead a second revolution that would result not only in the liberation of the workers, but, through the overthrow of the capitalist system, of mankind as a whole. Thus, the proletariat was the ultimate liberating class, expected not only to seize power, but to abolish class structures and exploitation entirely.

During the Chinese revolution of 1949, peasants had played a much more important role than the urban population. Urban workers, however, represented the future of the communist cause and a key element of the industrialized, socialist country the CCP was seeking to build. In line with the rest of the socialist bloc in Eastern Europe, the party in the 1950s saw workers as the most progressive class. Industrial laborers worked with advanced technologies in the factories of urban China, and their social relations were thought to be based less on kinship structures than on class solidarity, built through collective experiences of strikes and class struggle on the shop floor. The growth in the number of industrial workers in state industries after 1949 therefore amounted to an expansion of the pool of future socialists. After private ownership of land and means of production were abolished, everyone was to be a worker.

In short, the CCP's descriptions of "mastery of the country" grew out of the workers' theoretical role in the construction of socialism and the expectation that, as the new China modernized, the working class would inexorably expand with it. On these terms, "mastery" did not necessarily equate to governing authority. In fact, the party constitutions of 1945, 1969 and 1973 defined the CCP not as the servant of the working class but as its "vanguard."[6] The party was the mouthpiece, not of the transient, subjective desires that workers might themselves express, but of their deeper, objective interests. Building a communist future required the party to inculcate "class consciousness" into the workers,

---

5 Karl Marx and Friedrich Engels, *Manifesto of the Communist Party* (1848), www.marxists.org /archive/marx/works/1848/communist-manifesto/cho1.htm#007 (accessed March 3, 2017).
6 Zhongguo geming bowuguan (ed.), *Zhongguo gongchandang dangzhang huibian* (Beijing: Renmin chubanshe, 1979), pp. 46, 206, 212.

encouraging them to act according to the laws of historical development that would lead mankind towards communism.

Hand in hand with this went a need to strengthen the proletarian character of the party, a goal that required continual struggle against the negative ideological influence of the petty bourgeoisie and peasant smallholders. Workers had to be systematically trained to become cadres and leaders to replace officials from the old regime. The CCP under Mao adopted a narrative that viewed purging "class enemies" and fighting against leftist or rightist deviation as a way for the party to purify itself. While only the most advanced and revolutionary workers could become party members, all workers in state-owned enterprises were automatically enrolled in official labor unions. These were the "schools of communism" that would educate and raise the political consciousness of all workers, acting, in Lenin's formulation, as the link between the vanguard and the masses.[7] This link worked in both directions. On the one hand, the best trade union talent could be recruited into the party-state apparatus. On the other, unions were expected to implement government policies, enforce labor discipline and organize welfare in work units.

Labor Unions: Conflicts over Representation

Conflicts over the role of the labor unions in 1953 show that the party did not always get its way when it came to the working class. A report by the official labor unions to the Central Committee in August of that year described a steady drumbeat of strikes, work slowdowns, and collective petitioning by workers. These incidents had taken place from January to June in major cities across the country, and workers in industries from construction to transport and mining had been involved. In some particularly severe incidents, party cadres had been rounded up and beaten by the massed workers. Even self-proclaimed "representatives of the workers," supposedly the party's people, were making demands on the state.

Most of the strikes and other incidents had grown out of dissatisfaction with wages and welfare, and cadres were criticized for dealing with them by official sanction rather than engagement – the twin errors of "bureaucratism" and "commandism." The August union report also singles out the actions of "counterrevolutionaries," who took advantage of wage and welfare problems in some industries to sow dissent. Further problems were allegedly being caused by "feudal labor contractors," some of whom continued to work actively on behalf

7 V. I. Lenin, "The Trade Unions, The Present Situation and Trotsky's Mistakes," (1920), www .marxists.org/archive/lenin/works/1920/dec/30.htm (accessed September 18, 2017).

of the enemy.[8] The report argued that strikes could be avoided by strengthening the leadership of party committees in the labor unions, alongside efforts to improve "management style" by paying better attention to workers' demands.

In the early 1950s, the role of labor unions under socialism was still controversial. Unions could represent workers' interests against private capital, but state-owned enterprises were another matter. In January 1953, the Central Committee dismissed the chair of the All China Federation of Trade Unions, Li Lisan, on the grounds of "trade unionism" and "economism" (*jingjizhuyi*). The first label meant that Li was guilty of seeing the unions, not the party, as the most important representative of the workers. Li had failed to respect the leadership of the CCP: as the decision put it, "he does not understand that in the state-owned enterprises no class antagonism and exploitation exists. The interests of the individuals and the state are similar."[9] "Economism," meanwhile, meant that Li had promoted workers' material interests, such as higher wages and welfare, above long-term goals such as increased production, which the party had designated as the "central task."

Following Li's dismissal, a wider campaign against "trade unionism" saw the unions brought under stricter party control. His departure also had a highly symbolic effect. Li was an old hand: in the first half of 1920, he had led general strikes in the mining area of Anyuan, giving the CCP its first experience with mass movements. In 1930 he had served as the leader of the CCP, and even in the 1950s he remained a potent symbol of the Republican era workers' movement. After the founding of the PRC, he served as the first Minister of Labor and chairman of the unions. His removal severed the new state's link to the old labor movement and established the primacy of the party. In Shanghai, other high-ranking union cadres who had been leaders in the pre-1949 days were removed from office in 1953 and replaced by cadres with no connection to the city's old communist unions.[10] In line with Beijing's wishes, the new crop of outsiders, none of whom

---

8 "Quanguo zonggonghui dangzu, 'Guanyu jiaqiang dang zaijianzhu, banyun, kuangshan deng chanyezhong de gongzuo, xiaochu gezhong zaocheng gongren bagong, qingyuan shijian de kongxi xiang zhongyang de baogao'," August (1953), in Song Yongyi (ed.), *Database of the Chinese Political Campaigns in the 1950s: From Land Reform to the State–Private Partnership, 1949–1956*, CD-ROM (Hong Kong: Universities Service Centre for China Studies, The Chinese University of Hong Kong, 2014).

9 "Zhonggong zhongyang, 'Zhuanfa zhonggong quanguo zonggonghui dangzu kuodahui guanyu quanguo zonggonghui gongzuo jueyi'," January 5, 1953, in Song Yongyi (ed.), *Database of the Chinese Political Campaigns in the 1950s: From Land Reform to the State–Private Partnership, 1949–1956*, CD-ROM (Hong Kong: Universities Service Centre for China Studies, The Chinese University of Hong Kong, 2014).

10 Nara Dillon, *Radical Inequalities: China's Revolutionary Welfare State in Comparative Perspective* (Cambridge, MA: Harvard East Asian Monographs, 2015), pp. 175–176.

enjoyed a wide base of local support, proved less able to challenge the central government.

The party leadership's attacks on "trade unionism" recall the debate on the role of labor unions in Soviet Russia in 1920 and 1921. Then, Leon Trotsky had argued that the main task of labor unions under socialism would be the enforcement of discipline through the militarization of the workforce. In the new "state of the workers and peasants," the extra protections afforded by unions under capitalism would be unnecessary. Other leaders, convinced that the working class should not be able strike against itself, called for industrial action to be outlawed. Lenin, on the other hand, argued against Trotsky, asserting that although the Soviet regime would be a "worker and peasant state," bureaucratic excess would still lead to occasional instances of injustice. The new Soviet state's small, poorly educated population of industrial workers could not necessarily be expected to hold their own against the government bureaucracy, particularly when that bureaucracy was largely still staffed with officials from the old regime. In addition to these obviously difficult holdovers from the tsar's day, new bureaucrats drawn from among the party's own had already begun to develop bad habits and were no longer focusing single-mindedly on the needs of workers. As a result, Lenin argued that during the transition from capitalism to socialism workers would still require unions to protect their interests vis-à-vis the state.[11]

In 1950s China, industrial workers were not able to access independent forms of representation. Nevertheless, many benefited significantly from the socialist transformation. For millions, the founding of the PRC brought safe jobs and entitlement to welfare. The number of Chinese citizens enjoying official worker status rose dramatically between 1949 and 1957, as relatively lax controls on internal migration allowed the urban population to boom. Over this period, the population of China's cities and towns rose from 57.6 to 99.4 million,[12] while the workforce in state-owned enterprises tripled from 8 to 24 million. For those who managed to become part of this permanent workforce inside the system, the PRC's promise of upward social mobility was a genuine reality. For the rest of their life, they were entitled to secure employment, welfare, food rations, free health care and cheap housing. Their official retirement age was 55 years for women and 60 years for men, and they could be reasonably confident that at least one of their children would be able to join their work unit in adulthood. Beyond the state sector, the workforce in collectively owned enterprises also expanded

---

11 For the debate see: Lenin, "The Trade Unions"; Leon Trotsky, "Terrorism and Communism: A Reply to Karl Kautsky" (1920), www.marxists.org/archive/trotsky/1920/terrcomm/ch08.htm (accessed September 18, 2017).

12 Lu Yu, *Xin Zhongguo renkou wushi nian* (Beijing: Zhongguo renkou chubanshe, 2004), Vol. 1, p. 633.

rapidly, from 230,000 in 1952 to 6.5 million people in 1957.[13] As we have seen, the work unit system was not an invention of the CCP, but had its origins in Republican China and the Soviet Union. Nevertheless, it was under the CCP's rule that almost the entire urban population became part of the system, with social life, sport and cultural activities all collectively organized by work units for their members. For those on the inside, the new regime brought tangible benefits, and these success stories of the early PRC should not be overlooked.

Capitalists and the Transition to State Socialism

In 1953, the government announced its first Five Year Plan, aimed at transforming China into a modern industrial nation. By that time, communist parties around the world had come to consider the Soviet-style planned economy as the most appropriate model for a poor agrarian country seeking to develop at pace. Rational, scientific planning of the economy was seen as more advanced than the "anarchy" found in capitalist markets, where periodic crises caused by over-production resulted in high unemployment, poverty, the closing of factories and the destruction of means of production. Communist parties argued that a planned economy could liberate mankind from the cycle of crisis and unemployment by defining prices for raw materials and consumer goods and setting production quotas for each sector and work unit. Chinese leaders, like their Soviet counterparts, believed that the development of heavy industry was key, not only for the country's industrial future but also to provide for the national defense. During the First Five Year Plan, 88.8 percent of all investments in the industrial sector went towards heavy industry, with only 11.2 put into light industry.[14] Soviet experts played an important role in advising on the design of key projects. Of these projects, 156 in total, forty-four were related to the defense industry, twenty to steel, fifty-two to energy, twenty-four to machinery, and ten to chemical industries.[15] In particular, steel was seen as the industry of modernity since it provided the raw material for machines, railways and tanks.

In September 1954, the National People's Congress passed the first Constitution of the PRC, defining the state's immediate goals as transformation to socialism, the elimination of exploitation in general, the elimination of the rich

---

13 Zhonggong zhongyang shujichu yanjiushi lilunzu (ed.), *Dangqian woguo gongren jieji zhuang-kuang diaocha ziliao huibian* (Beijing: Zhonggong zhongyang dangxiao chubanshe, 1983), Vol. 2. pp. 105–107.

14 Maurice Meisner, *Mao's China and After: A History of the People's Republic* (New York, NY: The Free Press, 1999), p. 112.

15 Wu Ping, "Diyige wunian jihua he guojia gongyehua jianshe," in Guo Dehong, Wang Haiguang and Han Gang (eds.), *Zhonghua renmin gongheguo zhuanti shigao (juan yi): kaiguo chuangye (1949–1956)* (Chengdu: Sichuan renmin chubanshe, 2004), pp. 409–412.

Figure 3.2: Demonstration on Tiananmen Square on the October 1 National Day holiday.
Source: Photograph by Eva Siao, Museum Ludwig.

peasant economy and the replacement of capitalist ownership. The constitution declared that all citizens aged eighteen and above were to have equal voting rights, regardless of gender, occupation, social status, education, religion or property. Articles 85 and 86 affirmed that all were equal before the law, although those suffering from mental illness could be deprived of their political rights, as could anyone who had been stripped of these rights through the appropriate legal procedure. Citizens were guaranteed religious freedom, along with freedom of speech, publication, assembly and demonstration (articles 87, 88 and 89); unlawful arrest was prohibited. All citizens were given the right to work, education and social welfare. All in all, the 1954 constitution was more inclusive than the "democratic dictatorship of the people," which Mao had spoken of in 1949, and his suggestion of a blanket loss of political rights for all "class enemies" was conspicuously absent (see Chapter 2 for detail).[16]

The government initiated a campaign to discuss the draft constitution in public, including through the press and the urban work units. Archival documents show that the content of the draft caused considerable confusion among

16 "Zhonghua renmin gongheguo xianfa (1954 nian)," www.npc.gov.cn/wxzl/wxzl/2000-12/26/content_4264.htm (accessed June 6, 2017).

both cadres and ordinary people. In the early 1950s, it remained common for critiques of the CCP's record to be aired quite openly,[17] and criticism of the 1954 draft centered around the obvious contradiction between the promise of civil rights for all and the repressive measures already being practiced by the state organs. Further unease was expressed over whether capitalists could really be equal citizens, as envisaged by the constitution, when the same document called for an end to capital's control of the means of production.

In the early days of the First Five Year Plan, private enterprises continued to exist, but by 1954 the government had mandated the establishment of companies based on so-called "joint public–private operations." Private entrepreneurs were promised leading positions in these new ventures, along with compensation with interest for their losses. Instead of a violent revolution, the transformation to socialism envisaged here was a gradual one. The next step was to transform the mixed companies into state-owned enterprises. In 1955, Liu Shaoqi declared that, rather than doing so by expropriation, China would adopt a less adversarial strategy for corporate acquisitions. In contrast to Eastern Europe, where governments had driven private enterprises into bankruptcy by denying them raw materials and contracts for work, in China the official media were full of reports of capitalists voluntarily joining public–private operations.[18]

Some of this apparent willingness to cooperate with the government likely stemmed from the fact that, by the mid-1950s, it had become extremely difficult to operate private enterprises without the goodwill of the party. The depredations of the Five-Anti Campaign had left many business owners in fear. By showing loyalty to the new order, they hoped to avoid being labeled enemies of the people and so escape the suffering that had been meted out to landlords in the countryside. Some may even have imagined a professional career managing a state-owned enterprise, where a combination of good salaries and the compensation package promised by the government would allow them to continue to enjoy high living standards.

Early signs were encouraging. In 1955, Mao declared that capitalists should be given jobs and keep their political rights, in contrast to "landlords," who constituted a threat to the new order and should be kept fed but lose their rights.[19]

17 Neil J. Diamant and Feng Xiaocai, "The PRC's First National Critique: The 1954 Campaign to 'Discuss the Draft Constitution'," *The China Journal*, Vol. 73 (2015), pp. 1–37.

18 Gao Huamin, "Nongye, shougongye he zibenzhuyi gongshangye de shehuizhuyi gaizao," in Guo Dehong, Wang Haiguang and Han Gang (eds.), *Zhonghua renmin gongheguo zhuanti shigao (juan yi): kaiguo chuangye (1949–1956)* (Chengdu: Sichuan renmin chubanshe, 2004), p. 463.

19 Mao Zedong, "Gongshangyezhe yao zhangwo ziji de mingyun," in *Mao Zedong Wenji* (Beijing: Renmin chubanshe, 1999), Vol. 6, pp. 490–491.

At the same time, the CCP promised that capitalists who agreed to work for the state would be reclassified as workers after three five-year plans.[20] Some entrepreneurs, particularly those whose businesses were struggling, welcomed the opportunity to be paid by the state rather than taking their chances on the open market. In many cases it was those on the very lowest rungs of the ladder, craftsmen and peddlers, who struggled the most. They were not counted as capitalists and were organized directly into collectives; between the mid-1950s and the 1970s, legal opportunities to conduct petty trade essentially disappeared. In industry, handicrafts and trade, the transition to socialism was a top-down affair, guided and organized by the CCP. Change was relatively peaceful, but those designated capitalists had little choice but to welcome socialism and hope that they could keep their citizen status.

"Reform through Labor" and the World of the Camps

As we have seen, the party's early approach to dealing with "capitalists" was in many cases relatively tolerant. Landlords faced harsh treatment, but in other areas the emphasis tended to be on New Democracy and gradual change towards socialism. Nevertheless, the first half of the 1950s saw a massive expansion of the state's public security capacity, in particular the penal system. Towards the end of the Qing dynasty and during the Republican period under the GMD, moves had been made to establish a modern prison system, including a network of workhouses and labor camps. These trends continued in the early PRC. Several hundred thousand people were formally executed during the campaigns of the new state's early years. However, most party leaders in this period favored giving "class enemies" a chance at rehabilitation. Mao's 1949 threat of forced labor for "reactionary people"[21] should be seen in the context of contemporary communist beliefs about the link between labor and so-called "Thought Reform." Not only was labor the only way to turn people into productive members of society, but, by experiencing the hardships and pleasures of creation through work, the former exploiter or criminal could come to understand the suffering of the masses and the "parasitic" nature of their own former life. Forced labor was not simply punitive but also instructive.

The new criminal justice system distinguished between "labor re-education" (*laodong jiaoyang*) and "reform through labor" (*laodong gaizao*, in short

---

20 Feng Xiaocai, "Zhengzhi shengcun yu jingji shengcun: Shanghai shangren ruhe zoushang gongsi heying zhilu? (1949–1957)," in Han Gang (ed.), *Zhongguo dangdaishi yanjiu (er)* (Beijing: Jiuzhou chubanshe, 2011), p. 120.

21 Mao Zedong, "Lun renmin minzhu zhuanzheng," in *Mao Zedong Xuanji*, Vol. 4, p. 1414.

laogai). "Labor re-education" was an administrative sanction and could be imposed by work units or the police for minor crimes. Offenders could be sent to "labor re-education" for a maximum of three years without any involvement from the courts. More serious crimes called for *laogai*, which involved longer sentences and internment in a labor camp. The CCP viewed the justice system as an extension of the "people's democratic dictatorship," and the class status of the offender therefore played an important role in sentencing.

By 1951, the new government had begun building a nationwide network of labor camps, with a total capacity far outstripping anything seen under the GMD. Many of these camps were located in remote areas in western China. In some locations in the desert, no walls or fences were built to keep inmates in, since conditions were so extreme that escape would mean almost certain death. Research on the *laogai* camps has been limited, especially compared to the *gulag* system in the Soviet Union, and a lack of access to archives has made any work on the topic a challenge.[22] It is clear, however, that the camp system expanded massively in the 1950s before collapsing during the early Cultural Revolution. The network was subsequently rebuilt in the 1970s and continues to function up to the present day, although the term *laogai* itself has now been abandoned.

In the early days of the PRC, the party was quite open about the existence of "reform through labor." CCP leaders touted the success of the system in re-educating, among others, the last Qing emperor Puyi. After more than a decade as the puppet ruler of Japanese-controlled Manchuria (1932–1945), Puyi was imprisoned by the PRC as a collaborator at the Fushun War Criminals Management Center in Liaoning, until an amnesty for the ten-year anniversary of the communist victory saw him released in 1959. The government declared him reformed and assigned him a job at the Beijing Botanical Gardens, and his case became the textbook example of PRC generosity and humanity to its erstwhile enemies. Puyi's autobiography, ghost-written by Li Wenda and including a favorable account of his labor reform experiences, was translated into several foreign languages.[23] Needless to say, ordinary prisoners tended to face a much less lenient system than that encountered by the former emperor.

Official regulations in the 1950s declared the goal of the *laogai* system to be "reform first, production second." Nevertheless, obvious tensions existed between Thought Reform – a desire to re-educate prisoners – and profit

---

22 Some works are dealing with the issue: Jean-Luc Domenach, *Der vergessene Archipel: Gefängnisse und Lager in der Volksrepublik China* (Hamburg: Hamburger Edition, 1995), translated by Cornelia Langendorf; Klaus Mühlhahn, *Criminal Justice in China: A History* (Cambridge, MA: Harvard University Press, 2009).

23 For example: Pu Yi, *From Emperor to Citizen: The Autobiography of Aisin-Gioro* (Beijing: Foreign Language Press, 1964).

generation – the pressure to exploit their labor for the benefit of the state. In May 1951 Liu Shaoqi spoke of a workforce of about 5 million people in the labor camp system, arguing: "[This workforce] does not need insurance or wages ... In the Soviet Union, prisoners were used to build several canals. If we do this well, it has economic and political benefits."[24] By 1960, Liu's estimate of 5 million labor camp inmates had risen to perhaps 12 to 20 million.[25] In the 1980s, at least one official Chinese publication claimed that the labor camps generated considerable profit for the state; the same publication also admits that between the period 1949–1953 and the Great Leap Forward, harsh working conditions and inadequate food rations led to unduly high death rates among inmates.[26] It is not universally accepted that the camps were profitable. One Western scholar doubts the ability of the *laogai* system to generate any real surplus, rightly drawing attention to its relatively small size (0.65 percent of national production).[27] We can only speculate as to how many prisoners died in the camps during the Mao era, but it seems unlikely that conditions would have convinced many inmates of the greatness of the new socialist society.

Eyewitness accounts describe a system in which rationing was used as a disciplinary tool. Inside the camps, prisoners were categorized based on a hierarchy of "ordinary" and "political" crimes. Prison brigades and individual inmates were ranked according to output and were required to supervise each other and report transgressions to the authorities. Under the 1954 *laogai* regulations, inmates could be kept inside even after their sentence had elapsed, meaning attachment to a labor camp could become essentially permanent. Those who were still considered a threat after serving their sentence became so-called "free prisoners," unable to return to their original work units but allowed to live outside the camp, draw a regular salary and bring their family to live with them.[28]

Beyond the *laogai* system, the less severe penalty of *laojiao* or "labor re-education" became increasingly important during the early 1950s as the government cracked down on urban crime. Among those sent for re-education were workers at brothels and opium dens, which were closed along with jazz clubs, dancing and gambling halls and most restaurants as the CCP attempted to stamp out "bourgeois and decadent" night life. Marginalized urban groups such as sex workers, beggars, drug addicts, street peddlers and the homeless were also subject to *laojiao*. All these groups were seen as victims of the old society, but their "parasitic tendencies" made them candidates for Thought Reform, and

24 Quoted by Mühlhahn, *Criminal Justice in China*, pp. 223–224.
25 Mühlhahn, *Criminal Justice in China*, p. 269.
26 Cai Yanshu (ed.), *Laodong gaizao gongzuo gailun* (Guangzhou: Guangdong gaodeng jiaoyu chubanshe, 1988), pp. 2, 9, 14.
27 Domenach, *Der vergessene Archipel*, pp. 366–370.
28 Mühlhahn, *Criminal Justice in China*, p. 258.

many were brought to newly established centers for vocational training and ideological education. Little is known about how these groups perceived the CCP's policies towards them. In 1957, the authorities claimed that the vast majority of beggars, prostitutes and petty thieves had already been reformed, but archival sources suggest that in many cases re-education failed to alter its targets' outlook.

By the late 1950s, it was no longer possible for those accused of prostitution and other petty crimes to defend themselves as "victims."[29] Instead, their apparent failure to respond to earlier rounds of re-education was taken as a sign of resistance to the new socialist order. Continued government pressure saw the commercial sex industry disappear until the early 1980s, along with the majority of drug use; both feats were lauded by the CCP's propaganda organs as major achievements of the revolution. There was an especially potent symbolism in the fall of Shanghai's sex and opium trades, which had served foreign customers as well as Chinese citizens and which were seen as relics of pre-revolutionary China's moral degeneration and semi-colonial oppression. It is worth noting, however, that sex as a survival strategy did not disappear even if professional sex work was no longer possible. The archives of the Mao era are full of stories of women trading sex with local cadres for food or better treatment, a practice that tended to become more common in times of crisis, such as the Great Leap Famine, or vulnerability, as with the young women sent to the countryside during the Cultural Revolution.[30] These practices, however, were seldom referred to as "prostitution."

As crime rates rose in the 1980s with the advent of the Reform era, a discourse of nostalgia arose in which the 1950s were celebrated as a kind of golden age, when cities were safe, doors could be left unlocked and lost items were invariably returned. Documentary evidence suggests more than a hint of wishful thinking to these accounts. Document 3.1 describes the situation in Baotou, a major industrial center, where in 1956 theft, armed robbery, murder, "hooligan" violence and sexual harassment apparently remained widespread, partly as a result of the pressures created by the CCP's still weak control of urban–rural migration. Reform through labor and labor re-education were both widely used against a variety of criminal elements, including "hooligans" and so-called "lumpen proletarians." As the CCP attempted to enforce its moral vision in the urban work units, even apparently private infractions such as extramarital affairs could also be punished with "labor re-education." Yet in spite of the enormous scope of the *laojiao* and *laogai* systems, we still know very little about the lives of those

---

29 Aminda M. Smith, *Thought Reform and China's Dangerous Classes: Reeducation, Resistance, and the People* (Lanham, MD: Rowman and Littlefield, 2013), pp. 201–203.

30 For detail see: Yang Bin and Cao Shuji, "Cadres, Grain, and Sexual Abuse in Wuwei County, Mao's China," *Journal of Women's History*, Vol. 28, No. 2 (2016), pp. 33–57.

who returned to society from the camps and almost nothing about those who never did.[31]

Collectivization of Agriculture and the Struggle over Grain

Land Reform was one of the central projects of the Chinese revolution, but it was never the final destination. By 1951 some parts of the country had already begun the next stage of the Communist Party's vision: the collectivization of agriculture. Initially, this process was called "cooperatization" (*hezuohua*) to distinguish the new organizations from the Soviet Union's collective farms. On paper, there were three steps to cooperatization. First, several peasant families would organize "groups for mutual aid" that would work together during the harvest seasons, with no change to the private structure of ownership. Second, a larger number of families would come together in primary cooperatives that produced as a collective. In these early cooperatives, more work was done in common, but the amount of land, labor power, cattle and agricultural tools that each household had brought into the cooperative affected the distribution of produce after the harvest. Finally, in the advanced cooperatives, land, cattle and machinery were collectively owned and grain was redeemed against work points earned on the basis of labor performance. Families were, however, permitted a plot of land "for private use" to supply their basic needs. Before 1957, the CCP promised the peasantry that joining the cooperatives was an entirely voluntary affair, and the decision to enter a cooperative remained theoretically reversible. Nevertheless, by late 1956 almost the whole rural population had been organized into full socialist cooperatives, at least in majority Han areas.

Why did the party decide to push ahead with collectivization so soon after the completion of the Land Reform? A major contributing factor was the CCP's belief, in line with contemporary Marxist-Leninist theory, that the formation of larger agricultural units would increase productivity. Land, labor and machine power could be used more efficiently at larger scales. Mao and other party leaders were also concerned about how rural society would develop in the aftermath of Land Reform. The leadership detected signs of new class divisions in rural society, and concern grew that groups of "new middle peasants" and "new rich peasants" would emerge and seek to exploit hired labor as their predecessors had done. In this new cycle of exploitation, "poor peasants" were again expected to be on the losing side. Collectivization, which would eliminate private property in

---

31 For reportage literature on the life and death of "rightists" in the desert in Gansu Province, see: Yang Xianhui, *Jiabiangou jishi* (Guangzhou: Huacheng chubanshe, 2008).

the countryside and turn everyone into an agricultural laborer, was the only way to break the cycle once and for all.

Collectivization and the Class Line

By comparison to the Soviet Union, collectivization in China was relatively peaceful, and this difference has long puzzled the scholarly community. The CCP never found it necessary to deport class enemies from the villages, as the Soviet Union had done between 1928 and 1931. Nor did China face the kind of civil war between the state and the peasantry that had broken out in the Ukraine during the collectivization process there. One possible reason lies in the party's gradualist approach, which allowed collectives to be formed step by step and gave peasants time to adjust to the new way of life. This is at best a partial solution, however, since the party's neat three-step program was by no means universally adhered to. Pressure to collectivize during 1955 and 1956 meant that huge numbers of villages never went through the process of forming mutual aid groups and primary cooperatives. Instead, many communities "made the step to a heaven in a single day," establishing advanced cooperatives directly out of mutual aid groups.

Another answer to the "peaceful transformation" problem lies in the recognition that, by 1955, the CCP had already removed most rival centers of rural power. In the Soviet Union, kulaks (affluent peasants) and the church still played an important role in village life in 1928. The Soviet Communist Party was therefore forced to destroy the rural elite at the same time as it implemented collectivization, with millions deported to Siberia during the so-called "dekulakization" campaign. By contrast, China's rural elites – indeed, virtually all rural organizations outside of Communist Party control – had been destroyed by 1951, when Land Reform came to an end. Moreover, the CCP had stronger roots in the countryside than its Soviet counterpart. In 1955, 170,000 party branches existed in 220,000 villages across China, boasting a combined total of 4 million members.[32] The Soviet party had a much more limited presence in rural areas, instead relying also on the so-called "25,000," a body of urban workers who were mobilized to support the collectivization process.

In the early part of the collectivization campaign, the CCP adopted a "class line" approach that limited entry to the cooperatives to those with good class status. This restriction caused significant problems, since those excluded tended to be wealthier villagers, without whose cattle and tools many cooperatives were left poorly equipped. Local party organizations raised the question of landlord

---

32 Yu Liu, "Why Did It Go So High? Political Mobilization and Agricultural Collectivization in China," *The China Quarterly*, No. 187 (2006), pp. 738–739.

and rich peasant participation with the Central Committee on several occasions, although by and large their concern seems to have been that a relaxation of the exclusion policy would allow these individuals to sabotage the socialist order from within. In 1954, the Central Committee partially relaxed its stance, decreeing that students and other young adults with bad family backgrounds should be allowed to become members of the cooperatives but should be given leadership positions only if they were members of the Communist Youth League.[33] It was not until the pressure for full collectivization increased in 1956 that all of the rural population, in Han areas at least, was required to enter the cooperatives.

The CCP's destruction of the old rural elites did not prevent all resistance to collectivization. During 1956 and in the first half of 1957, millions of peasants opted out of the collectives, and their withdrawal was accompanied by the slaughter of livestock on a massive scale.[34] In Tibetan areas of Sichuan and Qinghai, local governments attempted to collectivize groups of nomadic herdsmen under a policy to "unite agriculture and husbandry." These efforts, accompanied in some areas by attempts to force herdsmen to adopt a sedentary way of life, provoked a number of armed uprisings which the PLA was forced to suppress.

There were also divides within the party leadership over the speed of collectivization. A number of key figures suggested that the process should be slowed to create more space for voluntary participation, while others called for more rapid progress to break the back of rural resistance. Mao eventually adopted the second option, demanding a full socialist transformation of rural China. As in other campaigns, the Chairman argued that his choice was in fact no choice at all: in his view, peasants and local cadres had already seized the initiative, creating a "socialist high tide in the countryside" that left the party no alternative but to ride the wave.[35] Certainly the collectivization process enjoyed widespread support. Many local cadres, activists and peasants genuinely believed the party's promise that larger farming units would bring collective security during natural disasters, promote agricultural modernization and lead to a more prosperous future. Soon, though, local opinions on the matter became irrelevant. By the end of 1957 the

---

33 "Zhongyang guanyu dizhu, funong jiating chushen de qingnian xuesheng nengfou canjia huzhu hezuo zuzhi wenti de zhishi," August 27 (1954), in Song Yongyi (ed.), *Database of the Chinese Political Campaigns in the 1950s: From Land Reform to the State–Private Partnership, 1949–1956*, CD-ROM (Hong Kong: Universities Service Centre for China Studies, The Chinese University of Hong Kong, 2014).

34 Felix Wemheuer, "'The Grain Problem is an Ideological Problem': Discourses of Hunger in the 1957 Socialist Education Campaign," in Kimberley Manning and Felix Wemheuer (eds.), *Eating Bitterness: New Perspectives on China's Great Leap Forward and Famine* (Vancouver: University of British Columbia Press, 2011), p. 109.

35 Mao Zedong, "Guanyu nongye hezuohua wenti," in *Mao Zedong Wenji*, Vol. 6, p. 418.

Figure 3.3: A Chinese peasant.
Source: Photograph by Eva Siao, Museum Ludwig.

CCP had revoked the right of peasants to withdraw from the cooperatives, beginning an era of compulsory collectivization that would last into the early 1980s.

The Struggle for Grain

The pressure of feeding a rapidly growing urban population placed considerable strain on the early PRC government. Traditionally, it was the prosperous "rich peasants" who had produced much of the surplus grain that eventually made its way to the cities. Land Reform weakened this group, and the "poor peasants" who displaced them proved much less willing to sell. After years of shortages, many preferred to eat their fill rather than supporting their fellow citizens in urban areas. Agricultural production increased under the New Democratic order, but the extra grain went to feeding previously malnourished peasants, and by 1953 urban China faced a serious grain supply crisis. In response, the central government introduced a state monopoly, the system of "unified purchase and sale" (*tonggou tongxiao*), with a stated goal of feeding the urban population and supporting rural areas hit by natural disasters. By 1957, this monopoly had been extended to almost all agricultural products, including cotton and other non-food crops. Urban food rationing was introduced in 1953 and standardized across the country in 1955, giving urban citizens guaranteed access to cheap food and basic consumer products.

Purchase prices under the *tonggou* system were low, and state propaganda painted the sale of surpluses as peasants' patriotic duty. In some regions, the duty was a particularly heavy one, as the state not only extracted the surplus but also ate into the rural grain supply, creating shortages for the local population. Throughout the Mao era, and indeed until its abolition in the mid-1980s, the system of unified purchase and sale allowed the CCP to exploit rural resources to promote urban and industrial development. The ability to extract whatever surplus it saw fit at the price of its choosing allowed the government to export grain to other socialist states, either to finance imports of industrial technology or to repay debt to the Soviet Union. Rationing gave the state a further measure of control by limiting consumption "inside the system." While peasants' patriotic duty was to sell grain cheaply, urban residents were constantly reminded of their own duty not to waste food. In spite of the extraordinary level of control it exercised, maintaining the balance between rural production and urban consumption presented a significant challenge to the early PRC state. More mouths to feed in the urban rationing system inevitably meant more grain procurements in the countryside, but per capita food production was still low and many rural areas faced frequent natural disasters throughout the 1950s. (See Figure 3.4.)

Collectivization made state control of the agricultural surplus far easier to manage, allowing the government to deal with a limited number of larger production units rather than the ocean of smallholders produced by Land Reform. Some Chinese scholars have argued that this, rather than any purely ideological consideration, was the main reason for the party's push towards collectivization.[36] From the state's perspective, the practical benefits of collectivization were only made more obvious by growing resistance to the new monopoly on the grain trade. Document 3.2 describes mass protests against grain

36 Wen Tiejun, *Zhongguo nongcun jiben jingji zhidu yanjiu* (Beijing: Zhongguo jingji chubanshe, 2000), pp. 175–177.

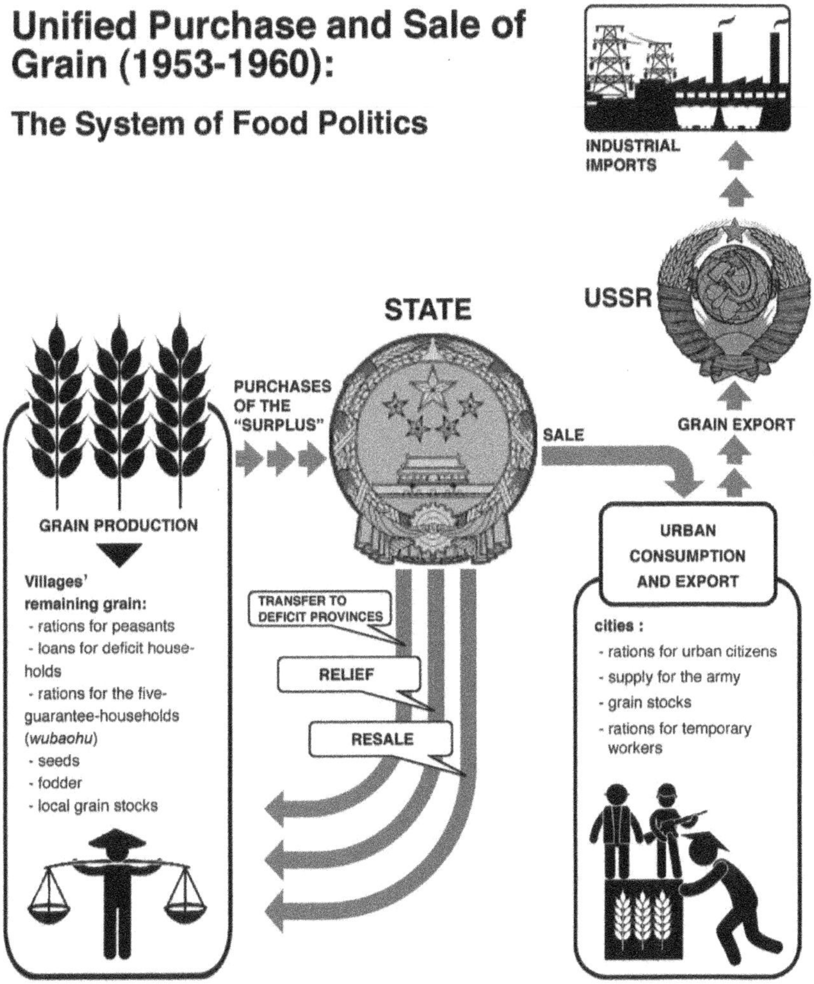

Unified Purchase and Sale of Grain (1953-1960):

The System of Food Politics

Figure 3.4: Unified purchase and sale of grain (1953–1960).
Source: Felix Wemheuer, *Famine Politics in Maoist China and the Soviet Union* (New Haven, CT: Yale University Press, 2014), p. 88. Reproduced with permission of the publisher.

shortages in Shaanxi Province in 1957, which saw peasants attack cadres and even force some to commit suicide. This incident occurred after collectivization, but less extreme examples could be found all across the country in 1953 and 1954 following the introduction of unified purchase and sale. Despite a rush of CCP propaganda hailing the system as a central plank of the socialist transformation, in many parts of the country peasants attempted to reduce their sale quotas by under-reporting land holdings and production. Others exaggerated the damage caused by natural disasters in order to obtain government relief.

Within each village, households were classified as either "surplus," "self-sufficient" or "grain deficit." Villagers went to great lengths to avoid being classified as a "surplus household," with the increased burdens that the designation entailed. In 1953, Mao estimated that "grain deficit households" accounted for 10 percent of the rural population, while around 20 to 40 million peasants would suffer from natural disasters in each two year period.[37] However, the CCP soon began to suspect that many claims of grain shortages and hunger were being faked. A narrative emerged in the press of peasants seeking to disrupt the grain procurement system and obtain relief under false pretenses, and the government became more and more distrustful of reports of rural shortage. CCP leaders blamed "landlords" and "rich peasants" for organizing resistance to state policies, with the result that claims of rural hunger became increasingly taboo as the 1950s wore on. When famine broke out on a national scale in 1959, this taboo would have a devastating effect.[38]

The 8th Party Congress and the System of Class Status

In September 1956, the CCP held its 8th Party Congress. It was the first since 1945; the 9th Party Congress would not take place until 1969. One function of the congress was to elect a new Central Committee, and 1956 was a contentious year in which to do so. The rise of Khrushchev in the Soviet Union had been accompanied by a campaign of "de-Stalinization," in which negative developments under the former leader's rule were attributed in part to the "cult of personality" that he had encouraged. In the USSR and the Eastern Bloc, cults around national party leaders were being scaled down. In China, Mao was not directly attacked, but the 1956 congress took the decision to delete Mao Zedong Thought from the party constitution (again unchanged since 1945).

The congress also announced the successful completion of the socialist transformation in industry and agriculture. China's new political conditions required further changes to the party constitution. The revised document permitted any Chinese citizen to become a member of the CCP, provided they did not exploit the labor of others. In theory, this definition encompassed nearly everyone in the Han Chinese areas, but in practice access was restricted by the need for candidates to serve a probationary period to prove their "reliability." The 1945 constitution had set this period of "candidacy" at six months for workers, poor

---

37 Mao Zedong, "Liangshi tonggou tongxiao wenti," in *Mao Zedong Wenji*, Vol. 6, pp. 296–297.
38 For more detail see: Felix Wemheuer, *Famine Politics in Maoist China and the Soviet Union* (New Haven, CT: Yale University Press, 2014), pp. 77–114.

peasants, revolutionary soldiers and the urban poor, but one year for middle peasants, office staff, and the self-employed.[39] The new constitution set a blanket probationary period of one year regardless of class status.

At the same time, questions were raised over the suitability of existing class labels for China's new socio-economic reality. Deng Xiaoping, the General Secretary of the CCP, explained the revisions to the party constitution as follows:

> The distinction hitherto made in admitting new members has been removed because former classifications of social status have lost or are losing their original meaning ... In recent years ... the situation has basically changed. The difference between workers and office employees is now only a matter of division of labor within the same class. Coolies and farm laborers have disappeared. Poor and middle peasants have all become members of agricultural producers' co-operatives, and before long the distinction between them will become merely a matter of historical interest. With the introduction of the conscription system, revolutionary soldiers no longer constitute an independent social stratum. The vast majority of intellectuals have now come over politically to the side of the working class, and a rapid change is taking place in their family background. The conditions under which the urban poor and professional people existed as independent social strata have virtually been eliminated. Every year large numbers of peasants and students become workers, large numbers of workers, peasants and their sons and daughters join the ranks of intellectuals and office workers, large numbers of peasants, students, workers and office workers join the army and become revolutionary soldiers, while large numbers of revolutionary soldiers return to civilian life as peasants, students, workers or office workers. What is the point, then, of classifying these social strata into two different categories? Even if we were to try to devise a classification, how could we make it clear and unambiguous?[40]

This statement represented a radical break with the old, hybrid class system, which as we have seen took account not only of the individual's place in the economic structure, but also their family origin. Deng was now arguing that, thanks to the expropriation of land owners and capitalists, the social classes that had been built on that particular ownership structure had disappeared or were in the process of doing so. The result was a system of class labeling that was actually closer to Marxist orthodoxy than the complex set-up the CCP had established after 1949.

---

39 Zhongguo geming bowuguan (ed.), *Zhongguo gongchandang dangzhang huibian*, pp. 49–50.
40 Deng Xiaoping, "Report on the Revision of the Constitution of the Communist Party of China," https://ia802609.us.archive.org/28/items/SelectedWorksOfDengXiaoping/Deng01.pdf, (accessed May 3, 2017), p. 183.

Deng's speech contained notable echoes of Stalin's arguments regarding the Soviet Constitution of 1936. Stalin too had claimed that, with the socialist transformation of industry and the collectivization of agriculture, the exploiting classes had been abolished. All that remained were two allied classes, workers and collective farmers, while the Soviet intelligentsia no longer existed as a separate class but was distributed between the other two. Class struggle would only persist, Stalin believed, if members of the former exploiting classes, "harmful social elements" and spies sent by hostile foreign powers were allowed to plot against the Soviet order.[41] During the Late Stalinist period after World War Two, the Soviet Union ended the policy of "class line," a system of affirmative action under which workers and peasants had gained preferential access to education and party membership.

Deng's speech and the announcements of the 8th Party Congress might have led observers to anticipate the imminent abolition of China's formal class system. However, this step did not take place until the early 1980s, in part because the party leadership was divided on how to deal with intellectuals. In 1960, critiquing a standard Soviet textbook on political economy, Mao complained that no mention was made of the necessity of re-educating "bourgeois intellectuals" to become "red and expert."[42] As he saw it, this was a major part of the process of socialist transformation.

Intellectuals: Necessary Reform for Much-Needed Experts

The relationship between the party and China's intellectuals had been a complex one ever since the founding of the CCP in the 1920s. Many early party leaders such as Chen Duxiu and Li Dazhao hailed from Peking University, where the former was on the faculty and the latter was head of the library. Others, such as Liu Shaoqi, Zhou Enlai and Deng Xiaoping, had studied outside of China, in some cases for many years. Mao himself had also been on the Peking University staff, albeit only as a librarian, and he was familiar with the leading intellectual circles of the day thanks to his political activism and the connections of his second wife Yang Kaihui. The party itself had fundamentally intellectual origins: although it relied on significant Soviet support in its early days, it grew initially out of the Chinese May Fourth Movement of 1919.

---

41 Josef Stalin, "Defects in Party Work and Measures for Liquidating Trotskyite and Other Double Dealers: Report to the Plenum of the Central Committee of the RKP(b)" (1937), www.marxists .org/reference/archive/stalin/works/1937/03/03.htm (accessed September 13, 2017).

42 Helmut Martin (ed.), *Mao Tse-tung: Das machen wir anders als Moskau! Kritik an der sowjetischen Politökonomie* (Reinbek bei Hamburg: Rowohlt, 1975), p. 26.

Today it is sometimes argued that Mao hated intellectuals, a hatred generally ascribed, with pop psychological simplicity, to an inferiority complex based around his lack of a university degree or formal academic education. In fact, I would argue that, from at least the late 1940s, Mao regarded himself as a great thinker whose practical study of warfare, revolution and social dynamics, combined with his success in leading the Chinese revolution to victory, had given him a level of theoretical understanding that far exceeded any university professor. In his own eyes, Mao was the ultimate practical intellectual. In keeping with this view, the party as a whole seems to have regarded itself as an intellectual movement well into the early days of the PRC. As one scholar has suggested, in most cases the leadership saw disagreements between the party and the intelligentsia as conflicts between one set of intellectuals and another.[43]

However, the composition of China's intellectual elite represented a real problem for the party. In the Republican era, university intake was limited and students were recruited mainly from the upper strata of society. According to one scholarly estimate, between 1911 and 1949, as few as 1.5 million students received a university degree.[44] Any of these highly educated young people who joined the communist movement were likely to be "betraying" their families' social class. Moreover, before 1949, major research institutions in China were dominated by scholars who had received their degrees in the United States, and a large proportion of the country's Christian universities and schools were financed with US money. Naturally, foreign sponsors had an impact on both the formal curricula and intellectual climate of these institutions. It is therefore unsurprising that some rural party cadres saw academics as an essentially alien group, influenced by Western imperialism and aligned with capitalist and landlord interests. In 1949, the CCP addressed these concerns with an announcement that "bourgeois intellectuals" had to be reformed (*gaizao*) and trained in Marxism-Leninism. At the same time, the party acknowledged the need for experts to conduct scientific research, build industrial capacity and run the country's universities. In keeping with the Soviet model, the CCP emphasized the importance of science and technology and of training engineers and scientists to secure China's industrial future. For these scholars, freedom of research within their disciplines was potentially more important than the general freedom of expression and publication afforded to writers, film makers or artists.

As early as 1942, in his "Talks at the Yan'an Forum on Literature and Art," Mao had emphasized the importance of the arts in China's revolutionary

43 Timothy Cheek, *The Intellectual in Modern Chinese History* (Cambridge: Cambridge University Press, 2015), p. 131.

44 Yu Fengzheng, *Gaizao: 1949–1957 nian de zhishifenzi* (Zhengzhou: Henan renmin chubanshe, 2001), p. 1.

struggle. In his view, writers and artists had to be willing to give up their privileges, unite themselves with ordinary people and produce art for the benefit of the masses.[45] However, a lack of compulsory education before 1949 meant that the new China would have to rely on "bourgeois intellectuals" until a new cohort of "red and expert" thinkers could be trained from among the ordinary population. The new state began this process with typical forcefulness. Missionary schools, private schools and universities were closed, and art production and publishing were brought under government control. Under the Republic, intellectuals of a political bent had a number of career options, ranging from professional service to life as an independent writer or commentator.[46] In these latter roles, success was driven by commercial considerations. In the PRC, by contrast, writers and artists who were accepted by the various official associations had none of these worries. Like all other urban workers, they were categorized as "inside the system," assigned work units and rations, and paid by the state. At the very top, "high-ranking intellectuals" could serve as cultural cadres and "teachers of the nation." Those in this position did not have to concern themselves with the commercial success of their works, but equally they had no avenues to earn a living "outside the system."

Intellectuals soon lost the freedom of expression and thought that they had enjoyed in the best days of the Republic. Under the PRC, not only was the content of their work controlled by the party, but form and style also had to conform to the standards of Socialist Realism. In line with doctrines imported from the Soviet Union, art and literature were required to illustrate the achievements of socialism and the future potential of socialist society. Abstract or avant-garde work was rejected in favor of popular and folkloristic forms designed to appeal to the masses. The state-controlled cultural industry distributed to millions of people the works of writers, artists and directors who were willing to serve the regime. This new dispensation was rejected by many, but huge numbers of intellectuals did agree to serve. Nor was fear of the consequences of resistance the only motivation: some intellectuals were genuinely enthused by the prospect of contributing to the rise of a strong, industrial China. It is often forgotten that academic research, art and science are not per se democratic, and recent history provides many examples of scientists and writers working quite happily with authoritarian regimes.

Between 1949 and 1957, the CCP's official attitude to intellectuals took a number of different turns. The class status of intellectuals, which we have

45 Mao Zedong, "Zai Yan'an wenyi zuotan huishang de jianghua," in *Mao Zedong Xuanji*, Vol. 3, pp. 807–808.
46 Cheek, *The Intellectual in Modern Chinese History*, p. 129.

already seen mentioned in Deng Xiaoping's speech to the 1956 party congress, was a regular point of contention. The 1950 regulations on the classification of classes declared that "intellectual" was not a separate class status,[47] but party leaders continued to disagree on whether intellectuals were part of the laboring classes or the bourgeoisie right up to the abolition of the class system in the 1980s. In general, "intellectual" had a much broader meaning under the PRC than in Republican China. The term encompassed all high school graduates, and in some cases it was applied to former GMD public servants and housewives. In the context of employment programs, even people with only a middle school education might be included.[48] Individual campaigns might focus only on certain subsets of these intellectuals, as with efforts to institute Thought Reform at universities from 1950 onwards. A few years later, writers rather than students were the focus, with mass arrests during the 1955 campaign against the so-called "Counterrevolutionary Clique of Hu Feng." A leftist writer, poet and literary theorist, who had failed to submit to the dogmas of the CCP, Hu had been criticized by the party several times before. The 1955 campaign, however, was significantly broader in scope, as the party called on intellectuals and even ordinary people to denounce this example of "counterrevolutionary" spirit.

The Hundred Flowers Campaign: Mobilizing Intellectuals to Rectify the Party

By 1956, the CCP was convinced that progress had been made in bringing intellectuals into the party fold. In February of that year, the Central Committee passed a resolution arguing that the majority of emerging new intellectuals were likely to have good family origins, and that as such intellectuals had now become part of the laboring classes. The document asserted that 5 percent of intellectuals were still "counterrevolutionary," while another 10 percent were alleged to be harboring backward or reactionary thoughts, but the majority were now supporters of socialist construction. The Central Committee therefore called for a campaign to encourage intellectuals to join the CCP, stating that by 1962 one-third of all "high-ranking intellectuals" should be party members. The leadership also criticized rank and file cadres for failing to appreciate the importance of intellectuals and assessed that a significant expansion in the number of intellectuals would be required to meet the needs of scientific and economic development. The resolution outlined an ambitious plan to cultivate

---

47 "Zhengwuyuan guanyu huafen nongcun jieji chengfen de jueding," in *JGYL*, Vol. 1, pp. 397–398.

48 Eddy U, "The Making of *Zhishifenzi*: The Critical Impact of the Registration of Unemployed Intellectuals in the Early PRC," *The China Quarterly*, Vol. 173 (2003), pp. 113–114.

new intellectuals, with a goal of allowing China to reach a high level of economic and cultural development relative to other countries within the next 12 years.[49]

The role of intellectuals became even more important during the Hundred Flowers Campaign. This now-infamous initiative grew out of Mao's worries over the anti-communist uprising in Hungary in autumn 1956. The CCP leadership welcomed the Soviet response, an invasion which crushed the revolt and returned Hungary to socialist rule. However, Mao was concerned that such an uprising could have arisen in the first place, and he became convinced that responsibility must lie with the Communist Party itself. He identified two major errors: a failure to deal with bureaucratism on the one hand and incorrect handling of what he termed "contradictions among the people" (*renmin neibu maodun*) on the other.

Hard on the heels of the Hungarian revolt came student protests in Beijing's schools. Then, in the spring of 1957, a wave of strikes broke out in Shanghai.[50] Faced with obvious dissatisfaction with CCP rule, Mao called on intellectuals to help identify the party's shortcomings and begin a period of "rectification." To encourage this free airing of views, a new slogan was adopted: "Let a hundred flowers bloom; let a hundred schools of thought contend." The campaign signaled that, across media, the arts and universities, a certain degree of pluralism was to be tolerated in an effort to identify problems and allow solutions to be devised.

Mao justified this new approach in February 1957, in a speech entitled, "On the correct handling of the contradictions among the people." He described two types of contradictions, antagonistic and non-antagonistic. Contradictions between the people and their enemy would inevitably be antagonistic and could only be solved by the suppression of counterrevolutionary forces. However, "contradictions among the people" – that is, disagreements among those loyal to the communist cause – were non-antagonistic in nature and could be resolved by discussion and persuasion. The CCP, Mao claimed, should not be afraid of criticism and open debate.[51] Mao also spoke positively of those involved in labor unrest and student demonstrations, since their actions had helped create pressure for the party to improve. However, he warned that if the CCP failed to handle these challenges correctly, non-antagonistic contradictions could quickly become antagonistic ones, as had occurred in Hungary.

---

49 "Zhonggong zhongyang, 'Guanyu zhishifenzi wenti de zhishi, zhonggong zhongyang zheng-zhiju huiyi tongguo'," February 24 (1956), in Song Yongyi (ed.), *Database of the Chinese Political Campaigns in the 1950s: From Land Reform to the State–Private Partnership, 1949–1956*, CD-ROM (Hong Kong: Universities Service Centre for China Studies, The Chinese University of Hong Kong, 2014).

50 See: Elizabeth Perry, *Challenging the Mandate of Heaven: Social Protest and State Power in China* (London: M. E. Sharpe, 2002), pp. 211–214.

51 Mao Zedong, "Guanyu zhengque chuli renmin neibu maodun de wenti," in *Mao Zedong Wenji*, Vol. 7, pp. 231–232.

This kind of distinction between "the people," who enjoyed the right to criticize, and "non-people," who did not, fit well with the rest of Mao's worldview. It was also notable that it was for the party to decide whether a particular criticism represented a "contradiction among the people" or a counterrevolutionary attack whose authors should be suppressed. Many other powerbrokers, including Liu Shaoqi and the Soviet leadership, remained skeptical of Mao's approach, and the resulting uncertainty discouraged intellectuals from speaking out during the early days of the campaign.

Mao, however, pressed on. His call for a relaxation of censorship in the press and academia saw several months of genuine openness between late April and early June 1957. As the weeks went by and no crackdown materialized, some intellectuals began to accept that Mao was sincere in his desire to hear critical opinions. Open debate broke out on a wide range of issues, including the lack of rule of law and the neglect of constitutionally protected civil rights. A number of commentators argued that the 1954 constitution's guarantees of freedom of speech, publication and demonstration should be taken seriously and urged others to exercise these liberties. Others questioned the control of universities by party committees and non-experts, dogmatism in the arts, the impact of agricultural collectivization, the dominance of Soviet experts and even the prosecution of innocent people in previous party campaigns.[52] The argument that non-experts, meaning party cadres from rural backgrounds, should not lead experts and intellectuals represented a particular challenge to the principle of CCP leadership in urban and academic institutions. Proponents of this critique also questioned the principle of the "class line" and the party's policy of affirmative action for people with little formal education. The CCP had consistently argued that art and academic research should serve the interests of the masses and the revolution, but some intellectuals now openly proposed that science should be subject only to academic rules. In the arts, they held that real creativity would be a result of individual expression by the artist, not contract work assigned by the propaganda department. Speculation and rumors spread of possible Hungary-style uprisings in China.

By June, Mao and the leadership had concluded that the campaign had spiraled out of control. Criticism from intellectuals had been much harsher than expected and had been directed not only against superficial problems, but also against the whole political system and even CCP rule in general. The party leadership's assessment in early 1956 that the majority of intellectuals supported socialism proved to be wildly optimistic. In an effort to regain the initiative, the government inaugurated the Anti-Rightist Campaign to attack and purge critical voices in schools, universities, the cultural industry, the minor parties and the CCP itself.

---

52 A documentary history is provided by: Roderick MacFarquhar, *The Hundred Flowers Campaign and the Chinese Intellectuals* (New York, NY: Praeger, 1966).

The Anti-Rightist Campaign: Crackdown on Dissent

Two explanations for the sudden turn from the Hundred Flowers to the Anti-Rightist Campaign dominate the academic literature. In the first, the Hundred Flowers Campaign is described as a calculated piece of political deceit, a trap set by Mao to bring hidden enemies into the open.[53] In the second, Mao is understood to have genuinely underestimated the level of discontent in society at large and to have been shocked by the harshness of criticism directed at the party. In this account, claims that Mao had been cynically attempting to uncover counterrevolutionary elements are dismissed as disinformation, spread by the Chairman himself to cover his own misjudgment. This second version of events – Mao surprised rather than Mao supreme – is supported by newly discovered archival documents, and it is notable that it was not until mid-May 1957 that Mao first claimed to be acting tactically to "coax the snakes out of their holes."[54]

In light of what followed, it is important to recollect just how severely threatened the CCP felt by the end of the Hundred Flowers Campaign. Labor strikes, student protests and rural unrest had all taken place at significant scale. In 1956 and the first half of 1957, millions of peasants had retreated from the rural collectives and returned to producing as individual farmers. Mao himself was enraged at evidence that even many rural cadres were still not convinced of the superiority of socialist agriculture. The wider party leadership feared that anti-socialist forces in the cities and countryside, which up to now had worked independently of each other, could link up in a broader national movement.[55] By cutting across classes, such a movement could potentially lead to questioning of the CCP's monopoly as sole representative of the workers and peasants. Whether or not this fear was justified in the autumn of 1957, the party moved swiftly to tackle the perceived danger. Alongside the Anti-Rightist struggle, a new Socialist Education Campaign, directed from the top down, swept through the countryside, factories, and minority regions.

Unlike previous campaigns, which had tended to move in cycles, the Anti-Rightist Campaign grew increasingly radical over time. By the end in 1958, over 550,000 people had been officially labeled as "rightists," many of them innocent victims of a poisonous dynamic of denunciations and "exaggeration."[56] Again,

---

53 For example see: Jung Chang and Jon Halliday, *Mao: The Unknown Story* (New York, NY: Anchor Books, 2005), p. 410.

54 Shen Zhihua, *Zhonghua renmin gongheguo shi, Vol. 3, Sikao yu xuanze: Cong zhishi fenzi huiyi dao fanyoupai yundong (1956–1957)* (Hong Kong: The Chinese University of Hong Kong, 2008), pp. 562–564.

55 Zhu Di, *1957: Da zhuanwan zhi mi: Zhengfeng fanyou shilu* (Taiyuan: Shanxi renmin chubanshe, 1995), pp. 238–239.

56 Bo Yibo, *Ruogan zhongda juece yu shijian de huigu* (Beijing: Zhongyang dangxiao chubanshe, 1991), Vol. 2, pp. 618–619.

quotas were imposed to pressure institutions to expose opponents of the system, with public announcements declaring that 5 to 10 percent of university teachers were rightists. In October 1957, the Central Committee issued a set of identifying markers to guide the hunt for enemies, including opposition to the political system or the socialist transformation of industry and agriculture, rejection of the leadership of the party in educational and cultural institutions and refusal to support the reform of "bourgeois intellectuals." The definition also included a section on the slandering of peasant and worker cadres or the socialist camp in general.[57] In the media and universities, "rightist" people and views were openly attacked and denounced. In the context of agricultural policy, statements such as "the life of peasants is bitter," "grain prices are too low and quotas too high" or "the peasants do not have enough to eat" were criticized as "rightist" thoughts.[58]

By the time this document was issued, many local governments in the countryside had already imposed the "rightist" label on some residents, often in large numbers. Eventually, the Central Committee decided that the label should not be applied to peasants and workers. In rural areas, a quartet of other labels, "landlord," "rich peasant," "counterrevolutionary" and "bad element," remained in place to single out enemies of the people more generally. In factories in the cities, cadres and technicians at higher levels could be labeled as rightists, but ordinary workers were protected. In cases in which peasants and workers had been labeled before the decision was handed down, the verdict should be corrected.[59]

For the most part, the label of "rightist" was reserved for intellectuals, but party cadres at the provincial and county level were also sometimes targeted. In Henan province in central China, the campaign developed a unique dynamic. In the summer of 1957, only 911 rightists had been identified, and the first provincial party secretary, Pan Fusheng, was accused of opposing the push for rapid collectivization and strict enforcement of grain procurement quotas. In summer 1958, Pan was dismissed from office and labeled as a rightist himself for his failure to prosecute the Anti-Rightist Campaign with sufficient vigor. This turn of events had severe consequences for the party in Henan. Elsewhere in the country, the campaign had already passed its peak, but Pan's successor, the former deputy party secretary Wu Zhipu, "rescheduled classes" and stepped up work against rightists in an attempt to make up for lost time. In 1958, 70,000 people – 14 percent of the total for the entire campaign in China – were labeled as

---

57 "Zhonggong zhongyang guanyu 'huafen youpaifenzi de biaozhun' de tongzhi," in *JGYL*, Vol. 10, pp. 615–617.
58 Wemheuer, "The Grain Problem is an Ideological Problem," p. 123.
59 "Zhonggong zhongyang guanyu zai gongren, nongmin zhong bu hua youpaifenzi de tongzhi," in Zhongyang dang'an guan (ed.), *Zhonggong zhongyang wenxian xuanji* (Beijing: Renmin chubanshe, 2013), Vol. 26, p. 146.

rightists in the province.[60] This late peak meant that the high point of the campaign in Henan overlapped with the beginning of the Great Leap Forward. Wu and his subordinates made their province into a model for the most radical policies of the Leap, and as a result Henan suffered particularly badly during the ensuing famine, starting from early 1959, as we shall see in Chapter 4.

In contrast to the fate of counterrevolutionaries during the 1951 campaign, rightists were not executed. Instead they were sent to the countryside, often to particularly remote areas, for a process of re-education that lasted in many cases until the early 1980s. Those who were sent away lost their urban household registration and found themselves "outside the system." The campaign had a devastating impact on relations between the CCP and intellectuals, and its effect on higher education, research, cultural production and confidence in the United Front was just as severe. Many Chinese citizens learned the hard way that it was better to keep their mouths shut when the party asked for "honest opinions." Critical remarks could be made inside the family or to very close friends, but never in public.

As ever with labeling of enemies, the identification of 550,000 "rightists" had a lasting impact on family members. Millions faced the burden of being known as the wives, husbands or children of rightists in their work units. The party demanded that they "draw a line" with bad family members. In some official documents, the umbrella term "the four elements" ("landlords," "rich peasants," "counterrevolutionaries" and "bad elements") was replaced by "the five elements," putting rightists in the same category as those who had opposed or been targeted in the New Democratic Revolution. Since rightists had usually been on the right side of history in 1949, since their crimes (having the wrong attitude to the socialist transformation) were supposedly less serious.

Official publications from 1957 onwards argued that, with the transformation of industry and agriculture, China had established socialism. The Anti-Rightist Campaign was seen as providing a parallel victory on the ideological front. Certainly, the CCP had won a much higher degree of internal conformity. However, this conformity also meant a fear of speaking out, and by the end of the campaign most people were nervous of telling the party anything other than what it wanted to hear. This would have disastrous consequences during the Great Leap Forward in the years that followed.

60 Zhang Linnan, "Guanyu 'Fan Pan, Yang, Wang Shijian'," in Zhonggong Henan shengwei dangshi gongzuo weiyuanhui (ed.), *Fengyu chunqiu: Pan Fusheng shiwen jinianji* (Zhengzhou: Henan renmin chubanshe, 1993), pp. 308, 316.

DOCUMENT 3.1 "Public security in Baotou is extremely poor."

Xinhua News 26th [October], Huhehaote: Many problems in public security have emerged in the iron and steel industrial base in Baotou. According to the most up-to-date report from the Public Security Bureau of Inner Mongolia, in line with the economic development of Baotou, the population of the city has increased from 230,000 last year to more than 300,000 this year (it is alleged that the number will further increase to nearly 400,000). However, development is unbalanced. In particular, public security is so bad that it has seriously affected production, daily work and the lives of local people. Statistics show that there were 137 criminal cases in the first six months of this year, a 25.5 percent jump for the same period last year. 65 criminal cases of all kinds have been solved, accounting for 47.4 percent of the total number.

Cases of theft appear frequently. Within one month, seven watches and two clocks were stolen from the department store in Xincheng district; and despite being locked in a document case, the camera of Fu Junyi, a cadre at the Baotou branch of the Anshan Construction Engineering Company, was also stolen. The 200 yuan bank deposit book of a worker at the 5th Bureau in the Baotou branch of the Hubei Construction Engineering Company was stolen, and when the worker realized the theft and went to his bank to report it, there was only 20 yuan left in his account. The most serious cases even threatened the lives and safety of the property owners. On his way back home after work, Yang Changxin, another worker at the Baotou branch of the Hubei Construction Engineering Company, was strangled to death by a criminal who robbed him of 30 yuan. This case caused panic among the workers, who were then afraid of going to work too early or going home too late.

Because of poor public security, there has been a rapid increase in hooliganism and cases of sexual offences. Within half a year, there were sixteen cases pertaining to hooliganism and sexual offences, such as the rape of women and young girls. During the day, sexual harassment of women by groups of hooligans in the street is also common. Sexual offenders show exceptional recklessness, not only cornering women where there were few people at night, but even breaking into the dormitories of female cadres. Not long ago a sexual offender broke into the women's dormitory of 477 Factory and sexually assaulted a female cadre. The offender only stopped when the victim started screaming and even stole the underwear of the victim as he escaped.

Recently, a number of hooligans were seen wandering through Xinxing Street in the new downtown of Baotou. They stopped at tea houses during the daytime and stayed in vendors' booths at night. A female hooligan often seduced small groups of jobless men into having unwarranted sexual relationships. More commonly, the hooligans knocked on the doors of workers' families at night and peeked inside in an attempt to catch a glimpse of women. This resulted in panic among the workers' families of the Baotou branch of the [above-mentioned] Hubei Construction Engineering Company, who became too scared to sleep at night. These cases also worried the workers, who could not concentrate at work, leading to increased concern about accidents.

Source: *Neibu Cankao*, October 26, 1956.

DOCUMENT 3.2 "Incidents caused by a shortage of grain supplies continued in Hanzhong Special District, Shaanxi Province."

Xinhua agency, Xi'an, news on the 8th [of May]: Since spring, in Hanzhong Special District, Shaanxi province, many peasants have protested violently because of issues with grain supplies. Peng Demao, a director of the Xiaolong cooperative, was dragged out and paraded through the streets by a few peasants who came to claim their grain rations; these peasants also spat in his face. Peng felt so humiliated that he cried for three days and stayed at home for more than a month. Another director, Chen Keyi, became furious after his mother was abused by members of the cooperative. Swearing that he would resign from his position, he tore up the certificate for his party membership dues and threw many commune documents at the township government buildings [a form of protest]. Half of the 26 directors and group leaders at the two cooperatives of Erliqiao and Wangziling also wished to quit, arguing that "without grain from the government, the members of the cooperative will crunch and swallow our bones!"

After numerous violent protests outside the township government buildings, the secretary of the Jiaoshan township government locked the gate and avoided returning to work. In the face of the same situation, the governor of the Changlin township government wept in front of his superior, the county governor, and refused to leave unless grain rations were immediately allocated. When he went to the countryside, the secretary of the district party committee of Lianxiang district was surrounded by people demanding grain rations; he was finally allowed to leave after using kindly words to persuade his audience [of his good intentions]. Having learnt that the county governor was coming for a conference related to irrigation works, more than 100 peasants in Yangwan town gathered together to protest; this petered out when the governor failed to show up. Qiao Jun, the deputy secretary of the county party committee, was also stopped by protesters when he went to check the water reservoir. After a difficult struggle, he finally escaped and later commented on this experience: "In all seriousness, I am afraid of going to the countryside. It is difficult to leave once you get there."

Several mass protests also took place in Chenggu, Lueyang, Nanzheng and Yangxian. In Dacaoba village in Chenggu county, more than 100 peasants crowded into the offices of the county People's Committee and claimed that "the Communist Party should not watch us suffering from hunger." At the Nankanying town in the same county, every day the county government received around 25 people who came angrily to claim their grain rations with statements such as the following: "Since joining, we have given everything, from our house to our land, to the commune. Who else will take care of us if you do not?" Thereafter, some peasants requested to withdraw from the commune. According to statistics from Chenggu county, within the three districts and one town under its jurisdiction, 220 households requested to withdraw, and around 10 households have already started plowing the land that had been taken by the commune to plant crops such as potatoes.

As far as is known, the reasons for the above problems are as follows: First, some regions of Hanzhong had a bad harvest last year and the year before last, and the total grain output was reduced compared with 1954. Second, many members of the cooperatives wrongly believed that once they had become members they could rely on the commune for everything. Thus they became less mindful of food waste. Some members of the agricultural cooperatives in Shulinping in Xixiang county paid little attention to the issue: they fed their pigs

DOCUMENT 3.2 (cont.)

with grain instead of food substitute. Other members were busy with construction projects and so employed construction workers, and consequently they required additional food. Furthermore, a number of members brought in money through food trafficking. 73 out of the 78 member households of Qishi agriculture cooperative in Yangxian county sold their own grain rations on the black market and then requested more from the state. Taking advantage of relaxed market regulations, some peasants in Hanzhong, Chenggu and Baocheng sold part of their rations on the black market, where the average price was one-third higher than the normal market price. Third, quite a number of peasants (in particular rich peasants) sent "false alarms." After investigation, of the 68 households in an agricultural cooperative in Yudongzi town, Chenggu county who complained about food shortages, only 16 had real problems and the rest were false alarms. Among the 432 households who protested to the government in Shaheying town in the same county, only 105 households were really suffering from a shortage of food. Although Zhang Bingqing, a member of Heping Agricultural Cooperative in Bocheng county, had grain stockpiled at home, he nevertheless went to cause trouble at the cooperative director's house, for no other reason than because the ration distributed to him last year was slightly less than he had received before joining the cooperative. [Once inside,] Zhang told his wife and two sons to eat at the cooperative director's dinner table and fight for food [with his family], while Zhang himself threatened the director, telling him, "If you do not believe me, you can search my house!" The director had no alternative but to do so, and he found more than 500 kilograms of grain there.

Source: *Neibu Cankao*, May 8, 1957.

4 THE GREAT LEAP INTO FAMINE (1958-1961)

超英赶美
Overtake England, catch up with the United States
共产主义是天堂，人民公社是桥梁
Communism is paradise, the People's Communes are the bridge to get there
吃饭第一
Eating comes first

Yu Dehong, a cadre working in agriculture in southern Henan's Xinyang prefecture, was just one of hundreds of thousands of party members to be criticized
for "right opportunism" for doubting the success of the Great Leap Forward.
In 1959, Yu began to feel that something was amiss in rural China, but it was not
until a visit to his home village in Huaibin county in December that year that he
realized how wrong things had gone. A few miles from his village, he was
confronted with a pile of perhaps a hundred corpses, some of which looked as
if they had been scavenged by animals. When he arrived home, he found that
several members of his own family had starved to death in the preceding weeks.
Cannibalism had affected almost every village in the region.

Back at his office in Xinyang, Yu did not dare to tell his superiors the truth. He
said only that some of his elderly relatives were sick. Later, when struggle sessions
were held against him, he told his interrogators that he was sure everything in his
village would turn out fine. In his memoirs, he wrote that the relationship between
the people who were struggled against and those doing the struggling was not equal:
"Even if he is wrong, he claims whatever he wants. If he beats you up, you just have
to take it. When he beats you to death, it is seen as just punishment. If he drives you
to suicide, they say that you betrayed the party and state by escaping punishment."[1]

---

1 Yu Dehong, "Guanyu 'Xinyang shijian' de yishu," in Zhongguo nongcunyanjiu bianji weiyuanhui (ed.), *Zhongguo nongcun yanjiu 2002 quan* (Beijing: Zhongguo shehui kexue chubanshe,
2003), p. 330.

In spring 1960, both Yu's personal situation and the local grain supply improved. Now the task for cadres was to organize the digging of mass graves, often for several hundred bodies. Yu describes seeing the corpses of those who had died during the winter rotting all across the countryside, as well as the appalling smell that went with them. Around this time he learned that in his uncle's family in nearby Guangshan county, ten out of eleven people had starved to death. According to an official report from the central government later that year, 1.05 million people had died in the Xinyang famine out of a total population of nine million. In official accounts, this catastrophe was referred to simply as "the Xinyang Incident."[2]

Xinyang had been at the vanguard of the Great Leap Forward. The first People's Commune had been established there in Suiping county, and in 1958 the national media had celebrated it as a model for other areas to imitate. Yu argued that the prefecture's rapid descent into crisis had little to do with natural disaster, as the party claimed, and everything to do with the state's failings. Climatic conditions in 1959, he argued, were nowhere near as devastating as those China had experienced in 1949, and the real issue was the local government's desire to maintain the illusion of progress, which led to an unwillingness to open grain stores to the hungry. Yu kept silent about his experiences until after his retirement, finally telling his story in 2003 in a short memorial article about the "Xinyang Incident." In it he expressed his dissatisfaction that local cadres had had to shoulder most of the blame for the catastrophe. In early 1961, the central government sent 30,000 PLA troops to Xinyang and dismissed the party secretary of the district, Lu Xianwen, from office. Over 100,000 local people were investigated, thousands were punished and some cadres were jailed. But, as Yu points out, Wu Zhipu, the party secretary of Henan and one of Lu Xianwen's chief backers, was punished only with a transfer to a new job in Beijing.

The years between 1958 and 1961 can be divided into two periods. 1958 itself was the heyday of the Great Leap, a radical attempt to find a Chinese road to socialism through rural industrialization and the founding of People's Communes (*renmin gongshe*) in the villages. In a mood of utopian enthusiasm, the party leadership declared that communism could be achieved quickly,[3] promising to build a rural welfare state and to "socialize housework." However, by early 1959, a combination of poor harvests and misguided policy-making meant that some parts of the countryside were already experiencing the famine that would turn into a national catastrophe the next year. From 1959 to

2 Ibid., p. 327.

3 "Zhonggong zhongyang guanyu zai nongcun jianli renmin gongshe wenti de jueyi," in Zhongyang wenxian chubanshe (ed.), *Jianguo yilai zhongyao wenxian xuanbian* (Beijing: Zhongyang wenxian chubanshe, 1992) [herinafter "*JGYL*"], Vol. 11, p. 450.

1961, 15 to 40 million Chinese people, mainly peasants, starved to death. This chapter will assess the impact of the Great Leap and the famine on peasants and cadres, progress towards women's liberation, and the United Front in Tibet. We will also examine why the Great Leap failed in the first place, along with the vexed question of the famine's size and demographic impact.

1958 and the Road to Dystopia

The Great Leap Forward represented a move away from the Soviet model of development emphasized during the First Five Year Plan. Heavy industry remained the focus of investment, but the system of planning was decentralized, as the ministries in Beijing delegated more and more responsibilities to the provincial governments. Nevertheless, the central government continued to set the overall tone. The party leadership, looking to accelerate China's economic and industrial development, sought to mobilize rural labor power to "overtake England [and] catch up with the United States." Their main target was steel production, a potent symbol of industrial modernity. In the first half of 1958, the leadership initiated a new campaign to set up "backyard furnaces" to smelt steel in villages across the country. The other major target was grain. In 1957, leaders such as Chen Yun had clearly said that it would take time to solve China's food problem. Now, hundreds of millions of peasants were mobilized to build dikes and dams to overcome the devastating impact of natural disasters on crop yields.

In the second half of 1958, the flow of information and rational economic planning collapsed. A mixture of genuine enthusiasm and political pressure from above saw local cadres report soaring figures for grain and steel production. Soon, competition developed at the county and village level to announce increasingly implausible levels of output, leading to a so-called "wind of exaggeration" (*fukuafeng*). Buoyed by this apparent success, the higher levels of government raised local quotas for steel and grain, which in turn placed even more pressure on cadres to inflate their figures. It was not until the onset of winter that Mao and the central leadership realized that many of the achievements they believed the Great Leap had delivered in fact existed only on paper. At this point, Mao called on cadres to report the real figures, but he refused to significantly reduce grain production quotas.

Production Armies and the Rural "Iron Rice Bowl"

The devastating impact of the "wind of exaggeration" was made all the worse because it did not strike immediately. The harvest of 1958 was relatively good, and this allowed the central leadership to push ahead with more radical transformation, believing, erroneously, that the grain question had been solved. At a conference at the coastal town of Beidaihe in August 1958, the Central Committee decided to organize the whole of the Han Chinese peasantry into People's Communes like those already established by local cadres in Henan. Each commune, often with a membership running into the tens of thousands, would take charge of agriculture, industry, government, finance, education and militia defense in the area under its control, with the potential to eventually replace the state apparatus entirely. The CCP promoted the notion of People's Communes as bridges to communism, and the official media were full of reports of peasants elated at the prospect of being able to eat as much as they wanted from the communal dining halls.

Party leaders envisioned the commune member as a kind of "all-rounder" who would be a worker, peasant and intellectual at the same time. To achieve this goal, peasants would have to "intellectualize," while at the other end of the spectrum intellectuals would be required to "proletarianize" and "peasantize."[4] By far the most pressing problem here was a lack of rural education. The CCP therefore began a nationwide campaign to rapidly eliminate illiteracy, and the new communes were encouraged to build elementary and middle schools. Villages competed to revitalize rural culture by collecting and writing folk songs. From the cities, college students and lecturers were sent to the countryside to support the Great Leap, and universities also built factories and established farms to contribute to the education of the new communist "all-around men."

In the early days of the Leap, the government promoted the slogan, "militarize organization, operate like on a battlefield and collectivize life." In some regions, the rural workforce was organized into "production armies" set up on military lines. The Central Committee also planned that, by 1962, 700 million Chinese citizens between the ages of sixteen and fifty would be armed as part of the militia, with only landlords, rich peasants, counterrevolutionaries, bad elements, rightists and the disabled excluded.[5] Women, who had fought in the militia during the war against Japan but been removed from front-line service after 1949, were called to arms once more. The task of the militia was to secure production, safeguard public security and support the PLA's national defense capabilities, and both it and the militarized rural workforce came under the leadership of local party committees. This rediscovery by the CCP of its traditions of "guerrilla-style" politics represented an indirect challenge to the USSR's highly centralized and professionalized military system.

---

4 For example see *Renmin Ribao*, October 8, 1958.
5 "Zhonggong zhongyang guanyu minbingwenti de jueding," in *JGYL*, Vol. 11, p. 469.

In 1957, some of the most stinging "rightist" critiques had focused on the CCP's creation of a "dual society" through restrictions on internal migration and the exclusion of the rural population from the welfare state. In early 1958, the household registration system was extended further, so that the entire population was divided between "agricultural" and "non-agricultural" *hukou* holders. Far from relaxing their grip on migration, the leadership now sought to control it more tightly, judging that the country still lacked the resources to allow unlimited access to urban welfare arrangements. Against this background, the People's Communes can be seen as a response to the problems of the "dual society." With their promise of plenty for all and a new set of entitlements for the peasant population, they represented a "new deal" for rural China that would bridge the divide between city and country and begin to erase the division of labor between the two.

The newspaper *People's Daily* described model communes that had moved from simple collective ownership to "ownership of the whole people," in which almost no private property remained. The bylaws of Sputnik Commune in Suiping county in Henan declared that all plots for private use, houses, trees and savings were to be owned by the commune. This statute was published by the *Red Flag* journal and was frequently reprinted as an example of best practice. Along with these reforms came the promised welfare entitlements. In September 1958, the *People's Daily* proudly declared: "Villages in Henan are complementing the distribution of grain with a wage system: a guarantee for a happy life." The same article assured readers that the "iron rice bowl" was to be introduced to the countryside.[6] Model communes claimed to guarantee food, material for clothing, medical care, education and housing and to bear costs for births, weddings and funerals. All over mainland China with the exception of Tibet, public dining halls were established by the People's Communes in autumn of 1958. In the early days, strict rationing of food and "distribution according to labor performance" were abolished in many places as the new era of bounty beckoned.

Dependency in the Communes

The CCP promoted the People's Communes as a way to gradually move peasants from "outside" to "inside the system," and their introduction met little resistance in the Han areas. Many local cadres and peasants appear to have responded enthusiastically to the war on rural backwardness and the promise of food security and welfare entitlements. However, the utopia of 1958 had dystopian

---

6 *Renmin Ribao*, September 29, 1958.

aspects from the moment of its inception. The loss of plots for private use and household food stocks left peasants devoid of any independent means of self-sufficiency and dependent on the communes for food security. One consequence of this dependency was an increase in the power of the local cadres who oversaw the public dining halls. The potential dangers of this new authority were already being foreshadowed before the famine struck, in decisions such as the declaration in Henan that local communes should ensure "whoever does not labor, should not eat."[7] When food became scarce in the winter of 1958, many peasants were left at the mercy of cadres. As shortage turned to famine, building and maintaining good relations with these power holders became a matter of life and death.

The militarization of the rural workforce meant that peasants were required to obey orders from above, and many people were essentially worked to death in 1958 as a combination of lack of food and insufficient rest took their toll. In addition to working the land, peasants were also required to make further sacrifices for the steel campaign. A wide range of metal objects, including woks and other kitchen implements, were collected from private households to be melted down in the backyard furnaces. While the houses of "class enemies" had often been plundered during Land Reform in the early 1950s, 1958 was the first time that those with good class backgrounds had had their possessions removed in this way. Communal resources were also targeted, with large tracts of forest cut down to fuel the furnaces. Output, however, proved underwhelming: a lack of knowledge and resources among the locals manning them meant that in many cases the furnaces produced little more than high-carbon pig iron. In the villages themselves, archival research has shown that many peasants lost not only their possessions but their houses, which were torn down to provide space and materials for public dining halls and new public accommodation. In some areas, thousands of people were left temporarily homeless as the Great Leap gathered steam. Graves were destroyed to create more agricultural land, sparking anger in a country where ancestor worship was still widespread.[8]

In official accounts compiled during the Reform era, the "wind of exaggeration" is mainly blamed on local cadres. The push for full socialization of rural property is also attributed to local factors. The official narrative stresses that "small peasant absolute egalitarianism," the ideology supposed to have whipped up the "wind of communism" in the villages, emerged spontaneously among the

---

7 "Henan Sheng nongcun renmingongshe shixing zhangcheng," in Zhongguo renmin daxue (ed.), *Renmingongshe cankao ziliao xuanji* (Beijing: Zhongguo renmindaxue, 1958), p. 27.
8 Wang Yanni, "An Introduction to the ABCs of Communication: A Case Study of Macheng County," in Felix Wemheuer and Kimberley Ens Manning (eds.), *Eating Bitterness: New Perspectives on China's Great Leap Forward and Famine* (Vancouver: UBC Press, 2011), pp. 160–162.

peasant population.[9] This attempt to paint the origins of the Great Leap disaster as fundamentally local seems to me to be rather too charitable to the central government. It is true that "ownership of the whole people" and the rural "iron rice bowl" were originally local innovations, but it was the approbation of official media such as the *People's Daily* and the *Red Flag* which turned them into national models. The party leadership initially refrained from ordering all villages to adopt the most radical Great Leap policies, but it gave local actors the clear impression that the transition to communism was achievable within a few years and that radicalism might therefore be desirable. Indeed, in the second half of 1958, several months went by during which local cadres, already under pressure to report swift progress in every policy field, might reasonably have believed that the People's Communes were intended to be fully communist institutions. It was not until December that the Central Committee clarified its expectations, indicating that although the communes were to include communist elements, they should still be socialist institutions based on collective ownership, not ownership of the whole people. The decision asserted that true communism – the abolition of commodity production and the replacement of "distribution according to labor performance" by "distribution according to need" – would have to wait until a later date. In the meantime, further increases in productivity would be needed to lay the groundwork for this final stage of the transformation.[10] The December decision was a blow to some of the headier visions of the early Great Leap. By early 1959, the utopian moment was over in any case, as several provinces began to slide into famine.

The Failure of the Second Women's Liberation

As we have already seen, the early Great Leap had social as well as agricultural and industrial components. With the establishment of the communes in 1958, the CCP launched a national initiative to "socialize housework," replacing some functions of the family with public institutions. This move, however, had less to do with gender equality per se than it did with the need for massive labor power for irrigation projects and the steel campaign. The party's motivations were reflected in official articles and documents, which largely spoke not of "liberation of women" but of "liberation of the female workforce."

---

9 Bo Yibo, *Ruogan zhongda juece yu shijian de huigu* (Beijing: Zhongyang dangxiao chubanshe, 1991), Vol. 2, pp. 1284–1285.
10 "Guanyu renmingongshe ruogan wenti de jueyi," in *JGYL*, Vol. 11, p. 602.

Figure 4.1: Daycare for Children in Zhengzhou, 1976.
Source: Photograph by Helmut Opletal.

The number of women in work had already expanded dramatically under Mao. In 1949, women had made up only 7.5 percent of the urban workforce, but this number increased more than threefold over the next decade to more than 25 percent in 1957. In the countryside, the labor participation rate for women working outside the home rose from 60 percent in 1952 to 90 percent in 1958.[11] During the Great Leap, the number of female workers in state-owned enterprises increased still more rapidly, from 3.2 million in 1957 to 8.1 million in 1958 and 10 million in 1960, more than double the overall rate of worker growth in the sector.[12] Nevertheless, until 1958 the gendered division of reproduction and care work remained largely unchanged. It was only during the radical heyday of the Great Leap that autumn that serious questions began to be asked about the relevance of basic family structures to China's communist future. As the Leap intensified, debate broke out over whether the family itself might not soon wither away.

11 Wu Hanquan, *Zhongguo dangdai shehuishi (1956–1966)*, Vol. 2 (Changsha: Hunan renmin chubanshe, 2011), pp. 288–289.
12 Guojia tongjiju shehui tongjisi (ed.), *Zhongguo laodong gongzi tongji ziliao, 1949–1985* (Beijing: Guojia tongji chubanshe, 1987), p. 32.

The Socialization of Housework

In August 1958, the CCP Central Committee stated that the communes should build public dining halls, nurseries for infants, kindergartens, middle schools, homes for the elderly and public shower halls to establish a new collective life and raise the collective consciousness of the peasants.[13] In party propaganda, one important argument for establishing dining halls was that to do so would result in the "liberation of the female workforce." An official brochure, "The People's Commune and Communism," argued that China's economic development was being held back by a lack of labor power in agriculture and industry, which could be partly alleviated by freeing female labor from domestic work. The author, Wu Ren, quoted an investigation that found that the "socialization of housework" had freed 20 million women in seven provinces to join production lines.[14] In Wu's telling, the New Democratic Revolution and the socialist transformation had already liberated women from political and economic exploitation. Now, the establishment of the communes would allow them to leave the "narrow circle of the nuclear family," marking a further step towards eliminating the feudalist and individualist thinking of the old China among both men and women. As Wu saw it, the family as an economic unit was on its way out. Another author called the establishment of public dining halls and kindergartens the "second women's liberation."[15]

Whether the CCP leadership ever actually intended to use the public dining halls and kindergartens to eliminate the family is a matter of debate. Both Mao and Liu Shaoqi were fond of referring to the late Qing philosopher Kang Youwei's *Book of Great Unity* (*Datong shu*), which imagined a world without states, classes or families. The central government never passed any resolutions calling for the elimination of the family. However, some model communes did advance policies in this direction, separating parents and children as well as husbands and wives into separate dormitories. Official documents indicate that many cadres on the ground were confused by such policies. An internal PLA report from December 1958 records cadres asking questions such as, "If we achieve communism, do we or do we not want to preserve the family? How will relations between family members look in the future?"[16] The All China Women's Federation received a number of letters from women asking whether a future communist society would neglect family life.[17]

---

13 "Zhonggong zhongyang guanyu zai nongcun jianli renmin gongshe wenti de jueyi," p. 446.
14 Wu Ren, *Renmingongshe he gongchanzhuyi* (Beijing: Gongren chubanshe, 1958), p. 31.
15 Zhongguo qingnian chubanshe (ed.), *Lun renmingongshe* (Beijing: Zhongguo qingnian chubanshe, 1958), p. 91.
16 *Xuanchuan Jianbao*, No. 22 (December 10, 1958), p. 6.
17 Hu Sheng, "Guanyu jiating," in Zhongguo funü zazhi (ed.), *Dang de zongluxian zhaoyao zhe wo guo funü chedi jiefang de daolu* (Beijing: 1960), p. 67.

Debates in the official media discussed the abolition of the nuclear family and considered whether a new kind of socialist family should replace the old bourgeois one, or whether the family model should simply be abandoned wholesale. Henan party secretary Wu Zhipu favored abandonment, writing with reference to the socialization of housework that:

> After the establishment of the People's Communes, the family is a unit neither of production nor of living. Family is one form of relations between relatives, and the boundaries between the families have been dismantled. The idea of the family is becoming weaker. Now, the commune, the society and the state are the family. In the future, the whole world will become a family and a Great Unity. The change caused by the collectivization of life is very significant. This is just the greatest reform.[18]

The (male) philosopher Du Renzhi argued that the commune would assume responsibility for educating children and caring for the elderly in old people's homes, and that in consequence the definition of the family should be restricted to the partnership between husband and wife. "Under these conditions," he wrote, "the responsibility of the mother for her baby is just a matter of breastfeeding."[19]

Other commentators viewed the socialization of housework simply as the replacement of one form of family by another. A September 1958 article in *Red Flag* described how the development of capitalism had destroyed the feudalist family. Now, the socialization of housework would destroy the bourgeois family as an independent unit of production and society, replacing it with a socialist family that would retain the traditional nuclear structure but allow its members to develop closer bonds to the outside world through the new public institutions. The family would survive, but in a new form that would better promote the wealth and happiness of China's citizens.[20]

After the Beidaihe Conference in 1958, many communes developed plans to construct new buildings intended for collective life. In Sputnik Commune in Henan, peasants were expected to live in multi-storey collective houses equivalent to those occupied by workers in the cities. The planners behind the new blocks felt that collective housing should replace traditional one-family buildings, and considerable care was put into their design. The first step was to separate the population into apartments by age and profession, and then to organize small children and primary school students into separate dormitories. For married couples, a private room would be provided, but all unmarried men

18 Wu Zhipu, "Lun remingongshe," *Xuanchuan Jianbao* (August 25, 1958), p. 6.
19 Du Renzhi, *Renmingongshe xiang gongchanzhuyi guodu de ji ge wenti* (Beijing: Kexue chubanshe, 1958), p. 66.
20 *Hongqi*, September 1, 1958, p. 30.

and women, including the commune's young manual labor force, would live in collective rooms with two or three roommates. Living space of 3.5 to 4 square meters per person was seen as sufficient, because residents would eat in the public dining halls and would therefore not require space for cooking and other domestic work. For the young manual laborers, the backbone of the commune, a separate dining hall was planned with capacity for up to 4,000 people.[21]

Patriarchy Resurgent: The Rural Family Survives

Most of these plans were never realized due to lack of resources, and many public institutions in rural China existed only on paper even at the height of the Great Leap. As we have seen, even before the famine began to bite in early 1959, the party leadership was already emphasizing that achieving communism was a goal of the distant future, and discussion of abolishing the family was also on the wane. The public dining halls seem to have been popular initially, and slogans such as "communism means eating for free" proved attractive to the rural population. ("Free" in this context meant that food was no longer rationed.) However, attitudes changed in 1959 as meals in the dining halls become sparser, and support for the new institutions fell still further in 1960, when distribution stopped completely in some areas. Instead of being liberated from housework, men and women now had to use their shrinking energies to search for or steal food. It was not only the dining halls that failed as the famine struck: provision of food and care in the kindergartens and old people's homes was often just as poor. Although nominally liberated, women faced pressure to pick up the slack as the care system began to fall apart, and working in the fields or on irrigation projects became, unsurprisingly, a secondary concern for many.

Mao himself continued to publicly promote the People's Communes and dining halls. Participation rates decreased in the first half of 1959, when the government reduced the pressure to communize, but increased again after the Lushan Conference that summer, when opposing public dining was designated as an act of "right opportunism." Only in 1961 were the public dining halls permanently shut down. By this time, it was clear that the "socialization of housework" had turned into a major disaster for rural China. This did not mean, however, that women simply returned to their old lives. Now they were called both to work in the fields and to perform care work at home. During the day, hard labor remained, while at night, spinning and weaving were done.

21 Hua'nan Gongxueyuan Jianzhuxi, *Guihua sheji – Henan Sheng Suiping Xian weixing renmin-gongshe diyi jicengshe* (Hua'nan Gongxueyuan Jianzhuxi, 1958), pp. 19–24.

Before 1949, young wives had often served essentially as the domestic servants of their mothers-in-law. As more young women started to work in the fields, the task of caring for the family's children and elderly fell increasingly on the older generation. In spite of these changes, however, the vision of Wu Zhipu and other radicals of eliminating the rural family as a unit of production and consumption never came to pass. By 1961, plots for private use had been reintroduced, and the return of distribution according to work points meant that the income of the family once again became highly dependent on young male labor power.

The feminist scholar Judith Stacey argues that:

> The Great Leap Forward ... violated the unarticulated terms of the patriarchal-socialist accommodation ... [Great Leap] policies attempted to bypass the peasant family economy in both production and consumption patterns, and peasants actively resisted the antifamily implications of these efforts. Their resistance, combined with natural and diplomatic disasters, wreaked havoc on the nation's economy. The regime was forced to capitulate.[22]

There is some merit to this reading, but it seems to me that peasants, male and female, had every reason to resist public dining on practical grounds, even before any questions of social structure are taken into account. Many communes that had taken over food management and distribution simply proved unable to feed their members. We can only speculate whether peasants would have accepted the "socialization of housework" if it had been effectively implemented, but in the face of famine it was understandable that many communities fell back on the survival strategies of past.

In the aftermath of the Great Leap the case for radical social reform was unavoidably tainted. As a result, the CCP was forced to make its peace with the rural patriarchy and the gendered division of labor. After 1962, party campaigns continued to attack "feudalist attitudes" such as preferring sons over daughters, but no new institution building took place to tackle the gendering of labor in the countryside. Contra Stacey, I would argue that the tragedy of the Great Leap was not that it was caused by patriarchal resistance, but rather that, by its failure, it ended up strengthening the patriarchs' hand. It was in part because of this failure that rural China remained trapped in a semi-socialist state for several decades to come.

The Great Leap in the Cities: Urban Communes and the Mobilization of Women

Before 1958, the state was reluctant to mobilize the "unused labor" of urban women for industrial production. State-owned enterprises generally sought to

---

22 Judith Stacey, *Patriarchy and Socialist Revolution in China* (Berkeley, CA: University Press of California, 1983), p. 253.

avoid accepting the family members of their male workers, in the belief that to do so would increase their expenses for welfare entitlements and housing. Older housewives generally had little formal education, and many work units were concerned that training them would impose additional costs. Taking on a mother with young children, meanwhile, required the unit to fund childcare places for the children she was leaving at home, increasing the expense of hiring her relative to a male worker. In some quarters, a belief that women were unfit for certain kinds of work doubtless also played a role.

The central government's attitude changed with the beginning of the Great Leap. Now, a large number of urban women were mobilized, including wives and other relatives of workers, along with students, former petty traders and women with bad family backgrounds. Between 1957 and 1958, the number of female workers in urban areas increased from 3 million to over 8 million. In some places, policies were promoted to replace men with women in the trade and service sectors.[23]

By the spring of 1959, the central government was calling for a reduction in the number of urban workers. Losses were intended to be spread evenly between male and female workers, but in June the authorities circulated a report by the party organizations of the Women's Federation and the Labor Unions complaining that, in some places, officials were seeking to lay off only women. The report steered clear of questioning the workforce reductions themselves, but it harshly criticized the gendered nature of the process. Married women, who made up about 10 percent of new female workers, were apparently at increased risk of being targeted because of a belief that the burdens of housework and childcare prevented them from focusing fully on their work.[24] The layoffs, however, did not last long. After the Lushan Conference, radicalism was once again the order of the day, and in the second half of 1959 the government began a new wave of mobilization. By the end of the year, the number of female workers in state-owned work units had increased to 8.4 million, around 18 percent of the total workforce in this sector.[25]

Another notable feature of the Great Leap in the cities was the CCP's push to introduce an urban version of the People's Communes. As was the case in the rural areas, this policy was intimately connected to the party's effort to bring more women into the productive sectors of the economy. Between late 1958 and

---

23 "Zhonggong zhongyang pizhuan quanguo fulian dangzu, quanguo zonggonghui dangzu guanyu caijian xin nüzhigong wenti de baogao," in Zhongyang dang'an guan (ed.), *Zhonggong zhongyang wenjian xuanji* (Beijing: Renmin chubanshe, 2013), Vol. 31, p. 415.

24 Ibid., p. 416.

25 "Zhonggong zhongyang pizhuan laodongbu dangzu guanyu nügong laodong baohu gongzuo de baogao," *Zhonggong zhongyang wenjian xuanji* (Beijing: Renmin chubanshe, 2013), Vol. 34, pp. 416–417.

Figure 4.2: Women on a tea production brigade at Longjing near Hangzhou, 1974.
Source: Photograph by Olli Salmi.

early 1960, a number of cities experimented with urban communization, encouraging residential districts to establish small factories alongside existing state-owned enterprises. In March 1960, the Central Committee issued an order that all cities should establish People's Communes. These new institutions were not counted as state owned, meaning that their workers and staff were not entitled to the high salaries and generous benefits afforded to their counterparts in the regular industries. The "five bad elements" were excluded from commune membership, but they were still required to perform labor.

The communes provided a way to mobilize women's labor without overburdening the state sector, and their workforce skewed overwhelmingly female. Data from eleven Chinese cities indicates that, on average, 76 percent of staff in the industrial communes were women, a figure which rose as high as 95 percent in Beijing.[26] In July 1960, the central government circulated a report from the party organization of the Labor Ministry that praised the mobilization of women in the urban communes and the expansion of childcare in work units and residential districts. The news was not all positive, however. The report criticized the failure of some factories to adequately consider the health of female workers

26 Li Duanxiang, *Chengshi renmingongshe yundong yanjiu* (Changsha: Hunan renmin chubanshe, 2006), p. 157.

when assigning labor, citing statistics suggesting that at least 14 percent of working urban women could expect to experience miscarriage if they fell pregnant. Many state-owned factories were not paying female contract workers during maternity leave, with some openly instructing any woman who reported a pregnancy to go home. Demand for daycare far outstripped supply, and social services in commune-operated work units remained weak.[27]

It remains unclear why the central leadership chose to establish urban communes at the height of the famine, when the state's capacity to successfully innovate was at its weakest. Whatever the motivation, the project was only short-lived, and by May 1962 the central government had determined that all except the most successful urban communes should close their factories. By the time the closures took effect, around 1.5 million people, including upwards of a million women, were working in these enterprises.[28] Women were also severely affected by the simultaneous downsizing of the state-owned sector. From a peak of 10 million in 1960, the number of female workers fell to 8.8 million in 1961 and 6.5 million in 1963.[29] Partly on this basis, a number of scholars have argued that urban women in effect constituted a "labor reserve," mobilized by the state when needed and then sent home when the workforce was downsized. For these women, the socialist welfare state was less an "iron rice bowl" than a fragile "clay rice bowl," liable to break at the earliest opportunity.[30] These arguments are in many ways compelling, and they provide a useful way to think about the state's attitude to the female workforce. Nevertheless, it should be remembered that, taken as a whole, the number of urban women working in "iron rice bowl" jobs in the state-owned enterprises more than doubled between 1957 and 1963, from 3.2 to 6.5 million.[31] This final figure represented a significant fall from the peak of 1960, but in aggregate it did represent some progress in integrating women into the urban workplace.

The Great Leap Famine

Why did the Great Leap end in famine, and why did that famine result in the deaths of so many millions? In the PRC, discussion of the famine was taboo until

---

27 "Zhonggong zhongyang pizhuan laodongbu dangzu guanyu nügong laodong baohu gongzuo de baogao," p. 418.
28 Li Duanxiang, *Chengshi renmingongshe yundong yanjiu*, p. 181.
29 Guojia tongjiju shehui tongjisi (ed.), *Zhongguo laodong gongzi tongji ziliao*, p. 32.
30 Tang Xiaojing, "Jia – Guo luoji zhijian: Zhongguo shehuizhuyi shiqi 'dayuejin funü' de 'nifan-wan'," *Funü yanjiu luncong*, No. 3 (2013), p. 67.
31 Guojia tongjiju shehui tongjisi (ed.), *Zhongguo laodong gongzi tongji ziliao*, p. 32.

the late 1990s. The Central Committee's authoritative 1981 resolution on party history makes no mention of the term, referring only to "great economic difficulties" and "damage to the people," which it blames on natural disasters, "leftist mistakes" by Mao Zedong and the sudden withdrawal of Soviet experts from China.[32] Alongside Mao, the rest of the collective leadership also came in for criticism for their handling of the disaster. Over the last ten years, the naming taboo has been partially relaxed, and some Chinese historians have begun to use the term "Great Famine" (*da jihuang*) in place of the officially sanctioned "three years of difficulties."

The Urban-Biased System of Entitlements

To understand how the famine unfolded, we must examine the system of food production and distribution as a whole. As suggested above, the rationing and distribution system set up in mid-1955 had a strong urban bias and was essentially designed to extract grain from rural areas to feed industrial development in the cities. Even prior to the famine, average consumption of grain was already low in many parts of the countryside. This was the background to the substantial fall in grain production that took place between 1958 and 1960, when statistics published in the Reform era indicate that China's overall grain output dropped by about one-third.

The decline in production was attributable to a number of factors: the chaos that accompanied the introduction of the larger communes; poor labor performance leading to reduced productivity; and general labor shortages in agriculture. Natural disasters and unfavorable climatic conditions also played a key role, but no serious Western or Chinese scholar regards bad weather as the major reason for the famine. A decline in production alone would not have been enough to cause tens of millions of deaths. It is striking that deaths from starvation occurred mainly in the countryside, where food was produced, and not in the cities.

The countryside bore the brunt of the famine in part because, under the unified purchase and sale system, the state could continue to appropriate as much grain as it saw fit, even under starvation conditions. Net grain procurement as a proportion of the harvest actually increased after 1956, rising from 14.9 percent to 28 percent in 1959, followed by a decrease to a still elevated 21.5 percent in 1960, the peak of the rural famine.[33] This supposedly surplus grain was used to

---

32 "Guanyu jianguo yilai dang de ruogan lishi wenti de jueyi," http://cpc.people.com.cn/GB/ 64162/64168/64563/65374/4526452.html, (accessed June 7, 2017).

33 Regarding production and procurement see: Zhonghua renmin gongheguo nongye bu jihuasi (ed.), *Zhongguo nongcun jingji tongji daquan 1949–1986* (Beijing: Nongye chubanshe, 1989), pp. 410–411.

feed the expanding urban population and rural labor power outside of agriculture, and some of it was also exported. Despite the enforcement of the nationwide household registration system, between 1957 and 1960 the population of China's cities and towns increased by over 30 million people, and industrial enterprises continued to recruit labor power from the countryside to fulfill the ambitious targets of the Great Leap.[34] This trend meant that fewer agrarian producers had to nourish a much larger urban population, even as crops began to fail.

From 1959 onwards, average grain consumption started to decline in rural areas. In response, in September 1960 the central government decided to cut rations. But while the cuts applied to both rural and urban areas, in the cities rations were only moderately reduced, while in the countryside a much larger fall brought rations down to starvation level. Even these modest rations did not always make it to the peasants, who technically had no defined entitlement to food. In many regions, the rural population received no grain at all, and people were left trying to survive on supplements, such as sweet potato stems or corn husks, which often lacked any nutritional value. Despite the famine, the central government continued to export large quantities of grain to the Soviet Union and Eastern Europe to service debts for industrial aid. In 1959, China exported 4.74 million tons of grain, and even at the height of the famine in 1960 another million tons were sent overseas. Although this represented only a small percentage of the overall harvest, in terms of the numbers who died it was potentially decisive. Based on a ration of 500 grams of grain per person per day (around 1,750 calories), the exports of 1959 would have been sufficient to feed 25.9 million people for a year. A further 5.4 million people could have been supported from the reduced exports of 1960.[35] Nevertheless, it was not until the end of 1960 that the CCP reversed direction and began to import food.

The average urban resident fared considerably better than the average peasant during the famine. Nevertheless, even within urban society, significant differences existed in levels of food distribution, influenced by a complex set of social and political hierarchies. Several decisions by the central government stipulated that the distribution of food to Beijing, Shanghai and Tianjin (and to Liaoning province, an important industrial center) were to be prioritized.[36] Inevitably, this resulted in severe famine in neighboring regions. To guarantee Shanghai's food

---

34 Lu Yu, *Xin Zhongguo renkou wushi nian* (Beijing: Zhongguo renkou chubanshe, 2004), Vol. 1, p. 633.

35 Felix Wemheuer, *Famine Politics in Maoist China and the Soviet Union* (New Haven, CT: Yale University Press, 2014), pp. 53–54.

36 For example: "Zhonggong zhongyang guanyu liji zhuajin liangshi diaoyun de tongzhi," in *JGYL*, Vol. 13, pp. 702–703.

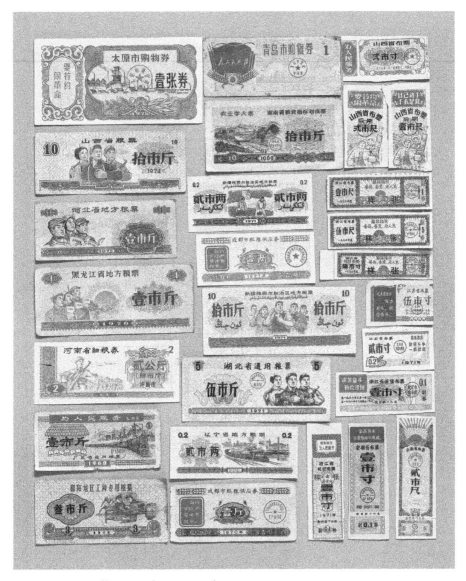

Figure 4.3: A collection of ration cards.
Source: Helmut Opletal (ed.), *Die Kultur der Kulturrevolution: Personenkult und politisches Design im China von Mao Zedong* (Wien: Museum für Völkerkunde, 2011), p. 228.

supply, grain was appropriated with special ferocity from Anhui, Zhejiang and Jiangsu provinces, leading to millions of deaths in Anhui in particular. Death rates in the hinterland around major cities varied with the quality of the provincial leadership. Some officials successfully sought to reduce the outflow of grain from their provinces through negotiations with the central government; others

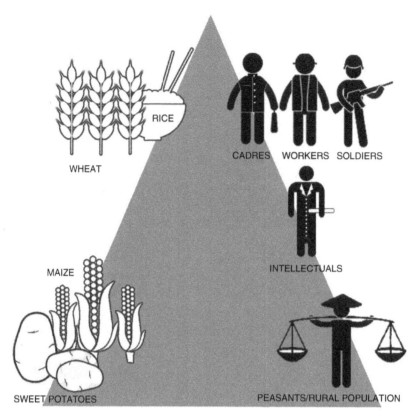

Figure 4.4: Hierarchies in the grain rationing system in China (1955–1983).
Source: Felix Wemheuer, *Famine Politics in Maoist China and the Soviet Union* (New Haven, CT: Yale University Press, 2014), p. 245. Reproduced with permission of the publisher.

chose to implement central directives without question, with predictable consequences. The zealotry of the leadership in Henan, Sichuan and Anhui saw those places continue to ship grain to other provinces, even when the extent of starvation became undeniable.

Within the cities themselves, some groups of people were prioritized over others. The army was one of the safest places to be, and its food supply remained stable throughout the famine. The government also provided extra rations to high-ranking intellectuals and workers in key industries.[37] Important officials who were provided with additional food were known popularly as "sugar and beans" cadres. In the universities, many teachers and students suffered from malnutrition-induced edema,

37 Bian Yanjun and Zhang Wenhe, *Li Xiannian zhuan, 1949–1992* (Beijing: Zhongyang wenxian chubanshe, 2009), Vol. 1, pp. 500–501.

but there were few deaths, and the first most heard of widespread starvation was when they visited relatives in the villages. As the famine worsened, the hierarchies established in the mid-1950s went from determining who received certain privileges to determining, in large part, who lived and who died. (See Figure 4.4.)

The CCP Purge and its Impact on the Famine

As the problems in rural China became steadily more apparent, Mao personally oversaw a "rectification" of the Great Leap in the first half of 1959, rolling back some of the policies that had disrupted agriculture over the winter. However, a power struggle at that summer's Lushan Conference resulted in another about-turn, contributing to a revival of public dining, a doubling down on the steel campaign and talk of a transition to full communism. The spark for this second slide into radicalism came from Mao's outspoken Defense Minister Peng Dehuai, a hero of the Korean War, who criticized the steel campaign in a personal letter to the chairman. Mao sensed an attack on the Great Leap and on his own authority, and a recent visit by Peng to the USSR and Eastern Europe, encouraged him to see hints of a Soviet-backed plot against his leadership. He responded with some force, dismissing Peng from office and attacking him and his supporters as an "anti-party, anti-socialist clique." It was the first time since 1949 that a member of the inner circle of the party leadership had been purged for expressing criticism internally.

Since the 1920s, the CCP leadership had used the concept of "left and right deviations" to criticize party members who strayed too far from the correct political line. Now, in the light of Peng's letter, a new category of error was devised to deal with opponents of the Great Leap. The Central Committee defined "right opportunism" as doubting the achievements of, or resistance against, the Three Red Banners, namely the general line of socialist construction, the prosecution of the Great Leap Forward and the establishment of the People's Communes. "Right opportunistic" tendencies inside the party were viewed as an expression of class struggle in society and as the result of residual bourgeois ideology. In November 1959, the Central Committee stressed that this label should not be used for members of the democratic parties, capitalists or bourgeois intellectuals. Through the United Front Work Department, the leadership made clear that these groups had already been re-educated during the Anti-Rightist Campaign and that the label of "right opportunism" should therefore be reserved exclusively for the struggle within the CCP.[38]

38 "Zhonggong zhongyang pizhuan zhongyang tongzhanbu 'Guanyu minzhudangpai, zichanjieji-fenzi he zichanjieji zhishifenzi zhong bu jinxing fanyouqing douzheng de zhengfeng yundong de yijian'," in Zhongyang dang'an guan (ed.), *Zhonggong zhongyang wenxian xuanji* (Beijing: Renmin chubanshe, 2013), Vol. 32, p. 33.

The anti-Peng campaign against right opportunists had a devastating impact. The Central Committee decided in 1960 that up to 1 percent of all cadres should be targeted and 1 percent of all party members expelled.[39] However, this quota was substantially exceeded, and, about 3.6 million out of 13.5 million members of the CCP were eventually labeled.[40] The effect of the turn from "rectification" to struggle against right opportunism is exemplified by the experience of a university investigation team sent to the provinces in November 1958. One hundred and sixty-two researchers from Peking and Renmin Universities, two of the most prestigious institutions in the country, were dispatched to Hebei and Henan to examine the progress of the People's Communes. Much of their work focused on Xinyang prefecture, soon to become the epicenter of the Henan famine. Instead of great achievements and an incipient utopia, the team found evidence of disaster in the offing. Chen Nianhui (ps.), a teacher from Renmin University, was part of the team. In an interview with me, he recalled that the 1958 harvest was good, but that after the establishment of the People's Communes the work ethic of the peasants collapsed: "No one was working hard anymore. Huge waste was widespread and many people ate without considering life or death. In 1959, nothing was left."[41] Cadres still had enough to eat, but some peasants had already succumbed to starvation-induced edema.

The head of the investigation was Zou Lufeng, the vice-dean of Renmin University. A "revolutionary cadre" who had fought in a guerrilla unit against the Japanese, Zou had impeccable communist credentials. His team's final report condemned the haste with which the People's Communes had been established and raised concerns over the abolition of distribution according to labor performance. At this stage, with Mao's "rectification" still ongoing and officials keen to identify shortcomings in Great Leap policies, the report's critical tone attracted little censure. After the Lushan Conference, however, the ground began to shift under the investigators' feet. The party leadership at the two universities re-evaluated the report, which was now declared to have "slandered" the Three Red Banners. Members of the investigation team were attacked as "right opportunists" and forced to perform self-criticism in internal struggle meetings. For Zou, the pressure and humiliation of the struggle process proved to be too much,

---

39 "Zhonggong zhongyang guanyu zai fanyou zhengfeng yundong he nongcun zhengdang yundong zhong duiyu fan cuowu de dangyuan ganbu de chufenmian de tongzhi," in Zhongyang dang'an guan (ed.), *Zhonggong zhongyang wenxian xuanji* (Beijing: Renmin chubanshe, 2013), Vol. 33, p. 38.

40 Thomas Bernstein, "Mao Zedong and the Famine of 1959–1960: A Study in Willfulness," *The China Quarterly*, No. 186 (2006), p. 432.

41 Interview with the author, Beijing, May 2002.

and on October 26, 1959 he drowned himself in a lake near Peking University. The party subsequently determined that this constituted "escaping criticism by committing suicide," and Zou was posthumously expelled from the CCP. Chen Nianhui fared rather better. He was criticized, but his punishment was limited to a transfer to a People's Commune near Beijing. He remembers being well treated by local cadres, who were all too familiar with the problems in the People's Communes that the report had identified. With the end of the Great Leap, the members of the Xinyang investigation team were rehabilitated. For Zou, however, it was too late.

Between the summer of 1959 and the first half of 1960, the CCP mobilized the propaganda apparatus to celebrate the "achievements" of the Great Leap and to demonstrate that the criticisms of the "right opportunists" were misplaced. For about a year, most officials, the memory of the purge fresh in their minds, avoided reporting deaths by starvation in the areas under their jurisdiction, and many covered up negative developments of any kind. Some reports about famine did reach the central government, but until the autumn of 1960 these continued to underestimate the extent of the disaster.

When Mao and the central leadership finally began to take the crisis in hand, local officials were made into scapegoats. Thousands of rural cadres were imprisoned for corruption or violence against villagers, while at the provincial level some leaders were punished with little worse than compulsory self-criticism. In December 1960, the party secretary of Shandong Province, Shu Tong, apologized at an internal party meeting for the massive number of deaths that had occurred in his province (see Document 4.1). His speech described 650,000 "irregular deaths" in 1959 and the first half of 1960, for which Shu admitted personal responsibility. His penalty was reassignment to Shaanxi Province, where he served as secretary of the provincial party secretariat. Certainly this represented a demotion, but as a sentence for half a million lives lost it was hardly earth shattering.

Where to place responsibility for a calamity on the scale of the Great Leap Famine? Some blame must inevitably fall on local and provincial cadres, whose actions account for much of the variation in local death rates. Mao, however, cannot be viewed as an innocent party. He personally devised or backed all the central policies of the Great Leap, from the People's Communes, the steel campaign and the public dining halls to the campaign against "right opportunism." His failure to act on reports of widespread starvation delayed the response to the crisis until the autumn of 1960. And his authority, reaffirmed by the events of the Lushan Conference, narrowed almost to zero the space for other actors in the leadership to address policy failures or seek to alleviate the famine. We will return to these issues below.

The Rural Population's Struggle for Survival

As famine struck in earnest in 1959, peasants in large parts of the country had to fight to survive. One option was to leverage personal connections to secure food. Village cadres, who controlled food supplies and organized separate canteens for their own use, could be valuable allies. A relative serving as a cook in the public dining hall could also prove helpful. When cadres' actions were investigated after the famine, many faced accusations of providing extra rations to relatives or lovers. Some had taken advantage of women who were willing to trade sexual intercourse for food rations, while others had simply raped women who were too malnourished to defend themselves.[42] Peasants, meanwhile, regularly stole grain from the communal stocks, the fields or their family members. Cadres tried to prevent theft as best they could, in some places by tying up and beating the thieves. Chen Chuwu (ps.), a peasant from a village near Luoyang in Henan, explained in an interview: "Even if you were afraid, you had to steal. If you did not steal, you would starve to death ... Everybody was a thief, even the old people and the children."[43]

Some peasants would sneak into the fields at night to steal unripe wheat or maize, a strategy known colloquially as "eating green." Doing so allowed the thief to take their share of the harvest before the state could collect the "surplus." The strategy was widespread enough to be mentioned in documents produced by the Central Committee,[44] but how to classify it remains the subject of debate. In particular, it is not clear whether "eating green" should be considered a form of anti-state resistance, since unless enough peasants engaged in it, it did not prevent the state from collecting its portion of the harvest. "Eating green" also did not lower grain quotas: cadres tried to prevent it not because it would interfere with appropriations but because it could harm the crop growth, and more abstractly because it challenged their monopoly on food distribution.

Another strategy that could be adopted at the level of the production team was to under-report grain yields. This required the cooperation of local cadres, or at least a willingness on their part to "turn a blind eye" and not report the deception to the higher authorities. It also carried a considerable element of risk, especially after several provincial governments launched campaigns against grain hoarding in 1959 and 1960. In the worst cases, peasants who were found to have hidden

---

42 Yang Bin and Cao Shuji, "Cadres, Grain, and Sexual Abuse in Wuwei County, Mao's China," *Journal of Women's History*, Vol. 28, No. 2 (2016), pp. 33–57.

43 Interview with the author, Henan Province, Xin'An County, February 12, 2005.

44 "Zhonggong zhongyang guanyu yadi nongcun he chengshi de kouliang biaozhun de zhishi," in *JGYL*, Vol. 13, p. 565.

grain in their homes faced being beaten to death, and some cadres confiscated all private food stocks and seed grain to fulfill quotas from the center.[45]

These village cadres were in a difficult position. Helping peasants to hide grain could lead to charges of "right opportunism" and arrest, beatings and imprisonment. If, however, cadres confiscated all the grain the central authorities demanded, they faced starvation themselves, since unlike their colleagues at the county level or above they were not entitled to government rations. Many county cadres were moved frequently from place to place and maintained few links with local people, but village cadres lived among other ordinary peasants whom they had known for many years. A misstep could invite reprisals from neighbors when the political winds shifted. The behavior of local officials had a direct impact on death rates during the famine, creating a complex patchwork in which even adjacent villages could fare wildly differently depending on the inclinations of their cadres.

As with almost every famine, food taboos disappeared in the face of starvation. Villagers ate tree bark, grass and pets. Some resorted to slaughtering cattle owned by the People's Communes, but this was a high-risk strategy that could invite accusations of sabotage. China's livestock numbers diminished significantly during the Great Leap, especially in the nomadic regions, but much of the wastage was due to the animals themselves starving to death rather than the intervention of hungry peasants.

In Henan, peasants attempted to survive on so-called "Guanyin soil," a kind of white clay named for the Buddhist goddess of mercy. All over China, many people died after eating inedible, indigestible or poisonous things. The search for food was easier in southern China and other regions with mild winters and diverse vegetation. Mountainous areas, where state control was weaker and black markets could flourish, offered some additional protection. Ironically, "grain deficit areas" sometimes fared better than "grain surplus areas," because the government avoided extracting too much grain. In the western province of Sichuan, long known as China's "land of plenty," the death rate was extraordinarily high. Grain transfers out of the province were facilitated by the new Chengdu–Xi'an railway, completed in 1958 to link the provincial capital to the North China Plain to its east. As recognition of the famine spread through the party leadership in 1960, the central government pressured "grain surplus areas" to deliver more food to support the major cities. In many regions, death rates rose significantly near transportation links and railways.[46]

45 Yang Jisheng, *Mubei: Zhongguo liushi niandai dajihuang jishi* (Hong Kong: Tiandi, 2008), Vol. 1, pp. 36–40.

46 For a systematic quantitative study see: Anthony Garnaut, "The Geography of the Great Leap Famine," *Modern China*, Vol. 40, No. 3 (2013), pp. 315–348.

A final survival strategy for peasants in rural areas was to flee temporarily to other regions. During previous famines, people from Henan would traditionally migrate to Shaanxi to escape hunger; people from Shandong would go to the northeast. Peasants could also eschew these time-tested escape routes and simply go where they had relatives. During the Great Leap Famine, different parts of the country were hit at different times, and some areas survived almost entirely unaffected. Many peasants from central China fled west to Qinghai and Xinjiang, where labor was needed as local authorities attempted to open up waste land for agriculture. Peasants I interviewed in Xinyang, Henan, told me that in their village all the young men, including cadres and militia men, migrated to Qinghai during the famine. After hearing rumors that plots for private use had been restored in their village, they returned home in 1961 to find that many of those they left behind – women, children and the elderly – had died of starvation in their absence.

Although no data is available to give us a clear picture, it seems likely that at least some of the new workers who came to the cities during the Great Leap were actually famine refugees. Attempts to escape hunger in this way were, however, limited by the constraints of the household registration system. In some regions government controls lapsed, but in other parts of the country local authorities used the militia to establish checkpoints at train stations and important intersections, creating what amounted to deportation hotspots. In Xinyang, many people who tried to escape were beaten to death by so-called "stick brigades."[47] At post offices in the region, the local government confiscated letters to prevent information about the famine from spreading beyond Xinyang's borders.

The massive movements of population created by the famine are documented in detailed reports and statistics produced by local officials. Table 4.1 is based on one such report, an archival file from Yixing county in Jiangsu province. Jiangsu was not one of the more severely affected provinces, but between October 1959 and March 1960, 9,418 peasants left Yixing county alone. Most were male "poor peasants" over sixteen years of age, but a number of children also apparently fled, along with a number of production team cadres. The author of the file recorded various reasons for the departures, from "worrying about agricultural production" and "difficulties with livelihood" to fear of punishment and criticism. Much of the movement was to the nearest major cities, Wuxi, Suzhou and Shanghai, but peasants also migrated to more far-flung locations such as Lanzhou in Gansu province or Dalian in the northeast. By July 1960 around two-thirds had returned home, presumably in response to improving local harvests.

---

47 For example see: Qiao Peihua, *Xinyang Shijian* (Xianggang: Kaifang chubanshe, 2009), p. 134.

Table 4.1 *Outward migration from Yixing County (October 1, 1959 to March 10, 1960)*

Outward migration	Total		9,418
	October, 1959 – December, 1959		2,568
	January, 1960 – March 10, 1960		6,850
Sex	Male		7,152
	Female		2,266
Age	Over 16		8,726
	10–16		517
	Children taken with parent(s)		175
Status	Poor peasant		4,885
	Middle peasant		2,880
	Upper-middle peasant		552
	Landlord		513
	Rich peasant		414
	Counterrevolutionary element		68
	Rightist element		15
	Other		91
Position	Cadre	Production brigade cadre	89
		Production team cadre	743
		Teacher	46
	Worker		111
	Commune member		8,429
Political status	Communist Party member		167
	Communist Youth League member		874
Main reasons for leaving	Cadres	Fear of punishment over the grain issue	154
		Not concerned over agricultural production	682
		Difficulties with livelihood	42
	Masses	Fear of criticism for serious capitalist words and deeds	658
		Failed to settle down for agricultural production	6,677
		Led astray by bad elements	775
		Life difficulties	430
Main destinations	Shanghai		2,433
	Jiangxi		4,169
	Baotou, Inner Mongolia		956
	Lanzhou (northwest China)		285
	Dalian (northeast China)		377
	Xinjiang		190
	Zhejiang		278
	Other		730
Progress at destination	Permanent occupation in place		3,830
	Not yet provided with fixed occupation		5,588

Table 4.1 *(cont.)*

Other departures	Visiting relatives and friends	350
	Natural fluctuation	266
	Involvement in speculative trade	147
	Within the county area	51
	Total	814
Returning population		2,297
Total of returning population until June 9, 1960		6,466

Source: County Archive Yixing, "Jiangsu Yixing xianweiyuanhui bangongshi, guanyu qunzhong jibing, renkou siwang, wailiu, qiying de zhongyao ziliao."

Document 4.2 suggests some of the ways rural people could attempt to survive in the cities. In July 1961, a report by the Department of Political Law of the Municipal Party Committee of Jinan in Shandong, expressed concern about the activities of female "hooligans," who were involved in theft and black market activities. These women were mostly around twenty years old and came from the countryside or from other cities. They would spend their time at train stations, markets, tea houses, parks or restaurants attempting to strike up what the report termed "chaotic sexual relations" with men – perhaps a euphemism for prostitution. While some of the women were known to have been involved in these activities previously, for others the move was a temporary one aimed at earning enough money to survive the famine. The report suggested that "hooligans" who were unwilling to mend their ways should be arrested, convicted and sent to labor re-education. In less severe cases, they should be sent back to their homes as soon as possible. The authorities in Jinan also had to cope with an influx of street children, some as young as five and a few younger still. By July 1961, the authorities had organized housing for 10,903 such children under the age of sixteen.[48] The document stresses the steps taken to lessen the suffering of these young people, but the orphans of the Great Leap remain a taboo topic in China, and little independent research is available on the experiences and fates of the millions who lost their parents as a result of the famine.

The CCP came to power on the back of peasant support and a promise that no Chinese person would ever starve to death again. We might then wonder why no major peasant uprising occurred during the Great Leap disaster. One possible answer lies in the speed with which the famine broke out. Only a few months elapsed between autumn 1958, when many communes declared that peasants

---

48 Archival File from Shandong Province County X, "Zhonggong Jinan shiwei zhengfa gongzuobu guanyu shourong chuli liulang ertong de qingkuang baogao."

could eat as much they wanted in the public dining halls, and early 1959, when some regions began to run short of supplies. At least in the modern period, "hunger riots" and protests over food have tended to occur when people are worried that they may soon starve, rather than when they are actually starving. People preoccupied by a life-and-death struggle for subsistence seem, unsurprisingly, to have little energy left for organized uprisings.[49]

The attraction of revolt was lessened still further in the Chinese case because of the effectiveness of the CCP's system of internal controls. Rationing, household registration and the strength of the militia all limited the population's ability to organize itself across social divides. At the local level, grain stores were well protected and attempting to loot them by force was a dangerous proposition. No organization capable of challenging the CCP had survived the campaigns of the early 1950s, and in any case the party's tight control of information and the media meant many starving peasants had no idea that the famine in their area was part of a nationwide picture. Even if there had been an appetite for rebellion, political alternatives to the CCP were few. The most plausible candidate to replace the Communist Party was the Republican GMD, but it largely lacked credibility on the mainland. In fact, the GMD leadership on Taiwan did consider an invasion, but the plan was shelved when US support failed to materialize.[50] With no prospect of outside intervention, the best that peasants could hope for was that Mao would institute relief measures to end the famine, even though it was the policies of the central government that had caused the disaster in the first place.

A final factor in the authorities' favor, perhaps connected to the party's control of information, was the fact that, in spite of the enormous destruction wrought by the Great Leap Famine, neither the CCP nor Mao seem to have suffered terminal reputational damage even in rural areas. To this day, some peasants continue to believe that the blame for the famine should be placed on local cadres. Mao, they argue, was misinformed by his subordinates and acted as soon as the true extent of the famine became known.

The Demographics of the Famine

Today, the question of how many people died during the Great Leap Famine has taken on considerable political significance. On the one hand we find the historian Frank Dikötter's claim, critical of Mao's leadership, that as many as

---

49 Cormac O'Grada, *Famine: A Short History* (Princeton, NJ: Princeton University Press, 2010), p. 55.
50 Jasper Becker, *Hungry Ghosts: China's Secret Famine* (London: John Murray, 1996), p. 288.

45 million people may have died during the famine, which he terms "one of the most deadly mass killings in human history."[51] On the other hand, some Neo-Maoists in China and elsewhere have argued for a total in the single figure millions.[52] For these writers, the famine is a major challenge to the narrative of Mao as a leader who loved the people.

No official document to which researchers currently have access states how many people the CCP believes to have died in the famine. It is entirely possible that no reliable data actually exists, given the way in which the system of reporting collapsed during the Great Leap, as supposed "achievements" of the Three Red Banners were invented out of whole cloth. Cadres at the local level were wary of reporting deaths by starvation, and villagers too had an incentive to conceal deaths and missing persons cases so that they could continue to draw the victim's rations. Likewise, over-reporting of the population could be used to secure additional food.

Government-backed investigations into levels of starvation during the famine were possible only for a short time. Between late 1960 and 1962, many county-level Public Security Bureaus produced detailed accounts of the numbers and causes of deaths. To take one example, archival documents from Wuwei in Anhui show that, of a population of around 950,000 in 1958, 280,000 people died in the county over the next three years.[53] As yet, however, we do not have access to enough of these local reports to be able to form meaningful estimates on the national level. Table 4.2, drawn from the archives of Yixing county and covering the period between October 1959 and the end of 1960, suggests how cadres classified famine deaths. It seems that in this case officials were keen to avoid mentioning starvation directly, instead giving causes of death such as "edema" or "emaciation" that obviously stemmed from severe malnutrition. Unsurprisingly, most people seem to have died between the winter of 1959 and the period before the 1960 harvest. People over sixty formed the largest group in the statistics, with famine deaths coming on top of natural losses due to old age. One thousand, seven hundred and sixty-one children below the age of sixteen also died, and sixty-seven people committed suicide by either drowning or hanging themselves. A national census was taken in 1964, but the results were not initially made public and only became available to scholars in the early 1980s. Moreover, this survey, along with the previous census of 1953, was of markedly inferior quality

51 Frank Dikötter, *Mao's Great Famine: The History of China's Most Devastating Catastrophe, 1958–1962* (London: Bloomsbury, 2010). See cover.

52 For example see: Yang Songlin, *Zong yao youren shuochu zhenxiang: Guanyu "esi sanqianwan"* (Haikou: Nanhai chuban gongsi, 2013).

53 Liu Shigu, "Tuishe yu wailiu: 'Dayuejin' qian de nongmin kangzheng: Yi Wuwei xian dang'an wei zhongxin," *Dangshiyanjiu yu jiaoxue*, No. 4 (2016), p. 74.

Table 4.2 *Population deaths in Yixing County (October 1, 1959 to end of March, 1960)*

Period	Deaths			Age				Cause							
	Total	Male	Female	1–16	17–50	51–60	Over 60	Old age	Disease	Edema	Weight loss	Cyanosis	Suicide (drowning or hanging)	Killed	Other diseases
October 1, 1959 – End of December, 1959	2,778														
January 1960 – March 10, 1960	7,420	7,276	2,922	1,604	2,014	2,587	3,993	4,385	1,904	1,529	830	275	59	2	1,214
March 11, 1960 – End of March, 1960	1,224	879	345	157	271	350	446	442	291	247	141	39	8	1	55
Total	11,422	8,155	3,267	1,761	2,285	2,937	4,439	4,827	2,195	1,776	971	314	67	3	1,269

Source: County Archive Yixing, "Jiangsu Yixing xianweiyuanhui bangongshi, guanyu qunzhong jibing, renkou siwang, wailiu, qiying de zhongyao ziliao"

to the 1982 census, another major source to which demographers have turned to estimate excess mortality during the famine. This later census was specifically designed to produce reliable numbers that would allow the government to plan and evaluate the one-child policy.

Mathematical modeling of these numbers by Western and Chinese scholars has produced a variety of estimates for excess mortality, ranging from about 16 to 30 million. The Chinese demographer Peng Xizhe gives a national figure of roughly 23 million excess deaths between 1958 and 1962. At the upper end of the range, a group of Western academics argue for 30 million excess deaths, including 12.2 million children under the age of ten years.[54] The main reason for this wide variation is the need to factor in unregistered births and deaths, two variables which by definition can never be dependably known. This need is particularly acute in the Chinese case given the imperfections in the state's population registration system, particularly in the early decades of the PRC. In addition, the introduction of the birth planning system, which penalizes parents who have more than the prescribed number of children, has resulted in millions of births going unreported – the so-called "black children" born illicitly in households across China. A final difficulty arises because the reliability of population data appears to vary from province to province.

Even with an accurate picture of births and deaths, excess mortality can only be measured compared to death rates in "ordinary" periods. How to define this baseline for the years between 1959 and 1961 is a complex question, since death rates in the years before the famine are by no means accurately known. Official statistics show that China's overall death rate and rate of child mortality were high before 1949. Thereafter, the years between 1949 and 1957 saw a dramatic decrease in the reported death rate, from about twenty-five per thousand to ten per thousand in less than a decade. If true, this would have meant over 30 million lives "saved" by the economic and social change of the early Mao years. The historical demographer Cormac O'Grada casts doubt on these figures, however, arguing that such a precipitous drop over such a short period is implausible. If we accept his claim that the reduction of the death rate between 1949 and 1957 was less significant than reported, then the overall death rate immediately before the famine must have been higher than has previously been acknowledged. The rise in the overall death rate (which peaked at 25.43 per thousand during the Great Leap) would then be correspondingly less severe, meaning fewer excess deaths attributable to the famine. Taking these

54 Peng Xizhe, "Demographic Consequences of the Great Leap Forward in China's Provinces," *Population and Development Review*, Vol. 13, No. 4 (1987), p. 649; Basil Ashton, et al., "Famine in China, 1958–1961," *Population and Development Review*, Vol. 10, No. 4 (1984), p. 619.

considerations into account, O'Grada estimates total excess mortality at 15 to 25 million people. Even this relatively low number still ranks the Great Leap Famine as the deadliest in modern history in absolute terms.[55] A higher estimate comes from the Chinese scholar Cao Shuji, who fixes the death toll at 32.4 million based on population statistics from official county gazetteers, discounting Qinghai and Tibet.[56]

Some demographers studying the famine have argued for taking account not only of excess mortality, but also of up to 30 million "lost births." The famine caused a significant drop in birth rates after 1958, as malnutrition led to reduced libido, amenorrhea (a temporary cessation of the menstrual period) for some women, and a decision by many couples to postpone marriage or pregnancy. Without this reduction in the birth rate, the death toll would likely have been significantly higher. It is certainly useful to recall that the demographic impact of the famine went beyond the actual recorded death toll. However, it is somewhat disingenuous to speak of all 30 million missing births as "lost," since the drop in birth rates during the famine was followed by a baby boom as the country recovered in the early 1960s. It is entirely possible that the surplus of births between 1962 and 1965 may even have exceeded the deficit of births between 1960 and 1961.[57] In the longer term, the famine had little impact on population trends. By 1964, the central government was already concerned enough about rising birth rates to introduce birth planning policies to control population growth (see Chapter 5).

Against the higher estimates cited above, some Neo-Maoist scholars have argued that it would be more appropriate to compare the death rate during the famine with normal death rates in Republican China. According to population surveys conducted by the GMD, the death rate in 1936 and 1938 was around twenty-eight per thousand. The death rate of around twenty-five per thousand during the Great Leap Famine was therefore lower than that seen during "normal times" in Republican China, making it unlikely, in the view of these scholars, that a famine causing tens of millions of deaths could actually have occurred.[58] The narrative of the Great Leap Forward as the "largest famine in human history," they assert, was created by anti-communist scholars bent on slandering the achievements of Mao era.

55 O'Grada, *Famine*, p. 96.
56 Cao Shuji, *Da jihuang* (Hong Kong: Shidai guoji chuban youxiangongsi, 2005), p. 282.
57 Cormac O'Grada, "Making Famine History," *Journal of Economic Literature*, Vol. 45, No. 1 (2007), p. 23.
58 Li Minqi, *The Rise of China and the Demise of the Capitalist World Economy* (London: Pluto Press, 2008), pp. 41–42.

A number of counter-arguments can be made here. First, and most obvious, the fact that millions of lives were saved due to the improvements in public health between 1949 and 1957, while welcome in itself, did nothing to prevent people from starving to death during the subsequent famine. Improvements in health care and hygiene meant that, by 1957, millions of babies had survived to the age of one who might otherwise have died. This does not mean, however, that the return to high levels of child mortality seen during the famine did not actually take place. Second, the comparison with death rates under the Republic has only limited validity in statistical terms. Before 1945, the GMD ruled over less than half the country. In this period of permanent violence, civil war and Japanese occupation, no representative population surveys were ever produced that can give us a reliable picture of death rates across China as a whole. Moreover, the comparison between death rates during the Great Leap and death rates as a whole under the GMD is not like-for-like. Although early deaths caused by poor living conditions in "normal times" are important, they must be distinguished from famines, when death rates suddenly sky-rocket and then decline after reaching a peak. Rough estimates for excess mortality due to famine and natural disaster under the Republic range from around 15 to 18 million people – that is, fewer deaths than the Great Leap Famine, spread over a much longer period.[59] It is certainly appropriate to view the Great Leap Famine in its larger historical context, as the Neo-Maoist camp attempts to do. However, we should not overlook what seems to me to be the key element of this context, namely that the famine of 1958 to 1961 broke out not in a time of war or limited state capacity, but during a period of peace and economic growth. The apologist argument that the Great Leap claimed only a few million lives flies in the face of serious demographic studies, backed by solid statistical analysis and survey data. It also fails to note perhaps the most tragic aspect of the disaster: that it could have been avoided.

The End of the United Front and the Uprising in Tibet

As we have seen, the CCP's accommodation with the Tibetan authorities had allowed the region to defer Land Reform and the establishment of the People's Communes all the way to the end of the 1950s. This made Tibet something of a special case. From 1958 onwards, other minority regions in the west, including Tibetan areas in Sichuan, Qinghai and Gansu, began to feel the effects of the Great

---

59 Xia Mingfang, *Minguo shiqi ziran zaihai yu xiangcun shehui* (Beijing: Zhonghua shuju, 2000), pp. 395–399.

Leap. In these areas, the rise of the communes often went hand in hand with CCP attacks on "backward customs." Among nomadic groups, the party launched a class struggle, mobilizing poor herdsmen against herd owners. Meanwhile, sedentary peasants in minority areas were organized into communes sometimes literally overnight, as the state adopted a "single strike" approach that bypassed the initial stages of collectivization. Many of the new communes were multi-ethnic bodies that broke down the borders between villages and increased the pressure for minorities to assimilate.

Perhaps the most striking example of the Great Leap's effect on minority areas was in the western province of Qinghai. In June 1958, the provincial government began an ambitious campaign to transform grasslands into farm land; a few months later, in April 1959, the leadership declared that each prefecture in Qinghai should become self-sufficient in grain, vegetables and fodder within two years. This campaign had extraordinarily severe consequences, leading to damage to vast swathes of grassland and an intensification of existing conflicts between sedentary peasants and nomadic herdsmen. Grain production on newly opened arable land remained very low, and the accompanying effort to settle nomads and "unite agriculture and animal husbandry" sparked the loss of more than a third of the province's cattle stocks, which declined from 15 million head in 1957 to 10.8 million in 1958 and 9.3 million in 1960.[60] As a result, the herdsmen's meat rations decreased without any rise in grain output to offset the loss. In some of the worst-affected parts of the province, starvation deaths were occurring even in the first half of 1958. By the end of the year, the nomadic areas were in a state of famine.

The 1959 rebellion in Lhasa is relatively well known, but it was preceded in the spring and summer of 1958 by a less widely remembered uprising, also linked to hunger, in minority areas over the border in Qinghai. The revolt began in April in Xunhua, a county populated by the Salar Muslim minority. The so-called "Xunhua Incident" eventually expanded into an armed rebellion among the Tibetan population of the province, covering six autonomous prefectures, twenty-four counties and 307 monasteries. Official statistics suggest that more than one hundred thousand people were involved, amounting to about one-fifth of the Tibetans in the province.[61] The situation deteriorated to such an extent that the central government was forced to send in the PLA, and battles between state forces and armed nomads continued for over six months in some areas.

---

60 Qinghai sheng difangzhi bianzuanweiyuanhui (ed.), *Qinghai shengzhi, 14, xumuzhi* (Hefei: Huangshan shushe, 1998), p. 48.

61 Li Jianglin, *1959 Lasa!* (Hong Kong: Xin shiji chuban jichuanmei youxian gongsi, 2010), p. 79.

The official *Short History of Modern Qinghai* asserts that the revolt resulted in 52,000 arrests in 1958 and 1959. In the CCP's account, the rebellion was able to garner substantial support primarily because the "reactionary classes" could use religion and the monastery network to mobilize forces. The nomadic population possessed large quantities of firearms, ammunition and spears, and the uprising was supported by "reactionary forces" both in Tibet and abroad. As the conflict progressed, the PLA seems to have treated all nomads fleeing the famine as "bandit rebels." A significant number of refugees, along with many genuine rebels, fled into Tibet after the suppression of the uprising, and Lhasa became the center of the anti-Chinese forces.

As these developments unfolded, the central government faced the real risk that the rebellion in Qinghai could spread to Tibet. Mao painted this prospect as an opportunity. In June 1958, giving his approval to the hard line taken by the provincial authorities, he declared: "Tibet should be prepared to handle the possibility of an overall armed rebellion. The greater the disorder is there, the better. If the reactionaries in Tibet dare to launch an overall rebellion, then the laboring people there can be liberated earlier."[62] On July 14, the Central Committee claimed that "reactionaries" in Tibet might be preparing to initiate an armed revolt, which the PLA should be prepared to crush. However, it stuck to its decision to postpone reforms in Tibet, expressing the hope that the local Tibetan government would continue to support the 1950 compromise. It was another nine months before the uprising Mao had envisioned actually broke out. After rumors spread that the PLA planned to kidnap the Dalai Lama, mass demonstrations erupted in Lhasa on March 13, 1959, and soon a full-blown rebellion was in progress. Among the rebels were both guerrilla fighters from Qinghai and the Tibetan army, which had remained independent of the PLA after Tibet's incorporation into the PRC. Chinese forces were able to quell the uprising after a few weeks, although guerrilla activities continued for some time thereafter in the remote mountain areas.

Later in the year, Zhou Enlai would suggest in a speech that 20,000 Tibetans had participated in the revolt.[63] This figure was revised significantly upwards in a later official publication, which spoke of 93,000 Tibetan rebels being either killed, wounded or arrested. Another official Chinese source claimed that as many as 5,000 people died on both sides.[64] Thousands more fled and followed

---

62 Mao Zedong, "Zhuanfa Qinghai shengwei guanyu zhenya panluan wenti de baogao de piyu," in Zhonggong zhongyang wenxian yanjiushi (ed.), *Jianguo yilai Mao Zedong wengao* (Beijing: Zhongyang wenxian chubanshe, 1992), Vol. 7, p. 286.

63 Zhou Enlai, "Zhengfu gongzuo baogao," in *JGYL*, Vol. 12, p. 225.

64 For these numbers see: Anne-Marie Blondeau and Katia Buffetrille (eds.), *Authenticating Tibet: Answers to China's 100 Questions* (Berkeley, CA: University of California Press, 2008), p. 89.

the Dalai Lama to India. The 1959 Tibetan uprising remains the most significant revolt against CCP rule since the foundation of the PRC. In the absence of social or ethnic unrest in other parts of the country, however, it was no more than a minor threat to the party's power.

More difficult than ending the rebellion was the task of winning peace. The government in Beijing attempted to win hearts and minds by painting the rebellion as the work of "feudal reactionary forces" among the old elite, who had betrayed the agreement reached during the peaceful liberation of 1950. In the CCP's account, the "pacification" of the rebellion was to be accompanied by a "democratic reform" that would destroy feudalism, the supposed social foundation of the uprising. The reactionary forces were accused of links with foreign imperialists and the GMD and of seeking to restore imperial and feudal domination over Tibet. By contrast, the laboring masses and patriotic elements of the elite were celebrated as having welcomed and supported the PLA's suppression of the uprising.

With this messaging, the government attempted to show that the uprising had not involved a cross-class alliance and that it had therefore not been in any sense a popular revolt. In the immediate aftermath of the rebellion, the CCP even claimed that the Dalai Lama had not gone to India willingly, but had instead been kidnapped by the reactionary forces.[65] In so doing, the party left the door open for him to return to China. The CCP leadership evidently understood that Chinese legitimacy in the eyes of the Tibetan population would suffer without the Dalai Lama's support, and official press coverage of his activities became very unfavorable in 1963, when he announced a constitution for the new Tibetan government-in-exile. By the end of 1964, he had been named as a "treasonous element" (*pantufenzi*) and discharged from his official positions in China.[66]

In the Dalai Lama's absence, the Panchen Lama, the second most senior figure in Tibetan Buddhism, became the main representative of the United Front among the Tibetan elite. In 1959, he was named chairman of the Preparatory Committee for the Tibet Autonomous Region. The promised "democratic reforms" began soon after with a series of land transfers from the monasteries and aristocracy to the peasants. These measures represented a counterpart to the Land Reform already instituted elsewhere in China, and it was for this reason that they could be referred to as "democratic" rather than socialist. The amount of land to be transferred was substantial: one Chinese scholar has claimed that the three largest monasteries alone owned 9,800 hectares of land and 11,000 head of cattle

---

65 Zhou Enlai, "Zhengfu gongzuo baogao," in *JGYL*, Vol. 12, pp. 224–226.
66 *Renmin Ribao*, March 13, 1963 and December 19, 1964.

Figure 4.5: 1959: Tibetan peasant women receive distributed land.
Source: Photograph by Eva Siao, Museum Ludwig.

in 1959, as well as supervising over 40,000 serfs.[67] The official media and the government-backed cultural industry soon began to propagate the narrative that the old Tibet had been "a hell on earth," whose slaves and serfs had been liberated by the intervention of the PLA.

The Panchen Lama's approval of the "democratic reforms" of the early 1960s led some Tibetans in exile to regard him as a Chinese puppet. The land transfers struck at the economic foundation of Tibetan Buddhism, which relied on mon- astery lands to nourish a huge number of monks and nuns. In the 1950s, 10 percent of the total population was part of the clergy, a figure that rose as

---

67 Ma Rong, *Xizang de renkou yu shehui* (Beijing: Tongxin chubanshe, 1996), p. 174.

high as 50 percent in the cities.[68] The party viewed this large group of Tibetans as "unproductive eaters" who would need to perform labor in order to transform themselves into representatives of socialism. Cooperation between the CCP and the Panchen Lama proved to be short-lived, however, and the party soon turned its fire on its new ally (see Chapter 5). Lip service continued to be paid to the United Front, but the uprising of 1959 and the subsequent crackdown spelled the end of the alliance between the CCP and Tibet's theocratic elite. Nine years behind the rest of the country, class struggle was belatedly enforced, and the New Democratic Revolution arrived.

The Failure of the Chinese Way to Communism

As early as 1958, Soviet experts had begun to express concerns over the Great Leap. Some were reminded of the Soviet experience with radical collectivization and over-ambitious plans during Stalin's push for rapid development between 1929 and 1932. Tensions between the Soviet and Chinese governments had been mounting for several years, but open attacks on the Soviet Communist Party were not seen until April 1960, the peak of the famine, when an article entitled "Long Live Leninism" appeared in *Red Flag*. Attacking the Soviet–American rapprochement and the notion of "peaceful coexistence" between capitalism and socialism, the CCP leadership insisted that US imperialism was inherently aggressive and that violent revolutions must be supported as the only way to "liberate" people in the non-Western world.[69] These critiques amounted to an indirect questioning of the USSR's leadership of the global communist movement. Given that millions of Chinese were starving to death as the article was published, the moment for open confrontation was, with hindsight, ill chosen.

On July 18, Khrushchev, the Soviet Premier, ordered the sudden withdrawal of about 1,400 Soviet experts from China. While the act indicated severe displeasure and harmed numerous industrial projects, the notion occasionally advanced that it was the withdrawal of Soviet support that led to the disaster in the countryside is largely without merit. None of the lost Soviet specialists appear to have been working directly on agricultural production.[70] Likewise, Mao's subsequent push to repay China's debts to the USSR within five years was a deliberate choice to reduce the country's dependency on its Soviet "elder brother." At least in the first half of 1960, saving the lives of famine victims was apparently not the chairman's top priority.

68 Ibid., p. 177.   69 "Lieningzhuyi wansui," in *JGYL*, Vol. 13, p. 279.
70 Lorenz Lüthi, *The Sino-Soviet Split: Cold War in the Communist World* (Princeton, NJ: Princeton University Press, 2008), p. 178.

The CCP's first attempt to find an alternative path from socialism to communism, the People's Communes, led only to disaster. In 1958, the party leadership had seen the peasants as the major force for achieving revolutionary transformation and had promoted rural industrialization. However, during the famine, the welfare of the peasants tumbled down the CCP's agenda, as the party followed the same path that its Soviet counterpart had taken during the famine of 1931–1933. Major cities and industries, soldiers, party cadres and high-ranking intellectuals were protected, while in many areas of the countryside ordinary peasants were left to starve to death. The urban bias of the food distribution system, already entrenched by the mid-1950s, was made painfully manifest in the response to the famine. In August 1960, the Central Committee issued a new slogan, "eating comes first." That same month, it gave several orders to transfer grain from the countryside to guarantee the food supply for key cities. Eating may have come first, but there could be no doubt who was first in line.

To lift the country out of the famine, all the major "new-born" institutions of the Great Leap were abolished by the end of 1961. The large, semi-communist rural communes, the public dining halls, the militarized rural workforce, the urban People's Communes and the backyard steel furnaces all disappeared. The smaller communes that remained in the countryside after 1961 were closer to the Advanced Agriculture Cooperatives of the mid-1950s than they were to the model communes of the utopian autumn of 1958. The push for urbanization was reversed, and about 26 million people who had come to the cities and towns during the Leap were sent back to the countryside in the early 1960s. The famine was a catastrophe for the peasants, but it was also the cause of a serious crisis for the CCP. Among the central leadership, there was a sense that control of the rural party organizations had been lost, and divisions emerged over the future direction of China's economy and society.

DOCUMENT 4.1 "My Self-Criticism" (December 10, 1960).

Shu Tong (Party Secretary of Shandong Province):

The situation in the countryside in our province has been worsening since 1959. This year, during summer and autumn, it developed to a serious and frightening degree. A large number of the population migrated away (1.09 million between August and today); edema and related diseases have been on the increase . . .; the death rate rose (between 1959 and the first half of this year, 650,000 people died unnatural deaths), [C]attle stocks were reduced (by 2.37 million head compared to 1955), and the constitution of many of the cattle is too weak to survive . . . This year, grain output was reduced drastically, down to the level seen under individual farming in 1949 . . . The supply of grain and goods in the cities is tighter still. The living standard of the general population is rapidly declining to a very difficult level. In some places, painful incidents of cannibalism have occurred. The political authority of the party has been seriously damaged among the people . . . In particular, the People's Communes are causing doubts among segments of the masses . . . The cause of the serious crisis in Shandong is not mainly the natural disasters of the past two years (though they have had a relatively important impact), nor that the Great Leap in industry was too fast . . . It is in particular my serious faults in work style and leadership. Over the last two years, and in particular over the last year, I have made serious mistakes regarding the implementation of the policy guidelines of the Central Committee . . . I apologize to the broad masses and cadres of Shandong.

Source: Archival file from Shandong Province X County, "1960 nian Zeng Xisheng, Tan Qilong, Shu Tong tongzhi zai wuji ganbu shengwei kuoda huiyishang de jianghua, 'Wo de jiantao'."

DOCUMENT 4.2 Report of the Department of Political Law of the Municipal Party Committee of Jinan regarding the situation with taking in and inspecting female hooligans (July 1961).

Report of the municipal committee to the provincial Department of Political Law:

Among those coming into our city who have recently been taken in to be deported are a group of women who display hooligan behaviors. These women were often active at the train station, free markets, tea clubs, restaurants and parks and other complex locations . . . To investigate and find out about these people, we research the countermeasures they take [against official policy]. We investigate the hooligan behavior of ten women. Among them, the home of one is in Qingdao, three are from Jimo county, two from Pingyuan, one from Jinan, one from Yanzhou, one from Beijing and one from Anshan . . . Six women have the status of poor peasant, two of poor urban dwellers, one of middle peasant and one is the daughter of a counterrevolutionary . . . There are four important reasons for their drifting about in this way.

1. They had already formed the bad habits of stealing and hooligan behavior. They are taking advantage of the current situation – namely that the free markets are blooming and the floating population is on the increase – to carry out their hooligan activities . . . Take one example, Wang Lihai, who is 22 years old, from Jimo County and has the status of poor peasant. Under the influence of her mother, she was infected with the bad habits of stealing and hooligan behavior when she was small. She often sleeps around with men . . . In July 1958, she started to drift around, first to Qingdao, Jinan, Tianjin, Shenyang, Harbin, Jiamusi and some other cities and towns, where she swindled and cheated . . .

4. Some have problems with the livelihood of their families. Two of the women are in this situation. Ma Meili is 22 years old, from Jimo county and has the status of poor peasant. At the age of 16 she graduated from primary school and married Zhang Haibin, a demobilized soldier, then 19. She gave birth to two children, one of whom is six years old and the other four . . .

Accordingly, we adopted the methods set out below regarding the female hooligans who have been taken in. Those for whom hooliganism was second nature, who steal often and refuse education, were arrested and punished. Those who have been deeply inculcated with the bad habits of hooliganism and who are unable to change were to be taken in for re-education through labor. Those who were experiencing problems of livelihood and who engaged in hooligan activity to eat and drink should be educated and deported to their birth place.

Source: Archive file from Shandong Province X County, "Zhonggong Jinan shiwei zhengfabu guanyu shourong shencha liumang funü qingkuang baogao."

Note: Pseudonyms have been used instead of the names in the original document.

5 THE POST-FAMINE YEARS: FROM READJUSTMENT TO THE SOCIALIST EDUCATION CAMPAIGN (1962–1965)

国民经济调整
Adjustment of the national economy
千万不要忘记阶级斗争
Never forget class struggle
反修防修
Fight against revisionism, guard against revisionism

Li Fu was born in 1938 in a small town in Shanxi Province. The founding of the People's Republic opened up new avenues for his education and career. After studying agriculture at a training institute, in 1960 he was selected by the provincial party school to study political theory, the first step towards becoming a cadre. His new role in the party-state apparatus brought him into contact with the worst aspects of the Great Leap. Before the year was out, the provincial government had assigned him to a team charged with investigating the "Shouyang Incident," in which huge numbers of peasants had starved to death or died at the hands of local officials in the county of the same name. Li's team was charged with examining the circumstances and replacing any officials found to be culpable.

Li joined the party in 1962 and after graduation served in the Department for Political Research in the provincial government. In 1964 he began a new role at the Central Headquarters of the Socialist Education Campaign. Over the following two years, he was part of a series of external work teams sent to rural villages to carry out the Four Clean Ups Campaign and investigate corrupt local officials. The teams mobilized villagers in struggle sessions against cadres, some of whom committed suicide under pressure. Li was particularly troubled by one case in Qi county, where a cadre who had recently killed himself was accused in a public struggle session of "committing suicide to escape punishment," despite there being no evidence of serious wrongdoing on his part. In the same county, the secretary of the party branch of the local work brigade was struggled against by the work team, but kept his position because no one was available to replace him.[1] Li recalled that particularly fierce grievances surrounded the Taoyuan brigade in Hebei province, which had been declared a national model in 1964. In Taoyuan, Wang Guangmei, the wife of Chinese President Liu Shaoqi, had organized violent and expensive struggles against local cadres involving huge outside work teams. Dissatisfaction with Liu and his wife was already evident among local cadres as early as 1966, according to Li.

In February 1967, during the Cultural Revolution, Li joined the leadership of a rebel organization within the provincial administration, later becoming a member of the Revolutionary Committee that replaced the provincial government. A reversal of his fortunes occurred in 1970, when along with other cadres and rebel leaders he was sent down to the countryside. There, he saw the lasting impact of the Four Clean Ups Campaign that he had taken part in a few years previously:

> The village where I went, Qinzhuang, still suffered from destruction of the Four Clean Ups ... The natural conditions were very good and the soil was fertile. In the past, [the village] would contribute two million *jin* of grain to the state ... [However,] they had carried out the Four Clean Ups in an ultra-leftist way and the secretary of the party branch of the brigade was labeled a counterrevolutionary. Four out of five people in the branch were expelled from the party. Hence, the leading group was destroyed. As a result, the new cadres were afraid and did not dare to do anything. It was disorder and a total mess. When the farm crops were ripe, they were stolen. At the end of the year, when I went there, production output was 640,000 *jin* ... From the original two million *jin* [surplus] sold to the state, total production had decreased to 640,000 *jin* in 1969.[2]

In 1971, Li was allowed to return to the provincial government, but was purged in 1977 after the arrest of the Gang of Four. In 1981, he was rehabilitated again and returned to government service as the party secretary of Pingyao county. In 1984, the political wind turned against him once more. Li was purged for his affiliation with the rebels during the Cultural Revolution and expelled from the CCP; he subsequently worked in a library until his retirement. His determination to write his memoirs grew out of a conviction that the party had treated him unfairly, and his experience exemplifies the roller-coaster-like trajectory of many

1 Li Fu, *Suosi suoyi qishi nian* (Fort Worth, TX: Fellows Press of America, 2012), pp. 182–183.
2 Interview with Li Fu by the author, Taiyuan, September 2015.

official careers in the Mao era. Cadres could rise fast as their superiors promoted them, but when they felt out of favor they quickly became vulnerable.

The years between the famine and the beginning of the Cultural Revolution are of great importance for the social history of Maoist China. Exactly how to categorize this transitional period is an open question. Some scholars consider it primarily a prelude to the start of the Cultural Revolution in the summer of 1966.[3] In this reading, the years between 1962 and 1966 represent a period of gradual intensification. Sino-Soviet conflict escalated in public with open polemics by the CCP against "Soviet revisionism." Mao warned of a "restoration of capitalism" in China. The threat of conflict also increased with the US move towards direct involvement in the Vietnam War, starting with the systematic bombing of socialist North Vietnam in 1965.

On the other hand, the period between 1962 and summer 1966 could also be considered a time of recovery. The rural population had been hit terribly by the famine, and many people had to rebuild families and homes. In some parts of the country the famine was still in progress in 1962. In Sichuan province, peasants continued to starve that year, and recovery would not begin in earnest until 1963.[4] At the same time, China as a whole experienced a baby boom in 1962–1963 that resulted in potentially worrying levels of population growth. In other words, the early 1960s saw contradictory developments in different policy fields and different sectors of society. A rough periodization of these years, which is perhaps the best we can hope for, could distinguish between two phases: 1. The time between early 1961 and late 1962, when the central government focused on the "readjustment" of the economy to overcome the famine. 2. A more radical period inaugurated with Mao's warning to "never forget class struggle" after the 10th Plenum of the 8th Central Committee in September 1962. This lasted until the beginning of the Cultural Revolution in summer 1966.

This chapter will address the great downsizing of the urban workforce and the student population that took place in the aftermath of the famine. These "austerity" policies severely curtailed social mobility by limiting opportunities for access to education and non-agricultural jobs. We will also examine why the government felt it necessary to enforce birth planning in 1963 in order to control urban and rural population growth. In the countryside, the famine had weakened the central state's hold over local cadres and peasants, and the government sought to regain the initiative with the Socialist Education Campaign

---

3 Regarding this debate see: Richard Baum, *Prelude to Revolution: Mao, the Party, and the Peasant Question, 1962–66* (New York, NY: Columbia University Press, 1975), pp. 156–158.

4 Yang Jisheng, *Mubei: Zhongguo liushi niandai dajihuang jishi* (Hong Kong: Tiandi, 2008), Vol. 1, p. 177.

(1963–1967), which targeted local "capitalist roaders in power" and also the underground "second economy." In the post-famine years, the CCP tried to revive the old policies of the United Front to regain the support of high-ranking intellectuals and ethnic minorities, two groups whose relationship with the party had deteriorated during the Great Leap. However, the party leadership quickly became divided on the question of how far any concessions should go. The policies of the "readjustment" resulted in economic recovery, but they also set the stage for many social conflicts that would escalate during the Cultural Revolution.

The Great Downsizing

A number of scholars have argued that the recovery of China's agricultural sector was primarily down to reforms to the ownership structure of the People's Communes. The key document in these reforms, the so-called "60 Points in Agriculture" of 1961, defined the structure of the communes as consisting of three levels. At the top sat the commune itself, and below it the production brigade and finally the production team, formed from several individual families. Under the "60 Points," collective ownership and the accounting of work points were to be managed primarily at the level of the production team, the lowest rung on the ladder. Commune members were entitled to plots for private use and a small number of livestock.

Although these reforms were important – primarily because they created greater incentives for peasants to increase production – they are only part of the story. The restoration of plots for private use and the strengthening of the role of the production teams in the communes were structural steps to increase future agricultural productivity. Their effect would only ever be felt a full cycle of planting and harvest after the famine; they did not offer any immediate increase in the supply of grain. In fact, according to official statistics released in the post-Mao era, death rates fell significantly in 1962 even though grain production was still lower than it had been in 1959.[5] In other words, no matter how important increased productivity was, China did not produce its way out of the famine. Instead, as I suggest below, the recovery was owed largely to a rebalancing of the supply system.

---

5 For grain production see: Zhonghua renmin gongheguo nongye bu jihuasi (ed.), *Zhongguo nongcun jingji tongji daquan 1949–1986* (Beijing: Nongye chubanshe, 1989), pp. 410–411; for the death rate see: Yuan Yongxi (ed.), *Zhongguo renkou zonglun* (Beijing: Zhongguo caizheng jingji chubanshe, 1991), p. 149.

Reduction of the Urban Population and Workforce

The architects of the "readjustment" of the national economy were senior party officials Chen Yun and Li Xiannian. Both argued for a reduction of the urban workforce and for importing grain to restore the balance between urban consumers and net grain producers in the countryside. Chen Yun in particular believed that the uncontrolled growth of the urban population had been the major reason, not just for the famine, but also for smaller dislocations in the grain supply in 1953, 1954 and 1957.[6] Fewer consumers entitled to urban ration cards would mean reduced pressure on the state to extract grain from the countryside to feed the cities. Not only would this rebalancing increase the number of agricultural workers, but crucially it would also reduce the overall amount of grain needed for the country as a whole, since much smaller rations were provided to rural residents than those with an urban *hukou* were entitled to. Chen also argued that the restoration of plots for private use in the People's Communes would allow those who were sent down from the cities to be self-supporting.[7]

Taking the volume of agricultural production and the numbers of urban consumers of trade grain into account, Chen estimated in 1962 that 20 million people needed to be sent back to the countryside from the cities and towns (*chengzhen*). Recent migrants who had come to urban areas during the Great Leap became the main target of the "downsizing" policy. In total, 26 million people were removed between late 1960 and 1963.[8] Table 5.1 outlines the reduction of the workforce of the state-owned enterprises: 8.7 million in 1961 and 8.6 million in 1962. By contrast, the number of workers in collectively owned enterprises, where entitlements were more restricted, actually increased slightly during these years. Assessing the exact effect of Chen and Li's recovery plan on the urban population is complicated by the fact that statistics from the period almost invariably count parts of the suburban population that were actually engaged in agricultural production as urban residents. Taking this statistical anomaly into account, it seems that non-agrarian urban residents never constituted more than 20 percent of the Chinese population during the Mao era. Within this already low percentage, the reforms do appear to have had a significant effect. The non-agrarian urban population's share of the national total decreased during

6 Shangyebu dangdai Zhongguo liangshi gongzuo bianjibu (ed.), *Dangdai Zhongguo liangshi gongzuo shiliao* (Baoding: Hebei sheng gongxiaoshe Baoding yinshuachang, 1989), Vol. 1, p. 314.

7 Chen Yun, "Dongyuan chengshi renkou xiaxiang," in *Jianguo yilai zhongyao wenxian xuanbian* (Beijing: Zhongyang wenxian chubanshe, 1992) [hereinafter "*JGYL*"], Vol. 14, p. 374.

8 Lu Yu, *Xin Zhongguo renkou wushi nian* (Beijing: Zhongguo renkou chubanshe, 2004), Vol. 1, p. 594.

Table 5.1 *Total number of employees in state- and collectively owned enterprises, 1960–1965 (all figures in millions)*

Year	Total workforce	Ownership by the people		Collective ownership	
		Workforce	Year-on-year increase	Workforce	Year-on-year increase
1960	59.69	50.44	4.83	9.25	2.11
1961	51.71	41.74	-8.70	10.00	0.75
1962	43.21	33.09	-8.65	10.12	0.12
1963	43.72	32.93	-0.16	10.79	0.67
1964	46.01	34.65	1.72	11.36	0.57
1965	49.65	37.38	2.73	12.27	0.91

Source: Zhonggong zhongyang shujichu yanjiu lilunzu (ed.), *Dangqian woguo gongren jieji zhuangkuang diaocha ziliao huibian* (Beijing: Zhonggong zhongyang dangxiao chubanshe, 1983) Vol. 2, pp. 105–106.

the 1960s, from 14 percent in 1964 to 12.9 percent in 1968, a figure it would not exceed until after Mao's death in 1976.[9] The government effectively capped the population of the towns and cities, limiting the number of people who were entitled to food rations, welfare and non-agrarian jobs. The leadership of the CCP had learned important lessons from the famine.

These measures alone, however, were still inadequate to stabilize the system of food supply in the post-famine years. Reform had to be coupled with immediate relief via grain imports. As Chen Yun argued: "If we import grain, we can take less from the peasants, stabilize their attitude toward production, and raise the enthusiasm of the peasants for production. If we take two or three years to develop agricultural production, the problems of the internal market can be solved."[10] Between 1961 and 1965, China imported on average 5 million tons of grain each year; net imports stood at around 4.18 million tons per annum.[11] Rather than being sent to famine-hit rural areas, this grain was used to supply Beijing, Tianjin, Shanghai and Liaoning. All four areas were part of the urban supply system administered directly by the central government, and the imports therefore constituted a kind of indirect famine relief, reducing the burden on peasants to meet grain quotas and allowing more grain to remain in the villages.

9 Yuan Yongxi (ed.), *Zhongguo renkou zonglun*, p. 277.
10 Quoted in: Jin Chongji (ed.), *Zhou Enlai zhuan* (Beijing: Zhongyang wenxian chubanshe, 1998), Vol. 4, p. 1565.
11 Luo Pinghan, *Da qian xi: 1961–1963 nian de chengzhen renkou jing jian* (Nanning: Guangxi renmin chubanshe, 2003), p. 118.

By opting for this method of relief, the government avoided imported grain passing through the hands of rural officials, thereby minimizing the risk of fraud and misappropriation. From 1962, quotas for grain procurement stabilized enough to bring rural communities out of famine. Strict enforcement of the *hukou* system helped maintain the balance between agricultural production and urban consumption.

Necessary as austerity policies and the downsizing of the urban population were, they nevertheless had a serious effect on morale in the cities. Even in Shanghai, which had one of the most secure food supplies in the country, workers complained about low food rations and a lack of household essentials such as toilet paper (see Document 5.1). An archived letter from one citizen expressed frustration at the limited information about the crisis available to ordinary people, who were not permitted to listen to the speeches of central leaders. The same document laments the practice of cadres "entering in through the back door" to acquire scarce goods such as meat and fish by corrupt means. It also asserts that the theft of children, a phenomenon not seen in Shanghai since the revolution, had become widespread. Little is known about how ordinary people reacted to the program of downsizing, or about differences in responses between rural and urban China. It seems safe to say, however, that many would have agreed with the words of one worker in Shaanxi: "The capitalists call it going bankrupt, we call it stopping production. The capitalists call it firing, we call it being sent down. The capitalists call it unemployment, we call it [workforce] reduction. In any case, we have no jobs and it is still the same as in capitalist countries."[12]

Work units throughout China were given quotas for reducing their workforce. Some urban residents tried to avoid being sent back to the countryside by petitioning the local government. Most petitioners argued that they were sick, pregnant or had to provide care for dependent family members. Others threatened to commit suicide if they were not allowed to remain in the cities.[13] The fact that targets for staff reductions were generally met suggests that these strategies tended to be ineffective. The central government's ability to enforce a large-scale population transfer hard on the heels of the famine crisis reflects the remarkable capacity of the early PRC state.

Little research has been done on how the arrival of returnees from the cities affected the villagers who had stayed behind. In contrast to the "sent-down youth" of the Cultural Revolution, many people who were hit by the downsizing of 1962 and 1963 were recent migrants who had left the countryside only a few

12 Quoted in Luo Pinghan, *Da qian xi*, p. 223.
13 For more detail see: Jeremy Brown, *City versus Countryside in Mao's China: Negotiating the Divide* (Cambridge: Cambridge University Press, 2012), pp. 86–99.

Figure 5.1: A view from Shanghai Mansion, 1974.
Source: Photograph by Carl Seyschab.

years earlier and remained familiar with agricultural production. They were not strangers in their home villages. Nevertheless, it remains an open question whether the returnees were welcomed as additional manpower or seen as competitors for scarce food. What is certain, however, is that under the influence of the CCP's new policies the countryside finally recovered. To achieve this recovery, the government sacrificed its push for rapid industrialization, which prior to 1961 had been primarily driven by imports of foreign technology financed by exports of grain. The state also raised the price it paid for grain to incentivize production, but in order to keep the peace in the urban areas the sale price remained stable. The losses from what was effectively a massive subsidy program would be a burden on the state's budget for the next two decades.[14]

In sum, the years between 1962 and 1966 saw a deepening of the urban–rural divide, caused by stricter enforcement of the *hukou* system and a deliberate reduction in the number of people entitled to access the urban welfare state. A side-effect of these policies was to limit social mobility for the rural population. Nevertheless, the party leadership remained united behind the new measures, and

14 Terry Sicular, "Grain Pricing: A Key Link in Chinese Economic Policy," *Modern China*, Vol. 14, No. 4 (1988), pp. 461–463.

Mao never questioned the *hukou* system in his lifetime, nor the various programs to reduce the urban population.

The Third Front and the Industrialization of the West

In 1961 and 1962, the central government's attention was focused on economic rebalancing. However, starting from 1963, Mao in particular pushed investment in heavy industry projects under the so-called Third Front. This program, designed to relocate parts of China's modern industrial base into the interior of the country, remained secret for many years, and much work remains to be done in analyzing it. Many official economic and industrial statistics from the period exclude Third Front construction. The strategic rationale that motivated the policy is clear, however. By 1963, the central government had become concerned by two major threats to national security, namely the US military's deepening involvement in the Vietnam War[15] and the Soviet Union's decision to mass troops near the Chinese border in Outer Mongolia. In a full-scale war against either power, China would have no realistic chance of preventing incursions by enemy marine or air forces. Any such incursion would leave China's modern industries vulnerable, since most were located in Manchuria or in coastal areas on the eastern seaboard. The CCP's thinking owed much to the GMD's experience during its costly retreat to Sichuan in the Second Sino-Japanese War (1937–1945). The Third Front envisaged a new industrial base in the west which would provide the economic foundation for a People's War against invading forces. Between 1963 and 1965, a remarkable 38.2 percent of national investments went to Third Front projects, and the program remained a priority for the central government until 1971.[16]

In the first phase of the Third Front, major projects were located in Sichuan, Guizhou and Yunnan, often in seemingly unlikely locations. The minor Sichuanese city of Panzhihua, for instance, was selected as a center for steel production. Parts of Qinghai, Gansu, Shaanxi, Hubei and Hunan were later included in the program as well. The relocation of industry accelerated the standardization of regional transportation networks. New railway construction linked up cities in the interior, adding over 8,000 kilometers of track to the Chinese rail system between 1964 and 1980.[17] Major trunk lines such as the

---

15 Lorenz Lüthi, "The Vietnam War and China's Third-Line Defense Planning before the Cultural Revolution, 1964–1966," *Journal of Cold War Studies*, Vol. 10, No. 1, (2008), p. 27.

16 Barry Naughton, "The Third Front: Defense Industrialization in the Chinese Interior," *The China Quarterly*, No. 115 (1988), p. 365.

17 Covell Meyskens, "Third Front Railroads and Industrial Modernity in Late Maoist China," *Twentieth-Century China*, Vol. 3, No. 3 (2015), p. 246.

Kunming–Chengdu–Guiyang and Xining–Golmud links were products of the Third Front, as was a new connection linking Tianjin to Guangxi in the south. The Third Front significantly altered China's spatial order, reducing the dominance of the eastern regions in industry and transport infrastructure.

The government mobilized millions of people to help build Third Front projects. Some were skilled workers from Shanghai and other developed coastal cities, while others were local peasants, "urban youths" or militia conscripts. Conditions on these projects were extreme, and Mao's slogan, "Don't fear hardship or death," took on an all-too-literal meaning in many cases. According to incomplete statistics, accidents during the construction of the Chengdu–Kunming railway – one of several new lines to pass through challenging mountainous terrain – caused the deaths of 2,100 members of the Railroad Corps and injuries to 5,687 others.[18] The party tried to maintain worker morale through appeals to patriotism. However, many Third Front projects were treated as military secrets, meaning that the workers involved received no public recognition. Beyond the risks to personal safety, other projects required Han workers to migrate to minority areas. The fact that the war the party was planning for never materialized has led some contemporary historians to question the practical value of the Third Front. The program was labor and capital intensive, and siting factories according to the needs of national defense meant economic efficiency tended to fall by the wayside. The social history of the Third Front largely remains to be written.

Reforms in the Labor Market and Education: Enforcing Dualism

In the years between 1962 and 1965, the government established a dual system in the labor market and education. In addition to the regular labor market and schools, a kind of "second-class" system with less funding and reduced entitlements was created to meet demand without overburdening the state. As a result, by 1964 the urban workforce had begun to increase again (see Table 5.1). The reason for the introduction of the so-called "dual system" in labor was simple. Many factories required new workers to meet their production targets. However, the central government was reluctant to increase the number of people on the state's payroll, a move that had backfired so spectacularly during the Great Leap. Between 1960 and 1963, the workforce in state-owned enterprises had decreased from 59 to 43 million. Some of these losses had been absorbed by the

18 Ibid., p. 257.

collective enterprises, whose workforce had increased from 9 to 11 million. Still, more workers had to be found from somewhere.

It was soon realized that one way to reduce government spending while enlarging the workforce was to allow an increase in the number of temporary workers. Short-term work had existed alongside lifetime employment since 1949. A decision by the Labor Department in 1959 had distinguished between three forms of urban work: long-term employment, temporary contract work undertaken by urban workers and a system of "peasant-workers" recruited from the countryside for short-term work in factories.[19] Between 1964 and 1966, the number of temporary workers in the latter two categories expanded significantly. "Peasant-workers" were an especially useful resource, since although their wages were higher than the average rural income, they remained poorly paid compared to regular urban workers.

It was clear from the outset that peasant-workers were not to be allowed to become part of the permanent urban workforce. A 1965 report by the Labor Department on the situation in Sichuan expressed concern that if wages for young peasant-workers were set too high, they would cause tension in the villages after their return. The report also recommended that production brigades should be able to claim compensation for lost work from members who took temporary jobs outside agriculture.[20] Both these conclusions rested on the assumption that a peasant-worker was and would remain part of his or her rural community, with no prospect of earning admission to the urban world. Although temporary workers were a minority, they were nevertheless a significant part of the urban workforce in the 1960s. By the end of 1965 China had over 33 million permanent workers and 3.18 million urban contract workers, an increase of 540,000 over the previous year. Another 2 million people were employed as peasant-workers. A contemporary report by the State Statistics Bureau praised the dual labor market for allowing urban work units to replace many permanent workers with temporary staff.[21]

In expanding the dual labor market, the government never planned to abolish the "iron rice bowl," but it did intend for a significant number of workers be temporarily employed and denied access to the welfare state. From 1964, President Liu Shaoqi was an important advocate for the dual system in the labor market and education. In an important speech on the topic, Liu argued that while the iron rice bowl was the gold standard, it introduced problems by making it difficult to "withdraw" workers, meaning to fire them. For seasonal

19 Zhongguo shehui kexueyuan and zhongyang dang'anguan (ed.), *1958–1965 Zhonghua renmin gongheguo jingji dang'an ziliao xuanbian. Laodong jiuye he shouru fenpei juan* (Beijing: Zhongguo caizheng jingji chubanshe, 2011), p. 5.
20 Ibid., p. 400.   21 Ibid., p. 459.

tasks, temporary employment was a more desirable route; as Liu put it, "If there is work, they come. If there is not, they can go home."[22] Liu argued against future increases in the permanent workforce. He also envisioned a system of obligatory labor to be used specifically in the mining industry. Mining was known to lead to severe health problems, and Liu therefore proposed that workers should be recruited into the mines only for a few years before being mandatorily discharged. While he was careful to frame his arguments in terms of workers' interests, "mandatory discharge" had the convenient side-effect of turning an entire industry into short-term contract work. His speech was rooted above all not in the socialist logic of worker entitlements, but in the government's desire to reduce costs.

The second strand of the dual system was education. During the Great Leap, the CCP's drive to expand schools and increase student numbers had created a tremendous additional burden for the central state and local governments. Nor was the money necessarily well spent. Standards in many of the new schools were low, and learning was often made more difficult by the fact that significant numbers of students were going hungry. In February 1961, the Central Committee circulated a document arguing that more young labor power was needed for agricultural production. To free up this labor, it was decided that students above the age of sixteen years should not exceed 2 percent of the total rural labor force over the next three to five years. Primary and middle schools should avoid enrolling students who had passed the regular age for schooling, and the number of students in regular and agriculture middle schools should be kept steady.[23] The decision significantly curtailed opportunities for peasant children to attend higher middle school. Table 5.2 shows the impact of the downsizing of the education system, although it should be noted that the figures do not distinguish between rural and urban schools. The number of elementary school graduates dropped from 7.3 million in 1960 to 4.7 million in 1963, and rates of progression between the different levels of schooling fell significantly. Only a slight increase was recorded after 1963.

Although the central government was keen to reduce costs and keep more labor power in agriculture to bolster food production, it also retained its ambition to universalize literacy and compulsory education in the countryside. To balance these competing aims, a system of "half studying, half producing" was introduced alongside the regular schools, allowing students to continue their education while also participating in either agriculture or industry. In the

---

22 Liu Shaoqi, "Guanyu liang zhong laodong zhidu he liang zhong jiaoyu zhidu," in *JGYL*, Vol. 19, p. 174.
23 "Zhonggong zhongyang pizhuan zhongyang wenjiao xiaozu 'Guanyu 1961 nian he jinhou yige shiqi wenhua jiaoyu gongzuo anpai de baogao'," in *JGYL*, Vol. 14, pp. 172-173.

Table 5.2 *Opportunities to continue schooling within the regular system, 1957–1965*

Year	(1) Elem. School graduates	(2) Jr. middle school entrants	(3) Elem. Graduate promotion rate (%)	(4) Jr. middle graduates	(5) Sr. middle entrants	(6) Jr. middle graduate promotion rate (%)	(7) Sr. middle graduates	(8) University entrants	(9) Sr. middle graduate promotion rate (%)
1957	4,980,000	2,170,000	43.57	1,112,000	323,000	29.05	187,000	105,581	56.46
1958	6,063,000	3,783,000	62.39	1,116,000	562,000	50.36	197,000	265,553	134.80
1959	5,473,000	3,183,000	58.16	1,491,000	656,000	44.00	299,000	274,143	91.69
1960	7,340,000	3,648,000	49.70	1,422,000	678,000	47.68	288,000	323,161	112.21
1961	5,808,000	2,218,000	38.19	1,892,000	447,000	23.63	379,000	169,047	44.60
1962	5,590,000	2,383,000	42.63	1,584,000	417,000	26.33	441,000	106,777	24.21
1963	4,768,000	2,635,000	55.26	1,523,000	434,000	28.50	433,000	132,820	30.67
1964	5,674,000	2,866,000	50.51	1,386,000	438,000	31.60	367,000	147,037	40.06
1965	6,676,000	2,998,000	44.91	1,738,000	459,000	26.41	360,000	164,212	45.61

Source: Suzanne Pepper, *Radicalism and Education Reform in Twentieth-Century China: The Search for an Ideal Development Model* (Cambridge: Cambridge University Press, 1996), p. 304.

countryside, students would work in the fields during the harvest and study during the growing seasons. In Liu Shaoqi's assessment, this dual system was the only way for the state to afford the general education needed to eliminate illiteracy.[24]

The President justified the dual systems in labor and education as a method to reduce the gap between city and countryside, and between intellectual and manual labor. The peasant-worker system was not simply a cost-saving measure, but an efficient way for peasants to improve their skills and knowledge by working temporarily in the urban industries. What this argument left unanswered was the question of where those extra skills would lead. Could people change tracks in the dual system? Would a peasant ever be given the chance to enter the permanent urban workforce, which accounted for only a very small percentage of the population? Would the basic skills to which schooling was restricted under the "half producing, half studying" system be enough to allow rural children to access higher education? These critiques would come to the fore during the Cultural Revolution, when the dual system was attacked as forming part of the "revisionist line" advocated by Liu and Deng Xiaoping. Liu stood accused of discriminating against the children of ordinary people, who were only allowed to learn the basic skills necessary to perform hard labor for others.[25] At the same time, critics alleged, children of intellectuals and urban cadres enjoyed a better education in the regular system or at elite "key-point" schools. It was disingenuous to direct these criticisms at Liu and Deng alone. Liu, after all, did not personally devise the dual system, and all the evidence suggests that Mao was initially supportive of it. Nevertheless, in my view the critique of the system itself was accurate. Contrary to Liu's assertions, the dual system entrenched rather than reduced the division between manual and intellectual labor and the gap between urban and rural China.

With regard to higher education, the central government decided in 1965 to place an additional focus on the issue of the "class line." A document circulated by the Central Committee argued that class status and political performance should be given more weight than academic standing in the admissions process, to allow universities to better "cultivate the successors of the revolution." The importance of examination results and academic performance was reduced compared to the early 1960s. The document instructed institutions to give the children of industrial workers, poor and lower middle peasants, revolutionary martyrs and cadres with the correct ideology favorable treatment in the selection process. Family origin was not to be the only criterion for admissions, and the

24 Liu Shaoqi, "Guanyu liang zhong laodong zhidu he liang zhong jiaoyu zhidu," p. 165.
25 "Chedi fensui Liu, Bo, Ma zhixing fangeming xiuzhengzhuyi laodong gongzi luxian de zuixing," *Laodong zhanxian* May 13 (1967), in *Chinese Cultural Revolution Collection*, Box 8, Folder "lao dong zhan xian," Hoover Institution Archives.

children of the exploiting classes could still be recruited provided they performed well and had drawn a line with their parents.[26] Nonetheless, the shift in emphasis was clear.

Did the stronger focus on status and political performance in higher education constitute an effective counterweight to the discrimination rural children faced under the dual system? I would argue that it did not. The aim of the dual system was to reduce the cost of providing rural primary education. Under the "half producing, half studying" model, most peasant children were filtered out of education before high school age. Adjustments to the university admissions system were a total irrelevance to these students, since they never made it far enough for higher education to enter the picture. Instead, the changes tended to give cadres' children an advantage over the children of the old intellectual elite, who performed better on examinations but were from less favorable social backgrounds. The communist elite, not the children of peasants, were the primary beneficiaries of the "class line."

The Limited Revival of the United Front

Even as the central government tightened control over the *hukou* system, it also sought to recreate aspects of the United Front with intellectuals, ethnic minorities and religious groups, all of whom had suffered during the Great Leap. Relations between the CCP and intellectuals had been tense since the Anti-Rightist Campaign of 1957. In the summer of 1961, the Central Committee attempted to win over this important constituency with the passage of the so-called "40 Points for Scientific Research" and "60 Points for Higher Education." Both documents signaled a renewed commitment to expert knowledge, book learning, formal institutions, quality of research and the authority of the teacher. The amount of manual labor expected of academics and their students was reduced from four to two weeks a year.

Some party leaders went further, arguing that it was inappropriate to continue to label the majority of intellectuals and technicians as "bourgeois intellectuals" or "bourgeois experts." In a 1962 speech, Zhou Enlai repeated the view he had previously expressed in 1956, that intellectuals in the new China constituted not an independent class, but "a social stratum of intellectual laborers."[27] The distinction was important, since it meant that intellectuals were to be

---

26 "Zhonggong zhongyang pizhuan gaodengjiaoyubu dangzu guanyu gaijin 1965 nian gaodeng xuexiao zhaosheng gongzuo de qingshi baogao," in Zhongyang dang'an guan (ed.), *Zhonggong zhongyang wenjian xuanji* (Beijing: Renmin chubanshe, 2013), Vol. 48, pp. 366–367.

27 Zhou Enlai, "Lun zhishifenzi wenti," in *JGYL*, Vol. 15, p. 224.

considered part of "the people" rather than as a separate group at risk of being designated class enemies. Like everyone else, intellectuals would still need to re-educate themselves to overcome bourgeois thinking, but shortcomings in their re-education should be considered as "contradictions among the people" rather than as a counterrevolutionary threat. Zhou's view was not universally shared, however. Later that year, Mao expressed opposition to dropping the label "bourgeois intellectuals," stating that such people still existed and that the term must therefore be retained.[28]

A key plank of the party's efforts to reach out to intellectuals was the revision of verdicts that had been handed down during the Anti-Rightist Campaign. As early as 1959 and 1960, 99,000 "rightists" had been allowed to "take off the hat" (zhai maozi), meaning that their negative label was suspended. This number increased to 300,000 in 1964, and most of those whose cases were revisited were intellectuals.[29] Permission to "take off the hat" improved living and working conditions not just for the individual concerned, but also for their relatives. However, it did not equate to full rehabilitation (pingfan), nor did it guarantee that the person could return to the same post that they had held before being labeled. Mao himself sought to limit the impact of the process by rejecting suggestions that all verdicts of "rightism" be re-examined automatically. When the hat was taken off, the original judgment remained on the record, and future shortcomings in labor performance and ideology could lead to an order from the party that an individual must "put on the hat" again. Those whose verdicts were revised therefore remained on a very short leash. The situation of many intellectuals improved in the early 1960s, but they were still at the mercy of the party.

For many ethnic minorities, the Great Leap had been experienced as an attack on traditional customs and religious institutions. While the Leap had not been enforced in Tibet, provinces such as Qinghai, Sichuan, Gansu and Yunnan, all of which had large Tibetan populations, were seriously affected by the famine. The Central Economic Work Conference of 1962 "readjusted" the state's policy towards the minorities. This included critically reviewing policies to settle nomads, as well as revisiting the closure or destruction of Buddhist monasteries. During the Great Leap, the rights of the "autonomous" minority regions had been restricted, and religious activities had stopped completely in some places. Official statistics suggest that 731 out of the 859 monasteries in Qinghai had been closed by the end of 1958, and 24,613 monks and nuns out of a total of 54,287 had been compelled to join agricultural cooperatives. Only 1 percent of

---

28 Bo Yibo, *Ruogan zhongda juece yu shijian de huigu* (Beijing: Zhonggongzhongyang dangxiao chubanshe, 1993), Vol. 2, p. 1006.

29 Ibid., p. 1001.

monasteries in the province had been fully preserved; in Gansu the figure was 2 percent; in Sichuan, 4 percent; and in Tibet, 6.5 percent.[30] These figures show that the closing of the monasteries in fact started many years before the Cultural Revolution, to which the decimation of religious worship under Mao has often been ascribed. The government did not plan to reopen all the closed monasteries, but it did concede that the number of closures had been excessively high. A second major Great Leap policy, the decision to "combine agricultural and husbandry" and convert grassland for cultivation, was now acknowledged as destructive. Nomads received compensation to replenish their herds, and class struggle in the nomadic regions was de-emphasized.

During the Great Leap, Han cadres had taken over many key positions in the minority areas. By 1961, the numbers of minority cadres had been reduced by 48 percent in Gansu and around 20 percent in Yunnan and Qinghai compared to the 1958 figures. The Central Economic Work Conference called for improvements in the training of minority cadres and for the rehabilitation of the vast majority of cadres purged for "localism" during the Great Leap. The conference document added that central regulations concerning the United Front with the "upper stratum" of the minorities should be respected, a provision that included improving the living conditions of their representatives. The conference also called for the restoration of "affirmative action" for minorities in higher education and for increased trade in minority goods. Given the shortfall in minority cadres, it was decided not to reduce the number of institutes devoted to the national minorities or to send minority cadres back to the countryside, in spite of the downsizing being pursued elsewhere.[31] The government seems to have viewed the need to "indigenize" cadres in the minority areas as urgent enough to override its efforts to reduce costs.

In the case of Tibet, the attempt to recreate the United Front had only limited effects. As we have already seen, the government's desire for smoother relations did not prevent it attacking the Panchen Lama, the region's most senior representative. In 1962, the Lama submitted a report to the central government detailing his visits to Tibetan-speaking areas outside Tibet. He argued that the famine was a "great threat to the continued existence of the Tibetan nationality, which was sinking into a state close to death."[32] This proved too much for Mao, and the Panchen Lama was dismissed from office and brought to Beijing for

---

30 "Zhonggong zhongyang pizhuan 'Guanyu minzu gongzuo huiyi de baogao'," in *JGYL*, Vol. 15, pp. 521–522.

31 Ibid., pp. 513, 517.

32 Panchen Lama, *A Poisoned Arrow: The Secret Report of the 10th Panchen Lama; the Full Text of the Panchen Lama's 70,000 Character Petition of 1962, Together with a Selection of Supporting Historical Documents* (London: Tibet Information Network, 1997), p. 103.

criticism. In 1965, a formal Autonomous Region was finally established for Tibet, along the lines of the existing Xinjiang Uighur Autonomous Region and the Guangxi Zhuang Autonomous Region in the south. This marked the end of the special arrangement with Tibet established in 1950, and the result was enhanced central government control. By the mid-1960s, the theocratic "old Tibet," a deeply religious society ruled by a clerical elite, was dead and gone. In addition to the institutional changes, the CCP began to recruit larger numbers of Tibetan poor and lower middle peasants as cadres to implement class struggle. These new cadres had joined the party during a period of radicalization, and they gained a reputation for their leftist leanings.

Not only did attempts to resurrect the United Front in 1961 and 1962 largely fail, but Mao also rapidly came to the conclusion that too many concessions had been made to intellectuals, ethnic minority leaders and religious communities. As a result, it was no surprise that the head of the CCP's United Front Work Department, Li Weihan, was criticized in late 1962 and 1964 before being purged from office in December that year. He and Ulanhu, the party leader of Inner Mongolia toppled early in the Cultural Revolution, were both accused of neglecting class struggle in the minority regions and supporting local nationalism.

The Socialist Education Campaign: Radicalization of Class Struggle

The clearest sign of a return to the "class line" and radicalization in the post-famine years was the Socialist Education Campaign. Beginning in spring 1963, this new movement aimed to reinforce discipline in rural party organizations. The CCP had in fact carried out several Socialist Education Campaigns in the countryside since 1957, but this was by far the most significant. Also known as the Four Clean Ups Campaign, the movement targeted local cadres' management of finances, bookkeeping, grain stocks and the distribution of work points in the People's Communes, all of which the CCP felt had been poorly handled during the famine years. The problems the party was seeking to address were real and serious problems – fraud, corruption and abuse of power by local cadres, all of which were widespread during and after the famine. On the other hand, cadres who had built up so-called "black grain stocks" to help prevent starvation in their local areas also faced investigation. The goal was not only to improve the relationship between the cadres and the masses, but also to restore the state's monopoly over the grain trade.

As in other campaigns, the movement alternated between periods of radicalization and moderation. Initially, the Central Committee stipulated that 95 percent of the local cadres had played by the rules, limiting the scope of the campaign to the remaining 5 percent. However, this quota was largely forgotten as the movement became more and more politicized. The central leadership's view that the campaign represented what it called a "two-line struggle" between socialism and capitalism set the stage for intense conflict at the local level. Beatings occurred at struggle sessions, and many cadres accused of being one of the enemy "four elements" committed suicide under the strain. In addition to cadres' administration of the communes, political attitude, economic management, party organizations and ideology were also investigated under the slogan of "the big Four Clean Ups." As the campaign progressed, huge work teams from higher levels of the system were sent into the villages to lead the attack on local cadres, adding to the increasingly radical atmosphere. The Four Clean Ups was also expanded to factories and universities, but the impact on urban society never matched the intensity seen in the countryside.

The Four Clean Ups did not proceed as smoothly as the CCP had hoped, and in 1965 conflict broke out between Mao and Liu Shaoqi over the source of the problems. Liu contended that resistance to the campaign was being driven by corrupt local cadres backed by "rich peasants." Mao, however, argued that local cadres were receiving support from high-level "capitalist roaders inside the party."[33] If the higher echelons of the CCP were complicit in maintaining the bad practices seen in rural areas, then the huge outside work teams being sent into the villages to promote the Four Clean Ups might themselves be compromised. Mao's view carried the day, and the strategy was abandoned.

Crackdown on the "Black Wind" in the Rural Economy

In 1961, Mao was willing to accept a relaxation of state control in the country-side in order to achieve economic recovery. Nevertheless, he was keen to set limits to ensure that central power was not reduced excessively. Soon after the release of the "60 Points for the People's Communes," he defined a "bottom line" for how far reforms could go. Experiments in several provinces, notably Anhui, had strengthened the household responsibility system, under which peasant families were the units of production and responsible for the grain fulfilling quotas, at the expense of the larger commune. In early 1962, these schemes were attacked as "revisionist" and "anti-socialist" and brought to an abrupt end.

---

33 Guo Dehong and Lin Xiaobo, *Siqing yundong shilu* (Hangzhou: Zhejiang renmin chubanshe, 2005), p. 346.

One important goal of the Socialist Education Campaign was to defend Mao's bottom line and to crack down on "capitalist tendencies" in the countryside. In summer 1963, the Central Committee complained that agricultural output had declined in some regions, because peasants were too heavily involved in more profitable "sideline production" at the expense of work in the collective fields. Collective goods and resources were also being misappropriated for private trade.[34] In some regions, local authorities had under-reported arable land to conceal part of the grain harvest. Campaigns were started to investigate land holdings and eliminate all "black land."[35] "Underreporting of production to distribute privately" remained widespread throughout the country, as Document 5.2 suggests, with extra grain concealed in so-called "black grain stocks." Large quantities of grain were being distributed by cadres without authorization or documentation, or else were being stolen or wasted as a result of improper storage. In one case, a factory facing external inspection called in staff to hide hoarded food and make false statements to the authorities.

There were other forms of grain fraud as well. In some places, small-scale black markets developed as peasants lent surplus grain to other villagers at high interest rates. For the party, such activities constituted not just misdemeanors, but an expression of the "two-line struggle" between socialism and capitalism. As the famine receded, the number of private food traders increased rapidly. Demand was strong thanks to restrictions on food in the official rationing system, and the downsizing of the urban workforce left a large pool of people willing to struggle for survival as "spontaneous traders." An "internal reference" report compiled in November 1962 estimated that there were 3 million such traders across the country.[36] As well as food, black markets also developed for cloth and cotton. Sometimes the factories themselves were involved in this business, appropriating raw materials from their stocks for sale on the black market. In the cities, even anti-socialist and erotic literature might circulate via such markets. In one county, 200 local schools were found to be using illicitly acquired Confucian tracts as textbooks (see Document 5.3).

During the Socialist Education Campaign, the Central Committee argued that these unauthorized economic activities reflected "capitalist tendencies." In April 1964, it called for the systematic elimination of illegal private trade. If a daily ration of one-and-a-half to two catties (*jin*) of grain per person could be guaranteed, the Committee argued, people would have easily enough to live off. Given the progress the government was making towards this goal, private food

---

34 "Fuye dangan shi dangqian nongcun liang tiao daolu douzheng de you yi tuchu wenti," in *JGYL*, Vol. 16, pp. 378–381.

35 *Neibu Cankao*, April 28, 1964.   36 *Neibu Cankao*, November 30, 1962.

traders could be replaced.[37] It is doubtful whether this level of nutrition, about 0.75–1 kilogram of grain daily, was ever actually reached during the Mao era. However, the government felt strong enough to reinforce its monopoly on the grain trade, believing that, even if rations were not as generous as claimed, the peasants already had enough food to survive.

During the early 1960s, Mao consistently pointed to a threat of the "restoration of capitalism" in the countryside. By this he meant the so-called "black wind" of individual farming that had sprung up in the years 1961–1962, but also the illegal extension of plots for private use, private trade and black markets, all of which challenged the new order of the People's Communes. Mao argued that peasants had a dual character, with tendencies towards socialism because of the exploitation they had historically suffered, but also towards capitalism because of their role as small producers. Landlords and rich peasants could abuse this weakness to gather supporters and undermine the socialist order. This was a classic, orthodox Marxist argument, made by Lenin on several occasions. Mao was also wary of "fellow travelers" within the Communist Party itself, who had supported Land Reform but never fully accepted the socialist transformation of ownership structures. In his view, reinforcement of the "class line" was the best way to counteract the "black wind" of resurgent rural capitalism.[38]

Reinforcing the Rural "Class Line"

By 1961, Mao was already seizing on arguments that violence against peasants by cadres during the famine was the result of "power seizures" by local class enemies. For example, a report by the party committee of Xinyang prefecture in Henan, site of the catastrophic "Xinyang Incident" (see Chapter 4), claimed that the disaster had resulted from a restoration of rule by the landlord class. Hidden class enemies had wormed their way into leading positions in local party organizations and had terrorized the rural population. The report, which was circulated by the Central Committee, spoke freely of the disastrous loss of life in Xinyang, acknowledging 100,000 deaths in one county alone and suggesting that more than a third of the population had died in some brigades.[39] The blame,

---

37 "Zhonggong zhongyang, Guowuyuan guanyu jinyibu kaizhan daiti sishang gongzuo de zhishi," in *JGYL*, Vol. 18, p. 430.

38 Bo Yibo, *Ruogan zhongda juece yu shijian de huigu*, Vol. 2, pp. 1087–1088.

39 "Zhonggong zhongyang dui Xinyang diwei guanyu zhengfeng zhengshe yundong he shengchan jiuzai gongzuo qingkuang de baogao de pishi," in Zhonghua renmin gongheguo guojia nongye weiyuanhui bangongting (ed.), *Nongye jitihua zhongyao wenjian huibian* (Beijing: Zhongyang dangxiao chubanshe, 1981), Vol. 2, p. 421.

however, was laid at the door, not of ultra-leftist cadres, but of the same enemies the party had been fighting since its inception.

Evaluations like this had consequences. Rural party organizations across the country began to set up campaigns to "reschedule classes in the democratic revolution." These reactions lent a real urgency to the battle against class enemies, and they help us to understand the atmosphere behind the party leadership's fevered reaction to perceived resistance against the Four Clean Ups. The leadership's first response was to reinforce the "class line." In July 1964, the Central Committee decided to establish Associations of Poor and Lower Middle Peasants. This was a striking move, given that the party had itself abolished similar peasant organizations after Land Reform in the early 1950s. The central leadership also called for a rebuilding of the militia, which had been downsized during the famine. It made clear, however, that arms should only be placed in the hands of reliable workers and poor and lower middle peasants.[40] The party leadership hoped that these two sets of organizations, both based on the "class line," would help to mobilize the masses against disloyal local cadres and the "four elements."

If the situation in the countryside was bad enough that "rescheduled classes in the democratic revolution" were required, it was only logical that a reinvestigation of class status might be necessary too. In the same year it revived the militia and the peasant associations, the Central Committee promulgated a series of orders calling for class files to be created for every rural family, based on the 1950 regulation on classification that had been used during Land Reform (see Chapter 1, Document 1.1).[41] Where new investigations identified members of the four elements who had "slipped through the net," they should be reclassified so that they could be purged from the party. The order had to be made repeatedly because, in contrast to the cities, most peasants, except those who were party members, still had no personal files by the early 1960s. Creating class files was an attempt to integrate the rural population into an urban-style system of bureaucratic registration by class status.

Classification was intended to make it easier to identify potential enemies of the system, but as might be expected the Central Committee's orders created considerable confusion at the local level. The attack on real landlords had ceased over a decade previously, and the four elements had been relentlessly targeted in the years since. Some cadres felt that as a result class struggle was a thing of the past, a claim they made openly in the face of central pressure. They even claimed

40 "Zhonggong zhongyang zhuanfa 'Minbing zhengzhi gongzuo huiyi jiyao'," in *JGYL*, Vol. 19, pp. 383–384.
41 "Zhonggong zhongyang yinfa 'guanyu nongcun shehuizhuyi jiaoyu yundong zhong yixie juti zhengce de guiding (xiuzheng cao'an)' de tongzhi," in *JGYL*, Vol. 19, p. 246.

that reclassifying some people as "poor and lower middle peasants" would lead to a drop in productivity by encouraging them to depend on government aid.[42] Many cadres found it difficult to classify people based on the 1950 regulation, given the significant changes in social structure that had taken place in the fourteen years since it was devised. The standards used to create the new class files, and the questions that cadres asked of rural residents in doing so, varied by region.[43] Given the time that had elapsed since Land Reform, the question of how to deal with the adult children of "landlords" and "rich peasants" was a major challenge. To address how these people should be treated, the Central Committee was forced to clarify the meaning of the "class line." The difficulty with these children, it argued, was primarily that they had been socialized by their families in negative ways, making them a political risk in the new China. However, given that they had never personally exploited anyone, they should be treated differently from their parents. The Central Committee argued that there should be no blanket exclusion of children with bad family backgrounds from the party, nor should they be forced to join their parents in struggle sessions. However, they were to be prevented from serving in leadership positions in local party organizations. Those with bad family backgrounds could participate in the new order, but they could never be fully trusted.

As had been the case during Land Reform itself, another point that required clarification was the relationship of family background to political status. Here the Central Committee took a relatively lenient approach. If parents were from a rich peasant background but were themselves revolutionary cadres or revolutionary soldiers, their children should be labeled according to the more favorable category.[44] A July 1965 document on the conduct of the Four Clean Ups Campaign in the national transportation network included a provision that technicians and workers with bad family backgrounds were to be evaluated mainly on performance. The same document reaffirmed the government's promise that the class status of laborers who had been capitalists or small business owners in the past could be changed after serious investigation. In addition, subject to the approval of the masses, landlords and rich peasants could be granted the status of "laborer" after ten years of service. Individuals whose status

42 Zhongguo shehui kexueyuan and zhongyang dang'anguan (ed.), *1958–1965 Zhonghua renmin gongheguo jingji dang'an ziliao xuanbian. Zonghe juan* (Beijing: Zhongguo caizheng jingji chubanshe, 2011), pp. 719–720.

43 Jeremy Brown, "Moving Targets: Changing Class Labels in Rural Hebei and Henan 1960–1979," in Jeremy Brown and Matthew Johnson (eds.), *Maoism at the Grassroots: Everyday Life in China's Era of High Socialism* (Cambridge, MA: Harvard University Press, 2015), pp. 60–62.

44 "Zhonggong zhongyang guanyu yinfa 'nongcun shehuizhuyi jiaoyu yundong zhong yixie juti zhengce de guiding (xiuzheng cao'an)' de tongzhi," pp. 264–265.

was changed would be allowed to become members of the trade unions, but not to serve as cadres.[45] The promise of a change of status as a reward for good conduct echoed the provisions of the 1950 regulation. However, it is doubtful whether this new undertaking had much practical impact. A permanent job in the railway network was one of the most desirable careers available in the Mao era, and it would be surprising if many landlords or rich peasants were actually serving in such posts in 1965.

As during Land Reform, inter-class (status) marriage again became a topic of debate during the Socialist Education Campaign. The Central Committee determined that members of the party and the mass organizations should be permitted to marry descendants of landlords and rich peasants, provided that the member concerned showed the correct class attitude. Nonetheless, such unions were still viewed by the party leadership as a possible source of moral corruption and treated with suspicion. Even non-party members faced barriers to inter-class marriage. For instance, anyone with ambitions to join either the CCP or the army had to be prepared to provide information about their "social relations" during the application process. At least during the 1960s, candidates therefore had to think twice about marrying someone with a bad class background. At the local level, the central leadership seems to have been caught between two extremes. On the one hand, some cadres wholly denied the continued necessity of class struggle; on the other, many made no distinction between the status of parents and their adult children, treating the two generations equally harshly. Both attitudes ran contrary to the official policy, which was to enforce the class line while providing a "way out" for young people with a bad family background but good performance. Perhaps the most important element of this policy was the control it gave the CCP over rural class status. Despite the apparent leniency of the leadership's approach, there was no automatic entitlement to changes of status or access to institutions, with the party organizations having the last word.

Academic studies on rural attitudes to the Socialist Education Campaign have been limited. In my view, however, it is doubtful that the reinforcement of the "class line" made much sense for most villagers, particularly in light of the Great Leap Famine. "Poor peasants" and "landlords" had starved together only two years before the campaign began, the victims not of the actions of class enemies but of grain appropriations by the state. The government's promise of food security through the public dining halls had been broken. Peasants learned the hard way that they could not rely on the state to survive. One of the first things to come under attack during the Socialist Education Campaign was the informal

45 Zhongguo shehui kexueyuan and zhongyang dang'anguan (eds.), *1958–1965 Zhonghua renmin gongheguo jingji dang'an ziliao xuanbian. Zonghe juan*, p. 739.

Figure 5.2: The CCP regime created a new master narrative of the Chinese people's struggle for liberation under the leadership of the party. Here a monument to that struggle is erected on Tiananmen Square.
Source: Photograph by Eva Siao, Museum Ludwig.

economy, which for many peasants had been the difference between life and death during the famine. Given this gap between CCP rhetoric and the actual experience of many villagers, are we to accept that people believed the old class enemies were the major problem? Was there real popular fear that the old order could be restored? It seems more plausible to suggest that the major contradiction was between the state and the rural areas from which it extracted resources.

We should note the efforts to which the party had to go to revive class struggle in the villages. The completion of collectivization in the late 1950s had left most rural communities socially relatively homogenous. Only by reinforcing a classification system based on the economic relations of the pre-Land Reform days could the CCP make class divisions operative again. What is most striking is that, following the famine, the state's ability to mobilize peasants for political campaigns of any kind seems to have been diminished. Outside work teams had to be brought in to break the power of local cadres because local people could not be persuaded to do so themselves. The enthusiastic response to mass campaigns seen in 1955 and 1958 did not reappear in the years after the famine.

The Introduction of Birth Planning

Much of the CCP's policy program in the post-famine years grew out of the renewed focus on the class line. Perhaps the most important exception was the birth planning campaign. This campaign was something of a departure for the party. Historically, Marxist thinkers had typically argued against the Malthusian notion that uncontrolled population growth was a primary cause of poverty and famine. Instead, their explanations concentrated on private ownership structures and the unequal distribution of wealth. In 1949, Mao himself had rejected the argument that the size of China's population would ever present a problem,[46] and the newly founded People's Republic introduced Soviet-style natalist policies that encouraged additional births (see Chapter 2). More children would mean a stronger nation.

Things began to change with the publication of a major set of population surveys in 1953. These revealed that China's total population was already above 600 million, a much higher number than had been anticipated. In response, some cadres from both the party and the Women's Federation began to call for birth control to improve the health of women and children. Mao himself expressed concern that the state would have difficulty feeding the rising population, but his attitude changed in 1958, when increasing the labor power of the masses became a central theme of Great Leap economic strategy. After the famine, the debate was reopened.[47] Despite millions of deaths, the birth rate rebounded swiftly, and the baby boom of 1963 and 1964 took the national population to 704 million, compared to 659 million in 1958. The evidence of the Chinese case undermines

46 Mao Zedong, "Weixin lishiguan de pochan," in *Mao Zedong Xuanji* (Beijing: Renmin chu-banshe, 1967), Vol. 4, pp. 1448–1449.
47 For an overview see: Tyrene White, *China's Longest Campaign: Birth Planning in the People's Republic, 1949–2005* (Ithaca, NY: Cornell University Press, 2006), pp. 19–41.

the Malthusian argument that famines serve as a check on population growth. Even in this most severe of famines, not enough people died to significantly dent numbers over the long term. Many peasants postponed marriage and birth during the famine, but in the following years they made up for lost time.

In 1964, the State Council established a new Birth Planning Commission and moved to insert targets for limiting population growth into the upcoming Third Five Year Plan (1966–1970). With these decisions, the state took on a new role, planning not only production, but also reproduction. One notable aspect of the new birth planning regime was that it was first implemented in the urban areas, where initial schemes started as early as 1963. Work in the cities was expected to provide the impetus for expanding birth planning to selected areas in the country-side. The rationale for starting with the cities came from a belief, shared by Zhou Enlai and a number of other central leaders, that the new policies would be easier to implement in urban areas because of their better developed public health systems and the comparatively high level of education of most urban women. The content of the birth planning policy was modeled on pilot projects in the northern port city of Tianjin, offering free sterilization and abortions.

A key argument for birth planning in the cities was that it would ease the burden on the peasants by reducing the number of urban consumers of grain. For instance, a document produced by the Urban Work Conference in 1962 explicitly stated that birth planning would "control the growth of the urban population; reduce the burden on the peasants; [and] relax the tight situation in the supply of essential goods, as well as in housing, schooling, and other facilities provided by the municipal administration."[48] In a speech in July 1963, Zhou Enlai argued that a socialist theory of population was needed to allow for effective government management. The first argument he offered in favor of birth planning was that the uncontrolled increase of the urban population between 1957 and 1960 had resulted in a high burden on the state.[49] The year after Zhou's speech, birth planning was extended to some of the more densely populated rural areas. Published documents never linked the new policies to the famine, but they made repeated references to the grain problem. As suggested above, another common argument was that birth planning and birth control would improve women's health. Ultimately, however, the introduction of birth planning should be seen in the context of the leadership's desire to control the growth of the population (particularly in urban areas) and the resultant expenses of the state.

48 "Zhonggong zhongyang, guowuyuan pizhun 'Di er ci chengshi gongzuo huiyi jiyao' de zhishi," in *JGYL*, Vol. 17, pp. 298–299.
49 Zhou Enlai, "Yinggai queli shehuizhuyi renkou lun de zhengque guannian," in *JGYL*, Vol. 16, p. 543.

Outside the cities, persuading peasants that it was necessary for the state to involve itself in their lives in such a dramatic way proved a challenge. A government that offered almost no sex education in schools found itself suddenly ordering its cadres to promote contraceptives, sterilization and abortions. The CCP was willing to make concessions to the peasantry on grain quotas and ownership structures in the People's Communes, but with birth planning the party seemed to have little problem with confrontation. Nevertheless, this early attempt at population planning was limited to a general effort to encourage lower birth rates. The more intrusive methods of the 1980s, when the state issued blanket regulations on the number of births allowed per couple, were not yet countenanced.

As with the Socialist Education Campaign, little academic research has so far appeared on popular responses to the introduction of birth planning in 1963–1964. According to rural tradition, many sons were a sign of prosperity, and the usual assumption has therefore been that birth planning was widely resisted as an attempt to limit couples' ability to conceive. This may have been the case in many places, but an archival report from Deng county in Sichuan from October 1963 suggests that responses to the new policy were more diverse than this view allows. Some peasant women argued forcefully for the merits of fewer children, often because of concerns over how many they would be able to feed. One woman put the case especially memorably: "One baby will be a fatty, two babies will be thin and three babies will be thin as monkeys." Another young peasant woman argued that too many births would be ruinous for women's health: "Formerly, I was a full labor force. In my three years of marriage, I gave birth to three babies, one after another. My body is broken apart. I ate a lot of bitterness."[50]

In spite of these sometimes favorable responses, local cadres in particular expressed their unwillingness to enforce the new policy. As one put it: "Agricultural production keeps us busy. Eating comes first. Why should we control other people's business?" Some cadres were afraid to alienate peasants by enforcing unpopular measures as they had done during the high noon of the Great Leap in 1958: "By giving orders and setting the plan, we will be compelled from above and cursed from below." Many peasants argued against birth planning on pragmatic grounds: "If we get more babies, they will distribute more grain rations." Others worried that "to get fewer children is not safe, because they may die. We must avoid having no children left."[51] Many of these concerns

---

50 "Zai Deng xian jinxing jihua shengyu shidian qingkuang de baogao," Chongqing shi dang'an-guan X qu, pp. 15–17.

51 Ibid.

reflected the experience of the famine. By the 1960s, rural cadres had learned the hard way that they should expect to take the blame whenever the central government made sudden policy changes. In the face of these difficulties, the first attempt to introduce birth planning proved to be short-lived. From 1966, implementation fell apart during the chaotic years of the early Cultural Revolution, and it was only in 1971 that population control again became a national priority for the CCP.

1962 to 1966: The Good Years?

For official party historians, the period between 1962 and the summer of 1966 has generally been regarded as the "good years" between the famine and the "ten years of chaos" of the Cultural Revolution. This view has much to recommend it. In these four years, the CCP leadership launched policies that rebalanced the national economy. The countryside recovered from the catastrophe of the famine, and the state acknowledged that the exploitation of the peasantry must have its limits. In the future, enough grain had to be kept in the villages for rural communities to survive unaided. Whether this was enough for the CCP to restore the regard in which it had been held in the pre-famine days remains an unanswered question,[52] but its new policies undeniably improved the national economic situation.

However, many lost out as a result of the "readjustment" of the early 1960s, for example the 26 million people who were sent back to the countryside from the towns and cities between 1961 and 1963. The downsizing of the permanent industrial workforce, the education sector and the government payroll put a brake on social mobility, especially for the rural population. The strict enforcement of the *hukou* system after 1962 further reduced the number of peasants who could seek a future outside agriculture. By 1965, party leaders such as Liu Shaoqi were explicitly promoting a dual system for the labor market and education that prevented parts of the rural population from participating in the regular school system, and which also reduced entitlements for workers. Groups who experienced downward mobility in the post-famine years were among the strongest supporters of rebellion against the party apparatus during the Cultural Revolution.

During the famine, peasants had to learn to survive by any means, and the early 1960s saw a growth in all manner of illegal economic activity. Some cadres

---

52 Regarding this question see: Ralph Thaxton, *Catastrophe and Contention in Rural China: Mao's Great Leap Forward Famine and the Origins of Righteous Resistance in Da Fo Village* (Cambridge: Cambridge University Press, 2008), pp. 344–346.

supported the under-reporting of production and the existence of black markets, while others turned into "local tyrants," visiting terror on villagers. The CCP tried to strengthen central control with the Socialist Education Campaign, which primarily targeted local cadres. The supposed "good years" were far from easy for the rural party cadres who fell victim to this new movement. However, the party's attempts at enforcing the "class line" with the creation of the League of Poor and Lower Middle Peasants and class files for rural households had only a limited impact. By 1966, Mao felt that the Four Clean Ups Campaign was insufficient. China needed a novel approach to properly "rectify" the party. The solution came in the summer of 1966: the Great Proletarian Cultural Revolution.

DOCUMENT 5.1 A Letter from Shanghai, July 7, 1962.

Lately, the minds of the people of Shanghai have been confused. They worry about the future of the state and how to escape life's problems, and they complain and curse the Communist Party. This pains me in my heart. Some people ask: "Is the situation really as good [as we are told]? There is an enemy in front of us [the United States], but no patron behind us [the Soviet Union]. [India's] neutrality towards us is gone. The market is tense and construction has declined, but prices are rising. Our standard of living has decreased and popular feelings have reached an alarming pitch." "In the past, we cursed the Nationalist Party because things would get worse every year. Today, isn't everything getting worse every year as well?" "Today we have socialism and it's rations, rations, rations. Even for toilet paper we need a ration card." "Last year, they called it 'three years of natural disasters'. This year, they call it 'four years of natural disasters'." "Shanghai may not be a disaster area, but they still only give us three liang of vegetables a day. If you want to buy a washboard, you have to wait in line through the night."

The workers should be informed of the reason for the current difficulties. Cadres are allowed to listen to the reports of Premier Zhou [Enlai], so why are workers not allowed to listen to anything? . . . We do not understand why the government and the big cadres eat and drink liquor every day at conferences while the country is facing great difficulties . . . High ranking cadres receive fish, meat and beans and "enter through the backdoor." "Big cadres receive gifts, middle ranking cadres 'enter through the backdoor' and petty cadres have their own tricks they can play. Only the workers have no doors to go through." . . . Lately, public security in Shanghai has been poor. Theft, robbery, and loss of children . . . have not taken place since Liberation but are now often heard of. Because of the current developments, people are worried that something bad is sure to happen.

Source: Zhongguo shehui kexueyuan and zhongyang dang'anguan (eds.), *1958–1965 Zhonghua renmin gongheguo jingji dang'an ziliao xuanbian. Laodong jiuye he shouru fenpei juan* (Beijing: Zhongguo caizheng jingji chubanshe, 2011), p. 783.

DOCUMENT 5.2 "Grain storage management in various places is in chaos and has led to serious losses."

According to documents from the central office in charge of checking grain stocks, poor grain storage management and cases of legal violations are now common in various places, with problems detailed as follows:

1. **Widespread "black" grain stocks**. According to reports, "black" stocks in Ji'an county, Jiangxi province held more than 5.5 million kilograms of unprocessed grain, as did those in the Jiujiang Special Region. These had been accumulated from unreported surplus grain, over-reporting of grain sales, under-reporting of rice yields, over-reported or misreported deficits and unreported surpluses.

2 . **Enormous deficits and losses**. Primary investigations conducted in more than 900 grain storage facilities, warehouses, factories and stations in Jiangsu province found a total shortage of 4.505 million kilograms of grain. A shortage of more than 35,500 kilograms, accounting for 41 percent of total grain storage, was found in Qinghan grain store in Gucheng county, Hebei province.

3. **Corruption and theft leading to serious grain losses**. In Taixing county, Jiangsu province, the grain shortage ran to 65,000 kilograms, of which more than 25,000 kilograms had been embezzled or stolen. The amount of grain and oil embezzled by the two corrupt groups operating in Wujin county and Nantong county exceeded 20,000 kilograms.

4. **Disorder in regulation and documentation resulting in a large amount of grain going missing**. From last November to this March, eleven rail cars of grain ordered by the Lanzhou Municipal Grain Administration Bureau from Xianyang, Shaanxi province went missing (a total loss of 315,000 kilograms). The case remained uninvestigated. Only 160 of the 320 bags of standard flour ordered from Fuyu Flour Mill by the Xi'an Baqiao District Grain Administration Bureau were received, and the remaining 160 bags went missing. A stock check revealed that the transportation unit had lost the bill of lading, and the delivery unit had no record of shipping that could be used for further investigation.

5. **Improper storage, serious deterioration**. Due to improper storage, 200,000 kilograms of grain have deteriorated in Huating county, Gansu province, while a further 810,000 kilograms are on the point of deterioration. In Zhen'an county, Shaanxi province, more than 2.4 million kilograms of grain have become infested, and over 3,000 kilograms are rotten.

6. **Unauthorized distribution of state-owned grain stores**. According to an investigation conducted by the Jiangsu Provincial Grain Administration Bureau into 13 work units, more than 94,950 kilograms of grain and oil have been lent out and distributed internally without authorization.

7. **Waste by managerial staff**. The staff of the Zhen'an County Grain Station in Shaanxi province did not obey the rules of grain rationing, and four of their temporary workers were able to obtain rations despite not being entitled to them. In Gansu province, Zhao Guoke, the manager of Taozhaizi Grain Station, exploited his authority to offer more than 120 kilograms of grain to his relatives and to lend more than 350 kilograms to members of his commune. At the Jiangdu County Grain Administration in Jiangsu province, over 600 kilograms of peanuts were used to make gift candies without authorization.

DOCUMENT 5.2 (cont.)

8. Unreported stores secretly transferred during stock checking. Out of 660,000 kilograms of sesame stored in Hucheng county, Hubei province, only 360,000 kilograms were reported by the county grain administration bureau. When news of a stock checking was received, the Changzhou Municipal Sauce Factory in Jiangsu province immediately called on all of its staff to hide an excess of 84,000 kilograms of rice, wheat and soybean cakes overnight, and then submitted false reports.

Source: *Neibu Cankao*, June 27, 1962.

DOCUMENT 5.3 "Free book markets" have appeared in several locations.

In recent years, "free book markets" have appeared in several locations in Hubei province. These book markets are disorderly and exercise a bad influence [on the population].

Recently, a large number of unlicensed book stores appeared in Wuhan. The number of bookstands selling illustrated story books alone has increased by 600 to 700, against a total of about 1,000 licensed bookstands. More bookstands became available during holidays. As a result, a trend has emerged of hoarding books to resell at "free markets." According to the Xinhua Bookstore, booksellers would take turns to queue up in front of their retail department to purchase books, which they would later resell in the markets at a mark-up of 30 to 50 percent. Some people held letters of introduction for purchasing their books, and some purchased books from places like Liaoning and Shanghai to resell in Wuhan. The political backgrounds of these booksellers are complicated, and they do not do business in a proper way. The books rented out by them include "The Legend of Jigong," "The Rosy House," "The King of Eagles," "The Flying Female Detective" and "Monster under the Water." From books related to martial arts and superstition to books on grotesque and pornographic subjects, they had everything one expects to find [from such stands]. Some bookstands even sell "The Membership Rules of the Guomindang."

In the last six months, a number of vendors appeared in Wuhan selling old printed or hand-copied librettos in the street. The majority of these librettos were related to "feudalism," superstitions, feudal codes of ethics and grotesque and pornographic subjects. It has been estimated that there are approximately 150,000 old librettos circulating in Wuhan.

Around stations and ports and at the places of entertainment in Wuhan, many people are selling images of political leaders which are shoddily produced and carry incorrect political indications. Also on the market are vulgar pictures of celebrities, tasteless vinyl records and roughly doodled landscapes. The "book market" in Jinzhou Special District is also chaotic. Some ridiculous books from this market are being used by quite a number of private elementary schools as textbooks. About 200 private schools in Gong'an county use books such as *The Essence of the Confucian Analects, The Principle for Children's Education, The Principle for Daughters, The Three-Character Classic* and *Wisdom in Chinese Proverbs* as textbooks.

In addition, during the Spring Festival, Chinese couplets and images of the door god and the family god are produced and sold in the street. One image of the family god costs about one to 1.5 yuan. In the face of the aforementioned problems, party committees and propaganda and cultural institutions at all levels of Wuhan city and of Jinzhou Special District have strengthened their supervision and regulation of these book markets.

Source: *Neibu Cankao*, April 16, 1963.

6 THE REBELLION AND ITS LIMITS: THE EARLY CULTURAL REVOLUTION (1966–1968)

造反有理，革命无罪
Rebellion is justified, revolution is no crime

抓革命，促生产
Grasp revolution, promote production

惩前毖后、治病救人
Learn from mistakes to avoid repeating them, treat the disease to save the patient

Liu Zhubing (ps.) experienced the Cultural Revolution as a sudden rise followed by a painful fall. In the summer of 1966, he was a chemistry student at Shandong University in Jinan, the province's most prestigious university. His family background, "poor peasant," was good, and his progression into university, something that would have been unthinkable a few decades earlier, made him a clear beneficiary of the Chinese revolution. He had made it from a village into urban society and was now "inside the system."

In autumn 1966, Liu became a leader in the student rebel movement and a member of the Maoist Red Guard Army of Shandong University. The following February, a provincial "power seizure" by rebel leader Wang Xiaoyu led to the establishment of a new order in Shandong and a change for the worse in Liu's fortunes. His organization, which had attacked the provincial Public Security Department building in an attempt to free arrested comrades, was labeled "counterrevolutionary." When Liu tried to return to his home village to celebrate the Spring Festival that year, he was arrested by the police and beaten. After his release, the new government twice mobilized "cudgel brigades" (*bangzidui*) of workers to attack Shandong University, the stronghold of the Maoist Red Guard Army.

Amid the factional struggle, Liu changed sides. He founded a new organization in support of Wang Xiaoyu, the February Third Red Guards, named for the date of Wang's power seizure. For a time, Liu was appointed vice-chairman of the university's Revolutionary Committee. However, his fate took another turn in summer 1968, when the government sent Worker Mao Zedong Thought Propaganda Teams to occupy campuses across the country and end factional struggles among students. Liu's memories of the episode are bitter:

> [The slogan] that "the working class should lead everything" definitely represented the strength of the workers. They clearly replaced the Red Guards, moving them off the stage of history ... All contrary opinions [from the students] were suppressed in the name of the workers and the dictatorship of the proletariat ... This was the most inglorious incident of the Cultural Revolution.[1]

In 1969, Liu was imprisoned on allegations that he was a member of the so-called "Counterrevolutionary Conspiracy of May 16." He was released, along with many other rebels, following the fall of Lin Biao, Mao's heir apparent, in 1971. During the subsequent campaign against Lin Biao and Confucius in 1973, Liu led a delegation of former rebels to Beijing to demand full rehabilitation from the central government, during which he recalls the group sleeping in front of the central petition office for weeks on end. On his return to Shandong University, his work unit finally assigned him a regular job.

This period of normality did not last long. After the fall of the radical Gang of Four in 1976, Liu was again arrested and sentenced to two years in a labor camp. Upon his release, he was allowed to return to his work unit, which assigned him to a post in the university library until his retirement. Liu remained "inside the system," but he could no longer entertain any hopes of an academic or political career. As he puts it: "I rebelled for half a year, was in power for two years and suffered from repression for fifteen years." Today, Liu remains a supporter of Mao and defends the rebel movement. His stories suggest the complexity that the turmoil of the Cultural Revolution brought to people's lives and political careers.

The Cultural Revolution is among the most important periods in the social history of the Mao era. As it unfolded, many social conflicts that had developed in the post-famine years or even earlier came suddenly and explosively to the surface. Especially during the short "People's Cultural Revolution" in the autumn and winter of 1966, grievances and demands regarding the system of class status, bureaucratic privileges and access to permanent jobs in state-owned enterprises were aired and addressed openly.[2] Between late 1966 and 1968, independent mass organizations of students and workers were given space to operate, a situation never seen before or since under the PRC. These groups published

---

1 Interview with the author, Jinan, September 17, 2013.
2 This term was not used at that time and was developed later, for example see: Liu Guokai, "Lun renmin wenge (yi)—wei wenge sishi zhounian er zuo," *Epoch Times*, December 12, 2005, www .epochtimes.com/gb/5/12/30/n1171757.htm (accessed December 3, 2015).

pamphlets and newspapers without the usual censorship. They were further empowered by the collapse by the end of 1966 of many urban party committees. The chaos of this period not only provided space to express grievances, but also led in many places to an outpouring of violence against members of the old elites, cadres or rival mass organizations.

The Cultural Revolution shook Chinese life to the core, particularly in urban areas. Nevertheless, it is important to understand the limits of the rebels' ambitions. Gender and the gendered division of labor were almost non-issues for the Red Guard movement that dominated the early Cultural Revolution, nor were they on the agenda of the central leadership. Workers and students sent down to the countryside made frequent demands to return to the cities and regain their urban *hukou*, but among the leadership the existence of the *hukou* system itself was never questioned. Nor did any meaningful debate develop around the usefulness of the system of ethnic classification. Instead, ethnic conflicts escalated in Tibet and Inner Mongolia, and large-scale purges were launched against so-called "local nationalists" within the CCP. Mao made occasional critical comments regarding the hierarchical wage system, but for party and government jobs he never questioned the distribution of wages and goods according to bureaucratic ranks. Even during the most turbulent period of the Cultural Revolution (1966–1968), the distribution system continued to function. Wages and salaries were still regularly paid in most cases, and ration cards continued to be issued as before.

The major feature of the early Cultural Revolution was a radical redefinition of the value of age and past political accomplishments. Before 1966, "revolutionary cadre" was one of the safest categories a person could occupy. Now young people and non-party members, who had contributed nothing to the victory of revolution of 1949, had an opportunity to prove their revolutionary spirit by participating in the rebel movement. Even leading cadres who had helped build the CCP and the PRC state became vulnerable to attacks on "capitalist roaders in power inside the party." As early as 1964, Mao had emphasized the importance of "cultivating the successors of the revolution."[3] The Cultural Revolution became a test of the new generation, providing a chance for people to change their social and political status. The personal stakes were high, and it is no surprise that, from the outset, one of the most controversial issues of the Cultural Revolution was who had the right to participate and who did not. The generation of young people who came of age in the late 1960s had been taught to hate hidden "class enemies" and to view violence as a necessary means to achieving the revolutionary liberation of mankind. Growing up, they had learned of the glories of the 1949

3 Bo Yibo, *Ruogan zhongda juece yu shijian de huigu* (Beijing: Zhongyang dangxiao chubanshe, 1991), Vol. 2, pp. 1158–1160.

revolution from books, plays and films. With the arrival of the Red Guard movement, they could finally prove their willingness to sacrifice their lives for Chairman Mao or to commit violence in the cause of revolution, just as the previous generation had.

The purpose of this chapter is not to retell the political history of Cultural Revolution in its full, dizzying detail. Instead, we will focus on four key narrative arcs: conflicts and social change in the system of class status; the rebellion of permanent and temporary workers; the place of cadres and workers in the new revolutionary order; and the early Cultural Revolution in the countryside. I will also suggest how the central leadership around Mao used the system of class status alternately to mobilize and dampen the movement. First, however, we will examine the issue of periodization.

The Question of Periodization in the Cultural Revolution

In general, existing literature on the Cultural Revolution has two main points of focus: the 1966 Red Guard movement in Beijing and the 1967 workers' movement in Shanghai. Much has also been written on Mao's goals and the shifts in his agenda. Our knowledge of the events outside the capital and the major urban centers is expanding, but it remains limited. There is an almost bewildering complexity to events in this period, partly caused by the convoluted internal dynamics of the movements themselves and partly due to several major adjustments in Mao's policies, which usually sparked similar turns from actors on the ground. Power struggles at the center overlapped with lengthy factional battles in local party organizations and with social conflicts at the grassroots. Different actors and places were not fixed in their roles, but interacted dynamically with the center and with each other. Victims and perpetrators, winners and losers changed over time. The center of events changed too, shifting from Beijing to Shanghai in early 1967 and then to Wuhan that summer. Between 1967 and 1969, China was wracked by armed conflict, some of the deadliest of which took place not in the major urban centers, but in poorer provinces such as Sichuan and Guangxi.

Given this confusing overall picture, scholars have found it difficult to agree on the question of dating and periodization. Those who consider the Cultural Revolution to be primarily a social movement from below tend to argue that it lasted only two or three years, from 1966 to 1968 or 1969.[4] Others follow the

---

4 Regarding this debate see: Jonathan Unger, "The Cultural Revolution at the Grass Roots," *China Journal*, Vol. 57 (2007), pp. 113–116; Susanne Weigelin-Schwiedrzik, "Coping with the Cultural Revolution: Contesting Interpretations," *Jindaishi Yanjiusuo Jikan*, No. 61 (2008), pp. 1–52.

official verdict of the CCP, which describes the Cultural Revolution as "ten years of upheaval" (*shinian dongluan*), lasting from May 1966 until the death of Mao and the subsequent arrest of the Gang of Four in the autumn of 1976. The Cultural Revolution of 1970 to 1976, however, bore little resemblance to the chaotic, bottom-up violence of the movement's early years. In this period, power struggles continued, but they were mainly confined to the top leadership of the CCP, first between Mao and Minister of Defense Lin Biao, and then between radical Maoists around the Gang of Four and senior leaders such as Zhou Enlai and Deng Xiaoping. Compared to the grassroots rebellion and factional fighting of 1966 to 1968, politics in the late Mao era commanded little popular enthusiasm. Most of the mass campaigns of the period were organized from the top down, just as they had been in the pre-Cultural Revolution years.

Given this turn away from grassroots movements towards more traditional elite conflicts, the description of the entire 1966–1976 period as a single "ten years of upheaval" does not seem to me to fit the historical circumstances. We should also not lose sight of the limits to this upheaval. Even during its chaotic early years, the Cultural Revolution did not cause the collapse of the central CCP leadership. No actor was willing or able to threaten the authority of Mao. From August 1966 to 1968, the party's Cultural Revolution Leading Small Group remained the acknowledged revolutionary headquarters for rebel groups across the country. Party media organs – *Red Flag, People's Daily* and *Liberation Daily* – defined the correct political line. A series of directives issued by the Central Committee and the State Council in 1966–1967 guided the development of the movement and the economy. Open factional warfare in the provinces had the potential to seriously challenge central power, but this had been suppressed by late 1969. Armed conflict at the grassroots enjoyed a short and less dramatic rival in 1974–1975, but this was confined to relatively peripheral areas such as Zhejiang province or Xuzhou in Jiangsu. For the vast majority of cities and provinces, "two years of upheaval," running from late 1966 to late 1968, would be a more accurate verdict.

Nevertheless, there were some continuities between the two periods of the "long" Cultural Revolution. Slogans and buzzwords such as "capitalist roaders inside the party" were used consistently across the period and were arguably not theoretically mature until the 1970s. It was 1974 before the radicals in the central leadership presented a truly rigorous account of how a "restoration of capitalism" might be possible even under the "dictatorship of the proletariat."[5]

5 Yao Wenyuan, "Lin Biao fandang jituan de shehui jichu," March 1 (1975); Zhang Chunqiao, "Lun dui zichanjieji de quanmian zhuanzheng," April 1 (1975), in Song Yongyi (ed.), *The Chinese Cultural Revolution Database* (Hong Kong: Universities Service Centre for China Studies, The Chinese University of Hong Kong, 2006).

In education, the reforms that first resulted in the closure of middle schools and universities in 1966 remained unfinished long after the turn towards top-down control in 1968–1969. Before late 1966, selective access to higher education had been one of the main mechanisms for the reproduction of the political elite. With the abolition of the university entrance examinations (*gaokao*) and the failure to recruit new university students between 1966 and 1971, this way to the top was blocked. A major aim of the university closures was to allow the authorities to devise a new selection mechanism that would include a higher number of children from families of "workers, peasants and soldiers," but this proved a more difficult task than expected, and higher education remained shuttered for years. Another bridge between the early and late Cultural Revolution was the restructuring of the public health care system. The centerpiece of these reforms was a transfer of resources and doctors to the countryside, which took a full ten years to effect. A further significant continuity was the integration of millions of temporary workers into the state-owned enterprises, a process which again spanned the two periods. Some promises of greater social equality that were "betrayed" during the power seizures of 1967 were fulfilled in the early 1970s. Formally at least, it was not until the accession of Hua Guofeng to the leadership in 1976 that the party declared an end to the Cultural Revolution, and it was only under Deng Xiaoping in 1981 that the movement as a whole was officially repudiated.

1966 to 1968: A Chronology

Periodization becomes more difficult when we begin to examine developments between 1966 and 1968–1969 in more detail. It may be useful to begin with a brief overview:

Purges in the cultural sector (December 1965 to May 1966): In the earliest phase of the Cultural Revolution, Mao's supporters took aim at the arts. Yao Wenyuan's famous polemic against the play *The Dismissal of Hairui from Office* was targeted against the cultural establishment in Beijing, and the resulting campaign led eventually to the dismissal of the Beijing party leadership around Peng Zhen. In the early days, what soon came to be known as the Great Proletarian Cultural Revolution appeared to be little different from previous purges against intellectuals and cadres. On May 28, 1966, the Central Committee's Cultural Revolution Leading Small Group was founded under the leadership of Chen Boda. It was to be one of the most important institutions in guiding the coming mass movements.

The early Red Guard movement (June to late August 1966): In this second phase, students at Beijing's universities and middle schools formed Red Guard organizations and began to attack school administrations and the old cultural elites. During the so-called "Red August" and into September, over a thousand people, many of them teachers, were beaten to death in Beijing alone.[6] Groups of teenagers hunted down and tortured so-called "class enemies," humiliating them by shaving their heads or forcing them to parade through the streets with placards naming their "crimes." The police offered little protection in these cases, either standing by as the Red Guards went about their work or simply ignoring them entirely. Struggle meetings against victims could last several weeks, and some committed suicide to escape the pressure. Allegations often had a sexual dimension. In addition to supposed political offenses, women were attacked as being of low morals or accused of having had extramarital affairs. Red Guards, both male and female, took to hanging shoes around women suspects' necks, a visual pun on the term "broken shoe" (*poxie*) for a promiscuous woman. Students also organized the deportation of tens of thousands of people with bad class status from the cities, supported by police who supplied them with information on targets. People were not safe even in their own homes. Mobs of Red Guards confiscated personal items such as books, photographs, letters or larger amounts of currency as proof of "counterrevolutionary activities." Watches, gold rings or other jewellery were considered evidence of a "bourgeois and decadent" lifestyle. The Red Guards tended to take quite a cavalier approach to this "evidence," much of which was either destroyed or disappeared, often not being returned to the original owners. At the same time, the campaign against "the four olds" – old customs, culture, habits and ideas – saw cultural relics, temples and monasteries destroyed all over the country. The movement lasted only a few months, but it had a devastating impact on China's cultural heritage.

Red Guards from Beijing played a key role in spreading the Cultural Revolution to other cities, traveling across the country to exchange revolutionary experiences in a process known as "the big link-up" (*da chuanlian*). The early Red Guards were dominated by members of the new revolutionary elite – children of high-ranking cadres from the party and army. Their potential influence was made clear in August 1966, when Mao gave his blessing to the Red Guard movement by receiving over 12 million young people from all over China on Tiananmen Square in a series of mass rallies. At this stage, however, many leading cadres considered the movement to be a kind of new Anti-Rightist Campaign, and few can have suspected that they themselves might become the next target. Although the Beijing municipal party committee had already fallen in May 1966, the provincial party leaderships remained in post until early 1967,

6 Wang Nianyi, *Dadongluan de niandai* (Zhengzhou: Henan renmin chubanshe, 2005), p. 57.

and there was no immediate sense that they might be under threat. In fact, provincial leaders tried to direct local manifestations of the Cultural Revolution themselves. The authorities supported the foundation of mass organizations known to the rebels as "official Red Guards" (*guanban hongweibing*). These official groups, however, tended to lack the self-confidence of children of high-ranking cadres from Beijing, and by and large they confined themselves to struggling against "enemies" hand-picked by their sponsoring party committees. In many places, the movement spiraled out of control only with the arrival of the Beijingers, who encouraged local actors to attack cadres and to make more extensive use of violence.

The *"People's Cultural Revolution"* (late August 1966 to early January 1967): An August 8 decision by the Central Committee on the direction of the Cultural Revolution marked the shift from a purge of cultural elites to an attack on "capitalist roaders in power inside the communist party." The decision emphasized the right to form mass organizations: "These Cultural Revolutionary groups, committees and congresses are excellent new forms of organization whereby the masses educate themselves under the leadership of the Communist Party. They are an excellent bridge to keep our Party in close contact with the masses."[7] One of the first leading figures to come under pressure was President Liu Shaoqi, who was finally purged that autumn. The major accusation against Liu was that he had suppressed the student movement by sending work teams to the universities to curb Red Guard activities. Many students who had been labeled as "rightists" or "counterrevolutionaries" by the work teams or school authorities over the summer fought for rehabilitation. Under the slogan "rebellion is justified," all manner of grievances against local party apparatus began to be aired. Revolutionary groups took the interpretation of Mao Zedong Thought, the core of CCP ideology, into their own hands. Mass organizations published unauthorized transcripts of speeches and quotations by Mao and other central leaders in their newspapers.

As time went on, conservative mass organizations (*baoshoupai*), also called the "protecting-the-emperor faction," were formed to defend local party committees against the rebels. Local cadres mobilized CCP and Communist Youth League members, labor activists and loyal workers. Some "old" Red Guards from the early days of the Cultural Revolution had grown disillusioned as they watched the movement turn against their parents, and they therefore supported the conservatives. This move to restore order was met, in October, by a new campaign

---

7 "Decision of the Central Committee of the Chinese Communist Party concerning the Great Proletarian Cultural Revolution," August 8 (1966), www.marxists.org/subject/china/peking-review/1966/PR1966-33g.htm (accessed June 19, 2017).

against "the reactionary bourgeois line," meaning the suppression of the rebel movement by officials. Widespread revolt broke out against cadres all over the country. As dissent against local authorities grew, the Central Committee finally allowed workers to join the Cultural Revolution, as long as they did so outside of work hours. As a result, the movement spread to the whole urban population.

During the "People's Cultural Revolution," the government's ability to control the fledgling rebel movement was tested. Young people who had been sent down to the countryside under the centrally mandated "up to the mountains, down to the villages" program demanded to be allowed to return to the cities. Many groups who had suffered in the campaigns of the pre-1966 period sought rehabilitation, and disadvantaged groups "hijacked" the rebellion to promote their own economic and political interests.[8] In Shanghai in particular, temporary workers were a major force in the Cultural Revolution, calling for secure, permanent posts in the state-owned enterprises. These multiple competing interests left Mao and the central leadership trying to propel some aspects of the movement while at the same time limiting others. They feared that strikes and factional infighting could put economic development at risk, and there was further concern that the formation of rebel organizations at the national level would call the CCP's monopoly on state power into question. By the end of the year, the central government had halted "the big link-up" and free train rides for Red Guards. The slogan of the day, "grasp revolution, promote production," gave some indication of the balance the party leadership was attempting to strike. Temporary workers, soldiers on active duty, public security staff and labor camp inmates were banned from forming their own rebel organizations; the occupation of archives and public security offices was also outlawed. The "People's Cultural Revolution" came to an end, and the rebel organizations shifted their focus to a goal acceptable to the leadership: "seizing power" from suspect local officials.

Power seizures (January 1967 to March 1967): At the beginning of the Cultural Revolution, neither Mao nor other actors had any expectation that the masses would "seize power." In early 1967, this was precisely what happened. At the start of the year, an alliance of worker rebels in Shanghai overthrew the municipal government in the so-called "January Storm." The national leadership acknowledged the power seizure soon after, although Mao refused a request to name the new authority the "Shanghai Commune," a choice which would have suggested independence from the party and the central state.[9]

---

8 Yiching Wu, *The Cultural Revolution at the Margins: Chinese Socialism in Crisis* (Cambridge, MA: Harvard University Press, 2014), pp. 97–104.
9 Ibid., p. 129.

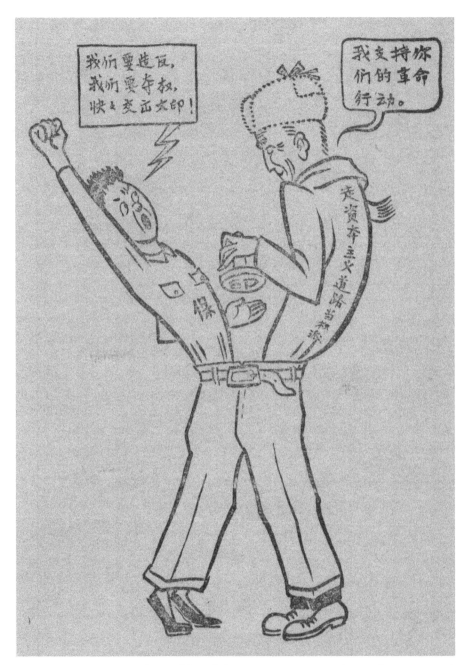

Figure 6.1: A 1967 attack on "fake rebels." A cartoon in a Red Guard newspaper shows a young member of a conservative faction receiving an official seal from a "capitalist roader in power." The conservative says: "We want to rebel, we want to seize power. Give us the seal quickly!" The cadre replies: "We support your revolutionary actions." Source: "Fei ming di," February 24, 1967, Chinese Cultural Revolution Collection, Box 4, Folder "Fei ming di," Hoover Institution Archives.

The Shanghai rebel government began a campaign against "economism" to curb individual demands for higher wages and better welfare. Mass organizations received orders to create "big alliances" and cease factional fighting. What this often meant in practical terms was the suppression of competing rebel organizations by the new authority, for example the Rebel Workers' Headquarters led by Wang Hongwen. In fact, some scholars have read the "January Storm" as the beginning of the *demobilization* of grassroots movements and the restoration of state order, as rebel leaders were integrated into the new leadership but the movements they led were gradually dissolved.[10] On January 23, the central government called on the PLA to "support the left" to "seize power" all over the country, essentially asking the army to take sides in local politics. The government eventually recognized four provincial power seizures in Shanxi, Heilongjiang, Shandong and Guizhou, all of which were effected with PLA support. In this period, Revolutionary Committees, composed of a "three-in-one alliance" of soldiers, rebel mass organizations and representatives of revolutionary cadres, became the new model of state order as provincial and local party committees collapsed. These new governments introduced policies to restore production and suppress other competing factions.

Revolutionary committees and final demobilization (April 1967 to April 1969): Full, government-backed power seizures did not succeed in any other provinces. Instead, factional fighting between rebel groups, cadres and army units escalated, as the central authorities failed to pass any clear verdicts on which takeovers were legitimate. The factional conflicts that rocked the provinces in this period bore little relation to the social contradictions that had exploded in the second half of 1966; instead, new groups rose and fell along often bewildering political lines. In summer 1967, the PLA in Wuhan mobilized the "Million Heroes," a mass organization of conservative workers and party members, for a counter-attack against the local rebel forces. Party orders for the army to stand down only inflamed the tensions, and in late July serious violence broke out. The attack of the conservative faction on the rebels and the following counter-attack resulted in street fighting leading to tens of thousands people wounded and over a hundred deaths.[11]

In response to the "Wuhan Incident," Mao called for a nationwide "arming of the left." Army units handed over weapons to rebel organizations, and arsenals were seized. In many places, armed conflict between rebels and army units

---

10 Ibid., p. 139.

11 For detailed numbers see: Roderick MacFarquhar and Michael Schoenhals, *Mao's Last Revolution* (Cambridge, MA: The Belknap Press of Harvard University Press, 2006), pp. 205, 214.

escalated between July and September to the point of civil war.[12] The severity of the violence made it necessary to rein in one side or the other. In the end, Mao proved unwilling to move against the PLA, the last institution that could guarantee domestic stability. He now turned against some of the radicals in the Cultural Revolution Leading Small Group. Qi Benyu and other members who had argued for a campaign against "capitalist roaders" inside the PLA were purged. By now, almost all the Revolutionary Committees that had been founded after the summer of 1967 had fallen under PLA control. Mass organizations and their representatives were left with almost no role, and many provinces, work units and ministries were brought under direct military rule. Even with PLA backing, establishing new state organs after the chaos of the preceding months was no easy task. It was not until August 1968 that the central government recognized the last Revolutionary Committees in Tibet and Xinjiang.

The new order enforced by the army generated significant resistance and gave rise to an opposition, "ultra-leftist" faction. The "ultra-leftist" label was mainly a term of abuse propagated by the government, but some of the individuals and groups that sprung up in late 1967 and 1968 also used the name themselves. These actors argued that China's problem was deeper than just a few "capitalist roaders in power." In their view, there now existed an entire "bureaucratic class" that exploited and suppressed the people and that needed to be overthrown. Some "ultra-leftist" groups, such as the Hunan Provincial Proletarian Revolutionary Great Alliance Committee, argued that the party bureaucracy should be replaced with a system of grassroots democracy along the lines of the Paris Commune of 1871.[13] The government was, to say the least, not receptive to this idea, and over the course of 1968 the "ultra-leftist" mass organizations were crushed.

A series of purges accompanied and consolidated the establishment of the new order. The campaign against the so-called "Counterrevolutionary Conspiracy of May 16" targeted rebels, many of whom were forced to make false confessions under duress. From May 1968 onwards, tens of thousands of people were arrested and executed as part of the brutal "Cleansing the Class Ranks" campaign. Many of the victims were from bad class backgrounds, while others were accused of treachery and spying. Based on a study of the official county and municipal chronicles, Andrew Walder estimates that a total of 1.5 to 1.8 million people were killed as a result of the Cultural Revolution. The large majority of the victims he identifies died as a result, not of the movement's chaotic early years,

---

12 See: Wang, *Dadongluan de niandai*, p. 203; Michael Schoenhals, "'Why Don't We Arm the Left?' Mao's Culpability for the Cultural Revolution's 'Great Chaos' of 1967," *The China Quarterly*, Vol. 182 (2005), pp. 277–300.

13 Wu, *The Cultural Revolution at the Margins*, p. 183.

but of state violence from above following the establishment of the Revolutionary Committees in 1968 and 1969.[14] However, deaths by mob and factional violence have tended to receive more scholarly attention than the official purges, in part because the breakdown of order in the early Cultural Revolution was so spectacular and represented such an extreme turn against previously all-powerful cadres. The official party history in particular is highly critical of the challenge to the state's monopoly on violence, but has far less to say about repression by state organs.

By the time of the 9th Party Congress in Beijing in April 1969, the central leadership had overseen the revival of party organizations at all levels. Rebel mass organizations had been dissolved, and the new, PLA-led order was in place across most of the country. The defanging of the Red Guard movements was hastened in 1969 by the fostering of an official cult of Mao, which successfully reasserted the authority of the center. Meanwhile millions of urban young people, mainly middle school graduates, were sent to the countryside under the revived "up to the mountains, down to the villages" campaign, allowing the party to reduce the temperature in the cities and restore order.[15] As these moves were unfolding, the conflict with the Soviet Union escalated into a border war in March 1969, leading China to consider rapprochement with the United States in an attempt to counter Soviet pressure. With this opening up to the old enemy, the period of the Cultural Revolution as a mass movement was over.

This overview gives some impression of the extraordinary complexity and speed of events during the early Cultural Revolution. The remainder of this chapter will focus on particular forms of social conflict during these years and on the differing experiences of students, workers and cadres. One of the most challenging questions of the period is why factionalism was not confined to the party leadership, but spilled over into factories, schools and universities. Some Chinese and Western scholars have explained the revolutionary factions according to the social background of the actors. People who benefited from the power structures of the pre-1966 PRC and had good political and economic status joined the conservative forces. Those with a bad or middling status or who had experienced repression were more likely to side with the rebels.[16] Other writers have pointed out that, at least initially, people with bad status did not dare to

---

14 Andrew G. Walder, "Rebellion and Repression in China, 1966–1971," *Social Science History*, Vol. 38, No. 4 (2014), pp. 535–536.

15 Daniel Leese, *Mao Cult: Rhetoric and Ritual in China's Cultural Revolution* (Cambridge: Cambridge University Press, 2011), p. 258.

16 Jonathan Unger, Anita Chan and Stanley Rosen, "Students and Class Warfare: The Social Roots of the Red Guard Conflict in Guangzhou (Canton)," *The China Quarterly*, No. 83 (1980), pp. 432–434.

rebel, and it was often students or workers with good status who took the lead in attacking party authorities. Walder argues that social background does not explain factional choices, because people had to choose sides in unclear political circumstances, with no way of knowing at the outset which groups would eventually be suppressed. After making their choice, most were left "fight[ing] not to lose," trying to escape the persecution that would inevitably follow defeat.[17] The situation was further complicated by the fact that mass activist groups were often backed or manipulated by party leaders. Picking sides on the basis of status became almost impossible in 1967, when violent factional battles were fought between large umbrella coalitions, in which clear social or ideological differences were difficult to discern. Walder suggests that splits in these blocs often centered around support for the newly created Revolutionary Committees; my own view is that too few cases have so far been studied to allow for any general conclusion. It may be most useful to focus on the social conflicts and opinions that were openly debated in the Red Guard and rebel movements. These do not tell us everything about why the Cultural Revolution unfolded as it did, but they do at least allow us to take these groups, which gave a whole generation its formative experience of political activism, on their own terms.

The Conflict around Family Origin and Class Status

One of the most famous debates of the early Cultural Revolution took place in the middle schools of Beijing in 1966–1967. At issue was the so-called "bloodline" theory, which addressed the meaning of the system of class status, and in particular the relationship between family origin and personal status. It was no accident that, in urban society at least, this question attracted such attention in 1966. By that year, the first generation to be born after the establishment of the formal class system had reached middle school age (twelve years). They would soon be told which of them would be allowed to continue on to university. In the cities, class status was directly relevant to this question. Unlike in the villages, where the majority of people occupied good class categories such as "poor and lower middle peasant," in the cities, especially those without a major industrial base, a large part of the population occupied the less favorable middle categories. An obvious tension existed between these groups, who needed a focus on political performance to overcome their bad class status, and those from better class

17 For the debate see: "Transcript—Grassroots Factionalism in China's Cultural Revolution: Rethinking the Paradigm," https://networks.h-net.org/node/3544/discussions/141257/tran script-grassroots-factionalism-china%E2%80%99s-cultural-revolution (accessed June 19, 2017).

backgrounds whose advantages might be eroded by the use of performance metrics.

This tension came to a head in the bloodline debate. A high percentage of students in Beijing's schools were the children of cadres from the central government, and it was these young people who formed the backbone of the early Red Guards. They considered themselves "born red," natural leaders of the Red Guard movement by right of birth. Many favored attending solely to class background as the ultimate determinant of political performance, an attitude captured by the popular slogan, "If the father is a revolutionary, the son is a good guy. If the father is a reactionary, the son is a son of a bitch."[18] Despite this rhetorical focus on the male bloodline, in many cases it was the daughters of high-ranking cadres who led the early movement. At Beijing Normal University's affiliated Experimental High School, Vice-Principal Bian Zhongyun died on August 5 as a result of beatings by her female students. Even today, this remains a highly sensitive case, largely because of the number of central government cadres who had children at the school, including Deng Xiaoping (two of whose daughters attended) and Liu Shaoqi (one daughter).[19] The violence committed by young female students during the Cultural Revolution challenged traditional stereotypes of women as passive, soft and gentle, and as a result it has been the subject of controversy ever since.

Pamphlets produced by the early Red Guards divided students into "the five kinds of red category" (children of cadres, martyrs, workers, revolutionary soldiers and poor and lower middle peasants) and "the five kinds of black category" (children of landlords, rich peasants, counterrevolutionaries, rotten elements and rightists). As we have seen, this categorization was at odds with central government regulations, which distinguished between family origin and personal status. Unsurprisingly, young people with unfavorable family origins pushed back against the early Red Guard view and fought for the right to join the movement and participate in cultivating the "successors of the revolution."

As the debate intensified, Yu Luoke and his Beijing Small Research Group on the Problem of Family Origin produced a seminal article on the tension between family origin and political performance. Yu and his comrades argued that, whether someone was a revolutionary or not, family was no guarantee of performance:

> "Family origin" (*chushen*) and "status" (*chengfen*) are two separate things. The status of a father becomes the class origin of his son. Feudal

---

18 For more detail see: Wu, *The Cultural Revolution at the Margins*, pp. 60–64.
19 Regarding this case see: Susanne Weigelin-Schwiedrzik and Cui Jinke, "Whodunnit? Memory and Politics before the 50th Anniversary of the Cultural Revolution," *The China Quarterly*, Vol. 227 (2016), pp. 734–751.

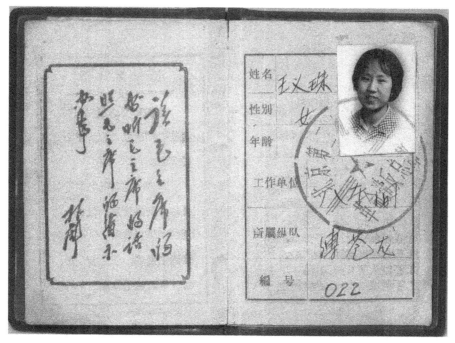

Figure 6.2: Membership card for the Red Guard Congress of the Middle Schools of Shanghai, issued in Beijing.
Source: Helmut Opletal (ed.), *Die Kultur der Kulturrevolution: Personenkult und politisches Design im China von Mao Zedong* (Wien: Museum für Völkerunde, 2011), p. 108.

families used to be an integral part of society, with succession from father to son as the norm, but even in capitalist society this situation already no longer applies. Family ties are loosened and the younger generation belongs to society [and is not exclusively influenced by family]. In socialist society, it is common for the young to accept proletarian education and to prepare themselves for serving the proletariat, and so it is out-of-date to judge the younger generation based on their family backgrounds.[20]

The article went on to point out that Marx, Lenin and even Chairman Mao all came from bad family origins, but proved to be great revolutionaries. In a true socialist society, social relations would not be based on blood. As Engels had argued, with the abolition of private property the family would eventually wither away. Yu and his group therefore fought to "acknowledge the equal right for

---

20 "Beijing jiating chushen wenti yanjiu xiaozu, 'Tan honggou'," February 27 (1967), in Song, *The Chinese Cultural Revolution Database*.

revolution of youths of bad family origin."[21] They reasoned that the "class line" (discrimination against people of bad background) would prevent many well qualified, pro-communist young people from joining the CCP or PLA. This was not an argument for the classical liberal notion of equal treatment under the law, but it represented a major challenge to the early Red Guard line.

The articles by Yu's group were written in summer 1966 and published in early 1967. This turned out to be almost the perfect moment. That spring, elitist Red Guard organizations in Beijing's city-wide United Action alliance began to come under attack for defending their parents, many of whom were now seen as "capitalist roaders." Theories circulated that cadres had used their children to divert attention from the real goals of the Cultural Revolution and to prevent the mass participation of ordinary people.[22] Yu's argument that the "bloodline" theory was being deployed to justify the privileges of a bureaucratic stratum of "capitalist roaders" struck a chord, and his group's ideas were widely disseminated and discussed in the newspapers of mass organizations. Yu, however, pushed the argument far beyond the ideology of the Maoist left within the party leadership. In his view former capitalists and GMD officials still described by the party as major threats, were little more than "political corpses." The struggle between the masses and the "capitalist roaders" now represented the most important contradiction in Chinese society.[23] To Mao, "Never forget the class struggle" had been a reminder to watch for the re-emergence of old class enemies. In Yu's retelling, the slogan was instead a warning against the new enemy emerging from inside the bureaucratic apparatus, an authoritative justification for his own political program. In fact, Yu and the Maoist left were a long way apart. The logic of his position required the abolition of the system of class status and an end to what he regarded as privilege-entrenching "affirmative action." This was something Mao and his supporters were never willing to countenance, and it took a substantial manipulation of the chairman's words to suggest otherwise.

21 Beijing jiating chushen wenti yanjiu xiaozu, "'Liandong' de saoluan shuomingle shenme – Jianbo qinghua fuzhong hongweibing ping 'chushen lun'," February 10 (1967), in Song, *The Chinese Cultural Revolution Database*.
22 Kangda "bayiba" zhanxiao Mao Zedong sixiang hongweibing sanzhanshi, "Zhi 'lao' hongweibing," *Bingtuan zhan bao*, No. 11, March 12 (1967), in Chinese Cultural Revolution Collection, Box 1, Folder "bing tuan zhan bao," Hoover Institution Archives.
23 Beijing jiating chushen wenti yanjiu xiaozu, "Chushen lun," January 18 (1967), in Song, *The Chinese Cultural Revolution Database*.

Figure 6.3: A cartoon in a Red Guard newspaper shows cadres including Politburo Standing Committee member Tao Zhu lifting a hat labeled, "Revision of class status in advance." Their action allows "ox ghosts and snake demons" (class enemies) to break free.
Source: "Pi liao zhan bao," August 1, 1967, Chinese Cultural Revolution Collection, Box 9, Folder "Pi Liao zhan bao," Hoover Institution Archives.

Against Equality for All

Many mass organizations' newspapers took a position between the two extremes of the "bloodline" theory on the one hand and total disregard of family origin on the other. The view of the "Third Research Group on the Issue of Class Origin in Beijing Families" (Document 6.1) exemplifies the centrist position. The group argued that performance was an important metric, but that family origin still played a key role, because it had an impact on socialization and also on access to education:

> Prior to the liberation, landlords and capitalists had money and power, and their children were frivolous and unbridled. Was their performance not directly influenced by their class origin? Today, seventeen years after the liberation, many children of landlords and capitalists progress into high schools and then into universities and pursue luxurious lifestyles. Is their performance not influenced by their class origin? There are hundreds of millions of workers and poor and lower middle peasants, so why

are so few of them able to go to university compared to the offspring of landlords and capitalists?[24]

This argument highlighted how the children of the old elites continued to profit from the pre-1949 education system and its structural discrimination against ordinary people. The impact of past injustices on life chances in the present was still too great to allow family origin to be ignored. Class-based "affirmative action" was still needed. According to this view, the exploitation the majority of the population had endured before 1949 more than outweighed the suffering that the small number of young people from bad family backgrounds now faced in the new order. Their difficulties were an acceptable price to pay for building a new, fairer society. The group accepted Yu's point that Engels and Lenin were from bad family origins, but it added that a precondition for them to become revolutionaries was that they had drawn a line between their families and themselves. In order to participate in the Cultural Revolution, Chinese children of class enemies would have to do the same. They should not expect a free pass.

Another Red Guard newspaper advanced a similar argument in an article published a few weeks earlier. It pointed out that family origin often shaped individuals' worldviews. Many children of intellectuals thought of workers as uneducated and believed that they were incapable of fully understanding Mao Zedong Thought. These attitudes, the article suggested, were a clear hangover from the views of the pre-1949 elite. If children from bad backgrounds worked to liberate themselves from the influence of their families, it was entirely appropriate for them to participate in the Cultural Revolution. However, as long as class struggle continued to exist, they should not expect full equality with children from families who still suffered from the legacy of the "old society."[25] In other words, such people could take part in the Cultural Revolution, but they should not be permitted play a leading role. At the same time, some Red Guards groups attacked the bloodline theory but argued that most children of high-ranking cadres, who were now widely regarded with suspicion, were actually still good. Their achievements during the early Cultural Revolution, most notably the "big link-up" to exchange revolutionary experiences, should be acknowledged, even if their theories on leadership were flawed.[26] Mao was even quoted as

24 Beijing jiating chushen wenti disan yanjiu xiaozu, "'Wei chushen lun' he 'chushen lun' doushi fan maliezhuyi fan Maozedong sixiang de," February 27 (1967), in Song, *The Chinese Cultural Revolution Database*.
25 Ping "chushen lun" xiaozu, "'Chushen lun' xiaozu," *Zhongxue luntan*, No. 2, March 11 (1967), in Zhongguo gong chan dang, Box 14, Folder "zhong xue lun tan," Hoover Institution Archives.
26 Benbao pinglunyuan, "Ganbu zidi hechu qu," *Xiangjiang Pinglun*, No. 1, February (1967), in Chinese Cultural Revolution Collection, Box 12, Folder "Xiang jiang ping lun," Hoover Institution Archives.

Figure 6.4: Cartoon: a "Little Red Guard" denouncing a class enemy.
Source: Helmut Opletal (ed.), *Die Kultur der Kulturrevolution: Personenkult und politisches Design im China von Mao Zedong* (Wien: Museum für Völkerunde, 2011), p. 173.

saying that cadres themselves were mostly good, with "capitalist roaders" representing only a small minority. This approach differed from Yu Luoke, who saw the new privileged stratum as the major target of the Cultural Revolution.

One notable feature of the early Cultural Revolution was that young people with bad family backgrounds invariably fought only for their own rights and not for their parents'. To my knowledge, no mass organization ever argued for the abolition of discrimination against the "four elements." Given the prevailing political climate, it is easy to see why. Rebels were under pressure to prove their credentials as good revolutionaries and not the representatives of class enemies. As a result, no matter which faction held the upper hand during the Cultural Revolution, the "four elements" were always a target of struggle. They were "non-people" with no right to defend themselves against humiliation or worse. Capitalists saw a particularly sharp decline in their fortunes. Before 1966, many capitalists were still receiving interest payments as compensation for the loss of their factories, and they had been shielded from the deadly struggle experienced by landlords during the Land Reform. This lenient treatment grew out of the CCP's initial assessment that the national bourgeoisie's departures from the socialist line represented merely a "contradiction among the people." However, the party's attitude changed during the Cultural Revolution. Former capitalists were now treated as enemies of the people. In the summer of 1966, Red Guards looted their homes and deported them from the cities. No group came to their defense. The debate on the "bloodline" theory took place across China, but it was at its most heated in Beijing's middle schools, and to a lesser extent in Shanghai and Guangzhou. The "bloodline" theory and the arguments of Yu Luoke represented the extremes of the argument, and many groups advocated more moderate positions. That such an open debate about the system of class status could take place was not only a product of the existence of Red Guard newspapers, but also a result of the central leadership's temporary support for attacking the "bloodline" theory and the old Red Guards. At the same time that this debate went on, the old United Action alliance was criticized for opposing the Cultural Revolution Leading Group and made a scapegoat for the worst excess of the "Red August" of 1966.[27]

The Leadership's Attitude to the "Class Line"

Mao himself did not participate on either side in the debate over the "bloodline" theory. He did not step in to prevent violence against teachers by the early Red Guard groups, but nor did he hesitate to disband those same groups when the agenda of the Cultural Revolution shifted to attacks on the party bureaucracy in autumn 1966. By the same token, ending discrimination against students with bad family origins was never a priority for him.

Between autumn 1966 and early 1967, mass participation in the Cultural Revolution expanded from students to workers and finally to peasants. One factor in this expansion was pressure from below: more and more groups showed a genuine desire to participate in the movement, with many keen to seize the opportunity to improve their political and social status. At the same time, the leadership understood that restricting participation to students from good family backgrounds would play into the hands of the party apparatus, since these young people were often related to high-ranking cadres. Members of the Cultural Revolution Leading Group, including Mao's wife Jiang Qing, publicly criticized the "bloodline" theory as providing potential cover for "capitalist roaders." In November of 1966, Jiang Qing said that the terms "five red categories" and "five black categories" were never used by the *People's Daily* or the Central Government. Performance would be the most important criteria and status only

27 Andrew G. Walder, *Fractured Rebellion: The Beijing Red Guard Movement* (Cambridge, MA: Harvard University Press, 2009), pp. 198–200.

secondary.[28] In the winter of 1966, hundreds of thousands of people who had faced repression for criticizing cadres during the summer were rehabilitated. These early rebels could now claim that they were victims of the "reactionary bourgeoisie line" and would openly "speak bitterness." Many people experienced this period as a time of liberation and opening up.

On January 1, 1967, an editorial carried jointly in *Red Flag* and *People's Daily* attacked the early Red Guards' use of the line, "If the father is a revolutionary, the son is a good guy. If the father is a reactionary, the son is a son of a bitch," as a reactionary plot to split the student movement. The slogan was decried as an expression of feudalist thinking in opposition to historical materialism, the CCP's guiding analytical doctrine.[29] In February 1967, the "Decision of the Central Committee regarding the Cultural Revolution in Middle Schools" clarified that the majority of Red Guards should be recruited from students from worker, peasant, revolutionary cadre and military backgrounds. However, students who were not from families of the working masses could also join the Red Guards provided they held Chairman Mao in high regard. The document also stated that teaching staff should be purged of the "four elements," but that teachers with bad family origins should not be excluded from work or participation in the Cultural Revolution if they showed themselves willing to reform.[30] For a time, it appeared that the central leadership was preparing to side with the rebels and that the days of discrimination against people with bad family origins were numbered. However, just as the elitist early Red Guards had lost out to a change of direction from the central leadership, many rebel activists would suffer when the government's policy reversed again in 1968.

This second reversal accompanied Mao's attempts to demobilize the student rebel movement in the wake of the remorseless factional fighting at the universities. Weary of conflict, the chairman now reinforced the importance of the "class line" and stepped up the party's rhetoric against the old class enemies. In summer 1968, he ordered so-called Worker Mao Zedong Thought Propaganda Teams and teams of PLA soldiers to occupy university campuses and factories across the country under the new slogan, "the working class must lead everything." The Propaganda Teams ruled the universities with an iron fist. Student rebel leaders, many of whom had been celebrated in the official media,

28 Jiang Qing, "Jiangqing tongzhi tan jieji luxian," *Huoju bao*, No. 2, February 15 (1967), in Chinese Cultural Revolution Collection, Box 7, Folder "huo ju bao," Hoover Institution Archives.

29 Hongqi zazhi bianjibu, "Ba wuchan jieji wenhua da geming jinxing daodi," January 1 (1967), in Song, *The Chinese Cultural Revolution Database*.

30 "Zhonggong zhongyang guanyu zhongxue wuchanjieji wenhuadageming de yijian," February 19 (1967), in Song, *The Chinese Cultural Revolution Database*.

suddenly came under attack. Mao's teams proved more effective in eliminating dissent than the work teams sent in by Liu Shaoqi in 1966. By the end of year, most of the graduating class of middle school students from 1966, 1967 and 1968 had been sent "up to the mountains, down to the villages." This was the end of the student Red Guard movement.

The Rebellion of the Workers

While the Cultural Revolution in Beijing was dominated by the student move-ment, in Shanghai workers played the major role. The first attacks on the local authorities were student-led, but in November 1966 workers began to press for their own right to form city-wide rebel organizations. Their request was refused, and on November 10 around a thousand workers led by Wang Hongwen's Shanghai Revolutionary Rebel Workers' Headquarters commandeered a train and set out for Beijing to petition the central government. They were halted at Anting on the outskirts of Shanghai, and their refusal to disembark resulted in all traffic on the Beijing line being halted for over thirty-one hours. As the Anting Incident unfolded, the mayor of Shanghai, Cao Diqiu, demanded that the work-ers immediately return to their units. Wang's rebels refused to stand down until their demands had been met: the recognition of their mass organizations and an acknowledgment that their actions were legal. They also demanded a public criticism of Cao Diqiu and the handling of the conflict by the higher authorities.[31] Zhang Chunqiao, the negotiator sent by the Cultural Revolution Leading Group, eventually signed off on the rebels' demands with Mao's support.

The Anting Incident showed that grassroots pressure could persuade the CCP leadership to ally with rebels against local party authorities, even in the country's most important industrial city. Only a few thousand workers had joined the Shanghai rebellion. After the success in Anting, however, worker rebel organiza-tions in other cities were emboldened, and many called for official recognition. On December 9, the Central Committee declared the right of workers to parti-cipate in the Cultural Revolution and to form their own mass organizations, with the proviso that production should not be disturbed.[32] For the first time since 1949, the central leadership recognized independent workers' organizations that

---

31 Li Xun, *Geming zaofan niandai: Shanghai wenge yundong shigao* (Hong Kong: Oxford University Press, 2015), Vol. 1, p. 333.
32 "Zhonggong Zhongyang guanyu zhua geming, cu shengchan de shitiao guiding (cao'an)," December 9 (1966), in Song, *The Chinese Cultural Revolution Database*.

were not integrated into the party apparatus. This might have represented a chance for progress in workers' rights, but the change did not last long.[33]

Many workers remained suspicious of the rebel forces. Between November and late December, the party leadership in Shanghai was able to mobilize significant numbers of workers in a counter-attack by the conservative Scarlet Guards. The demographics of the student and worker rebel movements were quite different. In contrast to many of their student counterparts, rebel workers often had good class status and more than a few had been party members even before 1966. These people had less to gain than the children of intellectuals and capitalists from a shake-up of the political order – industrial workers "inside the system" were one of the most privileged groups in China – but the Cultural Revolution nevertheless provided a rare chance to air grievances. In fact, the main demand of the rebel permanent workers in Shanghai was for the right to participate in the Revolution at all, since this would give them an opportunity to improve their political status through performance. The extent to which rebellion was about raising one's political status was made clear after the movement, spearheaded by Wang Hongwen's Rebel Workers' Headquarters, took power from the municipal authorities in January 1967. From this point on, activists from the heady days of the Anting Incident would claim the label of "old rebels," meaning that they had attacked the authorities when it was dangerous to do so and the fate of the rebel groups remained uncertain. This privileging of early participation recalled the boast of "revolutionary cadres" that they had joined the party before its victory was assured. The Cultural Revolution offered those born too late to be revolutionaries the chance to perform their own acts of political daring. For permanent workers, then, the main goal was participation rather than any critique of categorization or the system of class status.

Temporary Workers and the Attack on "Economism"

More specific demands came from those on temporary contracts. As we saw in Chapter 5, the debate over the various forms of contract labor was not new in 1966. The expansion and downsizing of the urban workforce between 1958 and 1962 had been a major source of conflict. In the winter of 1966, temporary workers used the Cultural Revolution and the ongoing critique of Liu Shaoqi to attack the system of contract labor as an anti-socialist form of exploitation. Liu was accused of masterminding the nationwide expansion of this system from 1964 onwards, with the aim of splitting workers into two classes and depriving temporary workers of their political rights. Particularly in Shanghai, temporary

---

33 Li, *Geming zaofan niandai*, Vol. 1, p. 379.

workers carved out a strong position within the rebel movement, and they used this platform to demand to be made part of the permanent workforce. By late 1966, the old municipal government of Shanghai had given in to demands including higher wages, access to welfare and public housing and financial support for a new "big link-up" to exchange revolutionary experiences. Strikes had already caused parts of certain industries to collapse.[34] In what became nationwide news, on December 26, 1966 Jiang Qing met with delegates of the All China General Rebel Regiment of the Red Laborers, an organization representing temporary workers, in the Great Hall of the People in Beijing. Jiang expressed her support for abolishing the system of temporary contract work and attacked the Ministry of Labor in a highly charged speech.[35] On January 2, the General Rebel Regiment, the Ministry of Labor and the official All China Federation of Trade Unions issued a "common announcement" that during the Cultural Revolution, contract, temporary and outsourced labor should be abolished. Soon temporary workers were rebelling against local authorities across broad swathes of China.

Central government leaders now began to worry about the immense cost of making all contract workers permanent employees – the very problem that had led to the expansion of contract work in the first place. Barely a few weeks had passed before the General Rebel Regiment fell victim to a Central Committee order that nationwide mass organizations be dissolved. Then, on February 17, the Central Committee and the State Council declared that the "common announcement" abolishing contract labor had no legal basis.[36] The two bodies stated that temporary labor could be acceptable in some cases and that full resolution of the problem should be deferred until a later stage of the movement. The decision emphasized the political rights of temporary workers to participate in the Cultural Revolution, and those who had been labeled as "counterrevolutionary" by their work units simply for joining a rebel organization were permitted to demand rehabilitation. However, infiltrators from among the "four elements" (which the decision stressed did not include the children of those elements unless there was evidence of personal wrongdoing) should be purged. Temporary workers were not to form their own rebel groups, but they could join the mass organizations of their work units. Participation was contingent on them returning to work in line with their existing contracts.

34 Ibid., pp. 649–657.
35 Jiang Qing and Chen Boda, "Jiang Qing Chen Boda yu quanguo hongse laodongzhe zaofan zongtuan daibiao de tanhua," December 26 (1966), in Song, *The Chinese Cultural Revolution Database*.
36 "Zhonggong zhongyang and guowuyuan, 'Guanyu linshigong, hetonggong, waibaogong de tonggao'," February 17 (1967), in Song, *The Chinese Cultural Revolution Database*.

This dampening of the demands of temporary workers was in line with the wider campaign against "economism," backed by both the central government and the new rebel authorities in Shanghai. In an "urgent notice" on January 9, 1967, the Shanghai Rebel Workers' Headquarters listed the restoration of production and the fight against economism as top priorities. Rebellion in the cause of higher wages or other material demands was attacked as risking the ruin of the economy and as an expression of the "reactionary bourgeois line" advocated by "capitalist roaders."[37] Concessions by the old party leadership to the workers were derided as a ruse to sabotage the Cultural Revolution. Some scholars have argued that Zhang Chunqiao and other radical leaders who assisted in the takeover in Shanghai were simply using temporary workers for their own political ends and were always set to betray their interests once the new government was formed. Others have pointed to a silencing of social and economic demands as a result of the campaign against "economism."[38] In January 1968, the Central Committee and the State Council reaffirmed their stance that the "common announcement" of the previous winter was invalid and that temporary labor should continue to be used.[39] However, as we will see in Chapter 7, many temporary workers did in fact become part of the permanent workforce in the early 1970s.

The Early Cultural Revolution in the Countryside

The effect of the early Cultural Revolution in the countryside remains an under-researched question, in part because the starting point and focus of the movement was in urban society. However, rural China was affected as well, albeit several months after the cities. In September 1966, the Central Committee passed a decision regarding the conduct of the Cultural Revolution in rural areas below the county level. The overthrow of cadres by the masses was strictly proscribed. Moreover, commune members and rural cadres were forbidden to leave their villages to exchange revolutionary experiences in other areas. A number of different regulations stipulated that urban Red Guards and rebels were neither to disturb agricultural production nor to mobilize peasants to participate in armed struggle in the cities.[40] After the experience of the Great

---

37 Li, *Geming zaofan niandai*, Vol. 1, pp. 668–669.
38 Wu, *The Cultural Revolution at the Margins*, pp. 140–141.
39 Dangdai Zhongguo congshu bianji bu (ed.), *Dangdai Zhongguo de laodongli guanli* (Beijing: Zhongguo shehui kexue chubanshe, 1990), p. 16.
40 For example, "Zhongguo Gongchandang zhongyang weiyuanhui guanyu xian yixia nongcun wenhua da geming de guiding ji fujian," September 14 (1966), in Song, *The Chinese Cultural Revolution Database*.

Leap Famine, the party leadership was keen to prevent any disruption to the food supply that could disturb political campaigning. The leadership also felt that rural party organizations had already been purged during the Four Clean Ups Campaign, which ended in 1967, overlapping briefly with the rural Cultural Revolution.

Despite the effort at central control, by early 1967 power seizures similar to those seen in the cities had begun to occur in the countryside. In March, the Central Committee declared that attempts to seize power at the level of production teams and brigades were to be prohibited during the plowing season.[41] The achievements of the Four Clean Ups should not be questioned by revising the verdicts of cadres against those suspected of wrongdoing. The government thus attempted to suppress the nascent rebel movement in the rural party organizations. However, the countryside was not immune to the chaos that swept China over the coming year. Much of the heaviest factional fighting in 1967–1968 took place in remote areas far from the cities. In some parts of the countryside, mass "community killings" occurred in 1968, targeting people with bad class backgrounds. Local cadres and militias slaughtered the "four elements" and their family members or killed rebels in revenge attacks. These acts of violence were not ordered by the central government, but nor did the authorities take any great steps to prevent them or punish the perpetrators.[42]

The rebellion in the cities also inspired similar acts among the "educated youth" in the countryside. Before 1968, a relatively small number of students had been sent "up to the mountains, down to the villages" – official statistics put the number at 1.29 million between 1962 and 1966.[43] Many of these were urban middle school graduates who had volunteered to make a patriotic contribution. But going down was a one-way ticket: even volunteers could not leave the countryside and return to the cities without the permission of the government. In autumn 1966, dissatisfied "educated youths" in a number of rural areas founded rebel organizations and returned illegally to the cities under slogans such as "return home to make revolution" or "we want an [urban] *hukou*, grain and work." Some argued that the program of "sending down" was a revisionist policy backed by the much-maligned Liu Shaoqi. Others tried to set up nationwide groups to unite the "sent-down youth." Multiple central government

41 "Zhonggong zhongyang guanyu nongcun shengchan dadui he shengchandui zai chungeng shiqi buyao duoquan de tongzhi," March 7 (1967), in Song, *The Chinese Cultural Revolution Database*.

42 Yang Su, *Collective Killings in Rural China during the Cultural Revolution* (Cambridge: Cambridge University Press, 2011).

43 Liu Xiaomeng, *Zhongguo zhiqingshi: Dachao 1966–1980* (Beijing: Zhongguo shehuikexue chubanshe, 1998), p. 863.

decisions stipulated that these students could not participate in armed struggle and should return to the villages to support agricultural production. Any urban *hukou* documents obtained illicitly by the students were to be declared invalid. Many evidently ignored these decisions, and the authorities' ability to enforce them was weak, since the central government was forced to reiterate its position in October 1967 and again in July 1968.[44] The rebellion of the "educated youths" was finally ended in December 1968, when Mao himself gave the order to enforce more large-scale deportations to the countryside (see Chapter 7). It was in large part because of this strategy that the mass movements of the early Cultural Revolution were finally broken.

The Fall and Rise of Cadres

From various groups of ordinary people, we now turn to the roles of cadres. Mao's principal objective in initiating the Cultural Revolution seems to have been to rectify the party. He was concerned that the CCP had lost its revolutionary spirit and ideology and was turning into a bureaucratic state apparatus. If the party continued to develop in the "revisionist" direction already evident in the Soviet Union, the result might be the restoration of capitalism in China. The Socialist Education Campaign had taken care of party organizations in the countryside, and Mao therefore focused the Cultural Revolution on the urban CCP. In addition, Mao was also concerned about his own loss of influence to leaders such as Liu Shaoqi and Deng Xiaoping, who had pushed to extend the economic reforms of the post-famine years. Nevertheless, the Cultural Revolution cannot be explained simply as a power struggle between Mao and Liu. Many factional conflicts in the provincial party organizations had local origins that were independent of Mao's personal battles against Liu, despite the consistent claim of all factions to be fighting for Mao's line.

High-Ranking Victims

The Cultural Revolution felled cadres at a higher level than any previous campaign. Prior to 1966, the most prominent official to die as the result of a purge had been Gao Gang, the head of the State Planning Commission and Vice-Chairman of the People's Government, who committed suicide in 1954. After 1966, however, the CCP leading group that had come together in Yan'an in the 1940s finally fell apart. Zhou Enlai, Kang Sheng, Chen Boda and Lin Biao

44 Ibid., pp. 91, 97.

became leaders of the Cultural Revolution, while their comrades were purged. Among the highest ranking victims of the Cultural Revolution were: State President Liu Shaoqi, who died in prison in 1969 as a result of maltreatment; Li Lisan, the former General Secretary of the CCP, who committed suicide in 1967; and He Long, the co-founder of the Red Army, and Tao Zhu, a member of the Politburo Standing Committee, both of whom perished under house arrest in 1969 due to a lack of medical care.

It is striking how many prominent critics of the Great Leap lost their lives to the Cultural Revolution. The first targets of the campaign against the cultural elite were Wu Han and Deng Tuo, both of whom fitted into this category. Wu's play, *The Dismissal of Hai Rui from Office*, and Deng's series of newspaper articles, "Night Talks in Yanshan," were read by many as references to Mao's failure to respond to the famine. Deng, the former editor-in-chief of the *People's Daily*, committed suicide on May 18, 1966, while Wu, the former Vice-Mayor of Beijing, killed himself in prison in 1969. The former Minister of Defense Peng Dehuai, one of the first internal critics of the Leap, died in prison as a result of torture and maltreatment in 1974. Tian Jiaying, the Vice-Chair of the Office of the Central Committee and Mao's former secretary, who had written long reports to the chairman regarding the famine in 1962, hanged himself in May 1966. Zhou Xiaozhou, the former party secretary of Hunan province and a member of the so-called "Anti-Party Clique" of Peng Dehuai that had challenged Mao at the Lushan Conference in 1959, committed suicide in December 1966. None of these individuals was officially sentenced to death and executed. They committed suicide to escape public humiliation and torture, or else they died a slow and painful death in hospital or under house arrest.

Clashes among Cadres and Divisions over "Power Seizures"

By early 1967, the rebel movement had brought about the collapse of the old party committees at the city and provincial levels, and also in most of China's urban work units. Of the twenty-eight provincial party secretaries who were in office in summer 1966, only two remained as chairmen of the provincial Revolutionary Committees in 1968.[45] Many had fallen in early 1967, when they endured mass struggle meetings and were paraded through the streets and in some cases beaten up. However, only a very few provincial leaders were actually killed at the hands of rebel organizations. Two of the exceptions were Wei Heng, the first party secretary of Shanxi, who died in the custody of a rebel

---

45 David S. Goodman, "The Provincial Revolutionary Committee in the People's Republic of China, 1967–1979: An Obituary," *The China Quarterly*, Vol. 85 (1981), p. 69.

Figure 6.5: The Gate of Heavenly Peace around 1966/1967.
Source: Collection Jean Moser, Gymnasium Leonhard, Basel.

group on January 31, 1967, and the party secretary of Yunnan Province, Yan Hongyan, who committed suicide on January 8, 1967, in the midst of a series of struggle sessions. In spite of these cases, it is important not to regard "revolutionary cadres" only as victims of the Cultural Revolution. Many not only participated in the movement but also served in key positions.

Early Cultural Revolution documents were targeted exclusively at "a handful of revisionists" or "a few capitalist roaders." This stress on limiting the scope of the campaign was repeated in the party's 16-point decision of August 1966, which defined the "main target" as "those within the Party who are in authority and are taking the capitalist road."[46] It continued:

> The party leadership should be good at discovering the left and developing and strengthening the ranks of the left; it should firmly rely on the revolutionary left. During the movement this is the only way to isolate the most reactionary rightists thoroughly, win over the middle and unite with the great majority, so that by the end of the movement we shall achieve the unity of more than 95 per cent of the cadres and more than 95 per cent of the masses.

46 "Decision of the Central Committee of the Chinese Communist Party concerning the Great Proletarian Cultural Revolution," August 8 (1966).

The percentages here are instructive. No official document claimed that the party as a whole had become a revisionist force or that the bureaucratic class should be overthrown. For Mao it was out of question that the CCP could be replaced by any other movement or institution. Even the Revolutionary Committees were based on so-called "three-in-one alliances," which included party cadres alongside soldiers and representatives of mass organizations. In fact, cadres themselves were also divided into factions along with the rest of the urban population. Some joined the rebel movement early on, while others sided with the rebellion only after it entered the mainstream. A significant proportion genuinely identified with the agenda of the rebel movement, while others turned against colleagues to save themselves. Many cadres who had been criticized and demoted in previous campaigns saw an opportunity for rehabilitation when their superiors came under attack. Much as they had done during the Hundred Flowers Movement, it seems that Mao and the central leadership underestimated the contradictions and conflicts sitting below the surface of Chinese society, both between people and officials and also within the party apparatus.

Attacks on leading cadres also met resistance at the central level. At a fractious meeting of the CCP Standing Committee in February 1967, its secretary Tan Zhenlin raged against the Shanghai radical Zhang Chunqiao's references to mass support for the rebel movement:

> What masses? Always the masses, the masses. There is still the leadership of the party! You don't want the party's leadership, and all day long you keep on talking about how the masses should liberate themselves, educate themselves and free themselves. What is all this stuff? ... Your aim is to purge the old cadres. You are knocking them down one by one, until there is not a single one of them left.[47]

This rare moment of open resistance was labeled by the Maoist faction as the February Countercurrent. The result was a nationwide campaign against opponents of the Cultural Revolution. While few cadres were as outspoken in their opposition as Tan, many had difficulty understanding Mao's purpose in destabilizing the party apparatus.

The Cultural Revolution is often remembered as a time when experienced cadres were replaced by incompetent young rebels. This may have been true for schools or work units locally, but when the government appointed officials at the provincial level following the "January Storm" of early 1967, it tapped only experienced "revolutionary cadres," albeit those who had sided with the rebels. This pattern was repeated across several different provinces, including

---

47 Quoted in: Frank Dikötter, *The Cultural Revolution: A People's History, 1962–1976* (New York, NY: Bloomsbury Press, 2016), p. 136.

Shandong, Heilongjiang and Guizhou. The first provincial power seizure, in Shanxi on January 12, was led not by an outsider but by Liu Geping, the provincial vice-governor. In Heilongjiang, Pan Fusheng, the provincial first party secretary, successfully sided with the rebels and was able to continue on as head of the new Revolutionary Committee. Wang Xiaoyu, who led the power seizure in Shandong in February, had not served in the senior provincial leadership prior to his elevation to chair of the Revolutionary Committee. He had, however, been Vice-Mayor of Qingdao, one of the largest cities in the province. In Guizhou, Li Zaihan, the head of the provincial Revolutionary Committee, was a rebel who had served as the vice-political commissar of the provincial military district.

All three of the civil rebel leaders had suffered in previous campaigns. Liu, a member of the Hui minority, had been purged on charges of localist nationalism during the Great Leap in 1960. The same fate had befallen Pan two years earlier in 1958, when as first party secretary of Henan province he had been labeled a "rightist" for his opposition to radical agricultural policies and to the Great Leap in general. In the same year, Wang had been labeled a "right opportunist" during the Anti-Rightist Campaign in Shandong. As chair of the provincial Revolutionary Committee, he won the support of many former colleagues who had suffered during the Anti-Rightist Campaign and who were eager to win rehabilitation. Wang was personally sympathetic to their cause, but from October 1967 his hands were tied by a decision from the Central Committee, which made clear that verdicts against landlords, counterrevolutionaries, rich peasants, "rotten elements" and rightists should not be revised.[48] The situation in Wang's province, where some of the strongest support for the rebellion against "capitalist roaders in power" came from cadres who had been hit in previous campaigns, was replicated across the country, for instance in Anhui province.

In March 1967, *Red Flag* carried an article calling on those involved in the rebellion to "handle cadres in the correct way." The view that all cadres in power were bad and had to be overthrown was attacked as "anarchist." A small number of capitalist roaders representing the interests of the four elements and rightists were blamed for intentionally deflecting the struggle onto good cadres. The article stressed that the vast majority of cadres remained loyal to the party and to Chairman Mao, calling them a "valuable treasure" of the party and people. It was crucial that revolutionary cadres should form part of the core

---

48 Qi Jinhua, *Qilu sannian xiaoxiong Wang* (Qingdao: unpublished manuscript, 2014), p. 56; "Zhonggong zhongyang guanyu buzhun di, fu, fan, huai, you chengji fan'an wenti de guiding," October 26 (1967), in Song, *The Chinese Cultural Revolution Database*.

Figure 6.6: A banner at a market denouncing Bo Yibo, circa 1966–1967.
Source: Collection Jean Moser, Gymnasium Leonhard, Basel.

leadership of the new order.[49] The writers in *Red Flag* also underlined that cadres who had made errors regarding the party's general line were for the most part not enemies of the people. Instead, conflicts with them should be considered as "contradictions among the people." In handling these cadres, the principle to be followed was that of "treating the disease to save the patient."

Statements of this kind, however, were too general to be directly relevant to problems on the ground. When the central government called for the integration of "revolutionary cadres" into the Revolutionary Committees, it gave no guidance on which cadres should be liberated and which should remain the target of struggle. In many places, this became the subject of intense factional infighting among the rebels. The temporary breakdown of provincial and local party organizations gave rebel groups considerable latitude, making top-down implementation of policies from Beijing next to impossible in many cases. Clarity was made even more difficult by the fact that it was often unclear who the legitimate representatives of power were at the local level. Moreover, radicals in the Cultural Revolution Leading Group oftentimes disagreed with Premier Zhou Enlai, the head of the State Council, over which rebel groups and cadres to

---

49 Hongqi zazhi bianjibu, "Bixu zhengque de duidai ganbu," March 1 (1967), in Song, *The Chinese Cultural Revolution Database.*

support. The center in Beijing had the last word in appointing new provincial leaders, but as long as it kept silent factional fighting continued.[50]

Backing the wrong horse in a provincial power struggle could be a fatal mistake. In Guangxi, the rebels believed that Beijing would approve the overthrow of the provincial party secretary, General Wei Guoqing. A similar situation occurred in Jiangsu, where rebels attacked General Xu Shiyou expecting the center's support. In both cases these expectations proved to be misplaced. The central government appointed Wei and Xu as heads of their provincial Revolutionary Committees, and both men took bloody revenge against the rebel organizations that had opposed them. In Beijing, factional contradictions between the rebels became so intense that in April 1967 the central government passed over the entire rebel leadership and appointed Xie Fuzhi, the former Minister of Public Security, as head of the municipal Revolutionary Committee. As we have already seen, in almost all provinces, soldiers rather than rebels headed the new state organs.

As the targets of the Cultural Revolution changed, many cadres who had been overthrown in late 1966 and early 1967 found themselves liberated again in the second half of 1967 and 1968. In late 1966, the major accusation against alleged "capitalist roaders" was that they were promoting a "reactionary bourgeois line" aimed at the suppression of the rebel movement. Articles accused capitalist roaders òf carrying their revisionist program into fields as diverse as industry, agriculture, education and foreign trade. In 1967, allegations began to be pushed back further in time, and cadres' historical records, including behavior in Nationalist or Japanese prisons, were reinvestigated. Those who had made confessions while in prison before 1949 could find themselves labeled as "traitors" (*pantu*), while members of the former communist underground movement in the "white areas" were accused of being nationalist spies (*tewu*). One of the most notable examples was Liu Shaoqi himself. In October 1968, the Central Committee announced that Liu had been a "traitor," a "spy" and a "strikebreaker" since the mid-1920s and that he was an agent of nationalist and imperialist forces. Liu, the most important figure in the underground movement and one of the CCP's most loyal adherents, was "permanently expelled" from the party. Many of his close associates were also labeled as spies.

As some scholars have argued, these accusations against cadres for historical misdeeds redirected criticism away from the privileged new bureaucracy to pre-1949 enemies.[51] Similarly groundless accusations were also common during the

---

50 Dong Guoqiang and Andrew G. Walder, "Nanjing's Failed 'January Revolution' of 1967: The Inner Politics of a Provincial Power Seizure," *The China Quarterly*, No. 203 (2010), p. 678.
51 Wu, *The Cultural Revolution at the Margins*, pp. 48–51.

Cleansing the Class Ranks campaign, and the confessions that accompanied them were often extracted under torture. In general, the campaign against cadres from 1968 onwards had more in common with Stalin's centrally organized Great Purge than the "People's Cultural Revolution" of two years previously. Cadres, after all, were being attacked not by rebel organizations, but by Revolutionary Committees mostly dominated by the PLA.

The forcefulness of the verdict against Liu made his return to politics unthinkable. However, many leading cadres who were attacked as "revisionists" in 1966–1967 were able to retain their party membership, as was the case with Deng Xiaoping, the economic planners Chen Yun, Li Fuchun, Li Xiannian and Bo Yibo, and the PLA marshals Yang Shangkun and Ye Jianying. The main movers in the February Countercurrent, Tan Zhenlin and Chen Yi, were able to return to leading positions even before the Cultural Revolution was over. In contrast to Stalin, Mao was largely not aiming to kill off the old party elite, but to "educate" them and ensure their loyalty to him and his program. He retained the option to reappoint those who were purged to leading positions at a time of his choosing. The Cultural Revolution made these leading cadres beholden to Mao, since up until his death their only chance at rehabilitation was to secure a revision of the verdicts against them by the Chairman himself.

Workers as Representatives in the PLA-Led Order

What role did workers play in the new order that was established in 1967–1968? Those who had participated in the rebel movement had the chance to become leaders or to serve as mass representatives in the Revolutionary Committees. Others would go on to play important roles in the Worker Propaganda Teams or the new workers' militia formed in 1968 under the slogan, "Attack with Words, Defend with Weapons." Only a few were able to make the leap from worker to cadre status while serving on the Revolutionary Committees, but a small number rose much higher. Wang Hongwen, the Shanghai rebel leader, enjoyed the most famous of these "helicopter" careers, moving from local politics to an eventual position as Vice-Premier of the PRC. After the early "power seizures," even workers without party membership could serve in high positions. In Qingdao, the twenty-eight-year-old worker Yang Baohua, a non-party member, became the head of the municipal Revolutionary Committee.

Many rebel representatives would live and work in government offices and compounds, but draw their salaries from their original work units rather than being paid as officials. In a sense this fulfilled the desire of some rebels to model the Revolutionary Committees on the Paris Commune, since it accorded with the

Commune's principle that a delegate should not receive a higher salary than the ordinary worker. However, the fact that so many representatives of the mass organizations were prevented from formally changing their status placed them at an enormous disadvantage, especially compared to returning "revolutionary cadres." Mass representatives at the city and provincial level were often systematically marginalized, and with the central government firmly back in control their political base was eliminated as the rebel mass organizations were dissolved. By late 1968, many Revolutionary Committees had stopped inviting representatives of the masses to participate in meetings. For those who remained, the authorities retained the ability to order them off the committees and back to their work units at any time, as occurred during the campaign against the "Counterrevolutionary Conspiracy of May 16" in 1967–1968 or the downfall of the Gang of Four in 1976.

Cadres were further empowered by the rebuilding of the local party committees, which gave them an organizational base, to which workers' representatives, who were non-party members, had no access. Increasingly, representatives of the masses seeking to play an important role in the new order had little alternative but to seek party membership. In the lead-up to the 9th Party Congress in April 1969, the CCP leadership concluded that the party contained too few rebels, workers included, and that without new recruits, "revolutionary cadres" and PLA members would dominate. In October 1968, the party journal *Red Flag* called for "fresh blood from the working class," declaring that more workers should be welcomed as party members and trained for senior government posts.[52] In the following months, large numbers of rebels were fast-tracked to party membership. After the end of the Cultural Revolution, the leadership under Deng Xiaoping would argue that many of these new memberships were illegitimate, since they had not been approved by their party committees as prescribed by the party constitution. As a result, the rebel memberships were canceled in the early 1980s.

In summary, in late 1966 and early 1967, worker rebel organizations were established within the CCP to provide an additional form of representation for the masses. In places such as Shanghai and Shandong, these bodies played an important role in the 1967 power seizures and in the new order headed by the Revolutionary Committees. However, by 1969 these mass organizations had been dissolved. Thereafter, rebel workers were forced to seek influence as individuals rather than as a movement, either through careers in the CCP or by sitting on the Revolutionary Committees. Cut off from their grassroots base, they

---

52 "Hongqi zazhi bianjibu, 'Xishou wuchanjieji de xinxian xueye – Zhengdang gongzuo zhong de yige zhongyao wenti'," October 14 (1968), in Song, *The Chinese Cultural Revolution Database*.

became reliant on patronage from above rather than support from below. (The notable exception was Shanghai, where Wang Hongwen was able to carve out a significant power base as leader of the Revolutionary Rebel Workers' Headquarters.) The Cultural Revolution opened up a path into politics for some workers and injected "fresh blood" into the party from the working class, but it failed to establish new forms of power for workers at the grassroots or to guarantee them substantive political representation.

The End of an Unequal Coalition

While the Cultural Revolution as a mass movement began with elitist Red Guards in Beijing, a variety of other groups including regular and temporary workers and young people with bad family origins fought successfully for the right to participate as part of one faction or another. In the party's campaign to "cultivate the successors of the revolution," many saw a unique opportunity to improve their social and political status. Cadres, too, splintered into factions. Many of those who had fallen victim to previous campaigns joined the rebellion in hopes of winning rehabilitation.

The exclusive approach favored by the elitist early Red Guards made a full-blown attack on "capitalist roaders" in the party bureaucracy impossible, especially given that these Red Guards themselves were often related to senior cadres. In late 1966, the CCP leadership under Mao threw its weight behind the popularization of the movement. The "People's Cultural Revolution" saw the agenda of rebel mass movements on the ground and the Maoist left in the central leadership briefly overlap in the power seizures of January 1967. However, the differences between these two forces were too great for the alliance to endure in the longer term. Temporary workers and young rebels with bad family origin sought to escape discrimination, while Mao focused on the need to rectify the party. Once that was accomplished, the Maoist left proved unwilling to countenance wider changes in China's political and economic structures, whether to the hierarchical rank and distribution networks, the *hukou* system or the policies of the class line. As factional warfare between competing rebel groups spiraled out of control, the central leadership reasserted itself and reinforced the system of class status in a bid to restore order.

The party's old guard, the revolutionary cadres, played an important role in the early 1967 power seizures. Many officials overthrown by the rebels returned to office, and in 1968 Worker Propaganda Teams were used to suppress the student rebel movement. The PLA, another crucial arm of party power, formed the cornerstone of most of the provincial Revolutionary Committees established in the first half of the year. As this new order bedded in, bloody purges were carried out across the country against people from bad class backgrounds, cadres accused of being "spies," and any rebels who failed to toe the line.

On the one hand, the Maoist left in the central leadership used the rebel groups of the Cultural Revolution for its own ends. On the other, it is equally true that many people at the grassroots hijacked the movement in an attempt to turn central policy to their advantage. Still, the balance of power remained with the center. By 1968, many rebel activists had grown disillusioned with the new order, in which they were increasingly marginalized as the party regained control. Mao himself had grown tired of the endless factional fighting and the unwillingness of the mass organizations to come together in "great alliances" to support the Revolutionary Committees. The union between the supreme leader and rebel movement, which at its heart was always an unequal coalition, finally ended. The mass organizations were dissolved and disarmed, and from 1969 China entered a new period dominated by the army and returning party cadres.

DOCUMENT 6.1 "On the Sole Focus on Family Origin" and "On Family Origin" are both Anti-Marxist and Anti-Mao Zedong Thought.

. . . In order to vitiate the impact of class origin, the authors of "On Family Origin" pay special attention to the terms "status" and "origin." As well as strictly differentiating "status" from "origin," they also outline the [nature of the] differences between the two, out of concern that others might confuse them. "Status" and "origin" are indeed different. Class origin is the essence of family origin, because the economic and political statuses of different families are a product of their different classes (which does not mean the family members' professional background). Class origin is only relevant for youths who have not yet left their parents and gained independent economic status. Once a person is employed, he has his own family and becomes economically independent, and he will live in his own class position and form his own class status. This status can be the same as his class origin but can also be different. And at this time his previous class origin becomes subordinate [to the class status that he builds for himself]. Therefore, class status is different from class origin. However, this does not mean that class status can be completely divorced from class origin, or that the connections between them can be deliberately cut off. In a class society, a person lives in a certain class position from the moment of his birth, while youths live in the same class position as their parents. Hence we can see that the class status of one's parents has a necessary connection with one's own class origin, and they should not be completely separated . . .

With regard to the relationship between class origin and performance, is it really only a minor connection? Is it only one's performance that matters, not one's class origin? Prior to the liberation, landlords and capitalists had money and power, and their children were frivolous and unbridled. Was their performance not directly influenced by their class origin? Today, seventeen years after the liberation, many children of

DOCUMENT 6.1 (cont.)

landlords and capitalists progress into high schools and then into universities and pursue luxurious lifestyles. Is their performance not influenced by their class origin? There are hundreds of millions of workers and poor and lower middle peasants, so why are so few of them able to go to university compared to the offspring of landlords and capitalists? Is it not due to the influence of class origin? Today, the children of capitalist roaders enjoy wealth and privilege. Is this not due to the influence of class origin? If it is due to the influence of class origin, and their performance is related to their class origin, how can we say that class origin does not matter? Is it not precisely because of the influence of class origin in a person's blood that his performance is sustained?

The authors [of "On Family Origin"] quote Chairman Mao: "Those who stand with revolutionary people are revolutionaries." They then ask: "Is class origin mentioned here?" We must ask the authors of "On Family Origin": how can a person originating from a landlord or capitalist family stand with revolutionary people, without first eliminating the strong influence of their class origin and erasing their capitalist ego? Wang Guangmei [Liu Shaoqi's wife, the child of an elite family] says that she has never exploited people and has stayed with the revolutionary forces for years, even acquiring the label of "CCP member," but is it not obvious that today she is still a capitalist and an enemy of the people? How can we deny the strong influence of class origin on her? . . .

[W]e should realise that "On Family Origin" has a deceptive face. In order to deceive people and provoke class hatred among the reactionaries, the authors devote a great deal of attention to how youths with bad class origin have been persecuted. We cannot help asking the authors of "On Family Origin": have you not seen the clear-cut reality that the broad masses of workers and peasants and their children were cruelly exploited by landlords and capitalists before the liberation? When the exploiting class oppressed workers and peasants, did they differentiate fathers from their sons and class status from class origin? How many *bona fide* proletarians and their children have had the chance to go to primary school, let alone university? Have you heard their voice in politics or seen them become officials? . . .

The third research group on the issue of class origin in Beijing families

February 27, 1967, first draft

Source: Beijing jiating chushen wenti disan yanjiu xiaozu, "'Wei chushen lun' he 'chushen lun' doushi fan maliezhuyi fan Maozedong sixiang de," February 27 (1967), in Song, *The Chinese Cultural Revolution Database.*

7 DEMOBILIZATION AND RESTORATION: THE LATE CULTURAL REVOLUTION (1969-1976)

批林批孔
Criticize Lin Biao, criticize Confucius
上山下乡
Up to the mountains, down to the villages
走后门
Entering through the backdoor

Ma Guanying (ps.) was born in 1952 in the city of Jinan in Shandong Province. Both his parents were "revolutionary cadres" and both served in the municipal government. When the Cultural Revolution arrived at his middle school, the fourteen-year-old Ma joined an early Red Guard organization, the Black Characters Guards, whose membership comprised the children of party and PLA cadres. Ma recalls: "We would look down on children from worker and poor peasant backgrounds."[1] Like many of his contemporaries, Ma participated in the beating of his teacher, an act he later regretted. His political fortunes changed when his father was overthrown in October 1966, on the basis of a confession made in a GMD prison in the mid-1930s that was now considered a betrayal of the party. Ma's mother was not accused of "historical problems," but she too was attacked as a "capitalist roader." In March 1969, at the age of sixteen, Ma went to the countryside as an "educated youth." By that time, the campaign to send young people "up to the mountains, down to the villages," which had been devised some years earlier as a voluntary scheme, had been made compulsory, and Ma had no alternative but to go. Three of his four siblings were also sent down, all to different places.

Ma himself was sent to the rural suburbs of Jinan, at that time a very poor area, and his *hukou* was changed from "non-agrarian" to "agrarian." From the moment of his arrival, the local peasants expressed their dissatisfaction at

---

[1] Interview with the author, Jinan, September 2016.

the "educated youth," who they viewed as unproductive parasites sent to "eat for free." Ma remembers that his short stature and lack of experience with heavy labor led the head of the production team to mock him for "working even worse than women." He was not far wrong: stronger women could earn eight work points a day, but teenagers such as Ma would only receive seven. The village where Ma was assigned was close to the city, and bus connections were good enough that he was still able to visit, at least once his parents were allowed to return home after investigation. In the countryside, his family background played no significant role in daily life, and Ma was able to escape from some of the political difficulties that had dogged him for the previous three years. He was also able to observe something of the conditions in rural China. He saw that peasants under-reported production and that some even farmed the land as individual households outside of the supposedly all-powerful communes.

In late 1970, Ma was able to return to Jinan and was assigned a worker's post in the local railway station, a state-owned work unit. Suddenly, the son of capitalist roaders found himself a member of the "upright working class." In his interview with me, Ma did not explain whether this desirable assignment was related to an improvement in his parents' situation, although this is certainly a plausible explanation. He did recall that labor discipline at the railway station was lax. Those workers who had been recruited in 1958 or later had not enjoyed a pay rise in the twelve years since, and overall their salary was less than half that of workers who had joined the unit before 1949. Ma remembers that it was common for workers to steal watermelon and other fruit from passing freight wagons.

The end of the Cultural Revolution brought another change in Ma's life. In 1978, he took the national university entrance examination, the *gaokao*, and was accepted. This success, however, was tempered by the death of his father a year later, after a long period of ill health that Ma links to his long imprisonment in a cow shed during the Cultural Revolution. Ma himself eventually became a public servant in the municipal government, where he remained until his retirement. His life is a case study of the multiple roles and statuses that one person could occupy during the Mao era.

The years between 1969 and 1976 can be divided into two major periods. Between the 9th Party Congress in 1969 and the Lin Biao Incident in September 1971, the military continued the political dominance it had established following the rise of the Revolutionary Committees. The second period, from 1971 to 1976, was marked by an escalating power struggle at the top of the CCP and by an intensification of social conflicts following the PLA's withdrawal from factories and universities. This chapter will address the transformation of the working class, developments in the countryside and the experiences of young people "sent down" from the cities. Finally, I will offer a brief evaluation of the achievements and failures of the Mao era.

Periodization: From Military Rule to the Death of Mao (1969–1976)

Green Dominance, Green Terror (1969–1971)

Between 1969 and 1971, the PLA played a central role not only in politics, but also in society more widely. Many government departments and ministries remained under military control, and at the 9th Party Congress large numbers of delegates turned out in the distinctive green uniform of the PLA. The new party constitution named Lin Biao, the Minister of Defense, as Mao's successor in the event of the chairman's death. The military was kept in the public eye by ongoing clashes on the Sino-Soviet border, and the government and media continued to stress the threat of war and the need to mobilize the whole country for national defense. Beginning in late 1968, staff from government offices at the central and provincial level were sent down to the countryside to so-called May 7 Cadre Schools, where they were to be re-educated by poor and lower middle peasants and participate in manual labor.

During these so-called "black years," the party leadership carried out multiple purges through movements such as the One-Strike, Three-Anti Campaign (1970–1972), resulting in a high number of arrests and deaths. The campaign was intended to expose "destructive counterrevolutionary activities" and to attack "corruption and stealing," "speculation and profiteering" and "extravagance and waste." According to one Chinese scholar, between February and October 1970 alone, over 1.2 million "traitors," "spies," and "counter-revolutionaries" were uncovered, with 280,000 people arrested and thousands executed.[2] At the same time, the campaign against the "Counterrevolutionary Conspiracy of May 16" continued to target rebels who refused to toe the line. Many rebels found themselves placed under de facto detention in so-called "study groups," often organized by the PLA. Army officers also controlled key factories and university campuses through Mao Zedong Thought Soldier Propaganda Teams.

Throughout this period, the management of much of the economy was placed in the hands of military officers, who were largely untrained for their new roles. The Third Five Year Plan (1966–1970) had directed 52.7 percent of national

---

2 Wang Nianyi, *Dadongluan de niandai* (Zhengzhou: Henan Renmin Chubanshe, 2005), p. 281.

investment to Third Front projects in Western China.[3] The military-backed Fourth Five Year Plan of 1970 continued the trend, directing most investment to heavy industry. Projects were designed with national defense, not economic efficiency in mind, and agriculture and light industry were neglected. Things began to change after the Lin Biao Incident in September 1971. The exact sequence of events remains unclear, but, according to the official account, Lin, Mao's "closest comrade-in-arms," was found to be planning a military coup with the support of his entourage, including his son Lin Liguo and supporters in the PLA Air Force. Members of the conspiracy were even accused of plotting to murder the chairman. Lin himself was killed in a plane crash during what was widely reported to be an attempt to flee to the Soviet Union. Whatever the truth of this narrative, the Lin Biao Incident damaged popular trust in Mao and the Cultural Revolution. The sense began to spread that something was amiss.

Power Struggles and Social Conflicts (1972-1976)

We can date the second part of the late Cultural Revolution from the Lin Biao Incident to the end of the Mao era, which was brought to a close with the Chairman's death in September 1976 and the arrest of the radical Gang of Four the following month. In 1972, the *People's Daily* published a document titled "A Summary of Project 571," which purported to be Lin's manifesto for the coup attempt. The document included harsh criticism of continued low living standards and political repression. The national economy, it declared, had been stagnant for over ten years. The state was rich, but the people poor; peasants did not have enough food and clothing; the "sent-down" program for urban youth was re-education through labor by another name; workers' wages were frozen; the May 7 Cadre Schools were a hidden form of unemployment. The document alleged that even the Red Guards now realized they had been cheated and misused, and that their repression was little more than scapegoating. The PLA itself was concerned about the direction of the country's development, while cadres who shared these concerns were afraid to speak up. The author called for the overthrow of "the modern Qinshihuang," linking Mao to the legendarily tyrannical first emperor of the Qin dynasty.[4] In the field of foreign relations, "Project 571" broke with prevailing policy to propose renewing the Sino-Soviet alliance. The publication of the document marked the first time since 1949 that an official newspaper had presented such fundamental criticisms of Mao and the

---

3 Barry Naughton, "The Third Front: Defense Industrialization in the Chinese Interior," *The China Quarterly*, No. 115 (1988), p. 365.

4 For the whole document see: "Lin Biao jituan '571 gongcheng' jiyao quanwen," http://history .sina.com.cn/bk/wgs/2014-06-16/155193265.shtml (accessed March 30, 2018).

PRC political system in print. Mao himself supported publication, hoping to use the document as further evidence of Lin's "betrayal." The unintended consequence, however, was to put into the public domain a ready supply of phrases and arguments for use in future protests and dissent.[5]

After 1972, the PLA retreated from factories and university campuses and returned to barracks. The CCP leadership now sought to rule through newly reconstituted party committees, but initially at least the withdrawal of the army left state capacity weakened. Black markets and the underground economy boomed in rural China, and workers gained more freedom on the shop floor. In some places, local labor unrest broke out.[6] As in the early part of the Cultural Revolution, the official campaign against Lin Biao allowed a wide range of persecuted people to claim to be "victims" of Lin and to demand rehabilitation, from revolutionary cadres and rebels to ethnic minorities and religious groups. Delegations from all over the country traveled to the provincial capitals or to Beijing to submit petitions for revised verdicts.[7] The Central Committee responded favorably to many of these requests. An official decision blamed Lin for exaggerating the campaign against "May 16 elements" and allowed many rebels to return from the "study groups" to their work units. The party leadership did not abolish the May 7 Cadre Schools, but it did permit most cadres to return to their offices in the cities.

Perhaps the most fundamental change in China's posture in the late Cultural Revolution was the remarkable rapprochement of the PRC with the United States. In February 1972, US President Richard Nixon visited China. The Shanghai Communiqué, signed by the US government during the visit, acknowledged the "One China" policy and cleared the way for the United States to transfer official recognition from the Republic of China on Taiwan to the PRC authorities in Beijing. This followed the Republic of China's loss of its permanent UN Security Council Seat – and indeed its membership of the UN itself – to the PRC the previous year. These changes together made Mao's China a global power, and by the mid-1970s American allies, including Japan, had begun to recognize the PRC as well.

After two decades of economic embargoes and threats of war by the US, rapprochement represented a foreign relations triumph for the new China. However, the leadership's strategic turn was not an easy sell in ideological

5 Yin Hongbiao, *Shizongzhe de zuji: Wenhua da geming qijian de qingnian sichao* (Hong Kong: Zhongwen daxue chubanshe, 2009), pp. 355-360.
6 Jackie Sheehan, *Chinese Workers: A New History* (New York, NY: Routledge, 1998), pp. 141-143.
7 For example see: Dong Guoqiang and Andrew G. Walder, "Nanjing's 'Second Cultural Revolution' of 1974," *The China Quarterly*, No. 212 (2012), pp. 905-908.

terms. Years of harshly worded propaganda against "US imperialism" made it challenging for the government to explain how America had suddenly become an ally against the Soviet Union. Theoretical justification for the renewed focus on Chinese "national interests" at the expense of world revolution and class struggle came in the Three Worlds Theory, officially outlined in 1974. In contrast to earlier Western models which divided the globe into capitalist, communist and non-aligned countries, the CCP now argued that the real division was between superpowers, developing powers and a third world of exploited nations, of which China was one. The party called for alliances between the third world and the "second world" – smaller European countries and Japan – against the "first world" powers, the Soviet Union and the United States. This equation of the United States and the USSR made it possible for the authorities to credibly describe the Soviet Union as China's most important geopolitical foe. However, relations with the United States remained difficult in light of Washington's continued military support for Taiwan, and diplomatic relations were not fully normalized until 1979.

As these moves were playing out on the international stage, a power struggle inside the CCP leadership led to a number of changes in domestic policy. The Maoist left argued for continuing the mass campaigns of the Cultural Revolution, while a more conservative faction around veteran cadres like Premier Zhou Enlai advocated for the restoration of the pre-1966 political and economic system. The Maoist left dominated the official media and the cultural industries, while the conservative faction was influential in foreign and economic policy and the military and party apparatus. For several years, Mao tried to maintain a balance between these two factions in order to prevent clashes that risked destabilizing the political system. The 1973 rehabilitation of Deng Xiaoping, and his subsequent elevation to Vice-Premier of the State Council and Vice-Chair of the Central Military Commission, severely challenged this balance. Deng demanded cuts to military spending and a reduction in troop numbers to support civilian economic development. He also stressed the need for economic efficiency and labor discipline, two goals obviously at odds with the participation of workers in endless political campaigns. In education, Deng argued for a return to selecting students by examination and for strengthening the role of experts and scientists. The Maoist left saw Deng's agenda as an attack on the "new-born things" of the Cultural Revolution and perhaps even as a plan to "restore capitalism." The conservative position was further reinforced in 1973–1974 by a new wave of rehabilitations for veteran cadres. Those who were allowed to return to power did not dare to question the Cultural Revolution openly, but in private many looked forward to opportunities to "settle accounts" with the rebels.

Figure 7.1: Slogan at the Summer Palace in Beijing, 1974: "Workers, peasants and soldiers are the main force to criticize Lin Biao and Confucius."
Source: Photograph by Emanuel Ringhoffer.

In this context, the campaigns to Criticize Lin Biao and Confucius (1973–1974), to Study Theories of Proletarian Dictatorship (1975) and to Repulse the Right-Deviationist Wind (1975–1976) can be read as last efforts by the Maoist left to "swim against the tide." All three campaigns attempted to push back against returning veteran cadres, but in contrast to the situation in 1966 and 1967, they elicited minimal enthusiasm outside of radical circles. Former rebels seeking to reactivate personal networks in their work units found themselves isolated with little wider support.[8] In 1974, the Central Committee made clear that the foundation of new mass organizations, the exchange of revolutionary

---

8 All rebels I interviewed in Shandong between 2013 and 2017 held this view. See also: Wang Shaoguang, *Failure of Charisma: The Cultural Revolution in Wuhan* (Hong Kong: Oxford University Press, 1995), pp. 247–248.

experiences between units and especially new local power seizures were not to be permitted.[9] The ban was rigidly enforced, as in the case of Qingdao, where on February 21, 1974 rebels occupied a government building and declared a "second power seizure." Those involved were soon arrested, and long prison sentences followed. Mao refused permission for a nationwide workers' militia outside the PLA's command structure, but he did approve the creation of such a militia in Shanghai, the last stronghold of the left.[10] The left also won further limited successes at the 6th National People's Congress in 1975, when Cultural Revolution policies such as the Four Democratic Freedoms ("Speaking out freely, airing views fully, holding great debates and writing big-character posters") and the right to strike were included in the new state constitution. The document also confirmed that education, sports, literature, science and administration had to be combined with production and manual labor. Finally, the focus on the "class line" was renewed, leaving "landlords," "rich peasants," "reactionary capitalists" and "other bad elements" deprived of all political rights.[11]

Despite these achievements, with the death of Zhou Enlai in January 1976 it became clear that large segments of the population were dissatisfied with the Maoist left in the party leadership, as well as with the overall direction of China's development. At the Tomb-Sweeping Festival that April, tens of thousands of people gathered on Tiananmen Square in Beijing, and in Nanjing and several other cities, in mourning for the Premier. Zhou was celebrated as the embodiment of the virtuous official, and thousands of workers, cadres, and intellectuals participated in marches in his memory.[12] Leftist leaders were publicly criticized. In response, Mao labeled this Tiananmen Incident "counterrevolutionary turmoil," and the government sent a stick-wielding workers' militia to "clean up" the square. Deng was accused of being the "black hand" behind the unrest and was forced from office.

The final end to the Cultural Revolution came with the death of Mao himself on September 9, 1976. Just weeks later, on October 6, the Central Security Bureau, the Central Committee's military guard unit, arrested the so-called Gang of Four (Jiang Qing, Zhang Chunqiao, Yao Wenyuan, and Wang

---

9 For example: "Zhonggong zhongyang, 'Guanyu pilin pikong yundong jige wenti de tongzhi'," April 10 (1974), in Song Yongyi (ed.), *The Chinese Cultural Revolution Database* (Hong Kong: Universities Service Centre for China Studies, The Chinese University of Hong Kong, 2006).

10 For detail see: Li Xun, *Geming zaofan niandai: Shanghai wenge yundong shigao* (Hong Kong: Oxford University Press, 2015), Vol. 2, p. 1546.

11 "Zhonghua renmin gongheguo xianfa," www.npc.gov.cn/wxzl/wxzl/2000–12/06/content_4362 .htm (accessed April 10, 2017).

12 For detail see: Sebastian Heilmann, "The Social Context of Mobilization in China: Factions, Work Units, and Activists during the 1976 April Fifth Movement," *China Information*, Vol. 8, No. 3 (1994), pp. 1–19.

Figure 7.2: School children commemorating the death of Zhou Enlai, Zhengzhou, May 1976.
Source: Photograph by Helmut Opletal.

Hongwen) with the backing of Hua Guofeng, the Minister of State Security and Zhou's successor as Premier. In the aftermath of the arrests, the relatively unknown Hua became, at least for a time, the acknowledged leader of China, taking the posts of party chairman and chair of the Central Military Commission. No rebel uprising or strikes occurred; even the 1 million strong workers' militia in Shanghai failed to come to the left's defense. The Cultural Revolution, which had begun as an explosive "social volcano" in 1966, ended ten years later with a silent coup. Permanent campaigns, mobilization, factional fighting and purges had left party and society alike exhausted.

The Working Class and the Expansion of the "Iron Rice Bowl"

Throughout the late Mao period, official media continued to celebrate workers as "masters of the country." Less visible but no less important was the social transformation and expansion of the working class that took place in this period. In 1967, radical leaders had reacted to the push for improved pay and conditions by accusing "revisionist cadres" of corrupting workers with economic demands. (In the Reform Era, roles would be reversed, with Jiang Qing and the rest of the Gang of Four blamed for wastefully expanding the "iron rice bowl" to temporary workers.)[13] This hostility to worker demands began to change in 1971, when the State Council issued a decision banning work units from using temporary labor for year-round production tasks. The Council also ruled that there should be no more than two and a half million temporary workers engaged even on short-term or seasonal tasks. As a result of this decision, over 8 million temporary workers were able to acquire permanent worker status (as against a total in 1971 of over 9 million).[14] The change in policy had a sharply gendered impact, because in many cases temporary workers were female relatives of existing permanent workers. The temporary worker rebels of the early Cultural Revolution had initially seen their demands rejected by the government, but those demands were now belatedly fulfilled. By 1971, no rebel mass organizations existed to pressure the government to improve workers' conditions, but it appears that the old argument – that hiring workers without political and social rights was in contradiction with the principles of socialism – proved eventually persuasive. The great divide between people inside and outside the system of the "iron rice bowl" remained, but the number of workers in precarious temporary employment was significantly reduced in urban China.

More difficult to assess is the impact of the Cultural Revolution on workers who were already in permanent, "iron rice bowl" positions at the outset. While the social prestige of workers was high throughout the last decade of the Mao era, wages were stagnant, rising once, and then only slightly, in 1971. Bonuses, an important part of the pre-1966 salary package, were decried as a "material stimulus" redolent of capitalist economics and attacked by the rebels as part of

---

13 Dangdai zhongguo congshu bianji bu (ed.), *Dangdai zhongguo de laodongli guanli* (Beijing: Zhongguo shehui kexue chubanshe, 1990), p. 16.
14 "Guowuyuan guanyu gaige linshigong, lunhuangong zhidu de tongzhi (gaiyao)," November 30 (1971), in Song, *The Chinese Cultural Revolution Database*.

Liu Shaoqi's "revisionist line." At the same time, wage cuts and penalties for poor labor performance were abolished, a decision which lowered the pressure on workers but also made it difficult to enforce discipline in some factories. Young workers who had entered the workforce since 1958 found it particularly difficult to secure promotions and wage increases, resulting in a widening gap between young and old. These income restrictions hardly pushed workers to the brink of starvation, but they did make covering daily expenses beyond rations more of a challenge. Workers at lower ranks, especially those with several children or elderly dependents, had to count every cent to provide for their living expenses.

The stagnation of wages went hand in hand with another, more striking trend: a massive expansion of the urban workforce. In 1966, state-owned enterprises employed 39.3 million people, but by 1976 the figure had risen to 68.6 million. The workforce in the collectively owned sector expanded from 12.6 to 18.1 million in the same period.[15] Meanwhile, the number of female workers and staff in the state-owned enterprises more than doubled, from 7.8 million in 1965 to over 20 million in 1977. Of these 20 million, 8.5 million worked in industry, 2.7 million in the trade, food and services sectors and 3.3 million in science, education and health.[16]

A survey circulated internally among the official labor unions in 1983 captures some of the major demographic shifts in the workforce during the Cultural Revolution. From a sample of eleven work units in key industrial cities, a picture emerges of a workforce that was larger, younger, more educated, and populated with greater numbers of party members than was the case before 1966. The work units surveyed had a combined staff of over 183,000, of whom only 3 percent had joined before 1949, compared to 37.8 percent (69,395 people) during the Cultural Revolution.[17] The breakdown of the backgrounds of the newer workers is particularly interesting. Of those recruited between 1966 and 1976, 1,213 were existing workers, 3,070 were young people leaving vocational training programs, 4,981 were peasants, 8,403 were demobilized soldiers and a full 18,039 were "sent-down youths."[18]

It is noteworthy that "sent-down youths" represented a plurality of the new workers. Permission to return to the cities, particularly to a job in a state-owned

---

15 Zhonggong zhongyang shujichu yanjiushi lilunzu (ed.), *Dangqian woguo gongren jieji zhuangkuang diaocha ziliao huibian* (Beijing: Zhonggong zhongyang dangxiao chubanshe, 1983), Vol. 2, pp. 106–107.

16 Guojia tongjiju shehui tongjisi (ed.), *Zhongguo laodong gongzi tongji ziliao* (Beijing: Guojia tongji chubanshe, 1987), p. 32.

17 Zhonggong zhongyang shujichu yanjiushi lilunzu (ed.), *Dangqian woguo gongren jieji*, Vol. 2, p. 1.

18 Ibid., pp. 26–28. This sample is based on 149,995 workers.

factory, was a highly desirable outcome for those who had been sent down, and it evidently remained an obtainable one. Demobilized soldiers, the second largest group, likely received their assignments in most cases more as a reward for service than because of any specific qualifications or education. The omission of bad elements such as landlords and capitalists from the data makes it difficult to determine how these less favored groups fared. One other obvious point in the data is a significant increase in the average new worker's level of education during the Cultural Revolution, compared to the years 1956–1965. The number of new workers who were illiterate or who had only a primary school education dropped rapidly, while the proportion who had enrolled in junior high school more than tripled, and the intake of workers with senior high school degrees increased almost fivefold.[19] For the workers of these eleven sample work units, at least, the Reform era narrative of a collapse in the education system during the Cultural Revolution simply does not fit.

By the time the 1983 survey was compiled, 16.9 percent of all 149,995 workers on whom data were available were party members, of which the largest group, about 44 percent, had joined their work units between 1966 and 1976.[20] Given that less than 4 percent of the population at large were CCP members, 16.9 percent represented a high degree of penetration. There are two possible interpretations of the figure: either workers had a higher "political consciousness" than the general population, or else the CCP had recruited too indiscriminately among this demographic, destroying the elitist "vanguard" status that had long been one of its chief strengths.

Across the eleven sample work units, 23 percent of the total workforce of 183,611 people were women. The figures show that, during the Cultural Revolution, the number of women in the factories more than doubled from 7,644 in 1965 to 16,944 in 1976. However, a gendered division of labor is still clearly visible in the data. Light industry and the service sector were dominated by women, while heavy industry, shipping, and mining were an almost exclusively male preserve (see Table 7.1). To take the extreme cases, the Shanghai No. 17 Cotton Mill had the highest portion of female workers at 64 percent, with the Guangzhou Ocean Shipping Company sitting at the other end of the scale with a 99.8 percent male workforce. The Changchun First Automobile Factory employed 26 percent women, an unusually high number for that industry.[21] Data from the Anshan Iron and Steel Company, a well-known national entity, suggest that the division of labor inside the factories changed during the course of the Cultural Revolution, with women moving into formerly male jobs. After 1966,

---

19 Ibid., pp. 42–25. This sample is based on 149,995 workers.   20 Ibid., Vol. 2, p. 6.
21 Ibid., pp. 18–19.

Table 7.1 *Number and percentage of female workers in eleven enterprises in 1982*

Work unit	Workforce	Female workers	% of workforce	By date of commencement of work				
				Pre-PRC	1949–1956	1957–1965	1966–1976	after 1976
Total	183,611	42,146	23.0	448	2,949	7,644	16,944	14,161
% of all female workers	—		—	1.1	7.0	18.1	40.2	33.6
Beijing No.3 Construction Company	8,495	1,711	20.1	9	83	158	848	613
Zhengzhou Railway Branch Bureau	45,947	7,769	16.9	14	287	1,781	2,528	3,159
Dalian Shipyard	16,822	4,690	27.8	84	344	743	2,165	1,354
Shanghai No.1 Department Store	2,436	1,183	48.6	15	139	159	676	194
Anshan Iron and Steel Company (eight subsidiaries)	12,778	1,822	14.3	8	112	223	783	696
Datong Coal Mining Company, Yongding county	8,143	853	10.5	1	21	97	390	344
Daqing Oil Field (13 subsidiaries)	15,000	3,504	23.4	6	50	302	1,696	1,450
Nanjing Radio Factory	5,505	2,071	37.6	17	163	668	771	452
Shanghai No.17 Cotton Mill	9,234	5,966	64.6	150	370	596	1,811	3,039
Changchun First Automobile Works	46,617	12,551	26.9	144	1,380	2,917	5,260	2,850
Guangzhou Ocean Shipping Company	12,634	26	0.2	—	—	—	16	10

Source: Zhonggong zhongyang shujichu yanjiu lilunzu (ed.), *Dangqian woguo gongren jieji zhuangkuang diaocha ziliao huibian* (Beijing: Zhonggong zhongyang dangxiao chubanshe, 1983), Vol. 2, pp. 18–19.

first women joined its primary steel and chemical production lines. In 1976, 26 percent of the new workers were female.[22]

Curiously, the data also shows that, not only during but also before and after the Cultural Revolution, work units with a high percentage of women tended to have fewer party members than those dominated by men. For instance, the Shanghai No. 17 Cotton Mill, Shanghai No. 1 Department Store and Nanjing Radio Factory all had very low numbers of party members, compared to heavily male units such as the Guangzhou Ocean Shipping Company, Zhengzhou Railway Branch Bureau and Datong Coal Mining Company. This may be a sign that on average the CCP considered female workers less qualified and less politically reliable as party members, or that a lack of support with childcare and other domestic labor presented a barrier to entry into political life. It is also possible that industrial workers simply enjoyed greater prestige than those in the light industry or service sectors, and that this status difference played out in the party's nomination process. The data from the 1983 survey suggest that some progress was made towards gender equality in the state sector during the Cultural Revolution. Nevertheless, even with these improved figures, women hardly "held up half the sky."

Peasants and the Countryside in the Late Cultural Revolution

Rural development during the late Cultural Revolution was wracked with contradictions, as different factions in the party promoted their preferred program. For some time, the CCP backed radical agricultural policies modeled on the Dazhai village brigade in Shanxi. However, the damage to state capacity brought on by the rebellion and chaos of the early Cultural Revolution made enforcement of the new model almost impossible. An underground "second economy" developed in the countryside, with black markets, underground factories, under-reporting of production and large-scale growing of cash crops all reducing party-state control. Document 7.1, an order from the Central Committee in May 1970, details some of the methods used by the authorities to combat illicit commercial activities. The Committee focused not just on individuals, but also on work units, which were able to leverage their connections to acquire goods "through the backdoor" and to embezzle collective funds and resources. The party leadership called for a mobilization of the masses and outlined a range of punishments for economic crimes ranging from simple criticism for less serious offenses all the way up to execution for the worst offenders.

---

22 Zhonggong zhongyang shujichu yanjiushi lilunzu (ed.), *Dangqian woguo gongren jieji*, Vol. 1, p. 4.

Figure 7.3: Fengqiao village near Suzhou, 1974.
Source: Photograph by Carl Seyschab.

Official statistics compiled in the Reform era indicate an annual growth rate for agricultural production of about 2 percent between 1966 and 1976. The 1968 and 1976 harvests were both affected by ongoing factional struggles in the party leadership, and 1972 saw the most serious drought in a decade.[23] Nevertheless, the slow rate of production growth, which failed to keep pace with the rising population, is striking given what were in many ways good conditions in the countryside. Rural taxation and procurement rates remained relatively stable over the period, with around 20 percent of total grain output purchased by the state.[24] Unlike in the late 1950s, no large-scale famine broke out, but slow growth coupled with natural disasters led to supply shortages and forced the government to continue grain imports well into the 1970s. According to one estimate, by the end of the 1970s 20 percent of all production teams were non-self-sustaining and reliant on emergency relief, while surplus grain for market came mainly from the top 20 percent.[25]

23 Zheng Yougui, "'Wenhua dageming' shiqi nongye shengchan bodong jiqi dongyin tanxi," *Zhonggong dangshi yanjiu*, No. 3 (1998), pp. 71–77.
24 Zhonghua renmin gongheguo nongye bu jihuasi (ed.), *Zhongguo nongcun jingji tongji daquan 1949–1986* (Beijing: Nongye chubanshe, 1989), pp. 410–411.
25 Flemming Christiansen, "Food Security, Urbanization and Social Stability in China," *Journal of Agrarian Change*, Vol. 9, No. 4 (2009), p. 552.

The Dazhai Model and the People's Communes

During the heyday of the Cultural Revolution as a mass movement, agricultural policy slipped down the CCP's list of priorities. However, this changed with the rise of Dazhai, a village in Shanxi's Xiyang county, as a national model. The *People's Daily* had first begun to promote the slogan "agriculture learns from Dazhai" in 1964, but it was only after 1968 that this small production brigade and its leader Chen Yonggui became national heroes. Early stories had portrayed Dazhai as a model mainly for its spirit of self-reliance and attempts to increase production without state subsidies. Now, as the Cultural Revolution kicked into high gear, the Dazhai brigade was described as a model of resistance to the "revisionist line" of Liu Shaoqi. In the aftermath of the Great Leap Famine, Liu had proposed rebuilding the countryside via the so-called "three freedoms and one contract," meaning free markets, expansion of private plots, individual financial responsibility and a "fixing of quotas for each household" rather than solely at the level of the production team. This last innovation was a forerunner to the household responsibility system that would allow families to produce independently from 1979 onwards. During the Cultural Revolution, Liu's program came to be seen as an attempt to introduce a "capitalist way" in agriculture. In Dazhai, his approach was disregarded. Plots for private use were abolished; attempts to increase productivity through material benefits ("putting work points in command") were attacked as revisionism. Instead of moving the major unit of accounting in the commune down from the team to the household, in Dazhai the move was in the opposite direction, from the team to the brigade. These decisions were lauded as a step towards a true socialist ownership structure.

Chen Yonggui enjoyed a similarly rapid rise in status to the Dazhai brigade he led. In 1966, Chen had been a labor model and the Dazhai party secretary. With the outbreak of the rural Cultural Revolution, he became heavily involved in the armed struggle in Shanxi and rose to a post in the provincial leadership in 1967. Two years later, he became a member of the CCP Central Committee; by 1973 he was a member of the Politburo; and in 1975 he was appointed Vice-Premier of the PRC. Only Wang Hongwen, the worker rebel from Shanghai, enjoyed a comparably rapid rise. The official media celebrated Chen as an honest and hardworking peasant fighting to save the countryside from revisionism. The Maoist left was particularly vocal, promoting Dazhai's success as a major milestone in the socialist transformation of rural China. Within the CCP, however, it remained controversial whether this radical version of the socialist model could be adapted to all of the country's diverse regions. The left also had only modest influence in the state's agricultural bureaucracy, limiting its ability to force change on a national scale.

The radical position was further weakened by Mao's unwillingness to support their agenda, a reticence perhaps influenced by the failure of rural reform during the Great Leap.[26] The CCP leadership's thinking on the issue was made clear in December 1970, when the Central Committee approved a report from the Agriculture Conference of the Northern Regions. This document continued the promotion of Dazhai as a national model, but it also sounded a note of caution:

> Chairman Mao personally supported the "60 Points for the People's Communes", which have had a great effect on the development of agricultural production and the consolidation of the collective economy. During the Great Proletarian Cultural Revolution, new developments and circumstances have come into play. However, at the present stage the "60 Points for the People's Communes" [remain] our fundamental policy ... they are applicable and must be enforced continuously. On 12 July 1967, the Central Committee made a clear decision: "The system of the rural People's Communes is based on the three levels of ownership [team, brigade, commune], with the team as the foundation. In general, the system of plots for private use should not be changed".[27]

Statements such as these underlined that the compromises made with the peasantry from 1961 onwards (see Chapter 4) remained in place. Nevertheless, the issue of plots for private use remained controversial. Supporters of the Maoist left often quoted Lenin's warning that "small production breeds capitalism and the bourgeoisie continuously, daily, hourly, spontaneously, and on a mass scale."[28] As long as peasants still produced on private plots, the radical view went, their capitalist tendencies would remain. These plots could not be eliminated immediately, but in order to lay the groundwork for their eventual removal the party needed to organize a permanent struggle that would raise the political consciousness of the peasant population.

In the end, despite the rhetoric around Dazhai, the CCP did not push for a new transformation of ownership structures on the national level. The state constitution adopted in 1975 declared that, for the present at least, the People's Communes were to be based on the three level ownership structure described

---

26 Yang Dali, *Calamity and Reform in China: State, Rural Society, and Institutional Change since the Great Leap Famine* (Stanford, CA: Stanford University Press, 1996), p. 101.

27 "Zhonggong zhongyang pizhuan guowuyuan guanyu beifangqu nongye huiyi de baogao (zhaiyao)," December 11 (1970), in Song, *The Chinese Cultural Revolution Database*.

28 Yao Wenyuan, "Lin Biao fandang jituan de shehui jichu," March 1 (1975) in Song, *The Chinese Cultural Revolution Database*; V. I. Lenin, *"Left-Wing" Communism: An Infantile Disorder* (Chippendale: Resistance Books, 1999), p. 30.

above, with the commune itself sitting atop production brigades and production teams. The collective economy was to retain absolute primacy, but commune members were permitted to work plots for private use, to engage in sideline production within their families and, if they were living in pasture areas, to raise small numbers of livestock for themselves.[29]

Whatever guiding principles the central government adopted, it remains controversial among scholars how much power the People's Communes actually retained in the late Cultural Revolution. It has been suggested in some quarters that peasant resistance may have significantly weakened the commune system in the 1970s. One Western observer has claimed that "large parts of the countryside had abandoned the planned economy" even before Mao's death in 1976.[30] In his study of peasant "counter-actions," the Chinese scholar Gao Wangling has shown that the rural population developed effective survival strategies to adapt to state demands, including under-reporting production and land, stealing or strategically lowering productivity. These counter-actions reduced the amount of grain that could be procured by the government, despite the fact that peasant households remained locked into the state-backed People's Communes until the early 1980s.[31] Another scholar has spoken of a "silent agreement" between peasants and local cadres, in which the authorities would often turn a blind eye to the under-reporting of land and production, as long as procurement targets were fulfilled.[32]

These forms of resistance were obviously important, but in my view they should not be overemphasized. No matter how many peasants were involved in small-scale "clandestine" economic activities, grain quotas and labor obligations still had to be met. Production teams remained the major gatekeepers of production and distribution. Even after Mao's death, the Dazhai model continued to be used under Hua Guofeng to promote a radical version of collective agriculture, and brigade accounting, which strengthened the commune's oversight of teams and households, was introduced in some places in the late 1970s. It would be an exaggeration to date the end of the planned economy to the early 1970s, instead of the early 1980s as was actually the case. A key inflection point came in 1980, when the Central Committee announced that the supposed "self-reliance" of Dazhai had in fact been a fabrication. During the Cultural Revolution, it was revealed, Dazhai had received subsidies from the central government; its famous

---

29 "Zhonghua renmin gongheguo xianfa," section 1, article 7.

30 Frank Dikötter, *The Cultural Revolution: A People's History, 1962–1976* (London: Bloomsbury, 2016), p. xv.

31 Gao Wangling, *Zhongguo nongmin fan xingwei yanjiu, 1950–1980* (Hong Kong: Zhongwen daxue chubanshe, 2013).

32 Jean C. Oi, *State and Peasants in Contemporary China: The Political Economy of Village Government* (Berkeley, CA: University of California Press, 1989), p. 229.

terraced fields, supposedly the work of committed, self-sacrificing villagers, had been built with assistance from the PLA. Chen Yonggui, one of the few heroes of the Cultural Revolution to have survived the purge against the Gang of Four, was finally dismissed from office. The Dazhai myth was broken.

The "Sent-Down Youth": Experiencing China "Outside the System"

As we have seen, the government's campaign to send educated young people from the cities to the countryside was not new, but it intensified as the Cultural Revolution continued, before becoming compulsory in 1969. CCP propaganda lauded the scheme as a chance for the urban youth to help develop the country-side and remote border areas while also receiving a second education from poor and lower middle peasants. In the party's telling, this would contribute to a reduction of the "three differences" which had been its focus since the 1950s, namely between city and countryside, peasants and workers, and manual and intellectual laborers. Sending young people away from the cities also provided an effective means to demobilize the radical Red Guards and rebels coming out of urban middle schools. The middle school graduates of 1966, 1967 and 1968 (known collectively as the *lao sanjie* or "old three-classes") were affected more than any other age group. In 1969 alone, over 2.67 million graduates were sent down. The numbers decreased between 1970 and 1972, but 1975 saw them peak again to 2.36 million people.[33] Of the 16 million young people sent down during the Cultural Revolution, half were able to leave the villages before 1976, usually to study, join the PLA or take up urban jobs. Others were able to return only after the death of Mao, or in some cases not at all.[34] Overall, the "sent-down youth" constituted around 10 percent of the urban population.[35] Beyond political concerns, scholars continue to debate whether the campaign was primarily driven by ideological motives, or whether economic considerations such as reducing the state's outlays on higher education, jobs, housing, and urban food rations also played a role.[36] The CCP did not publicly acknowledge any link between the

33 Liu Xiaomeng, *Zhongguo zhiqingshi: Dachao 1966–1980* (Beijing: Zhongguo shehuikexue chubanshe, 1998), p. 863.

34 Lu Yu, *Xin Zhongguo renkou wushinian* (Beijing: Zhongguo renkou chubanshe, 2004), Vol. 1, pp. 601–602.

35 Liu Xiaomeng, *Zhongguo zhiqingshi*, p. 848.

36 For example see: Thomas Scharping, *Umsiedlungsprogramme für Chinas Jugend 1955–1980: Probleme der Stadt-Land-Beziehungen in der chinesischen Entwicklungspolitik* (Hamburg: Institut für Asienkunde, 1981), pp. 425, 433, and Michel Bonnin (Pan Mingxiao), *Shiluo de yidai: Zhongguo shangshan xiaxiang yundong (1968–1980)*, translated by Annie Au-Yeung (Ou Yangyin) (Beijing: Zhongguo dabaike quanshu chubanshe, 2010), pp. 53–55.

sending down of 16 million people and the difficulties it was experiencing in feeding the population in the cities. It did, however, make some references to problems in finding employment for all urban middle and high school graduates.

Living Conditions in the Villages

Most of the "sent-down youth" worked in local People's Communes, while a smaller number were sent to the military construction corps or to state farms. Living conditions in the state institutions tended to be better than in the communes, since state farm workers, unlike their peasant counterparts, were inside the official supply system. Outside the system, living standards were heavily influenced by local geographic conditions, which varied from desert to remote mountains and from hard winters in Manchuria to the suburbs of Beijing. In the 1960s, the state hoped that the "sent-down youth" would become self-sufficient, increasing the productive capacity of the villages and "eating from their own strength." In reality, most urban young people showed little aptitude for agricultural work, which was both unfamiliar and physically taxing. Their productivity tended to be low, and at the same time they needed housing and land. The government therefore found itself providing subsidies for their resettlement, including housing, health care, transportation, study materials and agricultural tools. Between 1967 and 1972, the central government spent 1.7–1.8 billion yuan on these items, but the subsidies remained too low to cover the recipients' needs.[37] The income of the "educated youth" in the villages was often much lower than that of the local population, because peasants had access to better plots for private use and could earn extra income through economic sidelines. In grain deficit areas, cadres tried to keep the grain rations of the "educated youth" as low as possible,[38] and most peasants considered the newcomers a burden on their production teams. To make up the grain and income shortfall, many urban parents found themselves sending money to the countryside on a regular basis.

The harsh conditions the "sent-down youth" experienced in the countryside are captured in a widely publicized letter to Mao from Li Qinglin, an elementary school teacher in rural Fujian province, whose son had volunteered to be sent to a poor mountain region (Document 7.2). In addition to describing the difficulties his son faced, Li criticized the corruption which allowed cadres' children to be transferred away from the poorest areas, or out of the countryside entirely, on the grounds of "necessities of development and the course of the socialist construction of the state." Those without family connections, meanwhile, faced having to

37 Liu Xiaomeng, *Zhongguo zhiqingshi*, p. 192.
38 Scharping, *Umsiedlungsprogramme für Chinas Jugend 1955–1980*, p. 271.

remain in the countryside their whole lives. The letter struck a chord with Mao, who appreciated Li's attack on the abuse of power by cadres. In April 1973, he ordered the publication of the letter and sent Li 300 yuan to support Li's family. Later that year, the teacher from Fujian was admitted to the State Council's Leading Small Group for the Educated Youth.

As conflicts and tensions heightened in the villages and young people began to protest more vocally, the central government's National Conference on the Educated Youth decided in 1973 that monetary subsidies should be increased. The government also agreed to "top up" grain rations in areas where the sent-down youth received less on average than unmarried locals, or when the grain rations of a production team were extraordinarily low.[39] The decision also mandated that the "educated youth" were to be organized into their own production teams, rather than integrating into peasant teams as had previously been the case. Finally, the government ordered that the plots for private use given to the urban youth were to be of the same quality as those distributed to the local population.[40]

Marriage and Sexual Violence

Many of the "sent-down youth" had never experienced the level of poverty they saw in the villages. Not a few lost their faith in the revolution as a result, and many wished to return to the cities as soon as possible to escape the challenges of life "outside the system." However, the loss of their urban *hukou* system made it almost impossible to leave the villages without permission. Throughout the first half of the 1970s, "sent-down youths" could not be sure when, or even if, they would ever be able to return to their old lives. Even those who had volunteered to go to the countryside later came to feel trapped.

During the Campaign to Criticize Lin Biao and Confucius, the Maoist left celebrated "sent-down youths" as heroes in the national media. Particular praise was reserved for those who had decided to "put down roots" in the countryside by marrying peasants. These marriages were lauded as a way for young urbanites to integrate with the rural population and reduce the gap between urban and rural China. The pressure to marry in the villages was sharply gendered, thanks in large part to the difference in legal marriage age between men and women. For the purposes of birth planning, the government set the minimum marriage age for urban residents at twenty-five years for women and twenty-eight for men, and for

---

39 Liu Xiaomeng, *Zhongguo zhiqingshi*, pp. 401–403.
40 Liu Xiaomeng and Ding Yizhuang, *Zhongguo zhiqing shidian* (Chengdu: Sichuan renmin chubanshe, 1995), p. 517.

rural *hukou* holders at twenty-three and twenty-five years for respectively.[41] This meant that young women who were sent down and acquired a rural *hukou* between 1966 and 1968 would reach marriage age around 1973. Young urban men, by contrast, passed this milestone later in the decade, leaving a much smaller pool who were legally able to marry before their return from the countryside. Social pressure to marry soon after reaching the minimum age could be very strong, and some women from bad family backgrounds saw marriage to a poor peasant as a means to improve their social status. Overall, the urban youth in the countryside were confronted with competing messages. On the one hand, the official media criticized the oppression of women in the rural areas as a "feudal habit." On the other hand, the young people sent down to the villages were expected to accept "education" by poor and lower middle peasants, something which the Maoist left implied could well include accepting rural marriages.[42]

In some places, villagers tried to force urban women into marriage, and some were assaulted or even raped. Women from bad family backgrounds were especially vulnerable. "Sent-down youth" could often do little against the power and influence of so-called "local emperors." In August 1973, the Central Committee circulated a decision on the issue:

> Mobilize the broad masses to carry out a firm struggle against criminal activities that harm the educated youth who have been sent "up to the mountains, down to the villages". Criminals who use fascist methods of cruel persecution against the educated urban youth and who rape the female educated youth should be punished according to law. If criminals threaten the victim to cover up their crimes or make a show of taking revenge against people, they should be severely punished. If people who are guilty of terrible crimes are not killed, the anger of the people will not be curbed ... Reasonable dating and marriage among the educated youth should be protected, [but] forced marriage is strictly forbidden.[43]

It is difficult to assess the precise extent of rape and forced marriage suffered by young urban women in the countryside, but numerous references to the issue in central government documents of the period suggests the problems were severe. On the other hand, as was hinted at above, for some women marriage in the countryside was a genuine personal choice. A significant number decided to

41 Liu Xiaomeng, *Zhongguo zhiqingshi*, pp. 502–503.

42 For example see: Nora Sausmikat, *Kulturrevolution, Diskurs und Erinnerung: Eine Analyse lebensgeschichtlicher Erzählungen von chinesischen Frauen* (Frankfurt (M): Peter Lang, 2002), pp. 165–173.

43 Zhonggong zhongyang, "Zhuanfa guowuyuan guanyu quanguo zhishi qingnian shangshan xiaxiang gongzuo huiyi de baogao," August 4 (1973), in Song, *The Chinese Cultural Revolution Database*.

Figure 7.4: A village near Hangzhou in 1974.
Source: Photograph by Olli Salmi.

marry peasants or rural cadres to demonstrate revolutionary enthusiasm, improve their social status or even advance their political careers. By 1976, 4 percent of all "sent-down youth" had become part of the leading groups in their villages. 29 percent were members of the party's Youth League and 1.5 percent had successfully joined the CCP itself. Around 10 percent of all "sent-down youth" left in the countryside by the end of the Cultural Revolution had married.[44] The reasons for these marriages, however, were much more complex than the left's narrow focus on "putting down roots."

Leaving the Countryside

Starting around 1972, universities began to recruit new students again. Admissions were based not on central examinations, which would not return until 1977, but on "the recommendation of the masses." Mao argued for a system in which urban school leavers would work for several years in factories or agriculture, before the masses selected the best among them for higher education. After graduation, degree holders would return to factories or villages to avoid losing their connection to the ordinary people.

44 Liu Xiaomeng, *Zhongguo zhiqingshi*, p. 865.

The party leadership soon realized that, without standardized examinations, the admissions process was vulnerable to manipulation, especially by applicants with official connections. As a result, the Central Committee passed several decisions against "entering through the backdoor" in education.[45] Criticism was mainly targeted at those party and PLA cadres who had got their children out of the countryside illicitly by securing them job assignments or university places. The Maoist left used these decisions as ammunition against returning veteran cadres, who they described as nepotistic "capitalist roaders in power." The fact that some people could leave the villages while others could not led to exactly the kind of resentment that Li Qinglin had expressed in his letter to Mao.

Many of those who remained in the countryside came from disadvantaged groups: either their families were from bad class backgrounds or they were the children of workers and cadres who were still under attack. Among these young people trapped in the countryside, a kind of counter-culture developed, often influenced by memories, still fresh, of the Red Guard and rebel movements. A new activism took shape in which these exiled urbanites would read and write underground literature or meet in small groups to discuss political issues. Ideological purity and Mao Zedong Thought were no longer the focus, and debates often featured criticism of the program of "sending down" and even the political system more broadly.[46] Following Mao's death, "sent-down youths" all over the country took part in public protests. It would be some years before the program was finally ended in the early 1980s, but the level of discontent was clear.

Since the start of the Reform era, the sending-down campaign has been the subject of a voluminous literature, both in fiction and memoir. Narratives vary from memories of total neglect to a kind of rosy nostalgia for a lost age. It is important to note the skew in these accounts, which are almost always written by former "sent-down youth," and only seldom by the villagers among whom they lived. Access to the public sphere is much less readily available to peasants than to urbanites with professional careers, which is what those who were sent down tended to become. In the mid-1980s, these written accounts helped popularize the concept of a "lost generation." Some former "sent-down youths" wrote of how they and their peers had wasted the best years of their lives laboring in the dirt rather than preparing for university. With little formal education, they had difficulty competing in the labor market after their eventual return to the cities.

---

45 For example: Zhonggong zhongyang, "Guanyu dujue gaodeng xuexiao zhaosheng gongzuo zhong 'zouhoumen' xianxiang de tongzhi," May 1 (1972); Zhonggong zhongyang, "Guanyu 'zouhoumen' wenti de tongzhi," February 20 (1974), in Song, *The Chinese Cultural Revolution Database*.

46 For more detail see: Yin Hongbiao, *Shizongzhe de zuji*, pp. 215–340.

Some returnees preferred to view their "sent-down" identity as a source of pride. Under the slogan, "No regrets for the youth," they formed groups in the cities to share stories and keep their memories alive. For them, surviving the hardships of rural life and contributing to the development of the countryside was something to be valued; it was better to be sent down than to have been one of the Red Guards who caused so much destruction in the violent summer of 1966. This more positive narrative was also promoted by the state and the propaganda apparatus. Finally, some eyewitnesses emphasized the freedom they had enjoyed in the countryside. Away from the stricter state controls in the cities, they could read forbidden literature, listen to foreign radio programs or perhaps gain their first sexual experiences.[47] Personal views of the sending-down program were varied, but one thing that is clear is that the policy did not meet the political goals that Mao had originally envisioned. In 1966, when the Cultural Revolution began, many middle school students had been fanatical revolutionaries. A decade later, huge numbers returned from the countryside disillusioned, both with the Cultural Revolution and with socialism itself.

Achievements and Failures: Evaluating the Mao Era

It is not the purpose of this book to evaluate all of the key developments of the Mao era. I will limit myself here to a brief discussion of the achievements and failures of the early PRC in three areas: economic growth, access to basic entitlements, and social mobility and change. These issues are complex in themselves, and one of the first questions we must ask is how we are to judge success. On the question of, say, progress in human rights, should we confine ourselves to the CCP's own goals, or should we instead stress today's accepted metrics, such as the UN's Human Development Index (measuring life expectancy, education standards and standard of living)?[48] If we choose instead to make a relative judgment, what is the appropriate comparator? Should we compare the Mao era to pre-1949 Republican China, to the relatively peaceful Nanjing Decade under the GMD before the Sino-Japanese War (1928–1937), to the progress of Taiwan after 1949 or to developments in the Reform era since 1978? The CCP under Mao tended to prefer the first option, stressing the "sweetness" of the socialist present in contrast to the "bitterness" of the "old society." It perhaps makes most

---

47 For an overview see: Sausmikat, *Kulturrevolution, Diskurs und Erinnerung*, pp. 227–277; Emily Honig, "Socialist Sex: The Cultural Revolution revisited," *Modern China*, Vol. 29, No. 2 (2003), pp. 165–166.

48 For a detailed discussion on standards for measuring development see: Chris Bramall, *Chinese Economic Development* (London: Routledge, 2008), pp. 3–43.

sense to adopt this frame of reference, and to compare the situation at the founding of the PRC in 1949 to circumstances on the eve of Mao's death in 1976. The Taiwan analogy is tempting, but the difference in scale between an island of a few million people and a mainland of hundreds of millions makes meaningful comparison almost impossible. The comparison to the Reform era, meanwhile, is weakened by our inability to know how China would have fared over the last forty years had the Maoist left won out over the Deng Xiaoping faction.

Economic Growth

A lack of comprehensive national surveys prior to 1949 means we have little quantitative data from pre-PRC China, and statistics from the Mao era are often questionable and fragmentary. As a result, any attempt to evaluate developments in the economy, education, health care or food consumption remains fraught with difficulty. In the 1980s, the Chinese government published new and corrected statistics for the period between 1949 and 1976, but these have been subject to widely varying interpretations. I will focus here on two attempts to create an authoritative, statistically rigorous picture of Mao's China, one by Li Minqi, a Neo-Maoist and professor of economics at the University of Utah, and the other by Andrew Walder, professor of sociology at Stanford. Both attempt to evaluate China's economic performance and living standards between 1949 and 1976 in international perspective, and both rely on the same primary data set, Angus Maddison's 2006 compilation of historical gross domestic product (GDP) across countries.[49]

Based on this underlying data, Walder and Li reach divergent conclusions. Li argues that, under Mao, China's economic growth and rise in living standards were both outstanding compared to other developing countries. By 1976, the CCP was able to guarantee basic needs (food, health care, and at least primary education) to the entire population. It had also laid the foundation for China's conversion into a modern industrial economy. Li points to the country's rate of GDP growth between 1950 and 1976 – officially 6.7 percent per annum, which on his reading was the highest of any region during this period – as further evidence of the CCP's success. Even according to Maddison's corrected statistics, average annual growth was a strong, 4.7 percent, a figure exceeded only by West Asia and Latin America.[50] But these numbers, while impressive, fail to take

49 The data are from: Angus Maddison, *The World Economy, Volume 1: A Millennial Perspective*, Vol. 2: Historical Statistics (Paris: OECD, 2006).

50 Li Minqi, *The Rise of China and the Demise of the Capitalist World Economy* (London: Pluto Press, 2008), p. 29.

account of the simultaneous and substantial growth in China's population. The country's per capita growth rate was a much less striking 2.6 percent per year. Even today, after decades of sustained and rapid growth, China's GDP per capita remains far lower than that of the most developed countries, and the figure improves only slightly when controlling for relative purchasing power.

By contrast, Walder, who focuses mainly on GDP per capita, asserts that under Mao China fell behind compared to a wide variety of economies, including Japan, South Korea, Eastern Europe, the Soviet Union and Thailand. On the per capita metric, the PRC fared slightly better than some similar economies such as India, the Philippines and Indonesia between 1950 and 1973. The picture would have been far more positive had the high growth rates of the 1950–1957 period been sustained rather than being interrupted by the Great Leap. Instead, Walder suggests, standards of living and income saw little improvement during the Mao era as a whole. The newly established heavy industrial sector was unproductive and inefficient, and growth was achieved only with an enormous waste of investment and resources. While slums and other forms of highly visible urban poverty did not exist in China, this was primarily because the *hukou* system kept the poor permanently confined to the countryside rather than as a result of economic success. In addition to his skeptical evaluation of the early PRC's economic record, Walder stresses the high human costs of events such as the famine and the purges of the Cultural Revolution.[51]

Maddison himself supports Walder's assessment that capital productivity fell over time and that growth was achieved by wasteful allocation of resources. However, he also backs Li's description of the Mao era as laying the groundwork for the economic transition of the following decades. As he points out, China under Mao underwent an important structural change, from a primarily agrarian economy in 1952, when industry's share of GDP was one-sixth that of agriculture, to a more recognizably modern set-up in 1978, when industry was the larger sector.[52]

The economist Chris Bramall offers a similar view, arguing that that under-industrialization and high illiteracy rates acted as heavy brakes on China's economic development under Mao. The importance of under-industrialization is emphasized by the Third Front program, which worked much more efficiently in provinces with an existing industrial sector, such as Gansu, than in Yunnan or

---

51 Andrew Walder, *China under Mao: A Revolution Derailed* (Cambridge, MA: Harvard University Press, 2015), pp. 321–330.

52 Angus Maddison, *Chinese Economy: Performance in the Long Turn* (Development Centre of OCDE, 1998), pp. 55, 56 www.piketty.pse.ens.fr/files/Maddison98.pdf (accessed June 22, 2017).

Guizhou where the government was essentially building from scratch.[53] Bramall is skeptical of the economic benefits of Land Reform and the Soviet-inspired First Five Year Plan (1953–1957). However, he does detect a relatively coherent economic strategy in the period between 1964 and 1976, which he refers to as "Late Maoism." The new policies of this period did not necessarily produce significantly improved economic performance in the short term. However, echoing Maddison, Bramall suggests that Late Maoism bequeathed a range of positive economic legacies to its successors, including improvements in basic education and infrastructure and the foundations for a "green revolution" in agriculture. Local industries were often plagued by low productivity in their early years, but they also laid the groundwork for the rural industrialization of the 1980s and 1990s. The leadership under Deng did not start from scratch, but built on this positive legacy.[54]

It seems likely that China was among the poorest nations in the world in 1949.[55] To me, it therefore makes little sense to compare the PRC with countries such as Japan, which was already highly industrialized by this time, and more sense to compare the CCP's record to governments in other developing countries. For metrics such as individual income, this is exceedingly difficult, since throughout the Mao era basic goods and services were provided to the urban population either free or at nominal prices. Grain and housing, two major costs in other economies, were heavily subsidized, and the state monopoly on the purchase and sale of agricultural products allowed the government to keep prices and wages in the cities almost frozen for decades. As was noted above, little currency circulated in the countryside under Mao, with services such as health care or education mainly financed collectively by brigades and communes.

Despite these difficulties, comparisons between China and other developing economies have been attempted. Perhaps the most notable is a comparison of China and India by the Nobel Prize-winning economist Amartya Sen. He highlights the fact that, in contrast to authoritarian China, India did not experience deadly famine after 1949, in part because press freedom and democratic institutions helped avoid the spiral of misinformation and deference to power that served China so poorly during the Great Leap. However, with regard to long-term development over the three decades after independence in 1948, Sen suggests that India lagged behind:

> Because of its radical commitment to the elimination of poverty and to improving living conditions – a commitment in which Maoist as well as

---

53 Bramall, *Chinese Economic Development*, p. 281.   54 Ibid., pp. 318–319.
55 Cormac O'Grada, "Great Leap into Famine: A Review Essay," *Population and Development Review*, Vol. 37, No. 1 (2011), pp. 192–193.

Marxist ideas and ideals played an important part – China did achieve many things that the Indian leadership failed to press for and pursue with any vigour. The elimination of widespread hunger, illiteracy and ill health falls solidly in this category. When state action operates in the right direction, the results can be quite remarkable, as is illustrated by the social achievement of the pre-reform period.[56]

There is much to value in Sen's view, but we should not forget the caveat that he offers: state action, unchecked by meaningful institutional curbs, did not always work in "the right direction" in the early PRC. As Walder notes, China's economic and social development experienced painful setbacks during the famine and a less severe crisis during the chaotic years of the Cultural Revolution. For the tens of millions of people who died during the famine, and for their relatives, the overall picture of long-term improvements is cold comfort. The same state that was responsible for those improvements also ensured, by its own failings, that millions of its citizens never lived to see them.

Basic Needs: Nutrition, Health Care and Education

In terms of average consumption per head, peasants ate no better by the end of the Mao era than they had done in the early 1950s. One scholar has even argued for a slight overall decline, suggesting that by the mid-1970s a higher proportion of calories came from less popular coarse grains and sweet potatoes than from the staples, rice and wheat.[57] In provinces like Henan, peasants were still reliant on sweet potatoes and "eating green" to survive even in the late Cultural Revolution. People were no longer dying of hunger as they had during the Great Leap Famine, but their diet was exceedingly limited. Most of their calories came from grains with the addition of some vegetables. For large parts of the rural population, fruits, eggs and meat remained luxury goods, reserved for special events such as weddings and the Spring Festival. Improvements in housing were also quite modest over the nearly three decades of Mao's rule. Average per capita floor space in the cities declined from 4.5 to 3.6 square meters per person between 1950 and 1978.[58]

It could be argued that even to maintain the average level of grain consumption and housing over this period represented a major achievement, given the

56 Jean Drèze and Amartya Sen, *The Amartya Sen and Jean Drèze Omnibus, India: Economic Development and Social Opportunity* (Oxford: Oxford University Press, 1999), p. 77.

57 Robert Ash, "Squeezing the Peasants: Grain Extraction, Food Consumption and Rural Living Standards in Mao's China," *The China Quarterly*, No. 188 (2006), p. 990.

58 Lü Junhua, Peter G. Rowe and Zhang Jie (eds.), *Modern Urban Housing in China, 1840–2000* (Munich: Prestel, 2001), p. 19.

explosion in China's population from 551 million (1950) to 937 million (1976).[59] In absolute terms, many more people were fed than ever before, and the increase in mouths to feed was partly testament to the government's achievement in establishing peace within China's borders, and in improving public health. However, it is equally reasonable to say that economic and social progress were both "eaten up" by population growth.

Early birth planning policies, collectively referred to as "later, longer, fewer," succeeded in bringing birth rates down during the late Cultural Revolution by enforcing later marriage, longer intervals between permitted births and fewer births overall. From 1971, female sterilization, induced abortions and IUD contraceptive insertion increased rapidly. As a result, the total fertility rate (a projection of how many children the average women would be expected to have over her lifetime based on current trends) fell from close to six around 1970 to 2.7–2.8 by the end of the decade. One team of demographers has argued that at least 70 percent of the decline in fertility from 1970 to present had already been achieved before the introduction of the more draconian one-child policy under Deng Xiaoping in 1980.[60] However, even with these checks in place, the CCP leadership remained concerned that the increase in population was continuing to outpace economic and social improvements. It was this reasoning that lay behind the tightening to a one child per family system (with certain exclusions) during the Reform era.

Before 1949, modern hospitals were located only in the cities and in some county towns. There was nothing remotely resembling universal health insurance. In the villages, healers, some little better than quacks, practiced various kinds of traditional medicine. In this environment, epidemics caused huge numbers of early deaths, and the infant mortality rate was unrecognizably high. Even the generally skeptical Walder allows that the Mao era saw impressive achievements in public health and basic medical care. The crude death rate including infant mortality sank from 25.8 per thousand in 1953 (the first census) to 7.8 per thousand in 1976. Average life expectancy at birth rose from forty years to sixty-four years in the same period.[61] It should be noted that these overall figures hide significant regional differences. By the mid-1970s, life expectancy in the more developed coastal regions in the east was about ten years longer than in the poorer provinces in the southwest. Data from the 1982 census suggest that the urban population lived on average around three years longer than those in rural

59 Yuan Yongxi (ed.), *Zhongguo renkou zonglun* (Beijing: Zhongguo caizheng jingji chubanshe, 1991), p. 277.
60 Martin King Whyte, Wang Feng and Yong Cai, "Challenging Myths about China's One-Child Policy," *The China Journal*, No. 74 (2015), p. 152.
61 Walder, *China under Mao*, pp. 320–321.

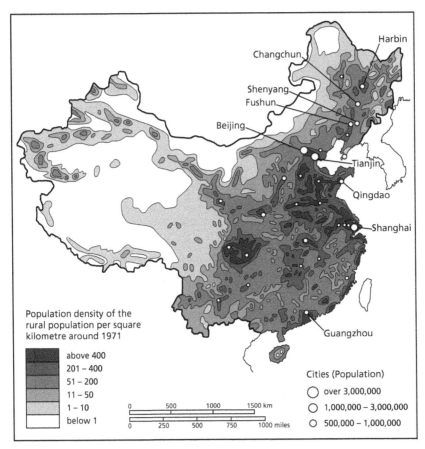

Map 7.1: Population density and large cities around 1971.

areas.[62] The rise in average life expectancy was partly achieved through campaigns to wipe out plagues and improve general hygiene in the cities and villages. Mass vaccination significantly reduced death by tuberculosis, which had been the most common cause of death in the 1930s. Public health in the Mao era had a strong focus on prevention. Midwives were trained to provide basic services in the villages, working alongside so-called "barefoot doctors" – peasants, students or "sent-down youths" who had received crash courses in basic medical knowledge. They were paid in work points by their brigades and lived alongside the local population. There has perhaps been a tendency to romanticize the "barefoot doctors." Students with little more than elementary training cannot be seen

62 Thomas Scharping, "Chinas Bevölkerung 1953–1982, Teil III: Sterblichkeit und Lebenserwartung," *Cologne China Studies Online*, No. 1 (1986), pp. 20–21, www.phil-fak .uni-koeln.de/fileadmin/chinastudien/papers/No_1986–1.pdf (accessed March 30, 2018).

as a substitute for a fully fledged, universally available health system. Nevertheless, the improvement in public health in China under Mao was a remarkable achievement.

Access to collective health insurance and hospitals changed over time. During the Great Leap, the central government attempted to expand social security to the countryside and pressured local governments to provide free treatment for peasants in county hospitals. Like other over-ambitious Great Leap projects, the main outcome of this policy was to overburden central and local actors. After the end of the famine, a system of collective rural health care, locally financed by production brigades, was gradually built up between the early 1960s and the end of the Mao era. Peasants no longer enjoyed free and unlimited access to hospitals at the county level, but their brigades would provide basic care and medication. Under this system, local cadres and barefoot doctors acted as gatekeepers, regulating access to more costly treatments in the county hospitals in cases of serious diseases. During the Cultural Revolution, specialized teams from urban hospitals were sent down to the countryside to support local doctors and clinics.

The quality of medical services in the countryside varied by location, depending on fiscal resources and other demands on local cadres' budgets.[63] Variations in quality of care also resulted from the state's decision to promote traditional Chinese medicine alongside Western methods. This not only played to a continued popular belief in the effectiveness of traditional remedies, but also chimed with the government's goal of reducing costs. On this point, it is interesting to note that it was the socialist state that institutionalized Chinese medicine, establishing training and research institutes for doctors and scientists to study traditional techniques.

In the field of education, China saw an impressive increase in elementary and middle school enrollment between 1949 and 1976, in both urban and rural areas. Some scholars have argued that rural enrollment at elementary and secondary level continued to expand even during the turbulent early 1970s. This trend had obvious benefits for the children of peasants, especially girls, whose education had rarely been a priority in rural China prior to the founding of the PRC. Official statistics published in the 1980s capture these developments, showing a rise in the rate of elementary school enrollment from 25 percent in 1949 to 84.7 percent in 1965 and 96 percent in 1976.[64] From the early 1970s, rural

---

63 For a general evaluation see: Sascha Klotzbücher, *Das ländliche Gesundheitswesen der VR China* (Frankfurt (M): Peter Lang, 2006), pp. 87–122.

64 Suzanne Pepper, *Radicalism and Education Reform in 20th-Century China* (Cambridge: Cambridge University Press, 1996), p. 483.

schools were permitted to develop their own curricula to fit local needs, for instance by focusing on agricultural science.[65]

Beyond the headline figures, the quality of education and changes in rates of literacy are harder to assess. A number of authors have claimed that children learned little beyond basic reading, writing and political ideology, the importance of which the party continued to stress. Rates of illiteracy do appear to have been high by the end of the Cultural Revolution.[66] One study argues that the disruption of schooling in these years had a noticeable negative impact on literacy, particularly for those children who turned eleven in the chaotic years between 1966 and 1968.[67] In 1971, officials claimed that the illiteracy rate was as low as 10 percent, or around 85 million people, but this number was disputed by the Reform era leadership. The 1982 census arrived at a much higher number, 236 million. This figure, however, is inflated by population growth and probably also by a further rise in illiteracy during the early Reform years, making it difficult to say what role the disruption of the Cultural Revolution may have played. What is clear from the 1982 data is that illiteracy, like so much else, was a gendered problem. More than twice as many women as men could not read and write, including the majority of women above the age of 50.[68] There was also a marked spatial divide, with far more illiterate people living in the poor minority regions in the west than in the more developed provinces on the coast.

In higher education, the impact of the Cultural Revolution was devastating. Most universities recruited no new students between 1966 and 1971, or in some cases even later. The Maoist left in the party leadership found the pre-1966 process for recruiting students, in which a national entrance examination reproduced the same urban, petty-bourgeois elite year on year, so problematic that a half-decade interruption of higher education seemed like the lesser of two evils. For the radicals, knowledge production and transmission was to be a combination of manual labor, participation in revolution and traditional study. Theory had always to be linked to production and practical experience. This understanding of education departed from the more formalized training that characterized Western and also Soviet universities.

---

65 Joel Andreas, "Leveling the Little Pagoda: The Impact of College Examinations, and their Elimination, on Rural Education in China," *Comparative Education Review*, Vol. 48, No. 1 (2004), pp. 19–22.

66 Dikötter, *The Cultural Revolution*, pp. 287–288.

67 Donald Treiman, "The Growth and Determinants of Literacy in China," in Emily Hannum and Albert Park (eds.), *Education and Reform in China* (London: Routledge, 2007), p. 149.

68 Scharping, "Chinas Bevölkerung 1953–1982, Teil II: Alter, Geschlecht und Sozialstruktur," *Cologne China Studies Online*, No. 2 (1985), p. 9, www.phil-fak.uni-koeln.de/fileadmin/chinas tudien/papers/No_1985-2.pdf (accessed March 30, 2018).

In addition to the shuttering of universities, most academic journals ceased publication during the Cultural Revolution. Recently, there has been a questioning of the established consensus that the last decade of the Mao era was a disaster for scientific development. Scholars such as Sigrid Schmalzer have pointed out that the "mass science" of this period, which saw teams of scientists, peasants, students and "sent-down youths" experiment with new seeds and creative farming methods, actually contributed to something of a "green revolution."[69] The Cultural Revolution also saw the development of a "people's archaeology" movement. Some of China's most important archaeological sites were first discovered during the 1966–1976 period, albeit often quite by accident. Notable finds included the Han tombs at Mancheng (1968), another remarkable set of tombs at Mawangdui (1971), the Neolithic Hemudu Site (1973), and most famously the Terracotta Army at the tomb of the First Emperor near Xi'an (1974). At the same time, there were also major achievements in scientific research, some in highly clandestine military projects. In 1967 China conducted its first hydrogen bomb test, while 1970 saw the launch of "The East is Red," the country's first satellite. The scientific achievements of the Cultural Revolution were thrust into the spotlight in 2015, when pharmacologist Tu Youyou received the Nobel Prize in Physiology and Medicine for her work in the early 1970s on "Project 523," which developed a now-standard anti-malarial drug from traditional herbal cures. The official narrative adopted during the Reform era continues to acknowledge and celebrate these achievements, but the sense remains that much more could have been achieved without the disruption to academic research and institutions.

Change of Status, Social Mobility and Political Participation

Another key criterion in evaluating the Mao era is social mobility. Some scholars have argued that society in the early PRC was structured around what amounted to semi-feudal "estates." People were born into an estate, such as "landlord" or "lower middle peasant," and had great difficulties trying to escape it; peasants remained tied to village and soil. As I have attempted to show, social mobility was intimately related to the state's systems of classification, in which securing a change in status could be challenging. Petitioning the government could produce results, and there was also some negative social mobility as middle peasants suspected of being "landlords who had escaped the net" had their class downgraded. However, to the best of my knowledge we have no overall statistics on

---

69 See: Sigrid Schmalzer, *Red Revolution, Green Revolution: Scientific Farming in Socialist China* (Chicago, IL: The University Press of Chicago, 2016).

the percentage of people whose class status changed over time. The government dropped this question from all major surveys in the 1980s, on the basis that class was no longer a relevant category. The abolition of the system of class status in the 1980s makes it challenging to assess social mobility from the official data.

Mobility can also be measured in terms of other metrics such as urbanization, the size of the workforce in the state sector or different groups' access to party membership. Unfortunately, the official statistics, produced under Mao and published in revision during the Reform era, are seldom disaggregated by categories such as class, gender and ethnicity. This makes it difficult to assess how different systems of labeling intersected. It is possible to look, for example, at how women or ethnic minorities fared on some particular measure, but if we want to narrow the question to, say, minority women with a rural *hukou* who were classified as "poor peasants," we find that the data simply do not exist.

The data also limits us in other ways. For instance, on the question of political participation, we have a reasonably clear picture of the membership of formal institutions such as the party or the Communist Youth League. During the early Cultural Revolution, however, the main engine driving changes in social status was not the party-state apparatus but a set of chaotic, fast-changing social movements. The membership of the rebel mass organizations fluctuated considerably, and many groups rose and fell in the course of a few months. Official organizations – the All China Federation of Trade Unions, the Women's Federation, the Youth League – collapsed and were only rebuilt in the early 1970s, or in some cases even later.

One of the most important determinants of a person's political status was the ability to join the Communist Party itself. In 1950, the CCP had 5.8 million members, equivalent to 1.1 percent of the total population. By 1977, this number had increased markedly to 35 million, or 3.7 percent of the population when population growth is accounted for (see Table 7.2). Despite this increase, it should be stressed that the CCP remained a highly selective organization – in Leninist terms, a vanguard party. In many other authoritarian regimes, ruling parties sought to co-opt the structures of the state by pressuring all public servants to become party members. While this method had its advantages, the usual result was that "opportunists" began to outnumber "true believers," diluting the ranks of the faithful and reducing the ability to pursue truly radical policies. Under Mao, the CCP appears to have avoided this trap. In fact, one of the hallmarks of the early PRC was the way in which real political power was centralized in the hands of a select, elite few. Cadres at the lower levels, and during the Cultural Revolution even cadres at the highest levels, faced a constant threat to their position from intra-party purges.

Table 7.2 *Communist Party membership figures, 1950–1977*

Year	Party Members (in millions)	Percentage of Chinese Population (%)
1950	5.8	1.1
1952	6	1.0
1953	6.4	1.1
1954	6.5	1.1
1955	7	1.1
1956	12	2.0
1957	12.7	2.0
1958	12.5	1.9
1959	13.5	2.0
1961	17	2.6
1969	22	2.7
1973	28	3.1
1977	35	3.7

Source: Ma Yuping and Huang Yuchong (eds.), *Zhongguo zuotian yu jintian: 1840–1987 guoqing shouce* (Beijing: Jiefangjun chubanshe, 1989), pp. 685–686. Chinese population figures extracted from Yuan Yongxi, *Zhongguo renkou (Zonglun)* (Beijing: Zhongguo caizheng jingji chubanshe, 1991), pp. 84–85.

One especially important avenue of social mobility in the Mao era was rural-urban migration. Urbanization – moving people out of the countryside into the cities – has often been regarded as a sign of social modernization, and many peasants in the early PRC sought to escape their villages for a more prosperous life inside the urban welfare system. Attempts to measure Mao era urbanization statistically are complicated by the fact that state definitions of "urban areas" were not consistent across the decades. Different datasets also disagree on how to treat the suburban agricultural population, which was sometimes considered part of the "population of cities and towns" and sometimes excluded.[70] Another quirk in the data is the Mao-era practice of including workers in factories located outside the cities in the non-agricultural (i.e. urban) population statistics.

With these caveats in mind, let us examine the figures. According to official statistics, the years between 1949 and 1961 saw an increase of the urban population from around 10 to 19 percent of the national total. The post-famine "sending down" of 26 million workers reduced this to 14 percent in 1964, before a slight uptick in the following years. During the Cultural Revolution (1966–1976), the urbanization rate held steady at around 17 percent.

70 Thomas Scharping, "Urbanization in China since 1949," *The China Quarterly*, No. 109 (1987), p. 102.

The increase in overall population meant that even this apparent stagnation still represented an increase in absolute terms. A little over 61 million people lived in the cities and towns in 1950, but by 1976 that figure had risen to 163 million (see Table 7.3 for detail). In two and a half decades, the urban population had more than doubled.

A slightly different picture emerges when we examine only those members of the non-agricultural population who actually lived in cities or towns. Between 1968 and 1976, the non-agrarian population in urban areas never exceeded 12 percent of the national total, suggesting an urbanization rate much lower than the 17 percent cited above.[71] This low rate is attributable to two major factors: the strict enforcement of the *hukou* system and higher rural than urban birth rates. If we think in terms of percentage rates rather than absolute figures, urban–rural mobility was low in the Mao era, especially considering the ongoing push towards industrialization, which tended to bring new migrants into the cities. During the Cultural Revolution, for instance, millions of peasants were recruited onto the state payroll and sent to work in factories. Yet, as one scholar has argued, this move was ultimately population-neutral, because it was almost exactly balanced by the number of middle school graduates sent down to the countryside under the "up to the mountains, down to the villages" program. One of the primary benefits of this policy was that it allowed the state to avoid the burden of integrating these students into the labor market and the welfare system, thereby helping to hedge against the costs of urbanization.[72]

Permanent employment, into which the new peasant-workers were recruited in the 1970s, was by far the most desirable form of work. It was also fast-growing. The workforce in the state-owned enterprises increased from 10 million in 1950 to 68.6 million in 1976, while in the collectively owned enterprises the rise was even more rapid, from 1.3 million in 1955 to 18.1 million in 1976. In total, about 75 million people were recruited into the socialist urban workforce during the Mao era. For most, access to the iron rice bowl would have meant a great improvement in their standard of living, especially compared to life "outside the system" or "before liberation." From their perspective, social mobility was a genuine reality. In consequence, it seems inappropriate to dismiss the class status and *hukou* systems as a form of medieval "estate." Certainly, people unlucky enough to be classified among the "four elements" were treated as outcasts, with few opportunities to improve their situation. However, they accounted for less than 10 percent of the population. For the rest, mobility

71 Yuan Yongxi (ed.), *Zhongguo renkou zonglun*, p. 277.
72 Bonnin, *Shiluo de yidai*, pp. 56–58.

Table 7.3 *Urbanization in China between 1949 and 1976 (all figures in millions)*

Year	Population	Population of Cities and Towns	Urbanization Rate (%)	Non-Agricultural Population
New Democracy				
1949	541.67	57.65	10.6	94.41
1950	551.96	61.69	11.2	91.37
1951	563.00	66.32	11.8	86.74
1952	574.82	71.63	12.5	82.91
Socialist Transformation				
1953	587.69	78.26	13.3	87.29
1954	602.66	82.49	13.7	92.29
1955	614.65	82.85	13.5	93.35
1956	628.28	91.85	14.6	100.02
1957	646.53	99.49	15.4	106.18
Great Leap Forward				
1958	659.94	107.21	16.2	122.10
1959	672.07	123.71	18.4	135.67
1960	662.07	130.73	19.7	137.31
1961	658.59	127.07	19.3	124.15
Adjustment of the National Economy				
1962	672.95	116.59	17.3	112.71
1963	691.72	116.46	16.8	115.84
1964	704.99	129.50	18.4	116.77
1965	725.38	130.45	18.0	121.22
Cultural Revolution				
1966	745.42	133.13	17.86	123.40
1967	763.68	135.48	17.74	126.37
1968	785.34	138.38	17.62	125.54
1969	806.71	141.17	17.50	124.03
1970	829.92	144.24	17.38	126.60
1971	852.29	147.11	17.26	133.50
1972	871.77	149.35	17.13	136.32
1973	892.11	153.45	17.20	139.92
1974	908.59	155.95	17.16	140.79
1975	924.20	160.30	17.34	142.78
1976	937.17	163.41	17.44	145.17

Source: Lu Yu, *Xin Zhongguo renkou wushi nian* (Beijing: Zhongguo renkou chubanshe, 2004), Vol. 1, p. 633.

Figure 7.5: Gulou East Street in Beijing, 1975.
Source: Photograph by Helmut Opletal.

might not come easily, but it was achievable, even if one's prospects were ultimately dependent on the goodwill of the party-state.

The regulation from the center of social mobility, urban–rural migration and access to jobs or political institutions produced many disturbing outcomes, but there was some logic to the CCP's methods, however unsavory they might appear to those coming from a different tradition. On occasions when the government relaxed controls on rural-urban migration, the number of workers in the cities tended to grow at unsustainable speeds, as was the case during the Great Leap and in the early 1970s. The center was then forced to tighten control again and to "adjust" access to the cities to preserve limited resources. It seems to me that struggles around the rural-urban divide and inclusion or exclusion based on class status were an almost unavoidable consequence of the way the CCP tried to manage resources. In establishing the party-state as a gatekeeper, it ensured that these conflicts would become politicized.

How did the Mao era impact on women, who Mao famously spoke of as "may hold up half the sky"? By the end of the Cultural Revolution, women had been integrated into the state-owned industries and were doing more "men's jobs" than had been the case in the 1950s. However, the division of labor remained gendered. In 1977, 20 million women were employed in state-owned work units out of a total workforce of 71 million, compared to 2.1 out of 18 million in 1953. This was a significant improvement, but of those 20 million only around 8.5 million worked in industry, a relatively low proportion. A further 3.3 million worked in science, culture, education and health, 2.9 million in agriculture, forestry, irrigation works and meteorology and 2.7 million in the trade, food and service sectors.[73]

In terms of political participation, women did not hold up even close to half the sky. In key political institutions, women accounted for well below half of the members. The proportion of women in the National People's Congress increased from 12 percent in 1954 to 22 percent in 1975, while on the Congress's Standing Committee women's representation rose from 5 percent to 25 percent in the same period. Women made up 4.1 percent of the CCP's Central Committee in 1956 and a marginally better 10.2 percent in 1975. In the same year, around one-third of all members of the Communist Youth League were women.[74] The state constitutions of 1954 and 1975 included the principal of "equality of men and women," but no concrete quotas were set for women's participation. As the above figures suggest, some progress was being made, and the level of participation was comparatively good for this period. However, it was far from outstanding, and it was certainly well below what the party claimed to aspire to. The (almost entirely male) party leadership consistently supported the training and recruitment of women, but there was never a concerted effort to share power equally. In part because of the failure to socialize care work in the cities, political life remained a particularly unfriendly arena for married women and those with children. The party provided maids for high-ranking female cadres, but for ordinary women hoping to begin careers as activists life could be challenging indeed. The situation tended to be worse in the countryside, where kindergartens and retirement homes did not exist on a large scale.

Turning to issues of ethnicity, we find that the ratio of ethnic minorities to the Han majority remained stable through the Mao era. The Han constituted 93.9 percent of the Chinese population in 1953, 94.2 percent in 1964 and 93.3 percent in 1982.[75] In terms of political representation, the CCP seems to have followed its policy on women's issues and to have avoided setting official

---

73 Guojia tongjiju shehui tongjisi (ed.), *Zhongguo laodong gongzi tongji ziliao* (Beijing: Guojia tongji chubanshe, 1987), p. 32. For the total numbers of employees in the state-owned industries see: Zhonggong zhongyang shujichu yanjiushi lilunzu (ed.), *Dangqian woguo gongren*, Vol. 2, pp. 105–107.

74 Based on: Zhonghua quanguo funü lianhehui funü yanjiusuo (ed.), *Zhongguo funü tongji ziliao* (Beijing: Zhongguo tongji chubanshe, 1991), pp. 571, 572, 575.

75 Yuan Yongxi (ed.), *Zhongguo renkou zonglun*, p. 439.

quotas for key institutions. However, the figures suggest that there may have been an unofficial quota policy. Ethnic minorities made up 5.2 percent of the 8th Central Committee elected in 1956 and 5.6 percent of the 10th Central Committee elected in 1973. In the National People's Congress, minority representatives decreased from 14.5 percent of the total in 1954 to 9.4 percent in 1975. Even with this decline, minorities remained over-represented in the People's Congress (though they were slightly under-represented in the Central Committee). This level of representation chimes with the CCP's efforts to manage minorities through a United Front strategy, which required that they be given a seat at the table even as the mostly Han central leadership retained overall authority.

The percentage of minority students enrolled in universities increased from 1.3 percent in 1950–1951 to 6.4 percent in 1975–1976. Over the next two decades, 7 percent appears to have been the ceiling for minority enrollment.[76] This number reflected almost exactly the minorities' share of the total population. Given that most of those classified as ethnic minorities came from poor, predominantly rural parts of western China, it seems unlikely that this could have been achieved without policies of affirmative action. The CCP's vision of a multi-ethnic society, with minorities represented according to their population share, was at least partially achieved. However, as with women, very few ethnic minority figures served in key positions in either the central party leadership or the government.

A Failed Succession

One of the most important projects of Mao's later years was the effort to "cultivate the successors of the revolution."[77] The Chairman was concerned that, after his death, China might fall victim to the same "revisionism" that he believed was afflicting the USSR. In Marxist-Leninist terms, China remained a society in transition, and true communism was a long-term aspiration rather than a present reality. The CCP's considerable achievements would be meaningless unless it could ensure that the revolutionary mission would outlast its leader. For Mao, this made it necessary to cultivate, not only his personal successor, but also new social forces that would ensure support for whoever

---

76 Barry Sautman, "Preferential Policies for Ethnic Minorities in China: The Case of Xinjiang," *Nationalism and Ethnic Politics*, Vol. 4 (1998), p. 365.

77 For example see: Mao Zedong, "Peiyang wuchanjieji de geming jiebanren," in Zhongyang wenxian chubanshe (ed.), *Jianguo yilai Mao Zedong wengao* (Beijing: Zhongyang wenxian chubanshe, 1996), Vol. 11, pp. 85–87.

was selected. Any verdict on the early PRC must acknowledge that, on these terms, Mao's leadership failed. Mao twice picked successors, only to subsequently abandon them. Liu Shaoqi, who in 1956 had seemed the obvious choice, was pilloried as "capitalist roader number one" a decade later. The party constitution of 1969 formally named Lin Biao as the party's next leader, but by the end of 1971 Lin was dead, having apparently been behind an abortive coup attempt.

Figure 7.6: The swimming pool at Beijing University, 1975.
Source: Photograph by Helmut Opletal.

Radicals such as Zhang Chunqiao or Jiang Qing seem to have been the most consistently loyal to Mao's agenda of "continuous revolution." However, the Chairman was aware that both were too politically isolated to hold the party leadership together after his death. We cannot be entirely sure who Mao eventually endorsed to succeed him, but the new leadership went to great lengths to prove the legitimacy of Hua Guofeng's claim. In hindsight, it is clear that Hua moved the country in a different direction than Mao would have anticipated. Not only did he order the arrest of the Gang of Four, but he also laid the foundation for the policies of Reform and Opening Up pursued by Deng Xiaoping, the man who displaced him in the late 1970s.[78] To be sure, Mao had criticized his wife Jiang Qing, but it seems unlikely that he would have approved the arrest of the radical leaders.

Outside the political elite, the radical forces were isolated and weak in 1976. Confronted with rural poverty during their time in the countryside, many of the 1966 Red Guards had lost faith in revolution. Students and workers who had led the rebel factions in 1966–1967 were in many cases disillusioned and exhausted within a decade. Some would join the CCP in the early 1970s, but only a few, such as Wang Hongwen or Chen Yonggui, ever served in important political positions. During the mass campaigns of the late Cultural Revolution, former rebels found themselves unable to recreate the revolutionary storm of 1966, and Mao himself turned back to revolutionary cadres and the party apparatus for support. In Shandong in 2014, I interviewed a former worker rebel, Li Huilin (ps.), who remains a Maoist activist to this day. As he put it to me:

> If we are talking about the chairman's mistakes, [the most important] is how he treated the Cultural Revolution. In the end, the masses and leading cadres who bravely defended and carried out his line never became a strong, unstoppable force. He did not achieve this goal. If he had achieved this, China would still have hope and would not have changed as it has done in the last thirty years.[79]

Mao's "continuous revolution" ended with his death. However, the CCP did not abandon the legacies of the Mao era wholesale. A quarter-century of his rule could not be entirely cast aside.

78 Fredrick Teiwes and Warren Sun, "China's New Economic Policy under Hua Guofeng: Party Consensus and Party Myths," *The China Journal*, No. 66 (2011), pp. 1–23.
79 Interview with the author, Jinan, September 22, 2014.

DOCUMENT 7.1 "Instruction from the Central Committee of the CCP to fight corruption, theft and speculative buying and selling," February 5, 1970.

Our written instruction from Chairman Mao is: this must be done.

At present, revolution and production are progressing well in our country. Along with the implementation of "struggle, criticize and transform," industrial and rural production have reached a new peak. We have won great success. However, the defeated classes are still struggling. A small group of class enemies not only seeks to counter-attack politically, but also launches offensives against the socialist economy. They collaborate with ne'er-do-wells who have lain concealed in state financial departments. Utilizing bourgeois factionalism and [hidden] anarchist potential, they have fuelled an evil fire against the revolutionary economy in order to damage the socialist economic foundation, to interfere with war preparation and to impede the dictatorship of the proletariat. Some of them have embezzled state property and occupied public housing and property; some have benefited from the dissolutions and mergers of public or private institutions and sectors, dividing up the spoils of public property and possessions. Some of them have been involved in speculative selling and buying of [ration] tickets, certificates and state goods and materials; some have established black market factories and shops, formed illegal construction and transportation teams or opened "underground" clubs. Some of them offered or accepted bribes and split the gains, achieving their purposes "through the backdoor"; some developed black markets and made enormous profits. Applying the methods of "corrupting and encroaching, dividing and disintegrating, dragging out and bringing in," they have attempted to disintegrate the revolutionary group and destroy the new-born Revolutionary Committees. This is the trend of class struggle under the new conditions . . .

To crush the class enemies who are attacking us in the economic realm is a struggle to defend socialism and is therefore of the paramount importance for the party. It is necessary to treat this struggle as seriously as our struggle against active counterrevolutionaries. It requires the same broad mobilization of the masses and the same wide publicity. It requires that party leaders take the same responsibility for initiating a mass movement against corruption, theft and speculative buying and selling, for thoroughly revealing any types and levels of crimes in this regard, for educating and criticizing those whose cases are less serious and for dismissing, punishing, sentencing and even executing those whose cases are very serious, as the only way to solve the problem . . .

In order to eradicate corruption, theft and speculative buying and selling and leave no opportunities for class enemies, the Central Committee reiterates:

1. Except for state commerce, cooperative commerce and franchised businesses, work units and individuals are prohibited from engaging in commercial activities.
2. Market regulation must be enhanced and irregular goods should be barred from coming onto the market.
3. Without permission from local authorities, no unit is permitted to purchase goods from markets or from rural communes and cooperative teams. Exchange of goods in the name of "cooperation" is prohibited; "entering though the backdoor" is forbidden.
4. All underground factories, stores, construction and transportation teams and clubs should be eliminated.

DOCUMENT 7.1 (cont.)

5. It is necessary to strengthen business management and enhance supervision by the masses in all units, to establish and improve rules and regulations. Financial and economic discipline must be strict and loopholes must be filled.

The Central Committee calls on the entire party, army and nation to follow the teachings of the great leader Chairman Mao to never forget class struggle, to act forcefully under the leadership of the party, to unite and to fight resolutely against the attacks of the capitalist class, to reinforce and develop a socialist economic foundation and thus to reinforce the dictatorship of the proletariat.

2 May 1970

(This document shall be passed down to the county/regimental level)

Source: Song Yongyi (ed.), *The Chinese Cultural Revolution Database* (Hong Kong: Universities Service Centre for China Studies, The Chinese University of Hong Kong, 2006).

DOCUMENT 7.2 Li Qinglin's letter to Mao Zedong.

Respected Chairman Mao,

Firstly, I want to express greetings to you.

I am a primary school teacher and my home is in the town of Chengguan, Putian county, Fujian province. My family background is that of a poor peasant. I have been a teacher for 20 years now.

My son, Li Liangmo, graduated from middle school in 1968. In 1969, he heard your instruction, "It is necessary that the urban educated youth should go to the countryside to receive a second education from the poor and lower middle peasants." He registered without hesitation to go "up to the mountains, down to the villages." The government dispatched him to Shuiban production brigade in Qiuliu Commune in the mountainous areas of Putian, to settle and work on farm land . . .

In the first place, his grain ration [in the commune] has been consistently inadequate. For six months or more every year, he has to come home and get grain on the black market in order to survive. Even during the best year, when he received 200 *jin* of mixed rice crops and about 230 *jin* of wheat, he still had no food. After drying, the mixed rice crops came to only about 100 *jin*. On this small food ration, my son has to survive and perform hard manual labor in wet fields. This is impossible, all the more so since he is young and full of energy and therefore needs to eat more.

My child is participating in agricultural labor in a mountain area, but the grain ration is too low for him to eat his fill, and he has never received a bonus or one cent of labor income. If he eats all of his food, he has no money to buy more. His clothes have worn through because of all the labor he has performed, but he has no money to replace them. If he falls ill, he has no money to see a doctor and cannot cover his other daily expenses . . . Since he went "up to the mountains, down to the villages," he has not had a separate room to live in and has been lodging in the rooms of poor and lower middle peasants . . .

DOCUMENT 7.2 (cont.)

Among those of our educated youth who have gone "up the mountains, down to the villages," some do not perform manual labor, do not keep self-discipline and do not seriously accept a second education by the poor and lower middle peasants. Instead they rely on the political influence of their relatives and friends, using personal connections to enter through the backdoor and get priority for job assignments, student enrollment or recruitment as cadres. Many relatives, friends and children of powerful revolutionary cadres are transferred out [of the countryside] in the name of "the necessities of development and the course of the socialist construction of the state." This can happen within only a few days of their going "up to the mountain and down to the villages," even if they are from rich peasant and landlord backgrounds . . .

Under these circumstances, the children of ordinary rural primary school teachers, who have no one to rely on on the political stage, have no choice [but to remain]. Naturally, they will not be transferred in the name of "the necessities of development and the course of the socialist construction of the state." They are qualified only to be down in the mud in the villages their whole lives, working for the revolution . . . I think it is correct that my child is following this road, going "up to the mountain, down to the villages" to perform agricultural labor . . . However, while practicing farming, he is facing real problems and difficulties that an individual alone is unable to shoulder. My demand is that the government will soon make a reasonable decision to allow my child to eat from his own strength [i.e. be self-sufficient]. I believe that I am not going too far and making unreasonable trouble or harsh demands.

Respectfully,
Li Qinglin

Xialin Primary School, Chengguan Commune, Putian county, Fujian province 20 December 1972.

Source: Song Yongyi (ed.), *The Chinese Cultural Revolution Database* (Hong Kong: Universities Service Centre for China Studies, The Chinese University of Hong Kong, 2006).

8 LEGACIES AND CONTINUITIES OF THE MAO ERA IN REFORM CHINA

拨乱反正
Bring order out of chaos
实事求是
Seek truth from facts
告别革命
Farewell to revolution

On August 17, 1979, husband and wife Emi and Eva Siao received documents confirming their rehabilitation. Both had spent seven years in prison during the Cultural Revolution (1967–1974), accused of being Soviet spies. For six of those years, all contact between them was cut, and the couple had no news of each other. In her memoirs, Eva Siao recalls the formal act of rehabilitation at Beijing's Friendship Hospital:

> Two representatives of the Ministry of Public Security were present, two from the Writer's Association and two from the Xinhua News Agency [her previous work unit]. One comrade from Public Security announced our rehabilitation and put two documents on the table, one for Emi and one for me. . . . Emi began to cry and sobbed the whole time from excitement, feeling deeply moved . . . To celebrate the day, I spoke a few words and expressed my joy that nobody and nothing can suppress the truth . . . All of our friends, relatives and colleagues, who had suffered because of us, were informed by the Ministry of Public Security about our rehabilitation.[1]

Eva and Emi had been released from prison in 1974, but prior to their rehabilitation they had had to "wear the hat" as "Soviet spies." In 1979, things were finally put right. The couple's money and personal effects, which had been confiscated

1 Eva Siao, *China: Mein Traum, mein Leben* (Bergisch Gladbach: Gustav Lübbe Verlag, 1990), p. 387.

by the authorities, were returned. They were allowed to move from low-grade housing into a modern apartment with seven rooms and hot water around the clock. Eva was permitted to return to her old unit, the Xinhua News Agency, where she had worked as a photographer in the early 1950s. Her husband received twelve years of back pay to cover the period of his persecution, and his party membership was restored. Emi had fallen a long way: he had been a school mate of Mao in Hunan, a party member since 1922, and a high-ranking official writer who had even compiled a biography of the chairman's early life in 1951. In the 1980s, his works were finally published again. He and Eva both became members of the Chinese People's Political Consultative Conference.

This book includes a number of photographs taken by Eva in the 1950s. Her life story is especially interesting in terms of classification, in part because her fate was intertwined with the question of citizenship. Born the daughter of a Jewish doctor in Breslau in 1911, she had fled Germany during Nazi rule, first to Sweden and then to the Soviet Union. There she met Emi in 1934, and the two fell in love and married, after which Eva took Soviet citizenship. From 1941 to 1944, the couple settled in the CCP's rural base area in Yan'an. After liberation, Eva initially worked for Xinhua, before becoming the Beijing film correspondent for East German television between 1958 and 1964. Her monthly salary, 500 yuan, was extraordinarily high for that time. After the Sino-Soviet split, in 1964 she decided to renounce her Soviet nationality for citizenship of the PRC. Soon, however, she was forced to give up her job, because, as the authorities told her, it was not permissible for the Chinese in her unit to work for foreigners. Her real difficulties began with the Cultural Revolution, when like many multi-ethnic couples and foreigners living in Beijing, including PRC citizens, she and Emi were accused of being spies. In later years, Eva recalled her eventual rehabilitation as a case of restorative justice. Despite spending seven years behind bars, she referred to China as "my dream, my love" in the title of her memoir. Her experience exemplifies the rehabilitation and change of status that many received in the 1980s.

This final chapter will discuss the lasting impact of the Mao era on China since 1978. After the end of the Cultural Revolution, the CCP leadership felt the need to reorder the classification system to legitimate social and political hierarchies. It also faced another challenge, namely constructing a narrative to explain which legacies of the Mao era were valuable and which were to be discarded. Under the leadership of Deng Xiaoping, the system of class status and the "class line" were abolished, but categorization of the population based on urban versus rural *hukou*, rank, gender and ethnicity are still in place today. This chapter will attempt to show how Chinese society has been transformed in terms of class and gender over almost four decades of reform. Finally, it will

Figure 8.1: Self-portrait of Eva Siao.
Source: Museum Ludwig.

explore the ways in which the new inequalities of "capitalism with Chinese characteristics" relate to the legacies of the Mao era.

Narrating the Legacies of the Mao Era

Overcoming the 1978 Divide

Xi Jinping, the CCP general secretary and state president at the time of writing, draws on Maoist rhetoric and the legacy of the early PRC more frequently and consciously than any other leader in the Reform era. Xi has pointedly stated that that no one should use the "first thirty years" of the PRC to deny the "following thirty years" or vice versa.[2] On the one hand, this declaration is directed against pro-Western liberals who downplay or deny the achievements of the Mao era. On the other, it also represents an attack on the Neo-Maoist view that since 1978 the country has been ruled by "capitalist roaders" who have turned China away from true socialism. Implicit in this view is the idea that China under Mao and China in the Reform era are not separate entities, but intimately connected. Identifying the extent of this connection remains a challenge for scholars seeking to understand how the two periods of PRC history relate to one another.

Some Western observers argue that continuity is the most important aspect of the story, suggesting that the "invisible hand" of Mao continues to exert a hold over China to this day. These scholars point out that the post-1976 political system in some ways still functions much as it did under the Chairman, albeit with more latitude for "guerrilla-style" and local experimentation in fields such as economics, health care and education.[3] In foreign relations, the continuities are even more striking. China had deeper trade links with capitalist countries than with the socialist Eastern Bloc long before the end of the Mao era. For example, the percentage of trade with the Soviet Union of China's total trade dropped from the peak in 1955 of 56 percent to 6 percent in 1966 and stood at 3 percent in 1976.[4] The PRC's rapprochement with the United States was not a Reform era innovation, but a Mao period strategy to counter Soviet pressure. Although it would be an exaggeration to describe China as having "opened up to the world" under Mao rather than Deng Xiaoping, it is important to recognize that the foundations for a multi-polar world order were laid in the early 1970s, well before the latter became paramount leader. I would go so far as to argue that the beginning of the end of the Cold War came in East Asia, not in Europe as has generally been suggested. On the other hand, the conflict had a much clearer end in Europe, where socialism in the Eastern Bloc collapsed entirely after the fall of the Berlin Wall in 1989 and the breakup of the Soviet Union in 1991. In East Asia, the Cold War arguably still continues on the Korean peninsula and across the Taiwan Strait.

Despite these continuities between the Mao and post-Mao periods, scholars have typically found it difficult to escape the "1978 divide." Historians, mostly in the West, have spent more than a decade trying to overcome the enduring

2 Wei Riping, "Zhidao sixiang shangde 'liangjian': Shibada yilai Xi Jinping guanyu jianchi Mao Zedong sixiang zhidao diwei de zhongyao sixiang shulüe," http://dangshi.people.com.cn/n/2014/0814/c85037-25467371-2.html (accessed June 26, 2017).

3 Elizabeth Perry and Sebastian Heilmann, "The Embracing Uncertainty: Guerrilla Policy Style and Adaptive Governance in China," in Elizabeth Perry and Sebastian Heilmann (eds.), *Mao's Invisible Hand: The Political Foundations of Adaptive Governance in China* (Cambridge, MA: Harvard University Asian Center, 2011), pp. 11–15.

4 Shu Guang Zhang, *Economic Cold War: America's Embargo against China and the Sino-Soviet Alliance, 1949–1963* (Washington, DC: Woodrow Wilson Center Press, 2001), pp. 282–283.

paradigm of 1949 as the watershed moment in modern Chinese history and to tease out continuities between Republican China and the PRC. This has proved more challenging for the Reform era. Partly the difficulty has stemmed from divergent disciplinary approaches: post-1976 China is seldom studied as history and is more usually viewed through the lens of the social sciences. Access to sources is another problem. According to China's Archive Law, documents should generally be opened to the public after thirty years, but many archives provide little access to files from the 1980s. For PRC scholars, the official narrative of the CCP – that the leadership around Deng made no serious mistakes – makes critical academic research on the 1980s a daunting prospect politically. Work on sensitive issues, such as the draconian early one-child policy, the disastrous war against Vietnam in 1979 or the Tiananmen Massacre of 1989, can pose real career risks.

Restoration and Reform

Since 1981, the CCP has stuck rigidly to a single official verdict on party history from the foundation of the PRC to Mao's death, essentially closing the lid on further discussion within the party.[5] The leadership around Deng also made a deliberate decision in the early 1980s not to pursue a "de-Maoization" to match the de-Stalinization seen in the Soviet Union in the late 1950s. In 1956, Khrushchev had drawn a distinction between a good Lenin, the founder of the Soviet party and state, and a more problematic Stalin, whose "cult of personality" had tainted the legacy of the 1917 October Revolution. The self-destructive Great Purge against party members (1937–1938) was presented as Stalin's major crime, and Lenin's example was used to criticize Stalin's mistakes. In China, the option to differentiate between a good and a bad supreme leader was not possible. Mao was both China's Lenin, founder of the state, and its Stalin, prosecutor of violent and destructive purges inside the party.

The official 1981 verdict recognized Mao as a "great proletarian revolutionary" and as the founder of the PRC, but added that he had committed serious "leftist mistakes," for instance by promoting the Great Leap Forward. The Cultural Revolution was described as a "great disaster for the party and the people," although responsibility for the persecution of innocent people was ascribed to a "counterrevolutionary conspiracy" by the Gang of Four in which Mao himself had no involvement.[6] The resolution declared that Mao had been

---

5 See: Susanne Weigelin-Schwiedrzik, "In Search of a Master Narrative for 20th-Century Chinese History," *The China Quarterly*, Vol. 188 (2006), pp. 1074–1075.
6 "Guanyu jianguo yilai dang de ruogan lishi wenti de jueyi," http://cpc.people.com.cn/GB/64162/ 64168/64563/65374/4526452.html, (accessed June 7, 2017); see also: Alexander C. Cook,

wrong to believe class struggle between the proletariat and bourgeoisie would be the major contradiction under socialism. It also stressed that this and other "ultra-leftist" ideas were not to be considered part of core Mao Zedong Thought. The notion that Mao Zedong Thought did not encompass all of Mao's personal views was an important one, since it allowed the CCP to flexibly reinterpret this key aspect of party theory according to changing ideological needs. Thus, even in the aftermath of the Cultural Revolution, Deng was able to characterize Mao Zedong Thought as the "collective treasure" of the party and even to draw his central slogan, "Seek truth from facts," from Mao's writings.[7]

Official documents from the early Deng era do not describe the new reform policies as a radical break with the Mao years. Between 1978 and 1982, one central slogan was "bring order out of chaos" (*boluan fanzheng*), or, more precisely, "set right things which have been thrown into disorder." This was partly a call for a return to the past, not a move away from it. The leadership argued that the Cultural Revolution had damaged China on almost every front, from the party apparatus and the planned economy to the United Front with intellectuals and ethnic minorities, the education and legal systems, and the correct understanding of Mao Zedong Thought. Now the party would remedy that damage and return to the order and progress of the state's early golden age.

In this context, it was essential to rehabilitate victims of the Cultural Revolution, as well as cadres who believed in the pre-1966 political system. One important step in this regard was the leadership's decision to abolish the label of "capitalist roader." Not all cadres who had been purged during the Cultural Revolution were rehabilitated, and the government did not offer a general amnesty. However, according to official statistics, of those cadres purged during the Cultural Revolution and earlier campaigns, over 3 million were rehabilitated, and 470,000 party memberships were restored.[8] The 1959–1961 campaign against "right opportunism" was labeled a mistake. The party also re-evaluated several major cases against cadres accused of "counterrevolution" during the Socialist Education Campaign (1963–1967). The official press argued that efforts to correct the wrongs of the Cultural Revolution would involve not only the revision of individual verdicts, but also a return to the policies of the "golden era" of the 1950s, when the major state and party institutions had been established.

The Cultural Revolution on Trial: Mao and the Gang of Four (Cambridge: Cambridge University Press, 2016), pp. 198–200.

7 Mao Zedong, "Zhongguo gongchandang zai minzu zhanzheng zhong de diwei," in *Mao Zedong Xuanji*, Vol. 2, www.marxists.org/chinese/maozedong/marxist.org-chinese-mao-19381014.htm (accessed June 29, 2018).

8 Zhang Shifei, *Zhongguo dangdai shehuishi (1978–1992)* (Changsha: Hunan renmin chubanshe, 2011), Vol. 4, p. 55.

As well as rehabilitations at the lower levels of the party, central leaders were also brought back into the fold. Those permitted to return to office included Deng Xiaoping (1977), Bo Yibo (1978) and Peng Zhen (1979), all of whom took up senior positions once more. Others such as Peng Dehuai (1978) and Liu Shaoqi (1980) were posthumously rehabilitated, a move which both restored their reputations and had an impact on surviving family members and close subordinates. The younger leaders charged with day-to-day administration in the early Reform era, such as CCP General Secretary Hu Yaobang and his successor Zhao Ziyang, were also "revolutionary cadres" from the old guard. To question the Mao era as a whole would have tarnished the legitimacy of the entire revolutionary generation and brought their contributions towards building the new China into doubt.

Competing factions inside the party deployed the legacies of the 1950s in different ways. After the chaos of the Cultural Revolution, cadres around Hua Guofeng argued for better institutionalization of the planned economy. Since 1958, mass campaigns and factional fighting at the top had often disturbed long-term economic planning, something Hua's supporters were keen to avoid. Meanwhile, the reformers around Deng revived the language of New Democracy to justify the recreation of the United Front with "bourgeois" intellectuals and private businessmen. The New Democratic order of 1949–1952 furnished abundant references to a mixed economy in which public ownership and central planning coexisted alongside private business and the free market. By the time of the 3rd Plenum of the 11th Central Committee in December 1978, the reformist faction had won out against Hua, and Deng was keen to press home the advantage. The emerging paramount leader had helped restore the prestige of the "revolutionary cadres," but he now sensed that many of those same cadres could not be relied upon to support economic reforms. Most agreed with him in rejecting the legacy of the Cultural Revolution, but many favored a return to more orthodox Marxist-Leninist policies rather than Deng's market-oriented approach. To reduce the opposition's power base, the new party leadership under Deng established a system of obligatory retirement for "revolutionary cadres," whom it took to describing as "old cadres." Official numbers suggest that, by 1986, 1.7 million "old cadres," 68 percent of the total, had taken retirement under this scheme.[9] The leadership justified the measure as a necessary step towards modernization and an opportunity to recruit younger, more educated and more professional cadres. Generous retirement benefits encouraged the old guard to accept an honorable retreat.

9 Ibid., p. 56.

The first radical break with the Mao era was the decollectivization of agriculture. The breakup of the People's Communes had already begun in some provinces by the late 1970s, but it was not until 1983 that the policy was adopted centrally. That year, the Central Committee announced the replacement of the communes with a so-called "household responsibility system." Collective land was to be distributed to individual families, who would have to fulfill grain quotas but could sell any remaining surplus on the open market. In practice this system was not actually new: a similar model had appeared unofficially at the local level at various points in 1956, 1961 and the early 1970s. Nor is it entirely correct to say that the rural family economy was "restored" under Deng, since even in the People's Communes plots for private use had continued to be distributed to individual households.

Mao had called the system of household responsibility "revisionist," but the leadership around Deng argued that it was merely another form of socialist economy. Land remained collectively owned even after the People's Communes were dissolved. From an orthodox Marxist-Leninist point of view, decollectivization was undeniably a step back on the road towards a full transformation of ownership structures. However, it should be stressed that Deng's reforms did not call into question the main achievements of 1949 revolution. Land distribution remained relatively egalitarian, and no new landlord class arose after decollectivization.

Undoubtedly, the legitimacy of the CCP since 1978 has been partly performance-based, with the party attracting support for its success in ensuring high economic growth, improved living standards, internal stability and the continued global rise of China. However, from the very start of the Reform era the CCP has pushed a narrative of continuity with the legacy of the Mao era. The legitimacy of the party rests not only on performance, but also on its claim to have succeeded in overcoming the less positive aspects of this legacy while preserving the better ones.

A further example of the way in which Mao-era concepts survive, reinterpreted, in contemporary party historiography can be seen in the use of terms such as "two-line struggle." During the Cultural Revolution, this referred to the struggle between the line of the "revolutionary headquarters" under Mao on the one hand and the alleged "revisionists" around Liu Shaoqi on the other. The clash between these two lines was regarded as an expression of the class struggle between the proletariat and bourgeoisie, as well as a symbol of the two potential roads that these forces represented, one leading towards fully fledged socialism and one to the restoration of capitalism. In the post-1978 narrative, this struggle was reimagined as a battle between "old cadres" such as Liu, Deng and Zhou Enlai and villainous ultra-leftists such as Jiang Qing or Wang Hongwen, who attempted to force out committed party leaders by branding them revisionists. This new narrative is of course a contortion of history. Liu, after all, was a chief supporter of the radical utopian projects of the Great Leap in 1958, and he also led a brutal attack on rural party organizations during the Socialist Education Campaign in 1964. The supposedly saintly Deng led the Anti-Rightist Campaign of 1957, while Zhou was deeply involved in the campaigns of the Cultural Revolution and the power seizures of early 1967. As is so often the case, official history in China has been written by the winners.

Reordering Classification

China's classification system today maintains striking continuities with the Mao era. Only one of the five major categorizations (urban/rural, rank, class, gender and ethnicity) has been abolished. In the early 1980s, the reformist leadership dismantled the system of class status, and with it the longstanding policy of "affirmative action" for workers and peasants. Beyond class, the population is still divided between rural and non-rural residents by the *hukou* system, resulting in differing entitlements to land, welfare and education. In state-owned industries and the party apparatus, distribution of goods and housing by rank is more hierarchical than ever. For high-level cadres and intellectuals, monetary salaries are only a part of a larger package of goods and entitlements. Gender is still classified according to a male/female binary, without additional options.

The ethnic classification system established in the Mao era, which divides China between the Han and fifty-five minority nationalities, remains in place and continues to reproduce itself as new generations are born into these categories. The state has not recognized a new minority since the Jinuo of Yunnan were added to the list in 1979. The government still regards ethnicity as something to be identified from above, leaving no space for identity politics from below. This contrasts with the situation in Taiwan, where groups of "indigenous people" (*yuanzhumin*), previously referred to as "high mountain tribes" (*gaoshanzu*) in Mainland China, can petition for Taiwanese government recognition without waiting for approval. While the CCP had abandoned the "class line" in higher education by the mid-1980s, "affirmative action" based on ethnicity continues to be practiced. This has even led to cases of Han students trying to illegally change the ethnic classification shown on their identity cards in order to gain easier access to university. The central government has also softened or granted exemptions to its birth planning policies in minority regions. As a result, between 1982 and 1985, ethnic minorities' share of the population actually increased in the five

Autonomous Regions of Guangxi, Inner Mongolia, Ningxia, Tibet and Xinjiang.[10]

Despite these continuities, what it means to be officially classed as a "woman," a "rural household" or a "Tibetan" has changed over time. Needless to say, the interpretation of these categories and of who gets what label has been the subject of abiding social and political struggles in Reform-era China. Classification has helped determine prestige, as well as access to resources and political power. However, it should be remembered that, by and large, official classification and its relationship to distribution by the state has become less central for people than it was in the Mao era. The deepening of market reforms in the late 1980s and early 1990s meant that those unable to get "inside the system" or be promoted once they were inside had other options. The possibility of success as a private entrepreneur meant that those "outside the system" were no longer necessarily confined to the margins of society. The state might not provide for you, but it became easier, though by no means simple, to provide for yourself.

Abolishing the System of Class Status

In abolishing the system of class status, the leadership under Deng did not argue that it had been an unjust policy in general, but that the re-education of intellectuals and the four elements (landlords, rich peasants, counterrevolutionaries and bad elements) had been so successful that the system was no longer needed. Class struggle would still exist under socialism, but it would no longer be a cause of major contradiction.[11] Between 1977 and the mid-1980s, class status was systematically eliminated from official life. In 1978, several provinces decided those who had been classified as "landlords or rich peasants who had escaped the net" during the Socialist Education Campaign (1963–1967) should be reclassified as ordinary peasants.[12] In January 1979, the Central Committee ordered that landlords, rich peasants and their children should finally be allowed to "take off the hat." As we have seen, this did not mean full rehabilitation, but it did mean that these people would no longer be treated as enemies or made "objects of class struggle." The decision stated that the vast majority of landlords and rich peasants had been living harmlessly as ordinary laborers since the collectivization of agriculture, nourishing themselves without exploiting others. Except for a few

---

10 Thomas Heberer, *China and its National Minorities: Autonomy or Assimilation?* (Armonk, NY: M.E. Sharpe, 1989), p. 100.

11 *Renmin Ribao*, May 15, 1979.

12 Xiao Donglian, *Zhonghua renmin gongheguo shi, Vol.10, Lishi de zhuangui: Cong boluan fanzheng dao gaige kaifang (1979–1981)* (Hong Kong: Zhongwendaxue chubanshe, 2008), p. 120.

reactionaries who refused any re-education, they and the rest of the "four elements" could be reclassified as ordinary commune members, subject to approval by the masses and local authorities. These statements carried unmistakable echoes of Deng's speech at the 8th Party Congress in 1956, in which he had argued that "family origin" had lost its importance after the socialist transformation and should be phased out as an official category.

For access to institutions, family origin remained important until 1979, when another decision made political performance the decisive factor once and for all: "Starting from today, if [commune members from landlord or rich peasant backgrounds] want to enter schools, the Youth League, the party or the army, apply for work or receive jobs, we should mainly consider their political performance. They should not be discriminated against."[13] The document declared that the children of these people should be classed as ordinary commune members, a clear statement that bad family origin would not be passed on to the third generation (see Document 8.1). These measures were a major step towards abolishing the system of class status as a whole. Classifying all peasants as "commune members" brought China closer to the position of socialist states in the Eastern Bloc and represented a move away from the complex system of class status (including individual status, family background and political performance) that had been in place since the founding of the PRC. With the dissolution of the People's Communes a few years later, the status of "commune member" also lost its meaning. The move away from the persecution of the "four elements" was billed as a way to address the damage wrought by the Cultural Revolution. Supporting the leadership's decision, the *People's Daily* accused the Gang of Four of causing mental and physical harm to second and even third generation "four elements" by promoting the "bloodline" theory.[14] It had of course been the Maoist left, including Jiang Qing, who had publicly criticized the "bloodline" theory in 1966 (see Chapter 6), but politically the accusation was a useful one.

In 1984, the central government finally decided to allow all the remaining "four elements" to "take off the hat." Numbers are unclear, but one Chinese scholar estimates that over 20 million people had been classified as "four elements" since 1949.[15] Many were already dead, but those who were left were now liberated from the label. The news usually reached them via a simple pro forma document. Document 8.2, sent to Liu Sanyi, who was twenty-seven when he was classified as a rich peasant in 1949, is a typical example. In 1979, after three decades of persecution in mass campaigns and struggle meetings, his only restitution was

---

13 "Zhonggong zhongyang guanyu dizhu, funongfenzi zhaimao wenti he di, fuzinü chengfen wenti de jueding," in Zhonggong zhongyang wenxian yanjiushi (ed.), *Xin shiqi nongye he nongcun gongzuo zhongyao wenxian xuanbian* (Beijing: Zhongyang wenxian chubanshe, 1992), p. 13.
14 Xiao Donglian, *Zhonghua renmin gongheguo shi*, p. 129.   15 Ibid., p. 130.

a piece of paper informing him of his reclassification as an ordinary commune member. He received no apology for his past treatment or the initial verdict against him. His only consolation was that his political problems were over.

In 1979, the party leadership also reclassified all those who had been labeled as capitalists. Deng argued that they, too, were now laborers in the socialist system and no longer lived off exploitation. By this point, only around 86,000 people were still classed as "bourgeois businessmen," which had always been a much smaller category than the "four elements." With the abolition of the label, the discrimination that had prevented their children from entering the party, universities and public employment was ended as well. The government also approved compensation for assets and apartments that had been seized during the Cultural Revolution. This expropriation had had wide-ranging effects: by 1981, most of those who had originally been classified as "bourgeois businessmen" were working as petty entrepreneurs, traders or handicraft workers.[16]

The abolition of the "capitalist" label and the end to discrimination against the second generation were important steps towards restoring entrepreneurial activity and the accumulation of private wealth in China. In the 1980s, private entrepreneurs were referred to not as "capitalists" but by the less emotive term "individual households" (*getihu*). Until 1988, they were permitted to hire only up to eight employees, while collective enterprises could hire as many laborers as they required. This disparity led many private entrepreneurs to "put on the red hat" (*dai hongmaozi*), bribing officials to register their businesses as collective enterprises. Especially at the beginning of the Reform era, some marginalized groups – "four elements," "sent-down youth" and women "outside the system" – chose to become "individual households," allowing them to earn money without having to seek admission to a work unit.

We have already seen that "intellectual" was never a separate class category in the Mao era. However, the exact status of intellectuals was a longstanding source of controversy. In 1978, the party leadership finally decided that intellectuals should be considered part of the working class. In January 1979, a commentary in the *People's Daily* argued that the number of intellectuals in China has risen to around 25 million, against 2 to 3 million intellectuals in the early 1950s. The article suggested that over 70 percent, more than 17.5 million people, were from worker, peasant and cadre backgrounds. Moreover, the majority of intellectuals from the "old society" had now been successfully re-educated and had become "intellectuals of the working class," in which category the paper also placed Marx, Engels and Mao.[17] The application of this label to Mao appears to have been a Reform-era innovation, and it helped to justify a redefinition of the

16 Ibid., p. 134.   17 *Renmin Ribao*, January 4, 1979.

political status of scholars and the intelligentsia. Under Deng's leadership, scientists, university students, professors and cultural producers enjoyed a dramatically improved social situation. Instead of attempting to eliminate the division between intellectual and manual labor, the CCP celebrated scientific modernization as the path to national salvation.

With some exceptions, the CCP was successful in integrating intellectuals into the new order and generating support for the reform agenda. The regime recognized that, in order to foster the creation of a modern technocratic elite, it would be necessary to re-establish meritocratic selection processes for higher education. In 1977, the leadership under Hua Guofeng had revived the national university entrance examinations. Ten million participants sat the first examination, with only 3 percent selected for admission.[18] The national examination had been abolished during the Cultural Revolution in 1966, and throughout the Mao era the party had struggled with the tension between selection by academic performance and "affirmative action" based on class and political considerations. After 1977, family background disappeared as criterion in the centralized admissions process. At the lower levels of the education system, examinations were reintroduced to select students for elite "key-point" schools, which received extra state funding. The new policies towards intellectuals and higher education significantly changed the social makeup of the party. In 1979, only 8 percent of new party members were "intellectuals," but in 1985 they made up 50 percent of the intake.[19]

The final element of the new classification system was the introduction of residential identity cards in 1984. Despite the government's avowed obsession with classification, nothing of this kind had been attempted in the Mao era. The regulation authorizing the creation of the cards limited the categories to be listed to name, sex, ethnic status, place of residence and date of birth, a decision which marked the end of the formal system of class status.[20] The *hukou*, however, remained in place as a separate form of registration.

Redefining Political Labels

One of the most important projects for the new party leadership was the redefinition of political labels that had been imposed during the Mao era campaigns.

18 Joel Andreas, *Rise of the Red Engineers: The Cultural Revolution and the Origins of China's New Class* (Stanford, CA: Stanford University Press, 2009), p. 224.
19 Ibid., p. 235.
20 "Guowuyuan, 'Zhonghua renmin gongheguo jumin shenfenzheng shixing tiaoli'," in Guowuyuan bangongting fazhiju (ed.), *Zhonghua renmin gongheguo fagui huibian (January 1984–December 1984)* (Beijing: Falü chubanshe, 1986), pp. 84–87.

The Anti-Rightist Campaign had officially seen 550,000 intellectuals branded as "rightists." Given that Deng himself had led this movement, it was not possible for its verdicts to be written off wholesale or for the campaign in its entirety to be declared a mistake. The 1981 official resolution on party history was therefore limited to criticizing what the leadership termed "exaggerations" in the campaign's conduct.[21] This opened the door to reassessments of individual verdicts, even as it foreclosed attacks on the Anti-Rightist movement as a whole. By the mid-1980s, the vast majority of accused "rightists" had had their verdicts revised (*gaizheng*). It is important to note here the distinction between *gaizheng* and the stronger *pingfan* or "rehabilitation," which the CCP reserves for cases where it is the integrity of a campaign (rather than an individual verdict) that has come into question.

As part of a program of so-called "practical policies" (*luoshi zhengce*), many former "rightists" were restored to the same positions and work units to which they had been assigned before their verdicts. Many received years of back pay, and their children were assigned better jobs. Responses to these moves varied. Some of those whose verdicts were revised felt liberated by the removal of their label, while others believed that the "practical policies" were grossly inadequate compensation for the destruction meted out to their careers, families or marriages. A significant number of "rightists" had already died by the time their verdicts were re-examined, as a result of anything from old age to hardships in rural exile, starvation or even violent struggle meetings during the Cultural Revolution. The party leadership also had to deal with cases from the 1955 campaign against the "counterrevolutionary clique" of the writer Hu Feng, which had directly affected over 2,100 people, most of them intellectuals. In 1979, Hu himself was released from prison after twenty-four years, and in 1980 the Central Committee announced that he and his "clique" had not in fact been "counterrevolutionaries." However, their actions were still considered "factionalist," and it was not until 1988 that the group was fully rehabilitated.[22] Hu did not live to see his name fully cleared: he had died in 1985.

Deng's unwillingness to revise the verdict on the Anti-Rightist Campaign as a whole did attract some controversy within the CCP hierarchy. In 1980, Li Yisan, who had argued for the rehabilitation of a "big rightist", wrote in a letter to Hu Yaobang that:

> I think now that the Anti-Rightist Campaign of 1957 was a product of the leftist line inside our party. Its characteristics were similar to those of the Cultural Revolution. It was a great mistake and disaster for the state and

21 "Guanyu jianguo yilai dang de ruogan lishi wenti de jueyi."
22 Xiao Donglian, *Zhonghua renmin gongheguo shi*, Vol. 10, p. 122.

occupations. The reform leadership invented new political labels and redefined old ones. "The four elements" and "intellectuals" were essentially defined out of existence as official categories, while the Maoist left and former rebels inside the party, who had previously held considerable prestige on account of their labels, now found themselves subject to purges. Under Hua Guofeng's leadership, the Gang of Four were attacked as "counterrevolutionary elements," "representatives of class enemies and capitalist roaders" and even "GMD spies" in a mass campaign that bore all the hallmarks of the Mao era.[26] One official publication suggests as many as 400,000 people were investigated during purges between 1976 and 1981.[27]

After the victory of the Deng Xiaoping faction in the late 1970s, the purge against the Maoist left underwent a subtle but significant change. In 1981, the party leadership opted for a public trial of the Gang of Four, placing the case against them in a legal rather than a political setting. As one scholar has argued, this choice went hand in hand with the CCP's efforts to establish a socialist legal system at this time.[28] In the event, two trials were held against the "counter-revolutionary cliques" of Jiang Qing and Lin Biao. Both groups, the Gang of Four and the generals around the deceased Lin, were convicted based on the new criminal code adopted in 1979. In their case, "counterrevolution" was not merely a political crime based on state-issued regulations, as it had been under Mao, but a criminal offense according to duly adopted laws. Important as this difference was from the perspective of legal procedure, however, in practical terms it was largely symbolic. The criminal code's definition of "counterrevolutionary activities" differed little from the state regulation of 1951, naming only one specific additional offense of "crimes to harm the socialist economy."[29]

Indeed, despite the move towards more formalized legal procedures, it is reasonable to view the trial at least in part as a political showcase. Jiang and her allies had purged and otherwise harmed large numbers of cadres and ordinary people, but it does not seem appropriate to describe them as "counterrevolutionaries." The trial verdicts outlined a conspiracy between the Maoist left and PLA generals loyal to Lin Biao. In fact, the relationship between these groups during the Cultural Revolution had been antagonistic for most of the time, and the idea that the Gang of Four had planned a conspiracy to overthrow, rather than remake, the party and government is weakly evidenced. Ironically, it was

---

26 Richard C. Kraus, *Class Conflict in Chinese Socialism* (New York, NY: Columbia University Press, 1981), p. 171.

27 Zhang Shifei, *Zhongguo dangdai shehuishi*, p. 56.

28 Cook, *The Cultural Revolution on Trial*, pp. 35–36.

29 "Quanguo renmin daibiao dahui, 'Zhonghua renmin gongheguo xingfa'," *Zhonghua renmin gongheguo fagui huibian (January 1979–December 1979)*, pp. 68–70, part 2, paragraph 2.

Hua Guofeng who came closest to organizing a coup with his decision to deploy the military in the arrest of leftists in the Politburo. Moreover, the new leadership around Deng was happy to use the "counterrevolutionary" label without court approval when it felt the need. Sometimes this occurred retroactively, for instance in the reclassification of the early 1967 "power seizures," which had severe consequences for former rebel leaders from places such as Shanghai and Shandong. The CCP also deployed the label against contemporary threats. The justification for the PLA's violent crackdown against the Tiananmen Square demonstrations on June 4, 1989 was that the participants' actions amounted to "counterrevolutionary turmoil." The label of "counterrevolutionary" continues to have negative consequences for those involved in both the 1989 and 1967 movements.

The purge against the Cultural Revolutionary left should be seen as a parallel process to the move to rehabilitate "rightists" and members of the four elements. Both cases involved significant changes inside the CCP. Between 1982 and 1985, the leadership launched an intra-party purge designed to "clean up three kinds of people." The target was party members who had joined the CCP during the radical campaigns of the Cultural Revolution: "three kinds of people" referred to followers of Lin Biao and the Gang of Four, people with strong factional views, and those who had "vandalized and plundered" during the populist phase of the movement in 1966–1967. Events during struggle sessions against "old cadres" in 1966 or during the armed struggle in 1967 were reinvestigated. Many of the new recruits who had joined in the 1966–1976 period were student and worker rebels recruited as part of Mao's attempt to inject "fresh blood" into the CCP. These recent members were viewed by the reformist faction as having poisoned the party with "ultra-leftist" people and ideas. In other words, the "three kinds of people" were not only punished for the actions of the past, but for the threat the leadership around Deng believed they posed to the new political order they were attempting to fashion.

In some provinces, only "representative persons," such as well-known former rebel leaders, were labeled and imprisoned under the "three kinds of people" designation. Elsewhere, ordinary rebels were labeled as well. Needless to say, only affiliation with the rebel movement or the Maoist left was counted as "factionalism"; support for Deng was acceptable. Sanctions on those found guilty included a ban preventing them being considered for political or professional leadership positions in their work units – essentially a political decapitation of the radical opposition. Deng offered further protection to his own faction by making clear there were likely to be only a few of the "three kinds of people" among the ranks of the "old cadres." Most of the targets of the campaign he suggested, would have been around twenty in 1966, and by the Reform era they would have been in their late thirties or early forties – too young, in other words, to have joined the party as an "old cadre" before 1949.[30]

During my interviews with former rebels in Shanxi in 2015, eyewitnesses expressed a deep frustration about their treatment during Deng's purge. Yang Yuanwu (ps.), already a party member before the Cultural Revolution, had been part of a rebel group that opposed the "power seizure" of January 12, 1967 out of suspicion of the new head of the province, Liu Geping. As tensions escalated, Yang became involved in factional fighting, and he later served in some minor cadre posts. In 1984, he was labeled one of the "three kinds of people" and sentenced to three years in prison. In his words: "As a communist, I was sitting in a communist party prison … I was a party member and a state cadre. I was willing to accept investigation by the party organs, but they should not have locked me up for three years and then placed restrictions on me for 30 years."[31] Yang felt especially aggrieved that his case had been moved from the party's judicial apparatus "inside the system" to an ordinary court "outside the system." He still considered himself a victim, and his attitude to his own involvement in the Cultural Revolution was filtered through this lens.

In 1982, the Central Committee clarified that the "three kinds of people" label could only be applied to those who had been of age in 1966. Actions committed by teenagers were not to be reinvestigated, even if they involved "serious mistakes."[32] In a 1984 decision, the Central Committee reinforced this point:

> Among the student Red Guards who were younger than 18 during the "Cultural Revolution," some were politically inexperienced or committed mistakes under the influence of "leftist" people or ideas, including serious problems such as collectively beating people to death during the campaign "to destroy the four olds". If they acknowledged their mistakes later, understand them correctly and now show good political performance, then the issue should not be raised again.

Only in a few very serious cases, where the offender had already been convicted of murder or plundering, should verdicts be upheld and the culprit face expulsion from the CCP.[33] These decisions protected most early Red Guards, who as we

---

30 Zhonggong zhongyang, "Zhuanfa Deng Xiaoping tongzhi guanyu ruhe huafen he qingli 'sanzhongren' de tanhua," November 16 (1983), in Song Yongyi (ed.), *The Chinese Cultural Revolution Database* (Hong Kong: Universities Service Centre for China Studies, The Chinese University of Hong Kong, 2006).

31 Interview with the author, Taiyuan, September 2015.

32 "Zhonggong zhongyang guanyu qingli lingdao banzi zhong 'sanzhongren' wenti de tongzhi (gaiyao)," December 30 (1982), in Song, *The Chinese Cultural Revolution Database*.

33 "Zhonggong zhongyang, Guanyu qingli 'sanzhongren' ruogan wenti de buchong tongzhi," July 31 (1984), in Song, *The Chinese Cultural Revolution Database*.

have seen were often the children of high-ranking cadres, from further prosecution, even if they were involved in extrajudicial killings during the Red August of 1966. Former rebel students and workers were purged, but the "old cadres" could continue to cultivate their children as political successors.[34]

The events of the Reform Era demonstrate that social control through political labeling played an important role in the PRC even after Mao's death. Today, there is widespread acknowledgment that the CCP remains the only authority able to define labels and revise verdicts. Many alleged "rightists" and members of the 1989 student movement continue to demand rehabilitation from the party.

Ethnic Classification and the United Front

Early Reform-era policies towards the national minorities were intended to "bring order out of chaos," and they showed a striking continuity with the formative years of the PRC in the 1950s. Between 1956 and 1964, scholars working on the government's behalf had carried out a massive research project to determine "the social history of the ethnic minorities," including extensive fieldwork in western China. In the 1980s, many of the reports produced during this period were either reprinted or published for the first time. The post-Mao state leant heavily on knowledge gained in the 1950s and early 1960s to inform its policy proposals. The leadership believed that some groups had been incorrectly labeled during the Cultural Revolution, and so the issue of classification returned to the fore. Encouraged by the government's apparent receptiveness, individuals and groups petitioned to change their classifications. In the late 1970s, eight groups comprising over 900,000 people in the Autonomous Region of Guizhou, perhaps the most ethnically diverse in the country, submitted requests for recognition as minorities, but without success. However, classification remained an unfinished project: the 1982 population census showed that there were still about 800,000 people for whom the government had no data on ethnicity.[35]

That year, the central government commissioned new investigations to reorder ethnic classifications, mainly in Guizhou, Sichuan, Hunan and Hubei. By the end of the year, 5 million people had had their minority status changed or restored. For instance, members of the Man and Tujia groups, who had previously been forced to change their status to Han, became official minorities again. In Sichuan, Gelao who had been wrongly labeled as Yi, Zhuang or Miao

34 Weigelin-Schwiedrzik, "In Search of a Master Narrative for 20th-Century Chinese History," p. 1081.
35 Heberer, *China and its National Minorities*, pp. 30, 37–38.

regained their old status. After the completion of this process, in 1987 the central government declared that ethnic classification was now generally complete. No further major changes would be allowed.[36]

In addition to defining ethnicity itself, the new leadership also had to set standards for the relationship between ethnicity and class. The question of whether class issues trumped issues of nationality had loomed over the CCP for decades. The problem had come to a head in 1964 with the dismissal of Li Weihan, the head of the United Front Work Department, and Ulanhu, the party secretary of Inner Mongolia, both of whom were accused of neglecting class struggle among ethnic minorities, especially in the nomadic regions. In 1977, the verdict on Ulanhu was revised, and he was elevated to Li's old post of head of the United Front Department. Li himself was also rehabilitated and went on to play an important role in policy developments in subsequent years. Shortly thereafter, in 1980, the Central Committee issued a decision that the argument that "the national question is actually a class question," which had been used to stress class struggle at the expense of minority interests, was wrong. The line was originally a quotation from Mao, but the leadership stressed that he had been referring only to the struggle of African Americans in the United States. The same argument could not be applied to the very different context of China's ethnic minorities. The Central Committee blamed the "ultra-leftist" policies of the Gang of Four for an over-emphasis on class struggle, which had harmed national interests by attacking the culture of the minorities and violating the principle of religious freedom.[37]

Inside the CCP, cadres who had been attacked as "local nationalists" were rehabilitated. Supporters of Ulanhu's so-called "anti-party treasonous clique" were rehabilitated, as were supposed adherents of the "New People's Party of Inner Mongolia." This last group had been subject to particularly ferocious treatment during the Cultural Revolution. A purge against it (1967–1969) affected at least 346,220 people, according to official numbers, including 16,222 killed and 87,188 seriously injured.[38] The victims were largely Mongolians, and the purge sparked severe ethnic tensions. Extraordinarily, it was now admitted that this party had never in fact existed, but had instead been invented out of whole cloth. Document 8.3 shows the kind of certification sent to rehabilitated "members" of

---

36 Huang Guangxue, *Zhongguo de minzu shibie* (Beijing: Minzu chubanshe, 1995), pp. 167, 157.

37 "Zhonggong zhongyang guanyu zhuanfa 'xizang gongzuo zuotanhui jiyao' de tongzhi," April 7, (1980) in Zhonggong zhongyang wenxian yanjiushi (ed.), *Shiyijie sanzhong quanhui yilai zhongyao wenxian xuandu (shangce)* (Beijing: Renmin chubanshe, 1987), Vol. 1, pp. 194–195.

38 For a detailed discussion of the numbers see: Qizhi, *Neimenggu wenge shilu: "Minzu fenlie" yu "wasu" yundong* (Hong Kong: Tianxingjian chubanshe, 2010), pp. 22–23.

the fabricated group. The standardized form simply lists the category of crime for which the comrade Zhao Dexuan was rehabilitated and gives his name.

The early Reform era government sought to restore the United Front with religious leaders and representatives of the old minority upper classes. The leadership continued to argue that the suppression of the 1959 Tibetan uprising had been justified, but it now accepted that the number of enemies had been "exaggerated," resulting in innocent people being victimized. The authorities therefore moved to rehabilitate "patriotic upper-class members of the national minorities," and to provide benefits and compensation to their family members under the same "practical policies" devised for former "rightists" and members of the "four elements." Among the beneficiaries of the new approach was the Panchen Lama, who was released from prison in 1977 and went on to serve as Vice-Chairman of the National People's Congress's Standing Committee, among other posts. The PRC government even opened confidential negotiations with the Dalai Lama, still in exile over the border in India. In 1979 and 1980, his representatives were permitted to visit Tibet as part of a "fact finding" commission, and the next year Hu Yaobang invited him to return to China and take up residence in Beijing. These overtures proved unsuccessful. The Dalai Lama remained unconvinced that the "facts" reported by his commission were signs of real progress in Tibet; he was also not willing to accept the leadership's conditions for his return.

Despite the only partial success of the reconstituted United Front, the 1980s saw a remarkable religious revival among China's minorities, and indeed among the Han majority. Many monasteries, mosques and temples that had been destroyed during or prior to the Cultural Revolution were rebuilt in this period. In Xinjiang, the number of mosques had shrunk from 14,119 in 1965 to only 1,400 by the 1970s, according to official statistics. By the end of 1981, 12,000 mosques were open again, bringing the region almost back to its pre-1966 total.[39] At the same time, economic reforms in the nomadic regions resulted in the expansion of herds and the revitalization of the nomadic way of life. Still, the wounds caused by the Cultural Revolution ran deep. Rehabilitation and compensation were often seen as insufficient to make up for the destruction of thousands of lives. Many members of minority groups believed that the Han Chinese had tried to obliterate their cultures entirely. In fact, the depredations of the Cultural Revolution had not been solely the responsibility of the Han. For instance, ethnic Tibetan Red Guards had participated in the destruction of monasteries alongside the Han, a development that remains a sensitive topic in

---

39 Zhang Xukai (ed.), *Boluan fanzheng, Xinjiang juan* (Zhongguo gongchandang lishi ziliao congshu, 1999, neibu ziliao), p. 103. I'd like to thank Daniel Leese for providing this source.

nationalist circles.[40] Whatever the rights and wrongs of the 1960s and 1970s, the rise of ethnic nationalism and separatism among Tibetans, Uyghurs and Mongolians today suggests that the return of the United Front in the 1980s had only limited effects.

The CCP still considers the minorities to be culturally and economically backward compared to the Han Chinese. In the official narrative, the party-state and Han settlers are presented as selfless agents of development. Ongoing unrest in Tibet and Xinjiang, now accompanied by remarkably brutal levels of government repression, shows that the CCP's attempts to create stability through economic development have not borne the fruit the leadership had hoped. In the early 1950s, many officially recognized "minorities" did not have a strong ethnic identity, and the state supported the development of written languages, written histories and distinctive customs for many of the groups it identified. Some minorities were in a sense state-created. The CCP supported moves by these groups to differentiate themselves from the Han, a strategy which helped increase backing for the newly created Autonomous Regions. At least in some cases, however, this policy backfired: not only local distinctiveness, but local nationalisms developed, and these continue to challenge the idea of the multi-ethnic unity in Tibet, Xinjiang and Inner Mongolia. The minorities in these areas have in common the existence of pre-PRC forms of ethnic nationalism that were at least partly developed by the 1920s. The former Tibetan and Mongolian upper classes and clergy were heirs to long local traditions of written scripts, written history and local religion. Nationalists could draw on these traditions to develop identities that cut against state narratives. Meanwhile, other "ethnic minorities" such as the Zhuang, Dong, Koreans, Miao and Manchus experienced ethnic revival in the Reform era without a rise in separatist tendencies.

New Gender Norms

We have seen that the binary division of gender into male and female remained unchanged in Reform China. Marriage is still considered to be a union between one man and one woman. Of wider relevance than the classification issue is the fact that, in the early Reform era, the party, media, cultural producers and society at large contributed to a substantial redefinition of gender roles. A powerful new discourse arose suggesting that the Cultural Revolution had placed too much emphasis on absolute equality between the genders and that this had resulted in

40 For debate see: Wang Lixiong, "Reflections on Tibet," *New Left Review*, No. 14 (2002), pp. 79–111; Tsering Shakya, "Blood in the Snows: Reply to Wang Lixiong," *New Left Review*, No. 15 (2002), pp. 39–60.

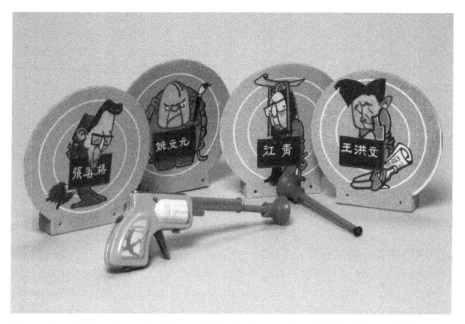

Figure 8.3: "Shooting at the Gang of Four": A game for children from the late 1970s. The cartoon of Jiang Qing echoes depictions of the Empress Dowager Cixi (1835–1908), another model of the danger of power-hungry women.
Source: Helmut Opletal (ed.), *Die Kultur der Kulturrevolution: Personenkult und politisches Design im China von Mao Zedong* (Wien: Museum für Völkerunde, 2011), p. 53.

the "masculinization" of women. Observers argued that the supposed "natural qualities" of women, such as gentleness, sensitivity and love of beauty, had been repressed by the events of the late Mao period. The "iron girls," the heroes of the Cultural Revolution who performed heavy labor in fields and factories, were suddenly recast as "abnormal." Jiang Qing became a byword for over-ambitious and malignant women with excessive political power. This new discourse was reflected in the widely praised 1986 film *Hibiscus Town*, the plot of which revolves around an unmarried female cadre, who colludes with the head of a work team and an alcoholic poor peasant to terrorize the local population during the Four Clean Ups Campaign. The film's heroine is a hardworking, happily married young woman whose husband is killed for attacking the troublemakers. The point is difficult to miss: the Cultural Revolution empowered deviant women and idlers to disastrous effect, before Reform policies restored good cadres and intellectuals to their rightful place.

The new discourse pressured women to conform to more traditional ideas of marriage and motherhood. Changing standards of beauty spawned new markets for fashion, cosmetics and weight loss, and later for plastic surgery and skin whitening products. As the scholar Wang Zheng trenchantly notes, traditional modes of femininity were repackaged as markers of modernity, while the "iron girls" were decried as having no freedom of choice in lifestyle or consumption patterns. This was not simply a case of men using a turn back to tradition to strengthen their privileged positions in the gender hierarchy. Many educated women from the urban middle classes also celebrated the supposedly "natural" femininity and beauty relayed in fashion magazines. For them, pale skin and indoor work formed a status marker distinguishing them from rural peasant women, who tended to be sun-tanned from labor in the fields.[41] The respectable urban middle class wife was also contrasted with the mostly poor rural migrants engaged in the illegal but booming sex industry. The CCP had celebrated the abolition of prostitution as one of the new China's greatest achievements, but commodified female sexuality now returned with a vengeance.

Undeniably, many women's lives improved in the Reform era in terms of living standards and consumption levels. The CCP never introduced formal policies to exclude women from the labor market, and women's participation in the urban labor force increased during the 1980s both in absolute and relative terms. In 1978, women made up around 32 percent of all workers and staff, but by 1988 the figure had increased to 37 percent. In the state-owned enterprises, the proportion of female workers rose from around 28 percent to 33 percent over the same period.[42]

However, the 1980s also saw serious setbacks in other aspects of gender equality. In particular, access to higher education and political positions was reduced. In 1976, 33 percent of all students in the regular higher education system were women, but by 1980 this rate had dropped to 23 percent. The late Cultural Revolution high was not reached again until 1988.[43] This decade-long dip in the percentage of female students coincided with the reintroduction of the national entrance examinations in 1977. To make up for the years of disruption to university recruitment, the government did not initially set an age limit for gaokao candidates. This was intended to allow returning "sent-down youth" and other members of the "lost generation" to apply to university, but the impact was not even across the genders. Many older members of the applicant pool had married and had children by the time the gaokao was reinstated. Among this group, men, who generally still performed less childcare and housework than their wives, were likely to have more time to study and prepare for the examinations. In the mid-1980s, China's female university enrollment rate (28 percent) was

41 Wang Zheng, *Finding Women in the State: A Socialist Feminist Revolution in the People's Republic of China, 1949–1964* (Berkeley, CA: University of California Press, 2016), p. 239.
42 Zhonghua quanguo funü lianhehui funü yanjiusuo (ed.), *Zhongguo funü tongji ziliao* (Beijing: Zhongguo tongji chubanshe, 1991), p. 239.
43 Stanley Rosen, "Women, Education and Modernization," in Ruth Hayhoe (ed.), *Education and Modernization: The Chinese Experience* (Oxford: Pergamon Press, 1992), p. 259.

strikingly low compared to other countries. In the capitalist countries of Western Europe, the rate was above 40 percent, and numbers were even higher in the USSR and the Eastern Bloc, where between 43 and 53 percent of students were women.[44] One question that remains open is how the impact of the new gender norms intersected with the abolition of class status. The disappearance of "family origin" as a category in the official record in the 1980s made class statistically invisible, and it is therefore difficult to quantify how changing norms affected different class groups. What is clear, however, is that from the first decade of the Reform era China was no longer a leader in gender equality.

In terms of political participation, women lost out as well. The number of women serving as full members of the CCP Central Committee dropped from an already unimpressive twenty out of 195 in the 10th committee (1973–1977) to eleven out of 210 in the 11th (1977–1982). (The Central Committees are numbered according to the party congresses at which they were elected.) Women's share of National People's Congress seats remained steady at around 21 to 22 percent between 1975 and 1988, but the number of women on the congressional Standing Committee dropped from 25 to 21 percent in the same period.[45] The early PRC model of the revolutionary leadership couple – Mao and Jiang Qing, Liu Shaoqi and Wang Guangmei – disappeared in the 1980s and has never returned since. In the Reform era, no spouse of a central leader has held a major position in either the party or the state apparatus. Xi Jinping's wife Peng Liyuan had a national profile long before her husband, but this was as a PLA singer rather than in any political role. Following Xi's accession to the state presidency in 2013, Peng ceased performing and has since acted more as a US-style "first lady" than as a revolutionary wife on the model of the Mao era.

At the same time as the new discourse of femininity arose in the early 1980s, a parallel view emerged arguing that the ideology of gender equality had "castrated" men and weakened the Chinese nation. The rediscovery of hyper-masculine values of competitiveness, physical strength, sexual potency and aggression was celebrated as a liberation from the "unnatural" order of the Cultural Revolution.[46] Arguments of this kind quickly became widespread in the media and popular culture.

Only a subset of men benefited from the rise of this new masculinity. In the Mao era, honest, hardworking urban *hukou* holders from good class

44 Ibid., p. 261.
45 Zhonghua quanguo funü lianhehui funü yanjiusuo (ed.), *Zhongguo funü tongji ziliao*, pp. 571–572.
46 For example see: Zhong Xueping, *Masculinity Besieged? Issues of Modernity and Male Subjectivity in Chinese Literature of the Late Twentieth Century* (Durham, NC: Duke University Press, 2000).

backgrounds were widely regarded as desirable matches. Since the 2000s, however, men have increasingly complained of the need to prove their "economic potency" to potential partners by buying apartments, cars or other trappings of wealth. Where women are called on to be pale, slim and attractive, men face unrealistic expectations of a different kind. Needless to say, most men are not "tall, rich and handsome," and standards of masculinity serve in part to reproduce and justify social inequality. Rich and powerful men can afford to keep "second wives" (*ernai*) and perhaps even third ones, while poor and rural male singles – so-called "bare branches" (*guanggun*) – may be unable to establish families at all.

The most important pressure on the bodies and lives of Chinese women in the Reform era has been the one-child policy. In the first half of the 1980s, the government tightened the previous birth planning regime, and quotas for reductions in births began to be enforced through draconian violence, forced abortions and sterilizations. In virtually all cases, the object of violence was the female body: men were sterilized in far lower numbers, although from a purely technical perspective they were equally effective targets. The restriction to one child freed women from family pressure to carry and care for large numbers of children, and in some circumstances that could prove liberating. By and large, however, the policy served to deny women control over their bodies and reproductive health. Nor did it do so to any especially spectacular effect. A number of scholars have argued that the one-child restriction did little to depress birth rates. Other developing countries in Asia have seen considerable reductions in births without national birth planning policies, although rates have tended to fall more slowly elsewhere than in China.[47] By 1979, the year before the policy was introduced, China's total fertility rate had already dropped to 2.75, from a previous peak of more than twice that number. By 1984, tens of millions of forced abortions and sterilizations later, the rate had fallen only slightly, to 2.35 expected births per woman.[48] The policy also created unintended side-effects. In the countryside, the CCP adopted a slightly looser standard of two births per couple, but even this has led to a significant gender imbalance. Peasants determined to bear sons have selectively aborted girls in their tens of millions, leaving enormous numbers of men – the "bare branches" referred to above – unable to find wives.

In short, it is emphatically not the case that every aspect of private life became more "liberal" and "free" in the 1980s. The birth limit adopted under Deng represented one of the most dramatic and violent efforts at social engineering in

---

47 Martin King Whyte, Wang Feng and Yong Cai, "Challenging Myths about China's One-Child Policy," *The China Journal*, No. 74 (2015), p. 157.
48 Tyrene White, *China's Longest Campaign: Birth Planning in the People's Republic, 1949–2005* (Ithaca, NY: Cornell University Press, 2006), p. 44.

modern history. In 2015, the PRC government under Xi Jinping relaxed the policy, declaring that all married couples would be allowed to have two children. It would be a mistake to regard this as an end to the birth planning experiment, however. In point of fact, the same target had existed in some regions, in practice if not in statute, during the late Mao era.

Redefining the Urban-Rural Boundary

The *hukou* system remains in place in China today, but during the Reform era its function has changed. Between 1962 and the early 1980s, the system worked to keep peasants in the villages. As long as distribution of goods was managed via state- or commune-organized rationing, it was difficult for potential migrants to access food and other necessities once they left their home area. The Mao era model of "primitive socialist accumulation" was designed to squeeze the countryside through the unified purchase and sale system, which kept prices for agricultural products low and prevented peasants from amassing the resources needed to move away. With the abolition of the state's and People's Communes' monopoly on the grain trade in the 1980s, peasants were "liberated" from this system and gained de facto freedom of movement. The end of the rationing system, which had been abolished by the late 1980s, also helped boost geographical mobility. Rural migrants still had no legal status in the cities, but they could buy food, rent housing and find jobs on the market. Train tickets could be bought without approval from the local authorities, and rising rural incomes made travel more affordable. Nevertheless, the government went to considerable lengths to counter uncontrolled "waves" of rural migration to the cities throughout the 1980s and 1990s. The leadership's refusal to allow all "sent-down youths" to return to the cities until years after the end of the Mao era was intended to reduce pressure on the urban labor market and welfare state.

Despite increased mobility in the Reform era, the agrarian *hukou* continued to count against people from the countryside, albeit in new ways. In the cities, migrants were welcomed as a source of cheap labor, but they still had no access to urban welfare and their children could not attend local public schools. The knowledge that migrants were sending money to families left behind in the countryside allowed employers to keep wages low, instead of offering pay commensurate with the urban cost of living. The urban authorities tolerated migrants to meet their labor needs, but they retained the option to use the *hukou* system to deport people classified as "rural" when necessary, usually in the guise of "cleaning up" the cities or reducing "illegal settlements."[49] Like those in other

---

49 For example see: Xiang Biao, *Transcending Boundaries. Zhejiangcun: The Story of a Migrant Village in Beijing* (Leiden: Brill, 2005), translated by Jim Weldon.

less favored categories, rural migrants lived precariously in the face of local governments prepared to deploy urban residency regulations in a highly selective way. Moreover, as in the "dual society" era under Mao, the central government continued to subsidize urban areas at the expense of the countryside. Rural officials, hospitals and schools were left to rely on heavy local taxation and high fees, increasing the burden on peasants. Agrarian *hukou* holders are still entitled to access collective land, but the state can easily remove this land for industrial or real estate projects, often with only minimal compensation. The structures and mechanisms of marginalization and exploitation have changed, but the agrarian population remain second-class citizens in contemporary China.

Capitalism with Chinese Characteristics

Much to the surprise of many Western observers, the PRC survived the disintegration of the Soviet Union and the Eastern Bloc after 1989. The state, the CCP as a Leninist vanguard party, and the PLA as that party's armed force, remain strong institutions. In contrast to the USSR, Czechoslovakia and Yugoslavia, the PRC did not split apart into new nation states either through ethnic conflict or civil war. Since the 1980s, China has consistently posted the highest rate of economic growth of any country in the world. The Chinese government has succeeded in gradually dismantling the Soviet-style planned economy while still maintaining overall control. The People's Communes were abolished by the mid-1980s, but there is still no private landownership in either the countryside or the cities. Land use rights may be traded on the open market, but ownership of the land itself rests with the state. In the state-owned industries, major waves of privatization occurred in 1992 and between 1998 and 2002. Tens of millions of workers lost their jobs, and the remaining state-owned enterprises were "restructured" to increase their competitiveness. However, the state continues to control key players – the so-called "commanding heights" – in important sectors such as finance, communication, the media and publishing, higher education, transport and any industries with national defense implications. Recent Five Year Plans have eschewed the detailed production targets favored in earlier periods, instead identifying strategic macroeconomic goals to be realized over the medium term. The CCP refers to the current system, with its mix of state and private ownership structures, as "socialism with Chinese characteristics" (*Zhongguo tese shehuizhuyi*). Certainly this arrangement is a long way from the omnipresence of central economic control in the Mao era, but it also differs from the neoliberal model seen in most Western economies because of the continued guiding role of the state. The current party constitution confirms that, at least in formal terms, the CCP has not abandoned Marxist-Leninist ideology or the goal of establishing full communism.[50]

Since the 1980s, tens of millions of peasants have escaped poverty under the Reform era system. In terms of consumption, Chinese under Mao famously dreamed of owning a bike, a watch and a sewing machine. Today, it has become the norm for the urban middle and upper classes to own their own apartment, drive a foreign car, consume Western branded products and travel as global tourists. In terms of diet, the proportion of calories derived from staple crops (rice and wheat) has significantly decreased, and eggs, vegetables, meat, soap, clothing and other necessities are affordable even for some of the country's poorest households. Elderly people in the countryside, most of whom have experienced severe famine and food shortages, sometimes claim that eating meat every day is a sign that life is good. On that measure, China's progress in the Reform era has been remarkable.

The Great Transformation: Chinese Society and the CCP under Reform

The improved living conditions celebrated in official CCP accounts of the Reform era have not been without downsides. In the 1980s, the CCP abandoned attempts to empower ordinary people in politics and to reduce the gap between manual and intellectual labor. As a result, the status of workers and peasants has declined precipitously, and the urban middle class has become the CCP's new social ideal. Groups who fall short of this ideal, whether through lack of higher education, failure to compete economically or simple refusal to conform to middle class social practice, are regarded by the party leadership as being of low "quality" (*suzhi*). Since the early 2000s, education, housing, health care and security have become highly commercialized, and those with limited resources have increasingly found themselves excluded from mainstream society. New problems such as low food safety standards and rampant air pollution have appeared as industrialization has deepened, and many have disproportionately affected the poor. In short, class and gender relations in China have been transformed since 1978. The major developments can be summarized as follows:[51]

1. While the pre-PRC capitalist and landlord classes had been eliminated by 1956, a new capitalist class emerged in the Reform era. The privatization of

---

50 "Zhongguo gongchandang zhangcheng," www.12371.cn/special/zggcdzc/zggcdzcqw/ (accessed June 23, 2017).

51 This section is indebted to: Alvin Y. So, "The Changing Pattern of Class and Class Conflict in China," *Journal of Contemporary Asia*, Vol. 33, No. 3 (2003), pp. 366–371.

state-owned enterprises was a golden opportunity for cadres, many of whom sought to transform themselves into owner-managers of semi-state businesses that blurred the boundary between collective and private property. Their political and social networks allowed them to enrich themselves by becoming, not merely "capitalist roaders" supportive of private interests, but actual cadre-capitalists themselves.

2. At the same time, a new class of private capitalists has developed out of the ordinary population since the 1980s. These new entrepreneurs have benefited from weak enforcement of labor laws and the lack of independent labor unions. The repressive machinery of the state continues to limit the bargaining power of workers by suppressing unionization or strikes that go beyond the confines of individual factories. Private capitalists have enriched themselves significantly, but they are reliant on the state's goodwill and patronage and are weak as a political force. While cadre-capitalists are almost all men, women made up one-quarter of all China's entrepreneurs in 2013.[52]

3. After two decades of attacks on those Chinese who had worked with foreign capitalists, the Reform era CCP decided to open the Chinese market to foreign direct investment. Initially, foreign capital could only be invested in Special Economic Zones, of which the most notable was Shenzhen, over the border from Hong Kong on the southern coast. Most early investment came not from Western capitalists, but from British-controlled Hong Kong, Taiwan and overseas Chinese communities in South East Asia. Since the 1990s, foreign direct investments have become increasingly important to China's economic growth, and the state has sought to maintain control by compelling overseas companies to form joint-venture enterprises with local partners to secure access to the Chinese market. Following China's accession to the World Trade Organization (WTO) in 2001, more and more sectors and regions have been opened to foreign capital, albeit still with these restrictions in place. In recent years, Chinese private and state-owned enterprises have become global players themselves, investing in and buying up firms all over the world.

4. The economic boom seen during the Reform era, along with a significant expansion of higher education in the late 1990s, has spurred the emergence of a new urban middle class. The creation of a white-collar middle class that is wealthy, professional and, critically, apolitical is a major state project. Historically, most Western theories of modernization have viewed emerging

---

52 "Female entrepreneurs account for one quarter in China: white paper," *Xinhua*, September 22, 2015, www.chinadaily.com.cn/china/2015-09/22/content_21947630.htm (accessed September 8, 2017).

middle classes keen to protect their privileges from government interference as potential drivers of democratization. By contrast, the CCP considers the middle class to be a stabilizing factor, reasoning that newly wealthy individuals will prefer not to risk their position by rocking the boat politically. Chinese sociologists estimate that the middle class accounts for 11 to 28 percent of the total population, depending on the definition.[53] Urban women have been particular beneficiaries of the expansion of this group. Wider access to higher education increases their prospects for career advancement, while the urban one-child policy has meant that daughters no longer face competition for resources from male siblings. It remains to be seen whether the move to a two-child policy will change things in this regard.

5. The semi-socialist peasantry of the People's Communes disappeared during the process of decollectivization in the early 1980s. (Semi-socialist seems to me an appropriate definition, since peasants remained entitled to plots for private use even inside the collectives.) The household responsibility system of the 1980s contributed to a boom in agricultural production and strengthened the family as an economic unit. However, over the four decades of the Reform era, millions of peasants have lost their access to land. There has been no re-emergence of the old landlord class, but the CCP's liberalization of the lease of land use rights has led to the rise of so-called "dragon head enterprises" (*longtou qiye*), which lease land from multiple villages to organize large-scale industrial agriculture and stock farming. Most "dragon heads" employ rural migrants, often from far-flung parts of the country, as wage laborers. In a departure from traditional economic theory in the West, Reform era China has instituted rural capitalism without any privatization of land ownership. The dissolution of the communes has been accompanied by an increase in the urbanization rate, which topped 50 percent for the first time in Chinese history in 2011. The government under Xi Jinping has underlined the need for further urbanization, which, absent major changes to the *hukou* system, seems likely to deepen demographic imbalances in the countryside. In most regions, those who move away to the cities tend to be working-age men, while elderly people, children and to a lesser extent working women stay behind in the villages. Elderly rural women are one of the most marginalized groups in China, at least among the Han majority.

6. Finally, the socialist working class of the Mao era, and the state-owned work units that formed the basis of working class communities, have largely been destroyed by the privatization of industry and housing. Urban working class

53 David S. Goodman, *Class in Contemporary China* (Cambridge: Polity Press, 2014), pp. 101–102.

districts have been demolished to make way for real estate projects targeted at the wealthy middle class. The workforce of the state-owned enterprises remains very large in absolute terms, but younger workers no longer see themselves as "masters of the country." Work has been commodified on the Western capitalist model: instead of being integrated into an "iron rice bowl" of permanent, well-remunerated jobs, labor is now a commodity sold by the worker and bought by the capitalist on the market. Even in the state sector, the "iron rice bowl" is well and truly broken.

Over the last two decades, a new working class of around 200 million "peasant-workers" has emerged. Its members are rural *hukou* holders, but their jobs are located in the cities. The first generation of "peasant-workers" was what might be called semi-proletarianized – they were only partly integrated into the urban labor market, and they retained close links with agriculture and the world of the villages. Many planned to save money from urban jobs before eventually returning home. By contrast, members of the second generation have often looked to remain in the cities and become part of urban society. As a result, these workers tend to demand higher wages than their parents' generation, a change that is reflected in the waves of strikes seen in the manufacturing hubs of the Pearl River Delta (Guangzhou and Shenzhen and nearby towns) since 2010. These strikes have been concentrated in new industries, especially the vehicle sector, and have affected private and foreign enterprises in particular.

The division of labor among the "peasant-worker" population is highly gendered. Men dominate in construction, automobile production and heavy industries, while in the textile, garment, electronics and service industries the workforce is predominantly female. The history of the Reform era suggests that, in contrast to the hopes of Deng and his fellow leaders, it is not possible to use marketization and capitalization as neutral tools of economic development. Both processes fundamentally reshape social structures. As Marx was the first to observe, the capitalist mode of production not only produces commodities and surplus value, it also reproduces the social relations of capitalist and wage laborer.[54] The 200 million disenfranchised "peasant-workers" and the capitalist super-rich are both unintended byproducts of Deng's market reforms.

The CCP and the Power of the Bureaucracy

The transformation of social structures after 1978 was accompanied by major changes in both the state and the party. The CCP today is dominated by urban

---

54 Karl Marx, *Capital: A Critique of Political Economy*, Vol. I (1887), www.marxists.org/archive/marx/works/1867-c1/ch23.htm (accessed June 23, 2017).

and white-collar members. In 2016, 36.9 percent of party members were workers or peasants, far less than the 45.9 percent who held a university degree.[55] Leading cadres are almost all university educated, and a significant number hold degrees from Western universities. Some scholars have argued that party cadres form what is essentially a "technocratic elite," and optimistic readings of Chinese politics suggest the country has established a "political meritocracy" in which holders of high posts are selected based on academic achievements and practical performance in office. More pessimistic observers speak of an evolving oligarchy that limits access to political power and wealth to a small elite with strong ties to both the state and private sectors.[56]

The party-state established under Mao is now more hierarchical than ever; the Chairman's long-term project to "rectify" the CCP and keep its revolutionary ideals alive can only be judged a failure. Under his leadership a sprawling new bureaucracy was created, which he was unable to tame in his lifetime. This was in part a consequence of the failure of the Cultural Revolution, which allowed the Dengist faction to win out over the Maoist left in the struggle for control of the CCP. Cultural Revolutionary policies to close the gap between urban and rural areas and between intellectual and manual labor did not bear fruit. Moreover, while Mao initially sought to temper the power of the party bureaucracy by encouraging rebel forces to attack the privileges of cadres and their children, after 1966 and early 1967 he backed down, sacrificing the rebels for the sake of stability and renewing the party-state. The rebel mass organizations had empowered students and workers to represent themselves outside the party apparatus, but it proved impossible to institutionalize these mass movements, and by 1969 the monopoly of the CCP had been restored.

In the Reform era, all attempts by Mao's successors to tame corruption, fraud, rent seeking, abuse of power and self-enrichment by cadres have proved unsuccessful. Even Xi Jinping's current anti-corruption campaign, by a distance the most far-reaching of these efforts, has generated significant skepticism. Social media buzzwords such as "princelings" and "the second red generation" (*hong erdai*) reflect the continued importance of "old cadres" and their families in networks of state power and capital. Both Western and Chinese observers have

---

55 Lea Shi with Kerstin Lohse-Friedrich, "Zentralisierte Führung – Hetrogene Parteibasis: Veränderungen in der Mitgliederstruktur der Kommunistische Partei Chinas," www.merics .org/fileadmin/templates/download/china-monitor/Merics_China-Monitor_KPC-2016_Screen .pdf (accessed September 8, 2017).

56 For example see: Daniel A. Bell, *The China Model: Political Meritocracy and the Limits of Democracy* (Princeton, NJ: Princeton University Press, 2015); Andrew Walder, "China's Evolving Oligarchy," in David B. Grusky (ed.), *Social Stratification: Class, Race, and Gender in Sociological Perspective* (Boulder, CO: Westview Press, 2014), p. 326.

long underestimated the importance of family clans in the PRC political system. In contrast to the two post-Deng party leaders, Jiang Zemin and Hu Jintao, Xi Jinping has built his authority in part on the legacy of his father Xi Zhongxun (1913–2002), one of the PRC's founding generation. With Xi's emergence, the Cultural Revolution era debate around "revolutionary bloodlines" has been shown to have continued relevance. In 1966, rebel students attacked the "bloodline" theory in the belief that it was unfair for children of high-ranking cadres to inherit prestige and privileges from their parents. Under Xi, that notion of inheritance suddenly appears very real.

Class Struggle from Below

Today, China has "changed its color" and become, in essence, a capitalist country, in ways beyond even the worst imaginings of the Maoist left. Nevertheless, the overlapping hierarchies of the Mao era still endure under "capitalism with Chinese characteristics," with the population still categorized according *hukou*, rank, gender and ethnicity. The gap between rich and poor continues to widen, and worker protests are on the rise, but the CCP and Chinese sociologists have largely abandoned the language of "class" (*jieji*) in favor of the less freighted notion of the "stratum" (*jieceng*), a borrowing from Western social science. The disappearance of class from mainstream discourse in the party and society at large is ironic, since it has occurred against a backdrop of sweeping changes in Chinese class structures and growing inter-class tension. Recent years have seen thousands of local protests across the whole sweep of the country, from worker strikes to peasant resistance against "land grabs" by local cadres and investors. Citizen protests target the most egregious cases of environmental damage by industry. Increasingly, these conflicts spark confrontation between ordinary people and local cadres and governments. In the Mao era, the state organized "class struggle" from above, using the system of official labels to identify targets. Today, workers are increasingly fighting for higher wages and better protections themselves, often bypassing the official labor unions. The new generation of migrant workers seeks to resist the restrictions imposed by the agrarian *hukou* and to establish a permanent foothold in the cities. Despite these instances of class struggle from below, the party-state has successfully prevented any workers' movements from gaining traction beyond the local level. The last serious attempt to establish independent national labor unions, made during the Tiananmen Square protests in 1989, was crushed first by military force and then by political and judicial repression.

In the late 1990s, workers protesting against privatization and factory closures in the state-owned sector sometimes carried posters of Chairman Mao on demonstrations. Parts of the old working class felt an abiding nostalgia for the era of job security and the "iron rice bowl." To them, the layoffs represented a violation of the social contract that socialism would always protect their livelihoods. The Mao era connoted a lost egalitarianism, and some people hoped for a return to Maoist campaigns to discipline corrupt officials.[57] These ideas still have some currency, but they are diluted by the fact that the overwhelming majority of Chinese in the active workforce today have no personal memory of the Mao era. In any case, as I have attempted to show, society under Mao was not egalitarian, but strictly hierarchical. Only around 20 percent of the population had access to the comfortable world "inside the system." The vast majority, including most of the enormous rural population, remained outside the socialist welfare state. Few elderly peasants have forgotten their suffering during the famine and the subsequent years. Memories in the countryside are generally far less nostalgic than those of urban workers, who after all led relatively privileged lives in the Mao era. Only a few Neo-Maoist intellectuals in the cities still argue for a return to collectivized agriculture. For most of the population, a revival of the planned economy holds little interest.

At the same time, the Cultural Revolution in particular remains a shorthand for more mainstream ideas, including resistance against abuses of power by the "bureaucratic class." The ruling elite continues to worry about selective, creative hijackings of the old Maoist slogan that "rebellion is justified," some of which, it believes, pose a real threat to its control. For this reason, and to avoid too great a focus on the CCP's past mistakes, the leadership around Xi has sought to tame memory of and research on the Mao era. Researchers are warned away from certain topics; access to archives is increasingly restricted. Still, the rich and powerful cannot be certain that those at the margins will not rebel, or that the promises of the Chinese revolution can be left permanently unfulfilled.

---

57 Ching Kwan Lee, *Against the Law: Labor Protests in China's Rustbelt and Sunbelt* (Berkeley, CA: University of California Press, 2007), p. 119.

DOCUMENT 8.1 Make correct decisions about the problem of the four elements "taking off the hat" by seeking truth from facts.

Comrade Zhao Cangbi, the Minister for Public Security answers our journalists' questions

Question: How should we treat landlords, rich peasants, counterrevolutionaries and bad elements after their hat is taken off? If they committed a crime should we not have them put on the hat again?

Answer: After the four elements have taken off their hats, they can be designated according to their work or profession as commune members, workers, teachers and so on. They should enjoy all basic rights as citizens as defined by the constitution. They should not be discriminated against in any way. They should not be called "landlords who have taken off the hat," "rich peasants who have taken off the hat," "counterrevolutionaries who have taken off the hat" or "bad elements who have taken off the hat," and even more importantly, they should not continue to be an "object of dictatorship." If anyone among them has committed a mistake, the method of handling contradictions among the people should be applied to educating them. If some of them have committed crimes, then they should be punished according to the facts of the crime and to law. But they should not put on their former hat again . . .

Question: Regarding practical policies for the sons and daughters of the four elements, what kind of problems should we pay attention to?

Answer: Regarding the sons and daughters of the four elements, we focus on their political performance. This is a policy of our party. Persons with the family background of "landlord" and "rich peasant" are part of all professions in society. Their parents belong to the exploiting classes, but they themselves are socialist laborers. The sons and daughters of counter-revolutionaries and bad elements are not responsible for the crimes that their parents committed. It is very clear that the phenomenon of discrimination against children with the family background of "four elements" is not in line with the socialist legal system and is an immoral version of democratic social life . . . According to the decisions of the Central Committee of the Communist Party, we should solve the problem comprehensively to define the status of the second generation and change the status of the third generation. From today forward, we must implement the party's policy of focusing on political performance. Children with the family background of "four elements" should enjoy the same treatment as persons with the family background of "worker" or "peasant" in terms of school admissions, recruitment, service in the army, joining the Youth League and party, distribution of work points and similar aspects . . .

Source: *Renmin Ribao*, January 30, 1979.

DOCUMENT 8.2 Revision of Class Status.

Note: italics indicate details written into the preprinted text (not italicized).

Revolutionary Committee of Fengshun County

Document Number 857

Regarding the investigation of *Liu Sanyi, male*, age *57, Tangnan* People's Commune, *Dongfang* Brigade:

> We agree that he may take off the hat of *rich peasant element* and that he will receive the treatment of an ordinary member of the People's Commune.

Hereby notified.

Revolutionary Committee of Fengshun County (12 September 1979)

To archive.

Source: Stanford East Asian Library, Collection of Contemporary Chinese Political Archives, 1949–1980, Box 74.

DOCUMENT 8.3 Notice of Rehabilitation.

Note: italics indicate details written into the preprinted text (not italicized).

Comrade Zhao Dexuan:

As result of cruel persecution caused by the counterrevolutionary line of Lin Biao and the Gang of Four, false evidence has been planted against you as a so-called:

> *Element of the "New Inner Mongolian People's Party"*

According to the two directives of the Central Committee of the CCP of April 20 and January 21 and the directive of the Party Committee of the Autonomous Region of Inner Mongolia, all accusations imposed against you are false, you receive full rehabilitation, your reputation is restored, negative impacts on your family, children and friends, who have been accused, will be eliminated and their reputation is also restored.

We express sincerest sympathies.

Hereby notified.

Bureau of the CCP for the Inner Mongolia Autonomous Region (July 23, 1979)

Source: Yang Haiying, *Cultural Revolution in Inner Mongolia: Documents related to the Mongolian Genocide during the Cultural Revolution in Inner Mongolia (2): The Purge of the Inner Mongolian People's Party* (Tokyo: Fukyosha Publishing, 2010), p. 777.

GLOSSARY OF CHINESE TERMS

Chinese Terms	
bangzidui	棒子队
baoshoupai	保守派
biaoxian	表现
bingtuan	兵团
boluan fanzheng	拨乱反正
chengfen	成份
chengzhen	城镇
chiqing	吃青
chushen	出身
da chuanlian	大串连
dai hongmaozi	戴红帽子
da jihuang	大饥荒
dang'an	档案
danwei	单位
datongshu	大同书
dazibao	大字报
ernai	二奶
fukuafeng	浮夸风
gaige kaifang	改革开放
gaizao	改造
gaizheng	改正

(cont.)

Chinese Terms	
gaokao	高考
gaoshanzu	高山族
geren shenfen	个人身份
getihu	个体户
gongfen	工分
gongren	工人
guanban hongweibing	官办红卫兵
guanggun	光棍
guanxi	关系
hezuohua	合作化
hong erdai	红二代
huidaomen	会道门
hukou	户口
jiating chushen	家庭出身
jiawu	家务
jieceng	阶层
jieji	阶级
jingji zhuyi	经济主义
laji ziliao	垃圾资料
laodong	劳动
laodong gaizao	劳动改造
laodong jiaoyao	劳动教养
laogai	劳改
laosanjie	老三届
longtou qiye	龙头企业
luoshi zhengce	落实政策
manchansifen	瞒产私分
minzu	民族
mo yanggong	磨洋工
neibu cankao	内部参考
pantu	叛徒
pantufenzi	叛徒分子
pingfan	平反
poxie	破鞋
renmin gongshe	人民公社
renmin neibu maodun	人民内部矛盾
renqing	人情
shehui guanxi	社会关系
shenfenzheng	身份证
shinian dongluan	十年动乱

(cont.)

Chinese Terms	
silei fenzi	四类分子
suku	诉苦
sushi	素质
tewu	特务
tie fanwan	铁饭碗
tieguniang	铁姑娘
tizhi nei	体制内
tizhi wai	体制外
tonggou tongxiao	统购统销
tuntian	屯田
xiaodao xiaoxi	小道消息
yuanzhumin	原住民
zhaimaozi	摘帽子
zhiqing	知青
zhishifenzi	知识分子
zhongguo tese shehuizhuyi	中国特色社会主义
zhonghua minzu	中华民族
zou houmen	走后门

SELECT BIBLIOGRAPHY

Bo Yibo, *Ruogan zhongda juece yu shijian de huigu*, 2 vols. (Beijing: Zhongyang dangxiao chubanshe, 1991).

Brown, Jeremy and Johnson Matthews (eds.), *Maoism at the Grassroots: Everyday Life in China's Era of High Socialism* (Cambridge, MA: Harvard University Press, 2015).

Brown, Jeremy and Paul G. Pickowicz (eds.), *Dilemmas of Victory: The Early Years of the People's Republic of China* (Cambridge, MA: Harvard University Press, 2007).

Cheek, Timothy, *The Intellectual in Modern Chinese History* (Cambridge: Cambridge University Press, 2015).

Diamant, Neil, *Revolutionizing the Family: Politics, Love, and Divorce in Urban and Rural China, 1949–1968* (Berkeley, CA: University of California Press, 2000).

Eyferth, Jacob, *Eating Rice from Bamboo Roots: The Social History of a Community of Handicraft Papermakers in Rural Sichuan* (Cambridge, MA: Harvard University Asia Center, 2009).

Gao Wangling, *Zhongguo nongmin fan xingwei yanjiu, 1950–1980* (Hong Kong: Zhongwen daxue chubanshe, 2013).

Han Gang (ed.), *Zhongguo dangdaishi yanjiu* (Beijing: Jiuzhou chubanshe, 2009; 2011), two volumes.

Hershatter, Gail, *The Gender of Memory: Rural Women and China's Collective Past* (Berkeley, CA: University of California Press, 2011).

Jin Dalu, *Feichang yu zhengchang: Shanghai "wenge" shiqi de shehui shenghuo* (Shanghai: Shanghai cishu chubanshe, 2011).

Joel, Andreas, *Rise of the Red Engineers: The Cultural Revolution and the Origins of China's New Class* (Stanford, CA: Stanford University Press, 2009).

Kraus, Richard, *Class Conflict in Chinese Socialism* (New York, NY: Columbia University Press, 1981).

Leese, Daniel, *Mao Cult: Rhetoric and Ritual in China's Cultural Revolution* (Cambridge: Cambridge University Press, 2011).

Li Xun, *Geming zaofan niandai: Shanghai wenge yundong shigao*, 2 vols. (Hong Kong: Oxford University Press, 2015).

Liu Xiaomeng, *Zhongguo zhiqingshi Dachao (1966–1980)* (Beijing: Zhongguo shehui kexue chubanshe, 1998).

MacFarquhar, Roderick and Michael Schoenhals, *Mao's Last Revolution* (Cambridge, MA: The Belknap Press of Harvard University Press, 2008).

Manning, Kimberley and Felix Wemheuer (eds.), *Eating Bitterness: New Perspectives on China's Great Leap Forward and Famine* (Vancouver: University of British Columbia Press, 2011).

Meisner, Maurice, *Mao's China and After: A History of the People's Republic* (New York, NY: The Free Press, 1999).

Mullaney, Thomas, *Coming to Terms with the Nation: Ethnic Classification in Modern China* (Berkeley, CA: University of California Press, 2011).

Perry, Elizabeth, *Anyuan: Mining China's Revolutionary Tradition* (Berkeley, CA: University of California Press, 2012).

Schoenhals, Michael, *Spying for the People: Mao's Secret Agents 1949–1967* (Cambridge: Cambridge University Press, 2013).

Smith, Aminda, *Thought Reform and China's Dangerous Classes: Reeducation, Resistance, and the People* (Lanham, MD: Rowman and Littlefield, 2013).

Thaxton, Ralph, *Catastrophe and Contention in Rural China: Mao's Great Leap Forward Famine and the Origins of Righteous Resistance in Da Fo Village* (Cambridge: Cambridge University Press, 2008).

Unger, Jonathan, Anita Chan and Stanley Rosen, "Students and Class Warfare: The Social Roots of the Red Guard Conflict in Guangzhou (Canton)," *The China Quarterly* 83 (1980), pp. 397–446.

Walder, Andrew G., *Fractured Rebellion: The Beijing Red Guard Movement* (Cambridge, MA: Harvard University Press, 2009).

Wang Nianyi, *Dadongluan de niandai* (Zhengzhou: Henan renmin chubanshe, 2005).

Wemheuer, Felix, *Famine Politics in Maoist China and the Soviet Union* (New Haven, CT: Yale University Press, 2014).

Wu Yiching, *The Cultural Revolution at the Margins: Chinese Socialism in Crisis* (Cambridge, MA: Harvard University Press, 2014).

Xiao Donglian, *Zhonghua renmin gongheguo shi, Vol. 10, Lishi de zhuangui: Cong boluan fanzheng dao gaige kaifang (1979–1981)* (Xianggang: Zhongwendaxue chubanshe, 2008).

Yang Jisheng, *Mubei: Zhongguo liushi niandai dajihuang jishi*, 2 vols. (Hong Kong: Tiandi tushu, 2008).

Yang Kuisong, *Zhonghua renmin gongheguo jianguoshi yanjiu*, Vol. 1 (Nanchang: Jiangxi renmin chubanshe, 2009).

Motion Pictures

Breaking with Old Ideas (Juelie), Li Wenhua 1975.

Coming Home (Guilai), Zhang Yimou 2014.

Farewell my Concubine (Bawang bieji), Chen Kaige 1993.

Hibiscus Town (Furongzhen), Xie Jin 1986.

In the Heat of the Sun (Yangguang canlan de rizi), Jiang Wen 1995.

Platform (Zhantai), Jia Zhangke 2000.

The Blue Kite (Lan fengzheng), Tian Zhuangzhuang 1993.

The Chinese (La Chinoise), Jean-Luc Godard 1967.

The Road Home (Wo de fuqin muqin), Zhang Yimou 1999.

The White Haired Girl (Baimao nü), Wang Bin, Shui Hua 1950.

To Live (*Huozhe*), Zhang Yimou 1994.
Two Stage Sisters (*Wutai jiemei*), Xie Jin 1964.
Xiuxiu: The Sent Down Girl (*Tianyu*), Joan Chen 1998.

Documentary Films

A Grin without a Cat (*Le fond de l'air est rouge*), Chris Marker 1977.
Chung Kuo, Cina, Michelangelo Antonioni 1972.
Morning Sun, Carma Hinton 2003.
Storm under the Sun, Peng Xiaolian, S. Louisa Wei 2009.
The Ditch (*Jiabiangou*), Wang Bing 2010.
The Revolutionary, Irv Drasnin 2012.
Though I Am Gone (*Wo sui siqu*), Hu Jie 2007.

INDEX